Skoob Books Publishing Ltd., **Lond**

Skoob *PACIFICA* is contributing
English, disseminating regional lite. ~~the Pacific Rim~~
and promoting understanding between continents.

At the turn of the last century, Europe developed a penchant for
novels set in lands afar which had a tendency to look **at** the
colonies whereas the Postcolonials view from within themselves,
experimenting with the deviation from tradition and affirming
the aesthetic of the sublime as against an aesthetic of the beautiful.

"The reality of cultural entity should be the simultaneous act of
eliciting from history, mythology, and literature, for the benefit
of both genuine aliens and the alienated, a continuing process
of self-apprehension whose temporary dislocation appears to
have persuaded many of its non-existence or its irrelevance
(= retrogression, reactionarism, racism, etc.) in contemporary
world reality."

Wole Soyinka, *Nobel Laureate*

"Storytelling, to the readers of a *genre* of novel, written by a
particular writer for a small group of people in a large and
fragmented culture, still survives in those places the English like
to call the Commonwealth. This idea of narration, of the active
voice is in the calypsonian as the ballad singer, the narrator,
the political satirist."

Derek Walcott, *Nobel Laureate*

As the *fin-de-millenium* approaches, the colonies have a voice of
their own, a new *genre* has developed. Ironically, this diachrony is
written in the language of the Imperialist. Behind the facade
of tropical, sandy beaches and factories of video games lies the
cross-cultural and interliterary tradition of two continents.

SKOOB *Pacifica* SERIES

Joint Series Editors: Ms. C.Y. Loh & Mr. I.K. Ong

SKOOB *Pacifica* SERIES

No. 2000

To paul

SKOOB PACIFICA ANTHOLOGY No.1
S.E. Asia Writes Back!

Best Wishes

Joint Series Editors:
Ms C.Y. Loh & Mr I.K. Ong

SKOOB BOOKS PUBLISHING
LONDON

First published in 1993 by
SKOOB BOOKS PUBLISHING LTD.
Skoob *PACIFICA* Series
11A-17 Sicilian Avenue
off Southampton Row and
Bloomsbury Square
London WC1a 2QH
Fax: 71-404 4398

ISBN 1 871438 19 5

Agents:
Skoob Books (Malaysia) Sdn Bhd.
11 Jalan Telawi Tiga, Bangsar Baru,.
59100 Kuala Lumpur
Tel/Fax: 603-255 2686

Graham Brash (Pte) Ltd.
32 Gul Drive
Singapore 2262
Tel: 65-861 1336, 65-862 0437
Fax: 65-861 4815

Typeset by Pearly Kok . Tel/Fax: 603-255 2686
Printed by Polygraphic, Malaysia. Fax: 603-905 1553

SKOOB PACIFICA ANTHOLOGY NO. 1
S.E. Asia Writes Back!

Contents

IN

MEMORY

OF

LEE KOK LIANG

(1927-1992)

Malaysian writer Lee Kok Liang died suddenly in Penang on the 24th December last year. Mourning his passing, his friends - indeed admirers of his accomplishments in literature, law and politics - celebrate the compassion, generosity, dignity and nobility with which he shared his life-gifts and communicated his visions. His person, like his writing, was imbued with a rare grace of hospitality.

Born at Alor Star, Kedah, Malaya, his father (whom Lee described as "a stern follower of the British Raj") was 4th generation Straits-Chinese, and his mother "a saronged woman, quick tempered with a mixture of Siamese, Chinese, Malay culture". His paternal grandfather was Chinese secretary of the Kedah Sultanate, and his maternal grandfather a Chinese Kapitan to the Malay Sultan of Kedah. The influence of this background is discernible in Lee's fictional studies of Chinese family life and the tenacious traditions and dynastic ambitions which have shaped it. Lee's description of himself as a "skeptical Zen Buddhist leaning towards Theravadaism and a sprinkling of Ganeshism" is vindicated by his thorough exploration of these belief-systems, embedded in Malaysia's multi-cultural society, in his novel *Flowers in the Sky* (1981). The theme of conflict between spiritual values and acquisitive, corrupting materialism in this work is also deftly etched into the plots of many of Lee's short stories.

Lee's schooling in Malaya's Chinese, Japanese, English and Malay education systems in the 1930s and 1940s laid the foundations of the cultural heterogeneity of his sensibility, the core of which is Straits-Chinese. This had important repercussions for him as a Malaysian who wrote in English and chronicled the private lives, phobias and passions of Malaysians from different ethnic backgrounds. Situating his characters in the Malaysian scene, Lee was subtly mindful of the politics of multi-racialism which are conveyed through hints and nuances rather than obtrusively or insensitively.

In the early 1950s Lee attended the University of Melbourne where he wrote and published short stories, a literary apprenticeship which culminated in his first collection *The Mutes in the Sun and Other Stories* (1963). He left Australia to study for the Bar at Lincoln's Inn, London; after graduating he returned to Malay to practise law. His documentary story "Return to Malaya", written for *Encounter* (1954), laid some of the foundations of his fictional method: detached-observer narration (at one point the narrator intently follows the conversation of children behind a closed door) and a meticulous rendering of physical, social and behavioural detail, as in a later hallmark image: "the bar where a group of young men sat like loose-limbed spiders on the stools" ("Not So Long Ago but Still Around" in *Death is a Ceremony and Other Short Stories*, 1992).

Politics permeate most spheres of human activity and relationships in Lee's fictional world: sex, marriage, family life, promiscuity, prostitution, religion, the colonial club, racial identity, funerals, violence (which is psychological as well as political), the professions, class hierarchy, the shadowy nation state. The corrupt and self-indulgent exercise of power for materialistic aggrandisement (or even sadistic self-satisfaction) is a reiterated theme. Lee had practical experience of politics, both as a former member of the Penang State Assembly and as a barrister who, in law cases involving labour politics, represented oppressed worker groups. He continued to practise law in Penang until the eve of his death, and undoubtedly some of the plots of his stories were suggested by legal and public cases with which he was familiar.

The stories in *Mutes in the Sun* present alarming, powerful profiles of individuals brutalised, ostracised, alienated by authority figures or fellow victims. These dark effects - paradigms of social evils, yet mitigated by gestures of compassion or love - suggest that Lee introduced to South-East Asian literature relevant adaptations of Dickens, Hawthorne and Dostoyevsky. The title story "The Mutes in the Sun", a novella, and "Dumb, Dumb, by a Bee Stung" (*Death is a Ceremony*) feature misshapen mutes whose characteristics are symbolic as well as naturalistic. In Lee's metaphoric narrative design, mutes and mutilators inhabit opposite sectors of the psyche and the society. His image of the mute (silenced by nature, fear, family, community, or authority) is potent with moral and political *angst*, and articulates a *malaise of silence* theme which is echoed, for instance, in Ee Tiang Hong's poem "Silence is Golden" ("A mute saw something / Shocking / And burst into speech"). *Death is a Ceremony* contains recent and previously published stories which extend the social and psychological range of Lee's compassionate melancholy. Two stories, for example, are sinister and sad versions of the same situation ("When the Saints Go Marching", "A Pack of Cards"): *Jane Eyre* Gothic without the Romance; *études* to complement Jean Rhys's symphonic *Wide Sargasso Sea* (1966).

Whereas "The Mutes in the Sun" is a Poe-like tale of tragic terror and mystery (is the murder suicidal provocation?), set in an equatorial Waste-Land, its affirmative coda (the mutes discovering the action, speech and liberation of compassion) anticipates the tragi-comedy of cultural reconciliation in *Flowers in the Sky*, in which suffering and celebration enjoy an equipoise previously unsustained in Lee's fictional world. In this novel tales of passion are juxtaposed to question and probe some of Malaysia's cultural and religious traditions. A Buddhist monk's torment of desire stimulated by a mute girl, and his consequential self-mortification, are counterpointed by Inspector Gopal's chaotic courtship and joyous marriage; a tale of passion punished contrasted by a legend of love consummated. It is as if, with the Gopal narrative, R.K. Narayan has incongruously challenged Kafka on Malaysian soil. As a writer of short fictions (*Flowers in the Sky* is four short stories woven into one) whose technique of applied introspection reveals the inward brooding of a world and its inhabitants, Lee may be rewardingly compared with many short-story artists in the new literatures in English, writers as diverse and distinctive as Henry Lawson, Alice Munro, Albert Wendt, Hal Porter, Vincent O'Sullivan, Olive Senior, and Witi Ihamaera.

Kok Liang's presence in Adelaide and at CRNLE are now in trust as privileged heritage.

Syd Harrex
The Flinders University of South Australia

With the kind permission of the Centre for Research in the New Literatures in English (CRNLE) *Reviews Journal, 1993 No. 1.*

PREFACE
by
IKE ONG

We were overwhelmed by the response of Malaysian/ Singaporean writers and had to extend this issue to illustrate the history of post-second world war prose writing to the **Skoob** *PACIFICA* Anthologies No. 2 and No. 3, particularly the kind contributors who have given their permissions to reprint material which were recently published. As such, the publication will be a quarterly periodical giving many writers a first opportunity to be published in Britain.

The First **Skoob** *PACIFICA Anthology* is an attempt to illustrate, evaluate, identify and understand the cultural mediation of South-East Asian Post-colonial literature in English of various forms, including, the traditional genres of novel, poetry and drama. Most literature in the English language today are not English Literature but Literature in English. This redefinition has given rise to 'New Writings' which we try to represent the variety of nations of the Pacific Rim in world literatures in English and the other literatures of the regions translated into English.

More than seventy-five per cent of the world's population come from nations who have been colonies. The term 'Post-colonial' applies to all the cultures affected by the imperial process and is concerned mainly with previous colonies of Britain. Applying this principle, the literature of the U.S.A. qualify to be in this category not for its neo-colonial foreign policy and assertion as a world power, but as the first post-colonial society to develop a national literature. This was achieved by revolution, political and economic success, as well as linguistic and cultural association with Europe. Initially, it was a branch of English literature and as the volume of literature with different characteristics developed, supported with literary criticism, a national literature was established.

"Post-colonial literary theory has begun to deal with the problems of transmuting time into space, and, like much recent

Post-colonial literature, it attempts to construct a future. The Post-colonial world is one in which destructive cultural *encounter* is changing to an acceptance on equal terms. The recent approaches have recognized that the strength of post-colonial theory may well lie in its inherently comparative methodology and the hybridized and syncretic view of the modern world which this implies. This view provides a framework of multicultural theories, both from within and between societies to be fruitfully explored.

What each of these literatures has in common is that they emerged in their present form out of the experience of colonization and asserted themselves by foregrounding the tension with the imperial power, and by emphasizing their differences from the assumptions of the imperial centre. It is this which makes them distinctly post-colonial."

Ashcroft, Griffith & Tiffin,
The Empire Writes Back: Theory and
Practice in Post-Colonial Literatures
Routledge New Accents, 1989

"There are also available alternatives, newly formulated traditions, such as those proposed by critics and scholars writing from previously marginalized points of view - most notably the feminist, black American, and 'post-colonial' perspectives."

Dennis Walder, *Literature In The Modern World,*
O.U.P./Open University 1990

Most nations throughout the world have achieved Independence and with it, the problem of national culture arises in their enthusiasm to decolonise and to establish their own imaginative culture. In the period of nationalist anti-imperialism, socio-political practice conflicts with ideological nationalism. At the same time, the native language undergoes a quasi-alchemical evolution e.g. Bahasa Malaysia and Singlish. With the post-second world war economic prosperity and industrialization, many nations retain their culture by keeping awake their consciousness of metaphysical questions. To depart from the historical world of Islam, Taoism, Confucianism, Buddhism, Hinduism and Christianity is to abandon history and would result in social deracination.

2

Amongst the Africans, E.K. Braithwaithe and Chinweizu regard a return to African roots as crucial to contemporary West Indian and Nigerian identity, but Soyinka and Harris espouse a cultural syncretism of ancestral affiliations with contemporary, multi-cultural reality (see Shirley Lim's, *Gods Who Fail*).

Other colonies achieve independence and consequently develop a 'new' literature which expresses the social and political process in establishing a national identity. The 'process of self-apprehension' as characterized by the Nigerian Nobel Laureate, Wole Soyinka is the most important stage in the process of rejecting the claims of the imperial centre. In order to transmit the self-apprehension of a race or a culture, it is necessary to liberate from and relate this collective awareness to the value of others. When the self-apprehending entity is based on the knowledge and exposition of the reference points of colonial cultures, the result is intellectual bondage and self-betrayal.

The Black Power movement and other institutions in the Sixties asserted and maintained 'Black Writing' as a concept of Negritude as developed by the Martinican, Aime Cesaire and the Senegalese, Leopold Sedar Senghor. It is based on the idea of race and not nationality to include Africans, Afro-Caribbeans and Black Americans. The social, economic and political origins of the writers were overlooked. Negritude claimed certain stereotyped identities e.g. being emotional rather than rational, upholds integration and wholeness as opposed to analysis and dissection, is rhythmic and temporal and upholds the African view of time-space relationships, ethics, metaphysics and aesthetics. Remarkably, it is the foundling adopted by European ideological interest as the antithesis to the thesis of white supremacy. Wole Soyinka perceived the inevitable since Negritude embraces the binary nature of western philosophical tradition.

Colonial Attitude in its heyday:

"The African is indeed my brother, but my junior brother."

Albert Schweitzer

"The latter day colonialist critic sees the African writer as a somewhat unfinished European who with patient guidance will grow up one day and write like every other European, but meanwhile must be humble, must learn all he can and to give due

3

credit to his teachers in the form of either direct praise or, even better since praise sometimes goes bad and becomes embarrassing, manifest self-contempt."

Chinua Achebe

With the achievement of Independence, various countries react differently and some choose the policy of decolonizing as a political motive. Some critics argue that the colonization is only a passing feature which will be overcome when full cultural independence is achieved. Other critics have argued that cultural syncreticity, the fusion of cultures which is implied in the use of English, is valuable, inescapable and characteristic of post-colonialism which is their peculiar strength.

"Syncreticist critics argue that even a novel in Bengali or Gikuyu is inevitably a cross-cultural hybrid, and that decolonizing projects much recognise this. Not to do so is to confuse decolonization with the reconstitution of pre-colonial reality."

Bill Ashcroft, Gareth Griffith & Helen Tiffin

Having attained nationalist independence, the previous colonies strive to achieve Liberation which is the transformation of social consciousness beyond national consciousness. Frantz Fanon explained the three phases of the evolution of post-colonialism. In the first phase, the native intellectual shows proof of his assimilation of the imperialist culture; his writings conform with those in the mother country; his inspiration is European and correlate with the literary trends of the mother country. This is the period of unqualified assimilation.

The second phase is when the native is troubled by the confusion of identity and trapped in imperialist cultural values. Having disassociated himself from the local community, he indulges in nostalgia and depends on his memory to recollect bygone days, reinterpretation of old legends with renewed enthusiasm and a redesigned concept of the world.

Finally, the fighting phase where the native creates a revolutionary national literature which awakes the people from their lethargy. Many people who have never written or spoken, and in the time of need or forced in circumstances on the eve of their execution release a discourse that would shake the nation to emotional disarray.

4

Some writers in their over-enthusiasm and willingness to forge a national identity are in danger of being mimetic. The result is to be reabsorbed into the English tradition. Derek Walcott criticised the West Indian writers obsession with the destructions of the historical past and makes a plea to escape to a 'historyless' world where a fresh but not innocent 'Adamic' naming of place provides the writer with inexhaustible material and new but not naive vision.

"...since after all many of the nationalist struggles were led by bourgeoisies that were partly formed and to some degree produced by the colonial power;...

These bourgeoisies in effect have often replaced the colonial force with a new class based on ultimately exploitative force; instead of liberation after decolonization one simply gets the old colonial structures replicated in new national terms."

Edward Said, *Colonialism and Literature,*
Field Day Theatre Co. Ltd., Derry 1988

There had been various attempts to give literature in English from different parts of the world a name. In 1965, Joseph Jones utilised 'terranglia' and about the same period, 'Commonwealth literature' emerged as a term for literatures of the British Commonwealth nations. This was in preference to 'Third World literatures' or 'new literatures in English' or 'colonial literatures'. Post-colonial literatures as defined by Ashcroft, Griffith and Tiffin is the new literatures in English and covers an area greater than the British Commonwealth. It also includes the settler colonies as well as the invaded colonies. In the first case, the settlers brought their own language and culture to a foreign land and in the second case, language and culture are brought to the indigenous people. In some areas where the majority of the populations are not indigenous but immigrants, e.g. the West Indies, etc., a large proportion of the contemporary population had been displaced and are in 'exile' (see Wong Phui Nam's, "Ways of Exile"). Other similarities among Post-colonial literatures of different nations are a distinctive use of allegory, irony, magic realism and discontinuous narratives. These common themes are due to the post-second world war industrialisation and political achievement and more recently the technological development which has shrunk the world. Many former colonies still react to the old masters and often adopt a neutral culture e.g. the music and television of the U.S.A. thus, giving rise to the new imperialism of the media.

Every literature must find its harmonious balance, in effect, have reference to a particular place, evolve out of its cultural heritage and history, and the aspirations and destiny of its people.

To change names of characters and places with colloquial dialogue of say D.H. Lawrence's, Lady Chatterly's Lover would not make the work S.E. Asian. The generalization of universality is thus non-existent. But the English centre makes the claim of universality whereas, the others must strain to achieve it. Western ideas and precepts exert an influence on other writers. Europe's charm of romance and its powers of persuasion have influenced many to adopt its values in the interpretation of their world. Thus creating a great confusion and in their attempt to imitate the West so as to associate with the progressed. The fulfilling of the ritual does not satisfy the intention.

As with African literature, there are three attitudes to the Asian colonial past: shamefaced rejection, romantic embrace and realistic reappraisal. Often the past is rejected and the wish is to have as little to do with it as possible, shamed by imperialist propaganda and ignorance, the need in excessive enthusiasm to be euromodernists. Since the past has been vilified by imperialism, there is a need to reclaim and rehabilitate the genuine past. Thus, a different history has to be established without misinformation or romanticism to achieve 'Devolution' in literature. To achieve this, we have to realise three important factors:

Firstly, a nationalist consciousness which revolts against European cultural imperialism. With this, we realise the wealth of our cultural heritage and Asian realism.

Secondly, with Devolution, the literary circle has the ability to retrieve the necessities of its cultural heritage previously deemed to be of no value in Western cultural terms.

Thirdly, to change the colonialist's image of the regions and to portray the true cultural heritage and its values.

We take our frame of reference from the European literary experience. Literary ideologies are the conscious formulation of the critic, not the artist. There is danger of it being an act of consecration and excommunication. Its formulation will develop into an instant capsule, which on consumption shall poison the creative process. Creative Art is non-prejudicial. The establishment of a literary ideology would result in incestuous inbreeding which limits objective enlightenment. When the artificial comprehensive adequacy is realised, the ideology is discarded. Fabricated evidence to substantiate a preconceived ideology will not survive the test of time. The literary ideology is what the art is defining.

Evolution, Revolution and now Devolution:

"It is in the literary Unilateral Declaration of Independence, despite its tendency towards narrow schematism, we achieve coincidence of literary ideology and a value expansion with a social vision. By turning the mechanics of creativity into a self-regulating domain, it elevates its sights to a regenerative social goal which makes continuing demands on the nature of that ideological medium and prevents its stagnation."

Wole Soyinka

The joint editors of the **Skoob *PACIFICA*** would like to thank the following for their help and support:
In Kuala Lumpur, a special thank you to Allan Kwok for his dedication beyond the call of duty; Lulu and Janice Kwok for understanding him; Pearly Kok for her inexhaustible dexterity to cope with the innumerous alterations to the various books; Yap Lock Too, Andrew Hwang, Satish, Suthan, Siew, Elaine, Oon Eam Kwee, William Harald-Wong, Allison Yap, Helen Ung, O. Don Eric Peris, Chu-Li and all who supported and enjoyed Malaysian/Singaporean literature.
In Singapore, Robert Yeo, the unofficial cultural ambassador whose selfless devotion which ought to be officially recognised, Prof. Koh Tai Ann, Arthur Yap, Lee Tzu Pheng, Kirpal Singh, Mr Mew Yew Hwa of Federal Publications, Mr Tan Wu Cheng of Cannon International, Mr Chuan I. Campbell of Graham Brash and the numerous writers who have helped to make the Anthologies possible.

In Australia, Annie Greet, Syd Harrex, Anne Brewster, Paul Sharrad, Bruce Bennett, Bill Ashcroft, Gareth Griffiths and Helen Tiffin.
In London, Prof. John McRae, Prof. Alan Durant, Dr. C.W. Watson, Dr. Peter Mayer, Dr. Barrie Buxton, John Madell, Paul Toy, Miles Lanham, Thomas Weinrich, Tina, Lucien Jenkins, David Houston, Chris Johnson, Mark Lovell, Jin Hin Neoh and Shirley Geok-lin Lim in Santa Barbara.

INTRODUCTION
by
JOHN McRAE

The term Pacific Rim has recently come to be widely used - but where is it exactly? From Alaska to Tasmania, from Sakhalin to Tierra del Fuego a large number of countries border the Pacific Ocean. The Pacific Rim is largely a question of perception rather than geography, however - the name invites the Eurocentric or the American-based world-view to shift its focus, and to take in that vast expanse of the globe which has been culturally ignored despite its growing economic and geo-political importance.

It comprises the whole of South East Asia, also known as the Asean countries, and necessarily reaches to Australia, New Zealand and the Pacific island nations, as well as stretching north to include Korea and Japan. It is somehow indicative that the American rim is *not* included in this perception, despite the ever closer ties between South East Asia and, for example, Chile and Argentina.

The countries of South East Asia, principally Malaysia, Singapore, Brunei, Thailand, Indonesia, and the Philippines (with Myanmar/Burma on the sidelines, it is to be hoped only for the moment) have found it useful to group themselves together for some political and economic purposes, and for tourism. And although each of these nations has its distinct and separate cultures, the grouping is also useful in terms of cultural identity and world perception.

If we see the whole Pacific area as taking in the United States and Russia, China and Japan, it becomes clear that any label will be misleading, as either too vast or too limiting. But if a shift of perception is possible, both from inside and from outside the area, it can only benefit the countries and cultures concerned, and attitudes to them locally and internationally.

South East Asia deserves to be considered as a cultural entity, just as much as the Caribbean or West Africa. That there are differences between the languages, literature and culture of Jamaica and Guyana or between Ghana and the many diverse areas of Nigeria is perfectly obvious. In the same way East and

West Malaysia are different, Singapore and Thailand are different, East Timor and western Sumatra have as many diversities as ties that bind.

If South East Asia is now beginning to see itself as embodying some kind of cultural and political unity, it is largely as a reaction to Western, colonial perceptions. The relationship has always been love/hate, dependence/independence. Now that economic factors have empowered the area it is no longer possible to recycle tired old concepts such as 'post-colonial' or even 'developing' to describe the cultural ferment South East Asia embodies.

Today Singapore is rushing headlong towards the realisation of its aim to become the new Manhattan; Malaysia is pursuing its vision of fulfilment to be reached by 2020, while Kuala Lumpur and the Klang Valley risk becoming the new Los Angeles, all high-rise blocks and blocked freeways; Bangkok is trapped between the image of sin city and gridlock, and Manila, deserted by the Americans, offers its young musicians the greatest of opportunities as copycat singers in every hotel and bar in the rest of South East Asia. Yet there is still desperate poverty, in countryside and in the city, and a huge mass of people who have no share in the region's success - as the writings of Thailand's Pira Sudham most memorable recount.

Imitation of western success sits uneasily with the vital necessity of local cultural, national, religious and political identity. It is fashionable to knock the West and plead that its values do not take account of local forces; at the same time the proliferation of shopping malls and multi-national companies marketing locally only reinforces the phenomenon of the newest cultural imperialism: the coca-colonisation of the universe.

The birth of pangs of a nation, or of a geo-political area, are never without violence. It is vital to remember that nations such as Malaysia and Singapore were born out of struggle and conflict, both against the colonial power and within the ethnic, political and religious contexts of the states themselves. Indonesia, East Timor, and Thailand have witnessed considerable violent upheavals very recently, and there is no guarantee that these struggles are over.

Literature might well have got lost in the rush to become more Western than the West. But there is a greater flourishing of new writing in South East Asia now than at any time in its history. The area has the inestimable richness of centuries of cultural and linguistic miscegenation at its beck and call: what is used to advantage to attract tourists, the multi-racial multi-cultural panoply of the area, is still not fully appreciated as also its greatest creative resource. Tagalog and Thai, Bahasa Malaysia and Bahasa Indonesia, Hokkien, Mandarin, Tamil, all are rich in potential to express the growing pains, the dreams and hopes and fears of a geographical region in its rush to maturity.

English was, traditionally, the language of culture, as the language of imperialism, when culture was defined in purely imperialistic terms. Now it has to be seen as the link language - more than just mere communication, more than just the necessary language of airlines and business, English can, ironically, become the language which will put South East Asia on the world map as a cultural presence.

In Malaysia, twenty and more years on from the anger which brought Bahasa to the fore as the language of education and politics, there is a growing culture in that language, a growing consciousness of language as identity. As the local strength of that identity matures, so also must develop an awareness of the polyglot strength of language: English has always been a polyglot language, and a polyglot culture, able like a chameleon to adapt to and incorporate myriad influences in every corner of the globe. South East Asian English is not only Singapore English: just as Indian English is different in Madras from Delhi, in Calcutta from Bombay, so there are many South East Asian Englishes, just as there are many South East Asian cultures, languages, and identities.

The geography of writing in English is extending its boundaries to grow far beyond the old colonial dimensions. Writing in English is not the prerogative only of countries which have emerged from British or American colonial domination. In Thailand, for example, Pira Sudham writes in English and is already, only in fifties and on the strength of only a few immensely important published works, being spoken of as a potential Nobel Prizewinner. In Indonesia, where the colonial presences were Dutch and Portuguese, linguistic identity and cultural roots are constantly under discussion and English writing, although very much the expression of a minority of writers and readers, is the major vehicle for international recognition.

Some writers find it necessary to write in English, some in their local language; some are torn between the two. For some, English is their first language, for some it is a second or even a foreign language. But expression will out, whatever the language. And a new, pressing need arises - for good, world class translations and translators, to bring local writing to a universal readership. Pira Sudham's *Monsoon Country*, for example, has the advantage over the great, and closely related Malaysian novel of peasant struggle *No Harvest But a Thorn* by Shahnon Ahmad, but the translation, by Adibah Amin should now bring that classic to a very much wider readership.

The writing of an area explores, defines, questions, subverts, affirms, and reinforces the human geography of its writers and readers. There would be no literature without questions, without searching, without pain. The writers who explore the sufferings inherent in the struggle of becoming are often criticised for painting a negative picture - but inevitably theirs is a search to move towards the affirmation of the positive. In creating a literature, any writer has to evolve his own background, almost indeed his own language. Too much of a stress on nationalism will be a limitation, but any serious writer is engaged in much more than simply affirming nationality - identity goes much deeper; humanity goes well beyond national boundaries, and identity is individual as well as universal. Local and universal, national and international must go hand in hand.

It is instructive in this context to remember the growth of American Literature, especially since South East Asia consciously and unconsciously imitates America in so many of its patterns. Writers like Fenimore Cooper and Mark Twain literally created the landscapes and the language of the country whose growing pains they witnessed and described. They took a nation and shook it into shape, bringing together a wealth of resources: racial mix, language and cultural variety, and innovation, the sense of the new, the challenge of growth and identity, the spirit of adventure and the indispensable sense of humanity and humour - they left a legacy which became America: not today's America, but the America of the soul, America as Americans want it to be remembered.

Appropriately, it is noticeable how big a part education plays in the process of self-discovery: school and university, breaking away from the traditional village background into a greater world awareness are fundamental to the novel of growth. It is hardly surprising then how often the *Bildungsroman*, the novel of growth, is the vehicle for self-examination both on the personal level and on a wider scale: K.S. Maniam's *The Return* shares this form with Dickens and D.H. Lawrence, with *A Portrait of the Artist as a Young Man* and *The Catcher in the Rye*. Growing pains are universal: individual, class, race and nation all have to undergo them. Similarities and differences are what make the universal experience unique yet common, shared but special, particular and universal.

This is the role of the writer in South East Asia now - to explore and define, to create and criticise, to evaluate and express the vast and varied culture which is emerging from the white heat of the melting pot. But in every growth, of empire, of nation, of an individual, there will somewhere be the seeds of decline. No empire, perhaps especially no Utopia, is forever. So if a sense of loss can be detected in a writer's work, it is no more and no less than the necessary accompaniment to growth: regret and hope are two sides of the same coin.

Thus the novels of Lee Kok Liang, Pira Sudham, Basanti Karmakar, Shahnon Ahmad, Lloyd Fernando, K.S. Maniam and many others depict struggles towards an unknown future - the struggles of recent decades, and the future which is also the present. Every writer is faced with the task of negotiating between past, present, and future. In Shakespeare's words, from *Hamlet*, creative representation, be it drama (it was "playing" in Shakespeare) has a clear "purpose...to hold as 'twere the mirror up to nature; to show virtue her feature, scorn her own image, and the very age and body of the time his form and pressure." The form and pressure of what makes the body of the present time are its past, its traditions, its roots, its culture, and all the components of its identity, local, national, and international.

The 'Three Beserah Fishermen' of one of Muhammad Haji Salleh's best known poems are not limited by the Malaysian geographical setting, in a small village in Terengganu - their plight is universal, their daily decision to trust themselves to the waves and the wind or to stay on a harsh shore just as much a universal predicament as Hamlet's "to be or not to be." The best and most universal writing starts out as local. Its universal frame of reference comes later. What unites readers and writers is the shared element of humanity, enriched by the endless diversity of culture, setting, and belief.

There has been, especially amongst the reading classes, a kind of inverted snobbery about local writing in many parts of the world. Somehow local writing is not so cosmopolitan (whatever that might mean); somehow the colonising culture and language have retained some kind of superiority.

But the only advantage that Western literature has is the length of its traditions, and the ever-expanding range of its terms of reference. Both the tradition and the terms of reference are in need of constant renewal and enrichment - otherwise they would stultify and die. The proliferation of pastiche and parody in recent years might be seen as a sign of an early stage in just such a process of atrophy. But exactly at that moment, when the institution of English literature began to question its own identity, other literatures in English, and in translation, began to contribute to a new tradition, one which is still in its earliest exciting days: world literatures in English, from sources as far apart as the Caribbean and New Zealand, Nigeria and Sri Lanka, Canada and the Philippines, Australia and South Africa, India and Tanzania have given the vital injection of new energy to writing in English for the world.

As a process of devolution this clearly started in the first countries to be colonised: Scotland, Ireland, and the United States of America. It was not just a case of the Empire writing back - in each instance it was an affirmation of local identity, local language and culture, local conditions and traditions. The discovery and rediscovery of tradition, especially age-old traditions of story-telling, the reaffirmation of what had always been, but was now seen in a new light, was the first expression of 'post-colonial' identity. And that was centuries ago. The world has now moved far beyond such patronising, belittling labels as Commonwealth, post-colonial, Third World or emerging, to describe the literatures of today. Each literature can, indeed must, be proud of its own cultural identity.

English is a universal language, and no country or culture has the prerogative of holding the major claim on it, either as a language, or as literature. By the same token, it is time that any English with a voice mature enough to produce a literature in its own context was welcomed onto the world stage as a participant in and a contributor to the ever-larger domain of world literatures in English.

This has happened with the literatures of many areas already - the Nobel Prizes given to such widely diverse figures as Rabindranath Tagore, Patrick White, Wole Soyinka, Nadine Gordimer and Derek Walcott attest the contribution of what used to be called Commonwealth writers to world literature. The process is on-going.

The question of 'maturity' arises in any discussion of 'new' literatures. But it is in many ways a false question, inviting invidious comparisons with pre-judged criteria of quality and standing. The true basis of any story-telling tradition in any culture lies in its reflection of the realities, needs, and aspirations of the culture it reflects. Ancient traditions of story-telling have rapidly accommodated the themes, sophistication and techniques of newer models, for better and for worse.

The discovery of new freedoms, especially sexual and political, has encouraged a rash of writings, especially in Singapore and the Philippines which revel in sexual explicitness and in the kind of violence and horror that the Oriental cinema so successfully celebrates. This the a parallel to the first flush of freedom which brought *Oh! Calcutta!* to the stages of London and New York in the late 1960s. So it is encouraging to find new themes being handled with the kind of maturity displayed in such texts as Johann S. Lee's *Peculiar Chris* and Simon Tay's *Stand Alone*: respectively the first gay novel to emerge from Singapore, and the best exploration of the other side of the yuppie success-oriented good-life philosophy which has made Singapore what it is. These newer writers, showing the way forward through the 1990s, with some of the more significant women's writing, will be featured in the next Skoob anthology.

The world will not sit up and take notice unless there is a spirit of creative power and tension, of constructive debate and self-evaluation, unless there is an ongoing process of creative development in the literature concerned. There is no merit in self-satisfaction, no honour without sacrifice. What we can see now is a rich tradition of writing together with a willingness to challenge and question, to face up to difficult issues and handle them with style and humour, with passion and sensitivity.

The material is all to hand: maturity brings with it responsibility, and the time is right for the area, and the world at large, to take cognisance of its role in the creative expression of its own local and international identity.

South East Asia must now begin to take its place as an active and vital force in the literature of the twenty-first century.

© John McRae, 1993.

JOHN McRAE is Special Lecturer in the English Department at Nottingham University and regular Visiting Professor at the Magistero Faculty in Naples, Italy. He is a leading figure in work on the interface between language and literature, and has published several books in this field. He lives in France and travels widely as a guest lecturer, theatre director, and consultant. He also edited the first critical edition of the suppressed novel *Teleny* by Oscar Wilde and others, and is co-author with Ron Carter of the forthcoming *Penguin History of Literature in English* of which the first volume is to be published in 1994.

The Journal of Commonwealth Literature

The Journal of Commonwealth Literature is published twice annually, usually in August and December each year. The first number of each volume consists of an issue of critical studies and essays; the second is the bibliography issue, providing an annual checklist of publications in each region of the Commonwealth. From 1993 it will be published three times.

All subscription enquiries/orders should be sent to: Bailey Management Services, 127 Sandgate Road, Folkestone, Kent CT20 2BL, U.K.

PART ONE

New Writings
of
the Pacific Rim

SKOOB *Pacifica* SERIES

Skoob Pacifica Anthology
is a quarterly publication featuring
contemporary writings of the Pacific Rim

The first issue
SKOOB PACIFICA ANTHOLOGY No. 1
S.E. Asia Writes Back !

Subscription of Five issues:
UK GBP20 post free
Elsewhere GBP25 post free surface mail

Subscription enquiries to Skoob Books Publishing Ltd,
11A-17 Sicilian Avenue, off Southampton Row and
Bloomsbury Square, London WC1A 2 QH
Fax: 71-404 -4398
Cheques payable to Skoob Books Publishing Ltd.
I enclose a cheque for GBP _____

Please debit my Access/Visa/Amex account
expiry date _____

Signature _____

Card No.

Name _____
Address _____
_____
_____

SHIRLEY GEOK-LIN LIM
"Why Do You Write?"

There comes a time when someone who has been writing steadily is asked, "Why do you write?" The question is never simple because is comes from and leads to fundamental assumptions concerning the nature of serious literature and the role of the writer.

With the journalist and the popular writer, there is little difficulty with the notion that they write for money and for the commonplaces of success: career promotion, social prestige and recognition. Many poets and fictionists would like these also, but if these were the reasons why they continue to persevere in their art, they would have abandoned their work at any early age. The chances of becoming rich or famous from writing a poem or a novel are so low that no respectable gambler would put money on a writer.

The best response to such a nosy question may well be, "None of your business" or "I don't know". Still, the question remains to intrigue and to irritate.

In an increasingly middle-class and professionalized society, there may be some hostility to the idea that someone is working out of a frame of references different or alien to the prevalent social norms. More often, the writer is simply ignored or mocked or invisible; what she does, after all, is unimportant, irrelevant, and essentially value-less. Her audience is minuscule or non-existent, her 'product' uncompetitive in the international market of literature. If she claims your attention, she is presumptuous. If you deign to give her attention, you are magnanimous.

Some writers, however, are unconcerned about being invisible. By 'unconcerned' I mean that they don't stop to think about it. It may merely be an illusion I have, but I tend to believe that when a writer has a poem in mind, her chief, if not only, concern is to make that poem visible. She sees her visibility, if not her actual substance, as taking shape in the piece she is writing. When the poem is completed, perhaps perfected, that finished form is the manifestation of her self as a writer.

It really doesn't matter if the poem is never published. Nor does it matter if it is and no one reads it. Of course, it would be very nice if some reviewer made a fuss about it and it got into anthologies and generations of students would have to write fulsome essays on it. That is the public life of poetry.

Inasmuch as the writer's piece is intended for a public, however, it becomes important for that piece to be published and read. Fiction more than poetry is an act of social communication; drama demands an even more immediate communal interaction, as live performance before an audience. So it is never so simple to separate the private motivations and act of writing from its public themes and reception.

But there is a fine line between writing that finds an audience and writing to find an audience. Just as we distinguish between people who genuinely like us and people who pretend to like us for their own manipulative purposes, so the discriminating reader, consciously or otherwise, distinguishes between writing that pleases because it has something to say or because it is aesthetically moving and writing that tries to please by saying what the writer thinks you want to hear in the way you want to hear it.

The distinction does not lie only in the integrity of the piece or in the disinterestedness of motivations. It is most remarkable in that with the latter the writer gives up originality; he has his sights on aims extraneous to his art and is guilty of the worst kind of imitation by second-guessing his readers and paying them the insult of pandering to their tastes. Writing for a society and writing to be read do not necessarily imply that the writer has to give up his independence and freedom of choice in subjects or style. Jane Austen, George Eliot and Gabrielle Marquez wrote about communities, societies and nations. But they did not defer their reflections and fictions to a public or consensual censor; their imaginations and their craft were the supreme centres in their novels.

It is this kind of self-centredness that many cynical observers cannot believe of the act of writing. They are either outraged, professing moral and ethical disgust, or they find it intellectually abhorrent. A cloistered nun may be forgiven her centredness in prayer as meditation between her self and her deity. But in the secular realm of art, such centredness smacks too strongly of the impure aesthetical argument.

I recall two indignant yelps from professional acquaintances. Years ago, a Canadian anthropologist and his knitting wife whom I was sharing an apartment with in Waltham, Massachusetts, said to me, "Why are you wasting your time writing poems? Why don't you take up basketry instead? At least you will be making something useful." More recently, an important academician said to me, "What do you mean, self-referential? How can a poem be self-referential?"

I too share their misgivings. I could probably use my time much better, volunteering for charity work or writing a scholarly article. And if a poem is self-referential, doesn't that make it self-indulgent, socially irrelevant, petty, boring, and all the other adjectives that go with self?

Perhaps these misgivings are the reason why writers need tradition, that larger-than-self body of authority that one can appeal to to make legitimate one's practice. It is pretty amazing how many writers will gladly talk about the major writers that have influenced them or how knowledgeable many of them are regarding literary traditions. There are very few English language poets who don't know what a sonnet is or who haven't read or heard of John Keats, T.S. Eliot, Wallace Stevens or Robert Frost. English language fictionists know of the Hemingway or the Faulknerian style. This interest in literary tradition is perhaps a kind of artistic professionalization and apprenticeship. If there is a strong tradition of local or national English language writing, writers in that region refer to books written within that tradition; Wole Soyinka, Chinua Achebe, Derek Walcott, R.K. Narayan, George Lemming are all figures in their own native traditions.

Of course, tradition is not public property in the way that a park is public. There still hangs over it the air of mystery and ritual associated with closed guilds or religious faiths for which the invited elite must undergo some form of initiation in order to approach it. But, sharing in a literary tradition, the writer is a member of a community. The self-referentiality of his work

21

lies in the way the circuits move: the poem's words work as poetry in the way they refer to themselves, as units of rhyme, internal meanings and imagery, succeeding only in the structure of the poem; and in the way they refer to the tradition of poetry, as intertextual weavings, connotations, associations, echoes, allusions, parody, the anxiety of influence and all that. Self-referentiality expands to include the self-referentiality of the art form.

As important, I believe, is the way tradition functions as an independent enlarged centredness in the writer's work. Authentic imagination, as opposed to imitation, emanates from the self. But craft, or aesthetic practice, or tradition (not always meaning the same things) is outside the self, has a degree of 'objectivity' which is partially tangible (you have the poem or the novel to refer to), partially transmissible, and, to a great degree, public in nature.

Which brings us back to the unanswered question, "Why does a writer write?" To answer that question fully, we have to ask how a writer writes and what kind of thing is a poem or a novel. To evade that question, I can try to respond honestly, "It depends". Every piece has its own particular genesis. This one came out of insomnia and feminist discontent; this from the recurrent pang of remorse over a much-loved father. This, however, was written after reading a wonderfully fresh poem by Czeslaw Milosz and being absolutely taken by the artful artlessness of the introductory passage. But none of these responses will do, for the question is not about particular origin. It is about the relation between self and art.

One can answer with the most recent theory from the school of psycho-socio-criticism, that writing is the act of obsessive self-conversation in which one works out one's neurotic anxieties and morbid emotions. Obsessions with death, sex, mutilation, shame, no matter how intellectually refined or abstracted, have their origin in "the rag-and-bone shop of the heart", in "The place of excrement". Writing can therefore be therapeutic, essential for psychic health. The artist is someone suffering an irredeemable wound, but unlike the ordinary neurotic he is saner and stronger for he finds redemption in his art.

Does one respond, therefore, "I write because I am obsessive and neurotic"?

Or one can idealize the process in another direction. Keats, as a consumptive, impoverished, frustrated and dying poet, believed it was the vague shapes of romance and fancy that moved his imagination to poetry. The passionate mind, mindful passions, are ennobled by a prescient imagination and a love of the language and its forms that language to engage in the creation of similar forms. There is not only a passion of feelings and thoughts but a passion of language and form which leads someone to enter into the life of writing. Without that singular passion, one writes obsessive letters or journals, or monologues in obsessive monotones.

Literature is, in a fundamental sense, an idealization of language. The writer, while he may write of the marketplace, writes from a dream of language, an ideal of aesthetic shape which is dynamic in process but static in realization. He must, after all, have a finished poem or novel to show, a form complete if not compact. His dream is both private and public, for while it is a subjective passion it is also shared by thousands of published and unpublished writers. Language and its forms have the peculiar characteristic of all arts, of being capable of the most interior, individual and intimate communication as well as the most communal and inclusive. Does one respond, therefore, "I write because I am in love with the deathless forms of literature"?

For myself, I would say all these and more. I write because I am moved by some powerful feeling which somehow wants to express itself in a specific shape. I write because I master these feelings when I utter them in the shape of a poem. I write in order to invent myself and my past. I write because I am moved by some idea of a beauty that is just waiting to be formed. I write because I believe some one needs to write down certain aspects of a communal past that would not be expressed otherwise. I write in order to communicate opinions, thoughts and feelings. It is usually personal urgency rather than social mission that leads me to write, but that doesn't mean I do not write from and of social concerns.

Finally there is a private elevation of mood, a certain plane of experience when I feel totally devoted in that time to the thing that I am doing, that comes upon me when I am writing a poem or a fiction. I'd like to think of it as a kind of zen focusness. Writing blesses me with this experience of connectedness: it is the act by which I am centred.

SHIRLEY GEOK-LIN LIM is currently Professor of Asian American Studies and English at the University of California, Santa Barbara. She received a Ph.D. in English and American Literature from Brandeis University, Massachusetts in 1973.

Her first book of poems, *Crossing the Peninsula*, won the 1980 Commonwealth Poetry Prize. She has published two other poetry collections. *No Man's Grove* (1985) and *Modern Secrets* (1989), and a book of short stories, *Another Country* (1982). Her critical book, *Nationalism and Literature: English-language Writing from the Philippines and Singapore* (New Day Press), appeared in 1993. She is co-editor of *The Forbidden Stitch: An Asian American Women's Anthology* which received the Before Columbus American Book Award in 1990; co-editor of *Reading the Literatures of Asian America* and *One World of Literature*, and editor of *Asian America: Journal of Culture and the Arts*. She has been published in numerous journals and collected volumes, including *Journal of Commonwealth Literature, New Literary History, Feminist Studies,* and *Poetry Review, Solidarity, Meanjin, ARIEL,* and *Massachusetts Review.* **Skoob PACIFICA** London will be publishing her new book of criticism on Southeast Asian literature, **Writing S.E. Asia in English: Against the Grain** and a revised edition of **Modern Secrets, Selected Poems** in **Spring 1994.**

SHIRLEY GEOK-LIN LIM
Shame

"Ta' malu!"

Mei Sim wriggled at her mother's words.

"You no shame! Close your legs."

Mother was standing five steps below the landing, the soft straw broom in one hand and her head on a level with Mei Sim's shoulders.

Mei Sim stared down her legs which she had spread apart the better to balance her body as she half-lay on the smooth wooden landing and thought her thoughts to herself.

Up came the broom and thumped against her knees. She pulled them together and tugged at her short skirt.

"What you do here all day? Go ask Ah Kim to give you a bath." Her mother's round pretty face was troubled. She had had a perm just last week, and the fat curls sat like waxed waves over her brow, wrinkled with vexation. "We're going to visit *Tua Ee*. And don't sit with your legs open there. She think I bring you up with no shame."

"Ya, ma." Mei Sim sidled past her mother's solid body down the stairs, glad for something to do. Every day was a problem for her until her brothers came home from school at three when they would shout at her to go away but still could be persuaded to give her a piggy-back ride or to let her hold their legs in a wheel-barrow run. The house was empty and dull until then containing only chairs, tables, beds, cupboards, photographs and such like, but no one to play with.

Ah Kim was scrubbing her brother's uniform on the ridged washboard. Drub, drub, drub, slosh, slosh. Mei Sim squatted beside her. Ah Kim's stool was only a few inches high and she had her legs thrust straight in front with the wooden board held firmly between. Her samfoo sleeves were rolled up high and the pale arms were wet and soapy up to the elbows. Taking the chunk of yellow laundry soap in her right hand, Ah Kim scrubbed it over a soiled collar. Then, seizing the collar in a fist, she pushed the cloth vigorously up and down the ridges. Her knuckles were red and swollen, but her face was peaceful. "You wait," she said, not turning away from the washboard. "I wash you next."

Bath-time was directly under the tall tap in the corner of the open-roofed bathroom. Mei Sim was just short enough to stand under the full flow of water pouring in a steady stream from the greenish brass tap while Ah Kim scrubbed her chest, legs and armpits with LifeBuoy. She was six and would soon be too tall for this manoeuvre. Soon, Ah Kim said, she would have to bathe herself with scoops of water from the clay jar in the other corner of the bathroom. Dodging in and out of the water, Mei Sim thought she would not like to have to work at her bath.

Mother dressed her in her New Year's party frock, an organdy material of pink and purple tuberoses with frills down the bib and four stiff layers gathered in descending for a skirt. She picked a red and green plaid ribbon which Ah Kim threaded through her plaits and, her face and neck powdered with Johnson Talc, she waited for the trishaw, pleased with herself and her appearance.

Mother had put on her gold bangles, gold earrings, and a long heavy chain of platinum with a cross as a pendant. Her kebaya was a pale blue, starched and ironed to a gleaming transparency under which her white lace chemise showed clearly. Gold and diamond kerosang pinned the kebaya tightly together, and the gold-brown sarong was wrapped tightly around her plump hips and stomach. She had to hitch herself up onto the trishaw and, once seated, carefully smoothed the sarong over her knees. When Mei Sim climbed in, Mother gave her a push to keep her from crushing her sarong.

Grand-aunty's house was all the way in Klebang. Usually Father took them there for visits in the evening after their meal. It was enough of a long way off for Mei Sim to always fall asleep in the car before they reached home.

The trishaw man pedalled vigorously for the first part, ringing his bell smartly at slow crossing pedestrians and hardly pausing to look before turning a corner into another narrow road. At Tranquerah he began to slow down. There was much less motor traffic, a few bicycles, and now and again a hawker's cart got in his way. Green snaky veins zig-zagged up his calves. His shaven coconut-round head was dripping with sweat. He didn't stop to wipe it, so the sweat ran down his forehead and got into his eyes, which were deep-set and empty, staring vaguely down the long road.

After a while, Mei Sim grew bored with watching the trishaw man pump the pedals. She leaned forward to stare at the houses on both sides of the road. What interesting things to see that she had missed on their evening car rides! Here was a small stall with bottles of *chinchaloh* and *blachan* neatly mounded on shelves. She glimpsed through an open door a red and gold altar cloth and bowls of oranges and apples before a dim sepia portrait. Two *neneks* in shabby sarong and *kebaya* sat on a long bench by the covered front of another house. Each woman had a leg pulled up under her sarong, like one-legged idols set for worship. Here was a pushcart with a tall dark *mamak* frying red-brown noodles in a heavy *kwali*. How good it smelled. Mei Sim's stomach gave a little grumble.

Now they were passing the Baptist Gospel Hall where on Sunday evenings she had seen many people standing in rows singing sweetly. In the morning glare the shuttered windows were peeling paint and a crack showed clearly on the closed front door which had a huge chain and lock on it.

"Hoy!" the trishaw man shouted. The wheels swerved suddenly and bumped over something uneven. Mei Sim hadn't seen anything.

Her mother gripped her arm and said aloud, "You bodoh. Almost fall off the trishaw. Sit inside all the way."

"What was that, ma?"

"A puppy dog."

She turned her head to peer behind but the canvas flaps were down.

The trishaw man was talking to himself in Hokkien. A small trail of saliva was trickling down the side of his mouth. Mei Sim could only hear mumbles like, "hey...*yau soo*...chei..."

"What is he saying, ma?" she whispered.

"Never mind what he say. He angry at puppy dog, bring him bad luck."

Mei Sim looked at the bare brown legs again. They were moving much more slowly, and the mumbles continued, sometimes louder, sometimes quieting to a slippery whisper. Her mother didn't seem to mind the trishaw's pace or the man's crazy talk. She had been frowning to herself all this time and turning the three thick bangles round and round her right wrist. Her agitated motions made a gentle jingle as the bangles fell against each other, like chimes accompanying the slow movements of the trishaw pedals.

They were on a deserted stretch of Klebang before the sandy rutted path on the left that led to Grand-aunty's house and the shallow sloping beach facing the Malacca Straits. Wood-planked shacks roofed with rusty galvanized iron alternated with common lots on which grew a wild profusion of morning glory, lallang, mimosa and sea-grape. A few coconut and areca palms leaned in jumbled lines away from the hot tarmac. The sky was a blinding blue, barren of clouds, and arching in a vast depth of heat under which the dripping trishaw man mumbled and cursed. The bicycle lurched forward and the attached carriage, on which Mei Sim crouched as if to make herself lighter, moved forward jerkily with it.

"Aiyah! *Sini boleh*," her mother said sharply, and almost at the same moment the man's legs stopped and dangled over the wheels. She pushed Mei Sim off the sticky plastic seat and stepped down carefully so as not to disarrange the elaborately folded pleats of her skirt.

The man took a ragged face towel from his pocket and mopped his face. Mrs. Cheung clicked the metal snap of her black handbag, zipped open an inner compartment, extracted a beaded purse from it, unbuttoned a flap and counted some coins which she clinked impatiently in one hand, waiting for him to take the change. She poured the different coins into his calloused palm, then walked up the path without a word. Mei Sim stood for a moment watching him count the coins and, at her mother's annoyed call, ran up the narrow lane just wide enough for a car to go through.

Waddling ahead of her, her mother was singing out, "*Tua Ee, Tua Ee.*" A wooden fence, newly whitewashed, separated Grand-aunty's house from the lane which suddenly petered out into a littered common compound shared with some Malay houses on low stilts. Beneath the houses and through the spaces between the concrete blocks on which the wood stilts were anchored, Mei Sim could see the grey coarse sand grading to a chalky white for yards ahead clumped by tough beach grass and outlined at stages by the dark, uneven markings of tidal remains, broken driftwood, crab shells, splinters of glass, red-rust cans, and black hair of seaweed.

Grand-aunty came out through the gap in the fence in a flurry of kebaya lace. Her gleaming hair was coiffed in a twist, and a long gold pin sat on top of her head, like a nail on the fearsome *pontianak*, Mei Sim thought.

"What's this?" she said in fluent Malay. "Why are you here so early without informing me? You must stay for lunch. I have already told that prostitute daughter of mine to boil the rice, so we have to cook another pot."

Grand-aunty had four sons, of whom she loved only the youngest, and a daughter whom she treated as a bought slave. She was not a woman for young girls and gave Mei Sim no attention, but she tolerated Jeng Chung as the niece whose successful marriage to a rich towkay's son she had arranged ten years before.

Mei Sim's mother visited her at least once a week with gifts of fruits, *pulot* and *ang-pows*, and consulted her on every matter in the Chung family's life. At six, Mei Sim was allowed to listen to all their discussions; she was, after all, too young to understand.

It was in this way she learned what men liked their women to do in bed, how babies were made and how awful giving birth was. She knew the fluctuations in the price of gold and what herbs to boil and drink to protect oneself from colds, rheumatism, overheat, smallpox, diarrhea, or female exhaustion. It was in this way she found out that women were different from men who were bodoh and had to be trained to be what women wanted them to be. If women were carts, men were like *kerbau* hitched to them.

This morning she settled on the kitchen bench behind the cane chairs on which her mother and grand-aunt were sitting close to each other sharing the *sireh* box between them, chatting and scolding in Malay and snatches of English, and she listened and listened without saying a word to remind them of her presence.

"...and Bee Lian saw Hin at the cloth shop...she told me he's been going there every afternoon when he's supposed to be at the bank...that slut is probably taking all his money but I haven't said a word to him. I thought maybe you can help me, what should I say to him. Oh, that swine, useless good-for-nothing. I scratch his eyes out, better still if I take a knife and cut her heart. These men always walking with legs apart, what does he want from me? Three children not enough, but she is a bitch - black as a Tamil and hairy all over. I keep myself clean and sweet-smelling, a wife he can be proud of. So itchified, never enough, always wanting more, more. That's why now he won't give me more money, say business bad. ha, bad! We know what's bad, I'll get some poison and put it in her food, and all my friends talking behind my back. She's making a fool out of me, but what can I do? I tell them better than a second wife, not even a mistress, just loose woman smelling like a bitch any man can take, so why not my Peng Ho."

It was Father Mother was complaining about! Mei Sim scrubbed her ears to clear them of wax, but quick tears had risen and clogged her nostrils, so her ears were filled with a thick sorrow. She knew all about second wives. Hadn't Second Uncle left his family to live in Ipoh because their Cantonese servant had bewitched him, and now he had three boys with her and second Aunty is always coming to their house to borrow money and to beg for the clothes they'd outgrown for her own children? And little Gek Yeo's mother had gone mad because her father had taken another wife, and she is now in Tanjong Rambutan where Mother says she screams and tears off her clothes and has no hair left. Poor Gek Yeo had to go to her grandmother's house and her grandmother refuses to let her see her father.

Mei Sim wiped her nose on her gathered puff sleeve. Grandaunty had risen from her chair and was shaking the folds of her thickly flowered sarong. Her Malay speech was loud and decisive. "All this scolding will do you no good. Men are all alike, itchy and hot. You cannot stop him by showing a dirty face or talking bad all the time. You will drive him away. The only thing that women have is their cunning. You must think hard. What do you want, a faithful man or a man who will support you and your children? Why should you care if he plays with this or that woman? Better for you, he won't ask so much from you in bed. No, you must be as sweet to him as when you were first courting. Talk to him sweet-sweet every time he comes home late. This will make him feel guilty and he will be nicer to you. Make him open the purse-strings. Tell him you need money for prayers at Hoon Temple to bring luck to his business. He will appreciate you for your efforts. Some men have to be bullied like your uncle, but..."

She stopped to take a breath, and Siew Eng, her skinny dark daughter, crept up beside and whispered, "Na' makan, 'mak?"

"*Sundal!*" Grand-aunty shouted and slapped her sharply on her thin bare arm. "Who asked you to startle me? You know how bad my heart is. You want me to die?"

Siew Eng hung her head. Her samfoo was faded and worn at the trouser bottoms, and the thin cotton print didn't hide her strange absence of breasts. She was already sixteen, had never been sent to school but had worked at home washing, cleaning and cooking since she was seven. All her strength seemed to have gone into her work, because her body itself was emaciated, her smile frail, and her face peaked and shrivelled like a *chiku* picked before its season and incapable of ripening, drying up to a small brown hardness.

Mei Sim had never heard her cousin laugh, had never seen her eat at the table. She served the food, cleaned the kitchen and ate standing up by the wood stove when everyone had finished.

Mother said Siew Eng was cursed. The fortune teller had told Grand-aunty after her birth that the girl would eat her blood, so she wouldn't nurse or hold the baby, had sent her to a foster mother, and had taken her back at seven to send her off to the kitchen where she slept on a camp bed. Mei Sim was glad she wasn't cursed! Her father loved her best, and Mother bought her the prettiest dresses and even let her use her lipstick.

"Now your uncle..." Grand-aunty stopped and her face reddened. "What are you waiting for, you stupid girl? Go serve the rice. We are coming to the table right away. Make sure there are no flies on the food."

Her daughter's scrawny chest seemed to shiver under the loose blouse.

31

"Ya 'mak," she mumbled and slipped off to the kitchen.

"Come, let's eat. I have *sambal blachan* just the way you like it, with sweet lime. The soy pork is fresh, steaming all morning and delicious."

Grand-aunty gobbled the heap of hot white rice which was served on her best blue china plates. She talked as she ate, pinching balls of rice flavoured with chillies and soy with her right hand and throwing the balls into her large wet mouth with a flick of her wrist and thumb. Mother ate more slowly, unaccustomed to manipulating such hot rice with her hand, while Mei Sim used a soup spoon on her tin plate.

"Your uncle," Grand-aunty said in between swallows of food and water, "is a timid man, a mouse. I used to think how to get male children with a man like that! I had to put fire into him, everyday must push him. Otherwise he cannot be a man."

"Huh, huh," Mother said, picking a succulent piece of the stewed pork and popping it into her mouth whole.

"But Peng Ho, he is an educated man, and he cannot be pushed. You must lead him gently, gently so he doesn't know what you are doing. Three children, you cannot expect him to stay by your side all the time. Let him have fun."

"Wha..." Mother said, chewing the meat hard.

"Yes, we women must accept our fate. If we want to have some fun also, stomach will explode. Where can we hide our shame? But men, they think they are datoks because they can do things without being punished. But we must control them, and to do that we must control their money."

Mei Sim thought Grand-aunty was very experienced. She was so old, yet her hair was still black, and her sons and husband did everything she told them. She was rich; the knitted purse looped to her string bag under her *kebaya* was always bulging with money. Father had to borrow money from her once when some people didn't pay for his goods, and she had charged him a lot for it. He still complained about it to Mother each time they drove home from Grand-aunty's house.

"But how?" protested Mother, a faint gleam of sweat appearing on her forehead and upper lip as she ate more and more of the pork.

Grand-aunty began to whisper and Mei Sim didn't dare ask her to speak up nor could she move from her seat as she hadn't finished her lunch.

Mother kept nodding and nodding her head. She was no longer interested in the food but continued to put it in her mouth without paying any attention to it until her plate was clear. "Yah, yah. Huh, huh. Yah, yah," she repeated like a trance-medium, while Grand-aunty talked softly about accounts and ton-tins and rubber lands in Jasin. Mei Sim burped and began to feel sleepy.

"Eng!" Grand-aunty called harshly. "Clear up the table you lazy girl. Sleeping in the kitchen, nothing to do. Come here."

Siew Eng walked slowly towards her mother, pulling at her blouse nervously.

"Come here quickly, I say." Grand-aunty's mouth was dribbling with saliva. She appeared enraged, her fleshy nose quivering under narrowed eyes. As Siew Eng stood quietly beside her chair, she took the sparse flesh above her elbow between thumb and forefinger and twisted it viciously, brea-thing hard. A purple bruise bloomed on the arm. "I'll punish you for walking so slowly when I call you," she huffed. "You think you can be so proud in my house."

Siew Eng said nothing. A slight twitch of her mouth quickly pressed down as the only sign that the pinch had hurt.

"What do you say? What do you say, you prostitute?"

"Sorry, 'mak," Siew Eng whispered, hanging her head lower and twisting the cloth of her blouse.

Only then did Grand-aunty get up from the table. The two women returned to the chairs beside the *sireh* table, where two neat green packages of *sireh* rested. Sighing happily, Grand-aunty put the large wad in her mouth and began to chew. Mother followed suit, but she had a harder time with the generous size of the sireh and had to keep pushing it in her mouth as parts popped out from the corners.

Mei Sim sat on her stool, but her head was growing heavier, her eyes kept dropping as if they wanted to fall to the floor. She could hear the women chewing and grunting; it seemed as if she could feel the bitter green leaves tearing in her own mouth and dissolving with the tart lime and sharp crunchy betel nut and

33

sweet-smelling cinnamon. Her mouth was dissolving into an aromatic dream when she heard chimes ringing sharply in the heavy noon air.

For the briefest moment Mei Sim saw her father smiling beside her, one hand in his pocket jingling the loose change, and the other hand gently steering an ice cream bicycle from whose opened box delicious vapours were floating. "Vanilla!" she heard herself cry out, at the same moment that Grand-aunty called out, "Aiyoh! What you want?" and she woke up.

A very dark man with close-cropped hair was carefully leaning an old bicycle against the open door jamb. Two shiny brown hens, legs tied with rope and hanging upside down by the bicycle handles blinked nervously, and standing shyly behind the man was an equally dark and shiny boy dressed in starched white shirt and pressed khaki shorts.

"Nya," the man said respectfully, bowing a little and scraping his rubber thongs on the cement floor as if to ask permission to come in.

"Aiyah, Uncle Muti, apa buat? You come for business or just for visit?"

"Ha, I bring two hens. My wife say must to puan, this year we have many chickens."

"Also, you bring the rent?" Grand-aunty was smiling broadly, the sireh tucked to one side of her mouth like a girlish pucker. "Come, come and sit down. Eng, Eng!" Her voice raised to a shriek till Eng came running from behind the garden. "Bring tea for Uncle Muti. Also, take the hens into the kitchen. Stupid girl! Must tell you everything."

The boy stayed by the bicycle staring at the women inside with bright frank eyes.

Curious, Mei Sim went out. He was clean, his hair still wet from a bath. "What school you?" she asked. He was older, she knew, because he was in a school uniform.

He gave her a blank stare.

"You speak English?"

He nodded.

"You want play a game?" She ran out into the compound, motioning for him to follow.

Mei Sim had no idea what she wanted to play, but she was oh so tired of sitting still, and the white sand and brown sea-nuts and blue flowers on the leafy green creepers on the fence seemed so delicious after the crunch, crunch, crunch of Grand-aunty's lunch that she spread her arms and flew through the sky. "Whee, whee," she laughed.

But the boy wouldn't play. He stood by the sweet smelling *tanjong bunga* and stared at her.

"What you stare at?" she asked huffily. "Something wrong with me?"

"Your dress," he answered without the least bit of annoyance.

"What to stare?" Mei Sim was suddenly uncomfortable and bent down to look for snails.

"So pretty. *Macham bungah.*"

She looked up quickly to see if he was making fun of her, but his brown round face was earnestly staring at the tiers of ruffles on her skirt.

"Want play a game?" she asked again.

But he said, "My sister no got such nice dress."

Mei Sim laughed. "You *orang jakun*," she said, "but never mind. You want feel my dress? Go on. I never mind."

He went nearer to her and stretched out his hand. He clutched at the frills around the bib, staring at the pink and purple tuberoses painted on the thin organdy.

"Mei Si-i-m!" Her mother's voice brayed across the compound. There was a confusion as the boy rushed away and the woman came running, panting in the sun, and pulled her at her arm. "What you do? Why you let the boy touch you? You no shame?"

Grand-aunty stood by the door, while the dark man had seized his son by the shoulder and was talking to him in furious low tones.

Mei Sim felt tears in her mouth, and wondered why she was crying, why her mother was shaking her. Then she saw the man pushing his rusty old Raleigh through the gate, without the hens, still holding the boy by his shoulder. She saw the look of hate which the boy threw at her, and she felt a hot pain in her chest as if she knew why he must hate her. A huge shame filled her and she was just about to burst into noisy weeping when she saw her mother's red, red eyes. "He did it, he pulled at my dress," she screamed, stretching her body straight as an arrow, confronting her lie.

Glossary

Ta'malu	No shame
Tua Ee	Eldest Aunt
kebaya	blouse
kerosang	brooches
Chincaloh	fermented shrimp
blachan	dried fermented shrimp paste
nenek	old women, grandmothers
mamak	Indian food peddler
bodoh	stupid
yau soo	cursed
pulot	sticky rice
ang pows	gifts of money wrapped in traditional red envelopes
na' makan 'mak?	Do you wish to eat, mother?
Sundal	prostitute
chiku	small brown tropical fruit
sambal blachan	piquant sauce
Tanjong Bunga	sweet-smelling beach blossom
Macham bungah	Like a flower
orang jakun	aboriginal; country bumpkin

THOR KAH HOONG
Divide and Rue

Divide and rule. Divide and rue.

South Africa is a land where division has gone wild and complex, much of it bloody and awful.

A visitor to South Africa must similarly divide himself into many minds, splinter into schizoid states to manage in different realities. Only in emphatic division could this visitor accommodate lunch accompanied by champagne and tart reds, spiced with dry, wry talk of the theatre and history, amidst austere winter gardens and vineyards, and... a shit-smelly shanty-town of scrap-shacks and tents pustulent on top of a dump, where the determined talk is of strikes and no schooling.

Division may be a fact of life and death in South Africa, but just like the yin-yang symbol, black and white are foetally, fatally, curled round each other in a historical whole. There is a common history that all parties would like to deny, at least selectively so, because no one likes reminders of loss and blindness.

But the hatred and love, frustration and guilt which are being expressed today are basic emotions rooting back to basic times when land was territory over which tribes and races fought; when a God-driven sense of being indomitable spilled a river of black blood which continues to course, poisonously, through the battered, shattered tribal and racial laagers of South Africa.

The situation encourages blinkered vision, either because a broad perspective reveals much that is guilt-ridden, disgusting or terrifying, or because the man has been reduced to a focused rage of despair.

(Division is seen even within South African officialdom. South African tourism authorities who wanted journalists in to see that there were fun places in the country, safely isolated, no trouble coming over the veld...and a South African consulate official in London coolly suspicious of the visa application of a journalist from Malaysia, one of those hit-Whitey countries she has been warned of, and thus promising an official response only after the flight had left. The situation was resolved by a friend from Commonwealth House who called to remind them that they needed friends, but they were not going to get any if they remain as mule-headed as...)

* * *

The Pits

Gold Reef City, a theme park centred round a gold mine and a model of early Johannesburg, exemplifies my divided experiences of South Africa.

Black help and white supervisors dressed in sun hats and layered flouncy dresses ala Gone with the Wind Down Swanee River. One corner of the park on entrance, is devoted to screaming people shooting into a watery plunge on logs or hanging on tight-fisted to a looping train. There is a sterile, lifeless model of parts of old Johannesburg: an early newspaper; buildings typically fringed with overwrought filigreed metal, looking like oversized garden furniture; an emporium of gold objects.

The main attraction is a tour down into the hollowed depths of an old gold mine. Armed with a helmet and a torch, a visitor is lifted down into a well-ventilated tunnel.

The tour takes in specks of gold and false gold glinting in the light of the torch. No romantic vision here of nuggets of gold hefted in a joy of discovery, but a voracious dissolution of one ton of rock to obtain about four grammes of gold. (Such an ugly waste - so many stunted, blunted lives and so many truncated pyramids of grey slag and gold waste which loom huge all over the fringe of Johannesburg.)

The echoing darkness, the bolts and beams jammed into the bedrock to hold things up, the patches of wet and the cubby-holes of rest evoke a sense of the daily routine down here in a richer past. But the sense is essentially false, another ignorant romance.

Near the end of the stretch of tunnel open to visitors, perched in a dark side-tunnel is a "miner". With just a lit candle for company, this man sits there, hour after hour, waiting for visitors. Visitors move him to stand up, at a lean in the confined space, to demonstrate the driving of spikes into the resistant rock to break up things. He moves to a drill and for a couple of ear-shattering minutes he shudders and hammers away at the rock-face.

Then he squats down again in the gathered dark, waiting.

A black man in a khaki uniform; a taciturn troglodyte crouching in his day of darkness.

What does he think all workday long? In that silence, punctuated by drips and the gurgling of rushing water and the approaching chatter of a tour guide heralding a shuffling of shoes, hushed giggles and whispers.

Only a poetically idle mind will hear the clangour of the mine when it was working, ghost roars of trains rumbling, machines clattering, drills shattering and explosions muffled in the depths.

No, the original work is over. No more pushing into the earth until it comes apart at the seams. Now the mine is just the main attraction in a side-show. Life glossed over for family entertainment and education in a Disney-formula of fun and money.

The man is ageless in the gloom. Is he old enough to remember eGoli, the city of gold, Johannesburg, when it was booming with the wealth underfoot? When thousands of black men were in the pits as far down as a mile and a half to worm through heat and noise and dark dust for less than US$5 a month? Was he just hired for this side-show or is he a remnant from the old mine? Did he have to go through acclimatisation in a giant steam-bath in simulation of conditions underground? Was he, together with hundreds of other men, placed in front of stepladders and told to climb up and down for hours on end, while sweat ran off their naked bodies and men in lab coats listened to their heart-beats and fondled their testicles checking for hernias?

* * *

South Africa does that to me - makes me have hallucinatory flashes of another world while in this whitewashed one my Asian upbringing conditions me to be either be a cliched, for convenience and defence, inscrutable Chinaman or always politely smiling in good-humoured tow of my hosts.

After all, the guide into the bowels of Gold Reef City was charming and informative (selectively) and there was no reason for me not to be smiling genuinely because everyone was so good-natured (so long as I did not do something so declasse as to ask for confirmation of my reading that up to fifty, sixty bodies would be chipping away amidst dust, crammed into that hole in the wall where one now disconsolately hunkers).

So I was a collaborationist - in maintaining the polite facade that papers over the divisions.

* * *

No Malice in Fairyland

You are now in Fairyland.

This flip line of graffiti scrawled on a wall in District Six in Cape Town seems to be particularly resonant with significance for South African writers.

In Richard Rive's collection of short stories, *Buckingham Palace, District Six,* about the "characters" of District Six - the fences and the pushers, the jive talkers and street stalkers - it was the epigraph. *Fairyland*, a musical conceived by David Kramer and Taliep Petersen, titled itself after this same inscription.

Fairyland is a joyous collection of songs and moves echoing the music popular in District Six in the Sixties: Motown funk such as "Papa was a Rolling Stone"; the smooth platter of "Smoke Gets in Your Eyes"; Malay choir "liedjies"; original numbers with risque double entendres.

The show must have hit the right chords because *Fairyland* is said to be the longest running show in South Africa, in the 21st month (in August 1992) of its run and still packing them in the night I caught the show.

It was easy to be drawn in by the slick ensemble portrayal of sidewalk choirs harmonising for the sweet mamas swaying by, and for the sheer joy and hell of it all; of the restless young ignoring the nagging love of parents; of last-row romances and front-row mayhem at the cinema.

In the beginning, *Fairyland* promised a bit of the edge, showing a fringe culture of a rich brown, yellow, black mix, fleeing from white strictures into the ethnic welcome of District Six or shoved there to mutate in exotic ferment. The musical delivered the flash characters, those trying to rise above the moneyless mob because poverty is anonymous and of grinding insignificance.

40

The cosy Dock Road Theatre in Cape Town packed in just over 250 people. Most of them looked comfortable, padded, well-fed. All of us laughed at the innocent energies of the young and even faked an ache or two for youthful promise unmet because the young grew into routine and family.

By the time of the sing-along clap and feelgood finale, however, I was tapping my feet by rote. I should have registered the tone of the notes in the programme.

District Six was a...place where music was important, where culture and tradition were revered. That it was impoverished and dilapidated, that there was crime and overcrowding, cannot be denied. But what is important is that it was a place where people had a sense of themselves as a community. The place had a spirit. A spirit that made it special. A spirit that is missing in the sprawling townships and suburban developments of today.

The last line betrays the sentiment. The eternal belief in a past idyll turned tawdry by growth and change. Nostalgia, the super good-natured pain-easer that rubs out the sharp edges that rubbed us the wrong way. Trying to bestow mythic stature on the daily and the ordinary, but only succeeding in making poverty and dilapidation and crime cute.

Kramer and Petersen may have wanted to create a musical memorial for a funky, spunky community, but their work exalts a spirit without any suggestion that its exuberance was essentially a frail flowering which fell to the bulldozing blades which flattened the District one morning because whites had decided it was a good location to set up their apartments and comfort.

District Six is an iconic point in the history of racial confrontation in South Africa because it is still there, in erased form, vacuously so because the authorities got discomfited by the outrage over the eviction and appropriation and did not get on with the building.

* * *

Down in the Dumps

It is a far drop from the down-at-heel raciness of District Six to the squatter settlement I visited at the edge of Soweto. According to the guide, it was called Dhlamini, but considering our fumbling

41

efforts at finding English sentences in common, I cannot swear that this settlement bears that name.

Anyway, such a dump (literally, since the thousand families are living on top of an old city dump) should not have a name. A name implies roots, permanence, a postal code, historical significance or familial attachment, and the residents, who have been there for four-and-a-half years, are there by lack of choice and would prefer to move out to the long promised but never delivered housing.

The place stinks...of geological layers of old rubbish, of the poor huddled in profusion, of clogged drains, of shit. A thousand families queue for water from just one standpipe.

I was in a tent, one of several pitched amidst the usual improvised collection of metal sheets, cardboard and bricks which passes off as houses for poor blacks around all the scabby edges of South African cities.

I was invited to sit on one of two beds/benches/tables which took up more than half of the space in the tent. Taking in too the guide and five women of the settlement's governing committee, the tent had just enough space left for a crucifix, a battered chest of drawers, assorted mugs, cups and glasses, several jars of spices and condiments, and a piece of tattered carpeting of indeterminate colour.

Despite the best efforts of my guide, I did not get the names of those women. More of a loss was the flood of fast and furious answers which was paraphrased by my guide to skeletal single sentences: "She says she has three children"; "Yes, it is difficult to get job."

What did come across was their despair over education for their children. A "chalk-down" by teachers in Soweto was threatened, if the Department of Education and Training did not recognise their union, reinstate two dismissed colleagues and withdraw the suspension of 127 others. There had been no effective schooling since the start of the third term. A "stayaway" on Aug 2-3, 1992, organised by the "comrades", was happily extended by the students into another three days of idle "action".

What is the point of studying anyway? Less than 50 per cent will finish primary school. Of those survivors, less than 10 per cent will matriculate. And of those, less than seven per cent will get jobs.

Not everybody has given up hope. This big mother, who spoke the most vehemently in our largely untranslated exchanges, was driven out of frustration over my inability to understand her to assert in English: "Teacher useless, teacher useless." She went on at length about her 12-year-old son, but an account which brought tears to her eyes had the others spluttering in laughter.

The translation of the intense outburst: "She says she will kill her son if he does not finish school. She is afraid she will die before she will get some money back after all that has been spent on him."

The guide felt that such blunt honesty about the mercenary rewards of bringing up a son would tarnish any romantic notion of the nobility of their oppression and proffered a platitude (which I am certain she did not say) about how she felt education was vital for the progress of...

She was a character. They all were.

The characters of *Fairyland* are endearing because they have charm and mean no real harm.

These people have character because only character can cling on in a dump, the tail-end of a city's digestive systems.

Fairyland is the soft white underbelly of the Beast.

* * *

Somebody is Out to Get Me

Over the weekend (of 23-24 August, 1992) at least nine people were killed in South Africa. In Silverton, near Pretoria, a young woman was burned to death. It is believed the woman was still alive when she was set alight, police said. The body of a young man was found behind a hostel at Durban Roodepoort Deep mine on the West Rand. In Alexandra, Sandton, a man was injured when gunmen fired several shots from a passing vehicle.

A policewoman, Constable Nhlapho, was injured when a crowd attacked her in Daveyton on the East Rand. An explosion caused extensive damage to the house of the deputy mayor of Soweto. The deputy mayor's daughter was injured in the blast.

In Natal, three people were killed and three seriously injured when unknown gunmen opened fire on a kraal in the Makwatini Reserve. One of the dead was detective-constable L.S. Mazipoliko. Unknown attackers opened fire on a taxi in Magabeni, killing two passengers.

The newspaper report above is of no particular significance ... and that is its significance. Nobody, except for those who must clean up after and weep over the remains, pays attention to the daily toll recorded in a perfunctory manner by the media. The victims are anonymous (except for members of the police). Gunmen are usually labelled "unknown" because the possible motives for the murderous assaults are many - political differences; faction-fighting; personal rage; random, spontaneous devilry; take your pick - and the authorities cannot find the time or the interest to probe the many and growing number of cases.

In an issue of *South African News*, a SATour spokesman noted: "South Africa is quite safe for holidaymakers. Those pondering a visit to the country should know that the violence is confined to areas well away from the main tourist paths."

There is a pernicious logic to this and other arguments for the comparative placidity of South Africa. Crime is as rampant and violent, if not worse, in the United States, yet tourists still flock there in planeloads. Only certain areas (meaning black areas) are dangerous. You will not be in danger if you hung around smug, snug suburbs (meaning white neighbourhoods).

Yes, every urban centre in the world is plagued by crime and life goes on. But how many cities have the entrances of their hotels locked by nightfall, opened again only to recognised guests? How many have traffic wardens exchanging AK-47 fire with car-thieves?

My hosts checked me into a hotel away from the centre of Johannesburg to avoid the mayhem in the streets. I found out later that it was next to the district with the highest crime rate in Johannesburg. Was I paranoid?

That very morning, just before I surfaced, someone had been mugged right in front of the hotel, and a German guest, who had been seized by an irresistible urge for bananas, had to be dissuaded from leaving the hotel with more than the couple of

Rands required for the purchase. He made it to the corner before his shirt-pocket was sliced open. Was I paranoid?

There we were, S.K. and I, strolling along the main shopping strip of Johannesburg, a transverse row of shopping complexes and stores bisecting the centre of town, ringing with the roar of the idle masses while shops rang empty. (Except for this so-called antique shop which had a traffic of drunks, washed-out women and young toughs, handing over thin bands of gold, gimcrack costume jewellery, worn dull old shillings and crowns, most of it junk, for evaluation, being finger-printed to try and keep the trade legit.)

So there S.K. and I were, outside the Johannesburg Sun, the poshest hotel in town and one which a colleague had recommended for my stay, to hell with the cost, it was safe. So there S.K. and I were, looking at the familiar sight of a couple of Chinese selling fake watches and jeans out of a shopping-cart, when...there was a murmuring of many, a roar in the background which clarified itself as a mob pursuing two men. One of these two had a man in tow, dragging him by his hair and one hand which was handcuffed to the other. The prisoner was kicking and screaming. The mob was alternating pleading with the two, presumably detectives, and threatening to attack them.

There S.K. and I were, our mouths open, our street-smarts having deserted us, just yards away, when passions building up to an overwhelming rush prompted the man dragging the shop-lifter (so we were informed by a fleeing man) to pull out a gun.

A gun! There, S.K. and I were, our mouths open, just yards away.

"Run, man, run," this frantic black man said, "trouble."

Run? That was undignified. S.K. and I managed a fast walk.

"Run, man, run, you wanna die?" the man said as he pushed his wife across the street.

We walked faster and looked back to see a knife falling out from the prisoner's waistband and at the same time, his captor dropping his gun. The mob rushed. The other man pulled out a gun. The mob backed off. We turned round a corner.

Later I teased S.K., pro photographer that he was, that he had snapped everything in sight in our travels the past few days but had not recorded the incident. And there were the two of us bravely insisting on taking along our cameras (tucked out of sight, hopefully, under our leather jackets) in spite of the fervent advice of the hotel manager not to set ourselves up as targets for muggers.

"What about you? Anyway, you think I'm crazy? We don't know the rules here, how they operate. I shoot them. He shoots me? No thanks."

Was S.K. crazy? Was I paranoid?

You bet, I was paranoid.

* * *

Confession time

I called upon the Lord in distress: the Lord answered me, and set me up in a large place ... All nations compassed me about: but in the name of the Lord will I destroy them ... They compassed me about like bees: they are quenched as the fire of thorns: for in the name of the Lord I will destroy them.
118th Psalm.

That was the kind of thunderous God and rhetoric which dominated early South Africa, when Boers trekked out to wrest the unknown from disease and natives. The 118th Psalm was recited to celebrate the victory of the Battle of Vegkop at the Orange River in 1837. It was the first big battle with the Matabele. The feverish vision of swarming enemies seemed confirmed in the heatwaves of the veld. The Boers cleared the land of threats and in their fear of subversion from within the bloodstream, planted the seeds of a fear of miscegenation.

That was then. Now, the religious strain seems to have shrunk to a pleading whine, the whispers of confession, *mea culpas*, the clicking of rosary beads, three Hail Marys, I am full of disgrace. The speeches of President de Klerk are full of references to "cleaning the slate", "burying the past", "closing the book."

Pick up a newspaper in Cape Town and amidst a page of ads touting phone services - call the *sangoma*, the witch-doctor for that mysterious ache, for a *muti*, a love-potion; many numbers to call for sexual advice, talking dirty; aural fantasies; dating/mating lines - there is one that tells you to "feel good about yourself again!"

For US$2 a minute, South Africans can dial-a-confession. Confidentiality is guaranteed. Just whisper all those dark guilts away. Purge yourself. Wipe clean your slate. Bury your past. Close the book.

"There's things to settle between us, and now is the time to do it," the white sinner tells the black sinner in Athol Fugard's new work, *Playland*. At the end of the play, the white man has cried out the memory of 27 men blown away in an ambush and the black man has defiantly confessed to killing the white boss of his wife because he demanded more than labour of her body.

"Forgive me or kill me. That's the only choice you've got," the white man says.

The play ends with the former option, both characters feeling good about themselves and each other. Sadly for everyone, more and more South Africans, blacks and whites, are choosing the latter mode of catharsis.

* * *

On the ride to the airport, Joseph the taxi-driver, talked about the difficulties of saving a deposit for a 50,000 Rand house, a two-room shack, one of many dotted over a bare-hard, almost treeless landscape. Then he had to find a financial institution which would be willing to lend him the rest; blacks are at a disadvantage because their stability, financial and otherwise, is suspect. After all that, the black house-owner is faced with an annual interest rate of about 20 per cent for many years to come.

On the plane, Joan Goode, on her way to visit her mum in London, demonstrates to me what a liberal humanist she is.

"I have nothing against blacks. An Indian doctor has just bought the house behind ours. I am not prejudiced."

I didn't ask her how many blacks or coloureds she knew who could afford to buy a quarter of a million Rand house.

Joseph and Joan. Still not seeing eye to eye. Still talking different languages. Still divided.

Revised from a three-part series published in the New Straits Times, 2-4 November, 1992, with their permission.

© The New Straits Times, 1992.

THOR KAH HOONG has a Masters from the University of Malaya for his study of Sylvia Plath and Anne Sexton. After 13 years as a journalist - as books editor, food columnist, film reviewer, editor, head leader writer - Thor has just quit to devote more time to being the artistic director of KAMIKASIH, a leading Malaysian theatre company he helped form in 1981, and to finishing a collection of short stories. His works include a recently concluded trilogy of plays under the common title of *Caught in the Middle*, a critical and popular success in Malaysia and at the Singapore Arts Festival. Mr Thor's prose work "Telling Tales" is forthcoming **Spring/Summer 1994** with **Skoob *PACIFICA***, London.

KARIM RASLAN
A New Year's Day Lunch in Kia Peng

"No, not the 'Queen Anne', Latifah. The **real** silver"

"Yes, Cik Bainun?" Latifah wrinkled her nose and frowned. Cik Bainun looked at her niece and shook her head - the woman was really awfully plain.

"Allah, don't look at me like that - the silver that's under my bed. It's got to be used some time. If we don't use it for the New Year's Day lunch we'll never use it. It's written in the Koran that it's very bad to have silver and gold which you never use - haram, you know?" The older lady wagged her forefinger at her niece. Cik Bainun knew she nagged Latifah far too much - it was her way, but she was fond of the woman and felt sorry for her.

"Adoi! Such a sour expression. Just because I ask you to fetch the silver from my bedroom. You young people (Latifah was forty-four), I don't know, you're all so ungrateful nowadays - Melayu Baru this: Melayu Baru that'. It doesn't mean we forget how to behave or our adat. Politician, politician." Latifah had already turned around and was walking out of the kitchen when Cik Bainun remembered that there was more that she wanted. "Bring the Noritake dinner service and the damask tablecloths as well." The guttural harsh-sounding vowels of her Mendelling ancestry rasped through her Malay.

"Yes, Cik Bainun," Latifah replied grumpily. She resented the way her usual unhurried day was being ruined by the preparations for the New Year's Day lunch. Her aunt had woken her for the 'suboh' prayers at five o'clock and kept her busy chopping vegetables, gutting fish, grinding chilies, stirring the laukes and curries ever since. She stormed off. Her heavy flat-footed walk could be heard thumping through the wooden house.

Her aunt, Cik Bainun was sitting cross-legged on a meng-kuang mat that had been spread over part of the kitchen floor. She was in her mid-seventies and looked rather like a dried-up Chinese plum: tough and chewy but not without flavour. She had a pronounced lower jaw that had made her look like a monkey in her youth. However as she had grown older, her face had filled out and her appearance had become less simian and more womanly. Still, when she laughed, which was very often the size of her mouth, lined with gold fillings, was quite astonishing.

There was a pile of blood red rambutans in front of her. She inspected each of the fruit in turn, as if on a factory line: those that passed her scrutiny were transferred to a second, more ordered pile, the damaged and the insect-ridden tossed into a plastic dustbin. When Latifah was not looking she would squeeze open a fruit and pop the egg-shaped orb into her mouth, depositing the seed surreptitiously under the mound of rejected fruit. Cik Bainun, like all her family suffered from diabetes and Latifah watched over her aunt's diet. Latifah was quick to scold her aunt if she found she had been eating cakes, mangoes or rambutans. As a result, Cik Bainun had had to employ an elaborate series of games and deceptions or else be deprived of her favourite foods. She chewed on the fruit defiantly, sucking at the sweet, forbidden flesh and thought, 'it's going to be a lovely day'.

Ten minutes later Latifah returned carrying the silver service.

"Yes that's it," she said excitedly, "pass the tray so that Cik Bainun (she always referred to herself in the third person) can have a look at it. Oh, but it needs a polish. Call Fuad and tell him to polish it up nicely. Polish first, lay the table second, then mow the badminton court lawn. Lay the table with the Noritake set, don't forget, uh?" She traced the finely engraved words on the centre of the tray as she spoke and thought of her late husband, Raja Zulkarnain for whom the tray had been a retirement present - "To the Director-General on his retirement from the grateful staff of the Ministry of Transport March 31st 1974". She tried not to think of her husband, (she had called him Zul) in the mornings because the memories would crowd into her thoughts and leave her almost paralysed with grief for the rest of the day. He had died only eighteen months before and the memories were still too fresh and sensitive to be touched on without causing pain. She handed the tray back to Latifah, wiped her face with her selendang and consoled herself with a rambutan.

For nearly forty years now Raja Zulkarnain's family and friends, or rather the **late** Raja Zulkarnain's family and friends, had gathered at his residence off the tree-lined Jalan Kia Peng, in order to herald in the New Year with a large lunch-party. He had been the eldest son of one of the wealthiest of Selangor's Territorial Chiefs, Raja Aziz, the Dato of Kajang who had had the foresight (a fact that the family were to hold out as an example of their greater cunning and intelligence: 'we're not ordinary Bumiputras, you know - we're clever') to stake a claim to the swamps of Sungei Besi long before the advent of the mining engineer and the gravel pump. Despite their princely status they were only very distantly related to the Sultan and that by marriage. There was a story, however, about a claim to the throne of a small Mendelling principality not far from the Sumatran town of Temiang - the exact name of which always seemed to escape their recall. It was a claim that was alluded to all the more readily as the ladies of the family replaced their brass jewellery with silver and then gold.

Despite his distinguished antecedents, Raja Zulkarnain, would have been a forgotten relic of feudal days (waxed moustache and all) living in a shabby mansion somewhere in Klang and mumbling about his ancestral 'terombo' had he not been the fortunate beneficiary of the enlightened colonial practice of the time. At the tender age of thirteen he was selected for entry to Malay College. His five years at that august institution had left him with an English accent as plummy as Noel Coward and a propensity to declaim passages from "Twelfth Night" (his Orsino in the 1924 school production had been highly commended). Understandably, perhaps his spoken Malay was never to recover from the onslaught of the Anglo-Saxon world. After Malay College he was sent to the London University to read Geography (predominantly concerned with those areas of the globe that were, at the time at least coloured red). He returned to a glittering career, becoming one of the first Malays to rise up through the ranks of the hallowed Malayan Civil Service crowning his distinguished career with a stint as Director General of the Ministry of Transport - a fact that was said to account for his collection of Ferrari's and Aston Martin's and his biannual trips abroad to parts of the world where the laws of banking secrecy were said to be as stringent as his iron-fisted control of transport licences had once been.

However, he had been made a 'Tan Sri' only the year before his death. Such was his character that he refused to use the title, claiming to have been slighted by the very tardiness of its award - "I am a Raja first, a prince - what is this 'Datuk, Datuk, Tan Sri, Tan Sri' to me? If they had given me the title when I fully deserved it I would have been proud of it: but they throw it out to me like scrap meat for the dogs! Bah!" He was not known for his humility and this streak of arrogance had, unfortunately been inherited by his children, though it was a trait they endeavoured to mask except of course, when they were amongst themselves.

So it was with a sense of honouring a tradition of considerable standing that the family reassembled at the house that New Year's Day. Tradition, adat and custom were the very oxygen of their lives and the grown-up children (though not their spouses) thought nothing of their dutiful trek to Jalan Kia Peng. It was not a religious occasion, nor a family one - none of the family celebrated their birthdays in January: it was a gathering sanctioned solely by habit. But if the truth be told the late Zul had once attended, when studying in England, the New Year's Day lunch of a university friend and having enjoyed the casual, rather louche meal had decided as he always did, (without discussing the matter with Cik Bainun) to introduce the gathering into his family life as soon as the opportunity arose.

Thus it became along with his solar topee (purchased at the 'Army and Navy' on The Strand), his MCS chortle, his subscriptions to "Country Life" and "Field", an aspect of his character and personality that his children had taken it to be a true sign of his aristocratic bearing, never for once sensing that what they took to be signs of his nobility were no more than affectations of a world long discredited. People wondered how Cik Bainun could have lived with such an affected prig and one or two had tried to needle her into a confession. Cik Bainun was wise to them: she kept her own counsel. In private, she was more critical of him than she made out in public. Nevertheless she had renewed the magazine subscriptions only the week before even though nobody in the family cared to read about the performance of Purdey's latest high velocity rifles.

She had conducted herself with considerable restraint at her husband's funeral - earning a lot of respect from among the princesses and ladies of the Istana. She had appeared small and frail alongside the catafalque and many of the mourners had thought she would not survive the grief. 'No way she'll stand the loss,' 'she's so tiny - sure she'll die within a month,' they had said. But they had all underestimated her resources. She emerged from mourning even more crumpled and bent-over but imbued with a strange passion to make the most of the days left to her. Within weeks she had departed for Mecca dragging along her none-to-willing architect son, Kam. They returned weighed down with gallons of holy water. Kam complained bitterly about having to carry the water but she ignored him. Thereafter, she made twice weekly visits to her husband's grave at the Royal Burial Grounds in Klang, sprinkling the precious water over the grave. When her eldest daughter Mahani had suggested that the New Year's Day lunch be cancelled she been so scathing in her reply that the matter had never been raised again.

In the days of Zul's Government service the house had seen the comings and goings of petitioners, licence-seekers, small-time Chinese businessmen and UMNO politicians: men who had waited patiently on his verandah for hours on end, accompanied sometimes by their families, knowing that in a simple flick of the wrist a licence, a taxi licence, a lorry licence could be granted that would lift them up from the uncertainty that clung to their lives.

On his retirement from the civil service Zul had entered the more rarefied world of business. He was appointed Chairman of the Board of McMurtie Estates Berhad, discovering a hither-to unexpected facility in the art of holding board meetings, for which his standard motto was - 'No agenda can possibly last more than half an hour'. He was a popular chairman. The house filled with more distinguished visitors: Chinese tycoons accompanied by gun-toting body guards, bankers, Malay princes and prominent politicians of all races, a roster of friends and acquaintances that were soon included as guests at the family's New Year's Day lunch. Cik Bainun had preferred the licence-seekers to the businessmen since there was no doubt as to their relative status vis-a-vis the family: they were supplicants and therefore inferior. With the businessmen such matters were far less clear. Civil servants, for example, had their defining rank and position - whether it be Grade H,I,J Superscale A,B,C,D,E,F or G. Businessmen were indistinguishable. Therefore they all merited equal treatment - a continuous headache for a woman who was expected to entertain them all with her best Noritake and silver.

There was a time then, in the early seventies when the lunch had become **the** invitation for New Year's Day as much for the company as for Cik Bainun's food, which Syed Jaffar Albar, 'The Lion of UMNO' had called the greatest cooking outside of Johore - quite a compliment for a Johorean. Tun Razak had come back year after year just to eat her laksa assam (she also knew exactly how he liked his Horlicks), Tun Sambanthan for her steaming 'teh tarik' and Tun Tan Siew Sin for her deep fried popiah. It was even said that much of the NEP had been thought up over her assam laksa. She remembered the time a troop of long-eared Sarawakian politicians (led or so she thought by Tun Temenggong Jugah) had descended on the house carrying jars of fermented rice wine. They had passed the jars around for everyone to try and Kam had drunk so much that he had been violently sick all over Latifah's toilet.

All that was left of those days, she liked to think, was herself - now a little hard of hearing, thirty seven cats (most of which appeared to have had their tails broken at birth) and her unmarried middle aged 'niece', Latifah, whose actual relationship to the family was never truly determined. She cooked, cleaned, polished and scrubbed from dawn to dusk certain of one thing alone - that the monotony of her life was alleviated by her association with Raja Zulkarnain's.

As Zul grew older the house too, had grown quieter, the noise and clamour of visitors subsiding and then totally disappearing when he relinquished the last of his corporate apppointments - much to the relief of the Belgian Ambassador who lived next door. The street returned to look of quiet sobriety and decorum that was its true persona: unrushed, sheltered by swaying raintrees and bamboo groves. But the calm was deceptive and shortlived. Within a few years the house, once so busy had become a rare, silent, redoubt amidst the nocturnal roar of cars arriving at one of the many discotheques and night-clubs that sprang up along the road. By day the awful noise was matched by the growl of the developers' bulldozers.

What had once been a quiet haven of houses and mansions, (the Loke's pink residence was nothing short of a mansion) ornamental gardens, lawns, badminton and tennis courts studded with parterres, tembusus, mimosas and raintrees had given way to the raucous growl of the concrete mixer, churned up red earth and fierce looking Javanese labourers. Still, as long as the redoubtable Zul was still alive it was impossible that the house should be sold and the garden torn up. He had thrown such a fit at the last estate agent who had the temerity to approach him, chasing the man off his property with a pitch fork that even the city's most insistent agents had drawn the line at No 17 Jalan Kia Peng.

The family home had become her husband's passion and she guarded the house with extreme care, directing its maintenance with a scrupulous eye. It was a large sprawling wooden structure set on nearly two acres, with termites in every beam and sinking foundations. She had treated and re-treated the timbers but no amount of effort seemed to be able to halt the destruction wrought by the white ants and termites. For a full forty years she had lain in bed at night listening to the steady crackle of insects at work. The house had been constructed on low stilts and visitors reached the large open drawing room by climbing a series of steps inlaid with colourful 'Nonya' tiles Zul had bought when stationed in Malacca. The furniture inside the house was eclectic, reflecting the owners particular passions during his more active years - there were the tiger skins and elephant's feet of his hunting days, the heavy rosewood furniture of his Malacca days, countless glass cases exhibiting gifts and awards that seemed to have attracted dust notwithstanding their airtight containers.

Zul had never been a man to throw anything away and the house benefited from this because it was stamped indelibly with his character - medals, framed pictures, a portrait by Husseim Enas and water colours crowding out all the surfaces, surfaces which his wife wiped and polished with a fanatical dedication.

For each of his three children then, the house was as suffused with memories as the santan scented kueh lapis his wife steamed every year for Hari Raya. For Mahani, the eldest daughter, a 'Datuk' in her own right and the Director of the University Hospital, the house, (or rather the garden) had been the scene of her first french kiss. This had taken place decades before - after a New Year's Day lunch as it happened. It was hard to imagine that the dignified and business-like fifty-five year old who always wore her hair in a snail-shaped bun was once a whisp of a girl with all the grace and delicacy of a mousedeer. Din, her second cousin had been the daring kisser (going on to surprise the family by becoming the most devout of religious teachers). He had lured her behind the chicken coop at the back of the garden, grabbed her hands and placed his mouth over her's. She had been shocked and pleased - he was older, wore drain-pipes and looked a lot like Cliff Richard. But the force of his embrace had left her shaking.

Mahani was married with four grown-up children, three grandchildren and one erring husband whose latest misdemeanour had been the acquisition of a second wife - 'to save me from committing zina' as he put it. She liked to relive her little encounter with Din: if only because it blotted out the awfulness of the present. It made her feel young, invigorated and desired again. She plucked flowers and crunched the sweet-smelling pandan leaves in her fingers as she thought about her little secret, relishing the almost girlish embarrassment she still felt - the kiss and his lizard-like tongue darting into her mouth. At the time it had seemed the height of sinfulness and wicked beyond belief: 'if only,' she thought, 'I had known better'.

Meriam, the second daughter (also a grandmother) was a more homely woman. She had large plump buttocks, the family jaw, her mother's laugh and the best 'onde onde' in all of Shah Alam. She gravitated towards the kitchen where she felt at ease among the smells and cumin stains. She peered into the store-room, examined the vegetables, pried open the fish gills to check their freshness, tasted the curries and questioned Latifah on the household expenses. Being the least well off of the family (she was married to a MARA lecturer) she considered it her duty to apply her own very stringent and parsimonious housekeeping principles to her mother's kitchen. What she failed to bestow in material terms she more than compensated - in money saved by re-using the frying oil and not throwing it away, by buying vegetables from the pasar tani and using beef shin whenever possible and cooking it for hours on end until it fell off the bone to the touch.

Finally there was the apple of Cik Bainun's eye, her Kam. He was her youngest child and only boy. Like all only sons, he was horribly spoiled and conceited. His self-absorption was made worse by his jaunty golf-tanned exterior and high pitched nasal voice. He was as thin as his sister Meriam was fat and laughed at her penny-pinching.

Whilst he laughed at Meriam endlessly - she was the 'Ratu Cheap Sale', Mahani was a different matter. People often referred to him as Datuk Mahani's brother. The mere mention of her name was enough to reduce him to a state of green-eyed jealousy. In private, he compared their respective newspaper coverage, counting the column inches (and photographs) with all the feverishness of an ambitious journalist. It was not that he was unsuccessful. Far from it. He detested the thought that people might think less of him the more they thought of Mahani. He was the of one of the city's most prominent architects and was well known for his distinctive trademark - deeply-pitched Minangkabau roofs. Even so, he had yet to be anointed a 'Datuk'.

He had married Chew Mei Mei, a Chinese girl, breaking his mother's heart in the process. At the time, the marriage seemed set to be a catastrophe: his mother had weeped disconsolately for weeks, mumbling the word "kaffir" in her dreams. "Fat Chew" as Mei Mei's father was called, was a follower of Confucius and a devoted eater of pork. He winced to think of his daughter's conversion to Islam - "all sembahyang, sembahyang - banging your head on the floor". But the marriage, oiled by the father-in-law's tin-mining fortune had been a quiet success and Mazlinda, as she was now called was as welcome in her in-law's houses as Kam was in his. Besides, her father's propensity for mistresses and concubines (he had had five on his deathbed) had prepared the daughter for her own husband's inevitable transgressions.

Raja Zulkarnain's death eighteen months before had freed the three children from the tiresome obligation of being nice to one another. In the past their father's looming presence had been enough to quell any outward display of anger or dislike. Every Sunday lunch they were expected to assemble and converse with one another notwithstanding their mutual antipathy. The old man had long favoured his eldest daughter, despairing, in turn of his son's bumptiousness. 'He may be my son Noon but that doesn't mean I have to like him', he would say. As if to compensate for her husband's favouritism Cik Bainun or Noon as he called her, lavished Kam with all her love and attention. Meriam was neglected entirely. She spent her days in the servant's quarters, learning how to cook and clean. As her father commented, "my daughter has learnt how to cook and mix with the lower orders: it was no surprise to me that she married Shahrir - who else would have her?".

A new source of misunderstanding had arisen between Kam and his two sisters. They had heard rumours that Kam wanted to knock down their father's house and build condominiums. Kam knew the sisters would be unwilling. Therefore he had chosen his first target well, mentioning the idea, in passing to Meriam's husband Shahrir. Kam had seen Shahrir buying cigarettes one stick at a time and knew it was only a matter of time before the money became too potent for Shahrir. He enticed Shahrir with figures that seemed obscene - enough, Shahrir had calculated to settle all his debts and buy a new terrace house in Subang Jaya's Phase 8. Having mentioned the subject to his perenially hard-up brother-in-law he had repeated the figures every few months or so. As expected Shahrir told Meriam who quite unexpectedly told Mahani who threw a self-righteous fit - thus upsetting his neatly laid plans.

Kam had dreamed of the idea from the day he first qualified as an architect. He had dreamed continuously of the apartments that he would build on the plot of the land (they transmuted into condominiums sometime in the early eighties), the ratios, the densities and the design: a simple, elegant structure with pitched Minangkabau roofs. Whilst he was sympathetic to his father's conservatism his dream of building, the overwhelming desire to plan, execute and construct was so ingrained in his psyche that it was impossible for him to look at the land without envisaging what he, the great Raja Kamarul could make of the spot. It was with these tantalising thoughts in his mind that he drove to his mother's house. He was determined to win them over.

"It won't be the same," Mei Mei said slowly, half to herself, "it just won't be the same without your father. The house, the gardens, Meriam's rendang, even the coronation chicken; it'll all be different. Like empty. No Ayah." Kam grunted. Twenty years of marriage had inured him to much of his wife's endless prattling, inured him to the noise but never the content. She continued, her chain of thought unbroken.

"Mak is so strong. I want to cry when I think of how she was when Ayah's body was brought back...she didn't cry, so brave. She stood all alone and she was so small in that house - she didn't want us to be with her."

"Sabrina, your mother is too sentimental. But she's right about one thing the house is too big for Mak," there was a note of irritation in his voice now and he rounded the corner in an aggressive manner, cutting so close to the curbstone that car shook from the jolt. He corrected himself angrily as if blaming his wife for his mistake. In the rear of the car, his teenage daughter, Sabrina was hurled across the backseat.

"Father!" But both parents ignored her.

"Kam, I would have been broken if it had been you."

"You, uh, always want to dramatise. We are not a 'Drama Minggu Ini' kind of family. Ayah was **my** father but I don't go on about it. Don't talk about it all the time. You're right though, I must talk to her about the house - it's just too big." Kam, her husband was not a man of great emotion - in fact his last mistress but one, 'Jamilah Jamboo' (on account of the firmness of her buttocks) had commented on Kam's determination to meet with her and have sex on the night of his father's death. 'That boy,' she had said later, shuddering in remembrance, 'he's like a grindstone: there's nothing soft, nothing gentle about him. Bang, bang, bang - finish. I don't know why he doesn't go to Chow Kit. Cheaper for him.' Unsurprisingly perhaps, 'Azizah Solid' forsook the fierce but clammy embrace of her rich architect lover for a demure Selangor State Assemblyman three times her age whose exaggerated devotion was as extreme as Kam's neglect had once been.

Kam had been deeply shamed by her desertion. Within an hour of hearing of her perfidy he had cancelled all her supplementary credit cards and changed the locks on their love nest in Wisma Stephens. He feared ridicule more than anything else in the world - the kind of ridicule that would ensue when people realised that he had been jettisoned in favour of a dithering YB old enough to be his father. From that hour on he excised 'Azizah' from his life acquiring a new mistress whose chief qualification was that she was pencil thin and without any discernible buttocks. It had all been achieved in as perfunctory and clinical a manner as possible, because for Kam, emotions - the messy things that women tried to blackmail him with in the morning, were a hindrance to the art of making buildings that made money that paid for the likes of 'Azizah Solid'.

Cik Bainun was making a final check of the preparations, as Kam's car pulled up the driveway. She had just rearranged the flowers and switched the cutlery around (Fuad, the houseboy had never been able to tell the difference between left and right). Looking up from the dining table she saw Latifah and smiled.

"I want you to wear that nice new baju kurung I bought you and put a bow in your hair - you can take one from my dressing table." It was a lovely day and she wanted everybody to be happy. She walked up to the maindoor repeating the words in English to herself, as she did - 'a lovely day'. She greeted Kam and Mei with the serenest of smiles.

"Assalaamualikum."

"Wa'alikumsalaam," Cik Bainun replied.

"Mak, you're looking lovelier than ever," he said in English and he hugged her. Sabrina bobbed down to kiss her grandmother's hand as Mei kissed her mother-in-law on both cheeks warmly.

"Kam, Mak is an old lady." She replied in Malay. She was touched, nonetheless, by his flattery and flushed.

"Mak, Kam's right you are looking lovely."

"You do 'Pah!" Sabrina joined in enthusiastically.

"Doesn't matter. The others are already here, come in, come in. Everyone except Mahmud - Mahani says he's got food poisoning." There was a moment's knowing silence before Kam spoke.

"Laksa assam, this year? I'm so hungry."

"Well there's no tapai," she teased, laughingly. Mei looked on and smiled. It still amazed her that her Kam could be so sweet and charming. Sabrina rushed ahead and salaamed each of her aunts and uncles, embracing her elder cousins and kissing their young children. Cik Bainun watched her granddaughter's energetic progress, the way she flicked the hair out of her eyes and twirled the babies up in the air. 'Just like Mahani,' she thought.

As with the year before and the years before that, there was an abundance of food. The conversation too, was no different from previous years: Meriam complained about her diets, 'they just aren't working' as she ladled a third helping of rice onto her plate; Kam gorged himself on his mother's laksa assam, belched very loudly and then light up an enormous cigar (to the delight of the young children who loved watching him roll the end of the cigar through the flame); Mahani, who watched her weight closely took some rojak, skimping on the sweet black sauce and the sayur lodeh. Cik Bainun insisted on taking some of the rich ayam percik and chicken kuzi even though Latifah looked on disapprovingly.

The conversation around the table ebbed and flowed. No one mentioned Mahmud's absence or the house. As Kam light up his cigar the conversation seemed to rise to a crescendo; everyone at the dining table save Cik Bainun seemed to have something to say. Mahani was telling her admiring nieces about the hospital, 'it's hard work - like running a hotel where every guest has a complaint'. Mahani's accent was the most English of all the children. Not one to be outdone, Kam started talking about his latest project as Sabrina, at the far end of the table, mimicked the rockstar Ella's singing style, 'like this-lah, Ciiiintaaaaaarghhh' and one of the babies - Cik Bainun's great-grandchild (who happened to be teething) started wailing.

Cik Bainun sat at the head of the table her face wreathed in smiles. She wasn't listening to any one particular conversation - as a mother, she had already heard everything her brood had to say. But rather, she was listening to the noise, to the disordered rush of conversation, children's cries and scraping chairs. And, like a bather on an empty beach during the monsoon she was enveloped in the all-encompassing roar of the ocean and the elements. Lost in the fullness of the sounds surrounding her, oblivious to the particular and the detailed.

"Take this house," Kam said expansively, throwing his arms out in a wide arc, "just imagine the potential." Mahani who was talking to Meriam's daughter Zarina, ignored his comment studiously.

"A job is a job. Being a doctor is more of a calling: you don't do it for the money - you do it for the love of it." She was a role model to her nieces and the one that they came to with their problems.

"How's the baby? Has he still got cholic?"

"It's been terrible Auntie Mahani. I've been awake every night for the past week - every time I put him down he cries and the husband refuses to get up."

"a beautiful shimmering block topped by with a Minangkabau roof set amidst landscaped gardens."

"- says he has work to do. As if I don't! I fell asleep at the office the other day and started snoring. That and the house-work, his family are always coming to stay."

"an Eden in the city".

"Don't you have a Filipino maid?"

"Yes, but she's so new I've got to show her everything."

"a dignified row of imperial palms with bougainvillea hanging from every balcony; lanais lined with black slate and shuttered windows."

"yesterday she put washing powder down the toilet and it foamed over every time we flushed it."

"You poor thing."

"Auntie Mahani, I wish I was more like you. You make it sound so easy."

"Two acres of land at thirty units per acre with a swimming pool and a squash court thrown in..."

"Easy? It's not easy, sayang. There are sacrifices." Mahani paused, not wanting to continue.

"Price the condos at four hundred thousand each and our profit margin is at least fifty per cent. That's the future - condo-living: all the facilities, security with none of the hassles. No snakes, no mosquitoes, no chicaks, Mak. So, Mak what do you think?" Kam spoke in Malay, smiling at his mother. But Mahani interjected before Cik Bainun could reply.

"Yes, Kam, kick your mother out of the only house she has known all her life so that you can build the condominiums of your dreams," Mahani said sarcastically. She had spoken in Malay; the language of all their arguments. Everyone else fell silent. Shahrir, Meriam's husband lowered his face into his coffee. Cik Bainun awoke from her reverie suddenly - the waters had receded: all around her there were rocks.

"Put your mother in a condo with all the mistresses and tarts!" she added aggressively. Kam smirked and replied.

"That maybe what Mahmud has done with his second wife Kak. I wouldn't do that to my mother."

"Astaghfirullah, my brother? Is this what it's come to? And who was keeping 'Azizah Solid' in Wisma Stephens until she ran off with the fat YB?" Brother and sister stared at each other in silent fury. But it was too much for Cik Bainun who called out angrily.

"Silence! Silence! I will not have this kind of talk at my table. Please for your late father's sake."

"I'm sorry Mak, but you heard her?"

"Both of you, apologise!"

"No!"

"Apologise, please," there were tears in her eyes.

"I'm sorry Kak."

"I'm sorry Mahani." But there was still enough malice in both their hearts to poison all the inhabitants of the putative condominium project.

"I think it's time the children had their badminton game," Cik Bainun said. Saddened she left the table and walked out onto the verandah, her heart heavy with foreboding. She had been able to stop them today. But she wasn't going to be around in the future.

She sat down on the cane armchair as if suddenly she had been made aware of her own powerlessness. She hugged herself. Zul was gone: his calming presence and authority all gone. She was alone - with no Zul to fend for her. She looked out across the verandah. There were memories of Zul all around her, pressing against her like gusts of warm rain-soaked winds. She wanted to be strong and willed herself not to cry - not to succumb on this, his favourite day of the year. An electric-blue kingfisher was perched on the raintree opposite the verandah. The bird twitched irritably. Even the birds, she thought were distressed. She looked away as the powerful gusts enveloped her. All she could think of was the hopelessness of the days that were left to her. Days and nights that would be filled with the petty squabbles of her own children. The ugly thoughts crowded in on her and she sobbed quietly on the verandah while the family prepared for the badminton match.

The match was another of the New Year's Day rituals. Each year the younger generation challenged the older to badminton. For the past two years' the children had actually won and everyone enjoyed the ramshackle match. The year before there had been fifteen players on the court: the numbers were augmented by Cik Bainun's great-grandchildren. There had not been enough badminton racquets to go around and her 'cit-cit' had had to make do with tiny hockey sticks, tennis and squash racquets as well as one small plastic spade.

As the children filed onto the court and knocked the shuttlecock backwards and forwards over the net Cik Bainun slowly regained her composure. She dabbed her eyes with her handkerchief and watched as Sabrina darted from side to side, tumbling onto the ground with her nephews and nieces in a good-humoured maul. Finally Kam, Meriam, Shahrir and Mahani emerged onto the court. Kam had a devilish slam that he had employed to good effect over the years, Shahrir was a drop-shot specialist, Mahani a solid defensive players and Meriam an unmoving presence in the middle of the court. The sisters were the "Sidek Brothers" in family parlance and Kam, "Ardy the Indonesian". Nobody had bothered to think of a name for Shahrir. When Kam was in a good mood, which he wasn't this year he would give a running commentary on the game in heavily accented Indonesian Malay - 'sekarang saudara Ardy menunggu serbis'. Even Latifah had laughed.

Mahani and Kam observed a frosty silence, ignoring one another on the court. When Kam miss-hit the shuttlecock making it land at his sister's feet, she ignored it and then trod on it just as he was about to bend down and pick it up. Meriam and Shahrir exchanged embarrassed glances: their cramped terrace house was more welcome than 'World War Three' on the courts.

"Everyone ready?" Sabrina and her cousin Zarina called out in unison.

"Yes," her father replied, "get on with it."

"No Uncle Kam," Zarina replied firmly, "we must repeat the rules - so no cheating or disagreeing." Kam grunted and Mahani swung her racquet through a wide arc before bringing it down in a mock smash. There was a curious half smile on her face. Zarina continued.

"Your court extends as far as the nangka trees at the back, the bougainvillea on the left and the path on the right. Auntie Mei is the line judge: all her decisions are final. Our court extends to the right as far as the flowers in front of the house and on the left as far as the path. The driveway is backside of the court (Sabrina giggled as Zarina frowned) - it's not funny Sabrina. If a shuttlecock is hit into the raintree that point shall be taken again." But another of the cousins objected.

"No, they always hit it into the tree: that's unfair." Kam scowled.

"Oh shut up and let's play."

"We'll serve first then."

"Just get on with it, Zarina."

"One: love," the youngsters chanted in unison as Zarina's drop shot of a serve fell beside Mahani, unnoticed.

"I wasn't ready!"

"Sorry Auntie Mahani, Uncle Kam said to get on with it." Mahani narrowed her eyes angrily and pulled up her sleeves.

Zarina served once again though this time the service was retrieved by Kam who knocked it back with a sharp tap. Sabrina intercepted the shot and lobbed it high over Uncle Shahrir.

"Duck," Meriam shouted, "I'll get it." And she did with a fierce smash that hit one of her grandchildren on the head.

"Hah," she cried - not noticing the injury, "love: one. Our serve." And so the game progressed with both sides notching up points as Mahani and Kam continued to ignore each other. As the game reached 13:13, both sides started taking things more seriously - Meriam took off her earrings and Mahani hitched up her baju kurung. Shahrir served a deft little shot that had Sabrina stretching to return it.

"Damn." She had pushed the shuttlecock high above the net and her father jumped up to smash the shuttlecock.

"14:13." This time Meriam served and her son-in-law smashed the shuttlecock back across the net. Embarrassed by her puny service she lumbered up to the shot.

"Alamak, is it an elephant?" Kam said in Malay under his breath as his sister thundered by. She rammed the shot back vigorously.

"Chelaka!" But the shot had not been firm enough to win the point and Sabrina had returned it with a drive straight down the middle of the court right between her father and Mahani. Since neither was talking to the other they rushed for the shot and crashed into one another with a dull thud and fell to the ground. Miraculously the shot was returned: the point and the game won.

Mahani was sitting on top of her brother and laughing. Kam, looked up and started laughing. As the adversaries laughed everyone else joined in, partly out of relief and partly because of the humour of the moment. From the balcony Cik Bainun clapped her hands excitedly.

"Better than the Thomas Cup, eh, Latifah?" she said.

The next game was an anti-climax as the youngsters took the lead and never lost their serve, winning 15:3.

"Daddy you're too old-lah," Sabrina said good-humouredly, "only good for one game." The third and final game was a more tense affair - the little ones with the squash and tennis racquets were told to sit down. The youngsters opened with the service but soon lost it when Sabrina hit the shuttlecock into the net at 4:love. The parents served carefully and smashed each of the returns to level the score.

"Too old, your father?" Meriam asked rhetorically. Kam was sweating profusely. The damp patched under his arms had expanded to reach the one in the middle of his chest as well as the one at the small of the back. When the score reached 8:8, Mahani loosened her hair bun, Meriam belched and Shahrir continued trying to look unobtrusive.

The game swung back to the youngsters as Kam's smashes grew a little inaccurate and Meriam was unable to run for shots that were more than a stretch away. At 12:8 Mahani spoke out angrily.

"Come on-lah Meriam we can't let them win!" Mahani was exasperated by her sister's inability to move.

"Yes, Meriam move your fat bottom!" Kam added, "no need to diet just run."

"You think it's easy. I'm a grandmother-lah, you know?"

"So's Mahani. Just move those fat thighs." Meriam's daughters giggled as their uncle and aunt teased their mother. They were sure of victory now. But in their over-confidence they lost their concentration and the parents were able to claw back four vital points to level the score. As Mahani or Kam smashed each of the winning shots all four of the parents shouted out excitedly.

"Yeh!" By this time Kam was drenched in sweat. His hair was dripping. Sabrina and her cousins were swearing at each other. They dearly wanted to extend their winning streak.

At 13:12, Shahrir missed an easy dropshot and the service passed back to the youngsters.

"This isn't sepak takraw. Hit the shuttlecock with your racquet not your kneecap." The shuttlecock had hit him on the knee. But the youngsters fluffed both their services (Sabrina was almost in tears). Cik Bainun shook her head in sympathy, thy'd been so close.

Meriam served at 13:12, her nephew-in-law returned the shot. Shahrir rushed up to net and slammed the shuttlecock into the top of the net where it was caught for a brief second before toppling onto the opposing side.

"Whoa!" he shouted, raising his fist in the air. Cik Bainun looked on in surprise. She had never seen him look so excited. Mahani and Meriam screamed in delight and Kam patted him on the back.

"Great stuff," Kam added. Mahani served for the match. A long, painfully drawn-out rally ensued as the two sides returned the shuttlecock with graceful shots that swept deep into both courts. By now everybody including Latifah and Fuad, the houseboy was gathered around the court gasping each time the shuttlecock was hit, their heads swivelling from side to side.

Sabrina was the first to falter. She miss-hit her father's attacking shot. The shuttlecock flew up into the air directly above Meriam's head. It was an easy smash and everyone knew it - unfortunately Meriam had missed every smash she attempted. Nonetheless she swallowed deeply and took a step back. Jumping up as best she could she smashed the shuttlecock with such ferocity that it crashed to the ground on the opposite side of the net.

Mahani threw her badminton racquet up into the air and hugged her sister, screaming "We won, we won". Meriam smiled exuberantly and ran up to Shahrir. They hugged and laughed. Meanwhile Kam looked at Mahani, tilted his head to one side as if to say 'I'm sorry, let's be friends'. Cik Bainun watched as they walked up to one another and hugged. She felt the tears in her eyes and pulled at the handkerchief that she kept in her sleeve. At last, she thought, we are one again, just as Zul would have wanted.

She remained on the verandah as the players trooped back into the house, calling for cold drinks. Sabrina and her cousins sulked, storming off to the kitchens. Though Cik Bainun was sorry for her grandchildren she was relieved that their parents had won and that the unpleasantness of lunch had been over-come. Maybe it was possible for the Mahani and Kam to live together - a bit more tolerance and thought would teach them both the importance of compromise. Kam was a forgiving and understanding boy. If only Mahani wasn't so headstrong. She knew that Kam would never touch the house - that it was all talk, silly talk. He was an architect! Of course he was going to talk about building things all the time. but she knew that he loved the house as much as her and that he wanted to keep it just the way it was - in memory of Zul. He was a fine boy. She sighed and looked off into the distance. Up in the raintree over-looking the badminton court, the kingfisher hopped from branch to branch. She watched as the bird preened itself, displaying sudden flashes of colour. This was the loveliest garden in the city. Where else could they play badminton? At the Lake Gardens? In Petaling Jaya? This was their home. She felt at peace once again - it had been a lovely day.

Just then she heard Kam's voice. He was speaking in Malay. The whispered the words angrily.

"There's no such thing as a free lunch Shahrir (he seemed to be speaking through his teeth). I've paid you already. You'd better work on your fat wife. Get her to persuade Mahani or I'll tell her about your problem with the English lecturer - abortion was it? Mak will have fallen for that little charade outside. She'll do whatever I want. Damn this house. I have to knock it down within six months and get building by the end of the year at the latest. Building costs are going up every week. I can't afford to hang around. I'm not putting up with another of these bloody lunches again...no sir."

KARIM RASLAN graduated from Cambridge with a degree in Law. He is now a writer and has contributed to both local, regional and international publications, newspaper and magazines. His novel, *The Bendaharas* is forthcoming in **Summer 1994** from **Skoob** *PACIFICA* London.

ROBERT YEO
The Further Adventures
of Holden Heng

Chapter 1

(I)

She was not dead, but she was in the Carmelite Monastery back home and she might as well be dead.

Funny, that a nunnery should be referred to as a monastery. A monastery was for monks, wasn't it?

Anyway, even if he had doubts whether Siew Fung would really remain a Carmelite nun, she was dead to him. Even if she should leave the Order, there was no way they would become lovers again. The past was the past was the past.

Nonetheless, he allowed the past to wash over him. In reality, he let thoughts about Siew Fung drip like ice-cream over chocolate mousse. He may not be mousse, but now that dinner was all over, he was prepared to allow that she was ice-cream. Then he switched to the airport departure scene.

(II)

As she tugged his red tie, Kim said, "I'm sure you're dying to go, Holden?"

"If every year is like this year, yes," Holden replied.

"And red tie some more. Whoever wears a suit and tie to fly anymore? That was me in the fifties," Kim teased.

Holden smiled. "I just wanted to be formal, to say a formal goodbye to the past."

Ray slapped him on the shoulder and cried, "That's my boy."

"Okay, but why red, eh?"

"Good luck, what else? After what I've been through, don't you think I deserve the luck, Kim?"

"You sure do," she agreed.

"Just remember the tricks I taught you, Ok," Ray said, "and keep away from spiritual women - "

"Stop it Ray," Kim said. "Holden's been through a lot this year." Turning to Holden, she asked, "So she's in the Carmelite Convent now, is she?"

"Yah," Holden replied without emotion.

"And did you see her, did you manage to see her?" Kim asked earnestly.

"Yes, last Friday."

"And how's she?"

"What can I say. She made up her mind."

"Do you think you've lost her for good."

"As far as I'm concerned, it's over."

"Hey, that's my boy lah," Ray burst in. "That's the style." And turning to Kim, he said approvingly, "He's ready for London."

"Funny thing, you know what?" Holden said.

"What?" Ray asked.

"She's now known as Sister Marie," Holden said.

Ray chuckled.

"And one of the last things she asked me to do was to call her Sister Marie."

Ray laughed.

"Sister Marie, Sister Marie, I can't believe it. What happened, why the name change?" Ray asked.

"That's what happens when a girl decides to become a nun. She's given a new name, a new identity and addressed as Sister. What's so funny, Ray?"

"It's not funny. I tell you especially when it happens to you," Holden said.

"And did you?" Ray asked.

"How could I, man?" Holden said, almost aghast.

"The things she did to you, Holden," Ray mused. "You know, it's strange, but I've never met her. I've given you tips about how to tackle her, I've listened to you moaning over her, but I've never met her?"

"Have you never met her?" Holden asked.

"No. Where's the occasion?" Ray asked.

Holden thought for a while and said, "I think you're right."

"She seems quite an unpredictable girl. I think you'll find her interesting, Ray, should you meet."

Ray nodded. "Which reminds me," he added, "there's someone who wants to meet you again before you go."

"Who?" he asked.

"Nan."

Kim remonstrated with Ray. "Darling, when are you ever going to stop interfering in Holden's affairs? He's leaving tonight, OK?"

"I know," Ray said, "but I just had to tell Nan about him." And he pointed to Holden. "She said she might come and see you off."

"Oh, OK, she's the past and I look forward to saying goodbye to the past."

At this stage, his publishing manager and boss, Mr Tan, joined them.

"I see I'm just in time to see you off, Holden," Mr Tan said.

"Hi, Mr Tan. I've just got a few minutes more," Holden replied.

Mr Tan handed him a wrapped-up book, saying, "This is what you want, I think. It came from London this morning."

Everyone laughed at the irony.

"Thanks," Holden said and bent down briefly to put it in his briefcase.

"Holden, Holden," a woman's voice was heard above the talk and everyone turned to see Nanette come into view, accompanied by a burly mustachioed Chinese. She burst through, kissed Holden on both cheeks and said, "So, you are leaving tonight?"

"Yes," he said, slightly embarrassed but pleased.

"But you come back soon, oui," she pleaded.

"Yes, in four month's time," he said.

"Oh, so it is only au revoir, not adieu."

"Oui, au revoir, not adieu. I'm sure I'll see you soon."

Kim and Ray exchanged what-is-going-on glances. Then Nan gently grabbed her companion with her left arm and thrust him forward to introduce him.

"Holden," she said, "this is my friend Jackie Cheung."

Jackie, looking cool and suave, did not offer to shake hands but merely said, "Holden Heng. I've heard a lot about you." His accent was clearly Hongkie. Holden said, "Hi Jackie." He then introduced Jackie to the rest and Nan to Mr Tan.

"I hear you're going to change your name? asked Mr Tan.

"Who told you," Holden demanded.

"Office talk," said Mr Tan.

"Hey, wait a minute," said Ray at the same time, "you can't do this, man, there is only one Holden, the one and only Holden Heng."

"Thanks," said Holden, "you're a big help, Ray. I thought you were helping me break with the past?"

"Wait till Siew Fung hears about this...I mean Sister Marie, it's enough to send her out of the convent."

Kim pinched him gently. "C'mon, Ray."

"You see what girls can do, lah," Ray went on, ignoring Kim and Holden, "make a guy change his perfectly good name. How can, eh Nan?"

"Of course you must not. I will miss calling you, Holden."

"No, no," Holden protested, "I'm not changing my name, I'm just not using it anymore."

"Then what name will you go by?" Kim asked.

"How Tan," said Holden.

"How what?" asked Nan.

"How Tan" he repeated firmly.

"How Tan. It sounds like how can. No it is not romantic, Holden is much better, more romantic."

"I'm through with romance," said Holden.

There were laughter all round. At this stage, the first announcement for his departure was heard and Holden excused himself and went to his mother, Mayo, Curtis and Aunty, to say goodbye. He hugged his mother and she kissed him.

"Write as soon as you can," she reminded him.

"Don't forget to write to me also," said Aunty.

To Mayo and Curtis, he said, "You two can have the phone all to yourself. Only don't quarrel over it, OK?"

"No chance, big brother, with you out of the way, the phone is going to be very quiet," said Mayo.

"Don't kid yourself, chea. The only reason it's going to be quiet is that you've got exams," said Curtis.

"As if you haven't got," said Mayo and stuck out her tongue to him.

"Looks like you both will fight over a quiet phone. Glad I'm going," Holden said.

"Betcha you won't be able to use your new name. The English sure cannot pronounce it," said Curtis.

"And even if they can," said Mayo, "it will sound like 'How Tan', and the last thing you will get in the English winter is a tan."

The second call came and Holden waved to his relatives and friends and strode towards the departure lounge.

© Robert Yeo, 1993.

ROBERT YEO has published three books of poems, one novel and numerous anthologies of short stories, plays and poems for both the general and school readers. In addition, he has written four plays, all of which have been performed in Singapore, Hong Kong and New York.

The poems are found in *Coming Home Baby* (1971), *And Napalm Does Not Help* (1977) and *A Part of Three* (1989). The novel, *The Adventures of Holden Heng*, appeared in 1986. The plays include *Are You There, Singapore?* (1974), *One Year Back Home* (1980, staged reading in La Mama 1985), *Second Chance* (1989, HK Arts Fest Fringe; 1992 Singapore) and *The Eye of History* (1992).

He is now Senior Lecturer in the Nanyang Technological University, National Institute of Education, Singapore.

A Beginning and a Middle Without an Ending

When it got to about ten o'clock, the incessant chatter started to peter off. Leng Eng turned to Elaine and asked if her sister would sing a song. Even in asking, Leng Eng was not herself convinced that it was a good idea. It was a dull gathering, a gaggle of girls who, like herself, had completed school a few years back. Similarly, if Jimmy had been free, why would she, Leng Eng, be with them?

Hurry up! Elaine's tone, while not as sharp as when rapping out orders at home, was commanding enough. Betty got up and walked to the centre of the room. She showed no awkwardness or embarrassment as being thus singled out. At twelve, she showed a resilience beyond her years. There was something rather vacuous about her face.

What's going on?

My sister's going to sing a song. You don't mind?

What's there to mind? Sing what?

Betty started singing a song in Mandarin. She had heard that song often enough to have learnt it by rote. When she first heard it performed by a Taiwanese singer, she there and then decided it would be a song she would sing forever. That Taiwanese singer had been sensational. At every performance, she ended the song with tears hosing down her face. To Betty, it was not only moving; it was like having access to an entire vista of human understanding that had so far eluded her.

Her earnest strong voice and impassive face struck the audience as comic. But she sang in obedience to the mannerly deployment of her heart. Her voice soared and, when she came to the end and had hit the last note, she fell onto the floor in a heap.

Bring a towel. Quick! Leng Eng screamed, more in anger than concern.

Elaine, bent over her sister, suddenly straightened herself. Betty stood up. And Elaine, who had heard her practising the song so often quickly understood what it was all about. Betty had wanted to extend the Taiwanese singer's presentation. In place of tears,

Betty had chosen the faint, the dramatic crumble. A sense of admiration, shame and anger welled up; Elaine got up and gave Betty a resounding slap.

The dull gathering ended on a merry note for nearly everyone. And Betty - who could tell what she felt? Leng Eng started praising Betty; the suppressed snigger and muffled laughter around her was ambient support.

You must come more often. Can't hide all that talent, you know. Elaine, you must enter her for the talentime. Whether she wins or not, sure to floor the judges.

Leng Eng was stacking glasses and plates on a tray.

Want some more coffee or not? Better say so, if not no time to make some more.

Later, thirty-five years later, Betty was the executive director of a modelling school.

Excuse me, Miss Wong, got two more enrolled this morning. Want to accept or not?

The new secretary did not last long.

You have to speak correctly. Above everything else, you must have poise. In speaking to you, the participants, the photographers, whoever they are, must feel as if you are confiding in them. Betty Wong, in her advice to the secretary being interviewed, was herself confident and highly poised. Her string of pearls secreted the wisdom of the sea. There is so much unhappiness in the world. If I could educate every woman to be elegant and charming, half the troubles of the world would be gone. You must understand, such education is the most difficult to instil in people. We have to work very hard. We have to make sacrifices.

Betty Wong levitated from her chair and, in crossing the room in regular, heart-felt steps, thought fleetingly of a song she could no longer fully remember.

Oh, hello, Vicki, Your show was fantastic! Such classical lines! Such poetry of motion!

Vicki held on the elegant white telephone, her hand a nubile technological extension. Oh, right, right! It doesn't matter. I'll call again. Hey Betty, you know what? Benny's going to have a show in Manila next month.

Who's financing it? I see, I see, and all expenses paid for. What! Twenty-five percent guaranteed sales.

Betty Wong inclined her head a little and both her hands described quarter-circles of beatitude. It isn't so much the financial success. Just imagine what Benny can and must do. What an educational experience it will have to be.

Betty returned to her office. In the eggshell splendour, a secondary thought raced through her mind. I must send Elaine some money. She is, after all, my sister. Should I send her a thousand? She wrote out a cheque for two hundred, lit a cigarette, buzzed the intercom, tore up the cheque and, when the new secretary came in, she was frowning over a letter like an octopus that had organized its tentacles over a sheet of sea-weed. She did not look up immediately; and when she did, the secretary's obedient eyes immediately rolled away. Betty Wong smiled an interior smile, a little mental zip had been pulled. An old trick, she thought, but how effective. The secretary was very brand new.

It wasn't Cent meditation I dictated. It was Zen meditation. Z for Zip. You have been very remiss.

> re: Miss Zatika
> I regret to inform you that the nominee you
> proposed for our course on Inner Poise and
> Cent Meditation has been unsuccessful.

Miss Zatika, prior to nomination, had been Au Lin Soo, a healthy fresh-face. Why would spring lamb want to pass off as meditative mutton? Such a thought was not in Betty Wong's ideational agenda.

> But if she likes, she could try again.

Her letter to the director of a lesser-known modelling school was one she had sent off hundreds of times. The difference each time was that the name was different. The name of the course was also different. Last week, she regretted the rejection of a participant for The Externalization Of Inner Light.

Betty Wong felt tired. All these trivial details. There is absolutely no one one can depend on. She had wanted, every single day, to plan and map out her Beauty Edification Project. A nearby file carried the inscription:

DhPP/II/16A
Physiognometrics - Within and Without
Beauty, the Art and the Science of, and the
    Philosophy of

Apart from the inscription, the file was empty, without.

An ending must be found. Without it, Betty Wong could only go on rejecting the Zatikas. The Zatikas are abundant. Somewhere in between the rejection and the realization that the Zatikas were being rejected for nothing, for things that weren't there; somehow, in between the chuckle and the choke, Betty Wong drew a conclusion. It was the collapse before the song started. And poor Elaine, the face, the recollection of the face that could not launch Betty Wong's hand.

© Arthur Yap, 1993.

ARTHUR YAP is a senior lecturer in the Department of English at the National University of Singapore.

His first collection of poems, *Only Lines*, published in 1971 was awarded by the National Book Development Council of Singapore in 1976. His other works include *Common Place*, published in 1977; *Down the Line*, published in 1980, was awarded the NBDC Award in 1982 and *Man Snake Apple & Other Poems* is his latest collection of poems. His **Collected Poems** is forthcoming **Summer, 1994.**

In 1983 he was awarded the Cultural Medallion in Singapore and the Southeast Asia Write Award in Bangkok. He was again awarded the NBDC Award in 1988.

Arthur has made seven solo exhibitions at the National Library and at the Alpha Gallery, Singapore from 1969-1977.

PHILIP JEYARETNAM
Making Coffee

On waking my thoughts are of the jungle, that half-hour before first light, shoulders numbly hunched over damp rifle, awaiting the dawn, air moist, bones cold. In the bathroom it is as if I have not shaved or showered for a week. I splash water onto my face with the eagerness of a young soldier back in camp after a week's patrolling. At least it has resisted the flab to which my friends have succumbed.

The maid has coffee ready downstairs, and Weixian packed and ready to meet the school bus. She's past the age when she might welcome a hug from her father, so I just smile and tell her to have a good day. I ask Nina if the mistress is up yet. She's not, so I open the newspaper and take a sip of coffee. I'm never fully awake till I've had my coffee.

Another day of meetings awaits me. The older I get the less real work I seem to do, the more it's just networking, pumping hands, that's what gets the business. There are always youngsters to keep the wheels turning, eager and bright, convinced that their big break is just around the corner. At four o'clock golf with the Minister. Mutual back-scratching, cooperation between government and business essential for the greater good of the nation. I tell him what the industry needs, he listens, adopts what he can, and projects to the public an image of assured competence. I am a man with connections, a man who gets things done.

On the green one often hears the crackle of small arms fire. I imagine young green bodies darting through the undergrowth, up, four seconds, down, cover, aim, fire, up, four seconds, on and on until nausea grips you in the pit of the stomach. Today the Minister is in a good mood, expansive, he tells stories of constituency dinners, when the garlands weigh him down like rubber tyres and he's introduced by some community worthy who keeps calling him Minister. He laughs at every story I offer, then nods solemnly when I say we really need more leadership if we are ever truly to go regional. "We're all small businessmen. Comfortable making the easy money, scared of taking risks. Government must take the initiative. Break the old mind-set."

Beers in the clubhouse turn into dinner. Without the Minister of course, he's off for some function or other. I eat with others who joined us over drinks, impressed not only by my nonchalant manner with the Minister, but also by the way I was on first-name terms with his bodyguard.

By the time I reach home Weixian is asleep. Shirley is awake in her room, watching TV. I enter, peck her on the lips, and after fielding the essential, dutiful questions retire to a glass of scotch. No massage interrupted my busy schedule today and my loins burn for a woman, even Shirley, but I leave it, knowing that I will only be rebuffed. One reaches a stage when things are too comfortable to risk any attempt at making things better.

This is not of course how it always was. Those were feverish days when I first met Shirley, a different faculty at the U but the same year, and so some three years my junior. I didn't feel comfortable with her at all, not at all. She was so good-looking, effortless in her movements, lively and charming. I felt leaden and dull beside her, old beyond my years...and challenged. I pursued her with a dogged single-mindedness, and when she finally consented to date me I did not stop until I held her naked in my arms. Touching the blood on the sheets I told her that now at last she was no longer a child, and now at last she was mine. She cried, and could not stop crying, though in between her sobs she told me how much she loved me. How good life felt in those days, to have a woman, to be doing well in studies, to have the world before me. Or even earlier, in Officer Cadet School, my whole life focused on graduating, obtaining a commission, not just in for me, but for each and every member of my platoon. We were cadets together, striving for excellence, breathing duty, honour, country as we ran together, singing of our nation.

Life has gone well. A pretty wife, a healthy daughter, a house my parents could never have dreamed of owning. My middle-aged unease is really the purest self-indulgence. What more surely could I ask for?

The next day I visit my parents. I am always gratified by mother's fuss. Father is gruff, as usual. He hardly speaks. No doubt he resents the impotence of old age, the dependency into which my success has thrust him. Looking at those tough hands that once wielded ever so readily a stout bamboo cane I cannot resist a certain satisfaction. This quickly passes however, for I want his approval more than his resentment. I know he is disdainful of the fact that Shirley has not accompanied me, that she would never tend me as mother does him. He cannot understand that it is a different world, that no woman, at least no worthwhile woman, can devote herself to a man in the way that once was universal. They want their own lives, their own identities, and Shirley does a lot of good in the community, with charities and women's groups, though sometimes I wish she'd spend more time with Weixian (but who of course am I to talk?). Mother gives me *bak chang* to take home, as if even after all these years away from her she must still make sure I'm properly fed.

She would certainly agree with the sentiments of the latest campaign to persuade people to marry younger and have kids earlier, that children bring purpose and direction to one's life, that one should live for one's children. The sentiments are noble ones, and yes I do love Weixian. When she's ill I ache inside at my powerlessness. But the campaign's message is fatally flawed, for if one human being lacks meaning, can find no purpose within his own life, how does it help, how does it supply that missing meaning, to bring another lost and lonely person into the world?

I wonder if Shirley's loins have welcomed other men since we married. She would be statistically anomalous if they had not, for she remains slim and pretty, and God knows what little sex we do have can hardly satisfy her. I marvel at my equanimity, my dispassionate contemplation of such matters, for it was only what some fifteen years ago when I had that fight, if one can call it that, with Dennis. He had been making passes at her, I'm sure of it, though she insisted it was only a matter of friendship. The bugger had not demurred when I accused him of dishonourable motives, nor put up any resistance to the two slaps I had given him, palm open, across his right cheek. These days I'd probably be glad if some man showed an interest in her. A welcome diversion, an amusement for her.

With the first person I pursued after our marriage I made the mistake of courting her, of pretending grand passions as in the days before I met Shirley, when I wanted a woman's body but not her heart, but knew one had to approach the average under-graduate, her head filled with romantic notions, from inside out as it were. I didn't realise the same rule does not apply to women who have broken free from adolescence, and so scared her into a kind, compassionate refusal of my advances. I did not make the same mistake again, and have enjoyed numerous desultory dalliances since.

I am interrupted in my early afternoon reverie, my usual eyes-open, day-dreaming nap, by Meng. He's one of my most enthusiastic young engineers. The sort of fellow who can be counted on for at least one useful incremental improvement to the production process every month, still young enough to enjoy the grand illusion that one of these days he'll come up with something really big, an idea or invention that will make him truly rich, and more importantly earn him universal fame and respect.

He needs my go-ahead on a proposal on which he sent me a memo a week ago. I can't remember having seen it until my secretary digs it out and reminds me that I'd KIVed it the week before. Ah yes, I rush to say, a very interesting suggestion, but it really needs to be passed through Ong and his team. Meng objects, he feels any delay is just a waste of money, but I silence him by asking him whose money is he talking about, and doesn't he understand the need to follow procedures in any organisation. He crawls away like a dejected puppy. My secretary raises her eyebrows at me, and I wonder if the two of them are having an affair for her to be so obvious about her sympathies.

I go home early for dinner, feeling the need to spend time with the family, only to find that Weixian has gone to stay at a friend's place, and Shirley's playing bridge at the Club. I watch TV, then read for a while. Nina comes by to ask if I need any-thing, and for a moment, idly turned towards her, I admire her curves, apparent despite the unshapely house dress, then quickly shut the door on such dangerous thoughts, the sort of thing that can ruin a man forever, and say no, thank you Nina, I can manage.

I think of my sisters, both overseas, one married to a Canadian doctor, another to an English lawyer. Both their husbands floated through Singapore sometime ago and were really blessed with remarkable good fortune in meeting and marrying my sisters. They were always devoted to me, and I am envious of their husbands, who have taken them away, so far from me.

They, and mother, were always on my side. No matter that I had tracked mud through the flat, they would happily clean it up before father's return. When he stood over me with report card in one hand, cane in the other, they were there to plead on my behalf. He probably felt his position undermined, his supremacy usurped, a long long time ago, long before I started work at twice the salary he had retired on.

Shirley comes home late. I hear her in the kitchen and go downstairs. There's alcohol, cognac I think, on her breath, and her eyes were a little wild. Where were you I ask, knowing what she will say, and that it will not be the truth. Playing bridge. The girls suggested a drink after. I nod, and help her with the coffee maker. We cooperate on the filter paper, the scoops of ground coffee, the water, and I think of late nights in the hostel, instant coffee then of course, nights of yearning before the net I cast had captured her, I think of stripping and assembling rifles, my section of cadets in one line, moving faster and faster with each practice until our fingers are rubbed sore, I think of late nights working through calculations, poring over designs, those early days of work. I kiss her hard on the lips, and then more gently, my tongue thrusting between her parted lips, her body giving as she leans back against the countertop. I taste the cognac, taste her and someone else, and feel myself harden against her. The coffee smells great in my nostrils as I stand here, enfolding my wife, mourning those days of grand illusion.

© Philip Jeyaretnam, 1993.

PHILIP JEYARETNAM is the author of *First Loves* (Times Editions Ltd., 1987) and *Raffles Place Ragtime* (Times Editions Ltd., 1988). His short story *Evening Under Frangipani* won 1st Prize in the 1985 Singapore National Short Story Competition. He has a new novel scheduled to appear before the end of the year. He is married and lives in Singapore where he also practises law.

ALFRED A. YUSON
The Music Child

When I first heard of the hair-string fiddlers from Fil, I thought it was just another of his blustery inventions.

But then the odd and curious never seem in short supply in these islands. Quickly have I learned to keep the brow down upon getting wind of possibly interesting copy.

I was in Southern Philippines for a follow-up story on *muro-ami* fishing, having already sent a report on the Manila end of the ecologically ruinous operations.

I had interviewed the big bosses of the Frebel Fishing Corporation, as well as a few legislators involved in a committee on natural resources. Easy enough to get into these high offices when one represents Western media.

It was a dying issue as far as the local papers went. Officials had upheld the ban on boy divers pounding the reefs with iron balls to drive fish into giant nets. All that the greedy operators could do was take it on the chin and shrug. But for the *Examiner* back home, the triumph of environmental concern would always rate a banner story in the features section. So had my editor assured me as soon as I faxed Part One of the series.

Ecology couldn't die as a cause in the world's leading democracy. And where better to flush out tales of horror than in Third World enclaves run by petty politicians?

Cebu City was a smaller Manila, just as dense, dustier, hotter, more humid, except at the seafront where I found the usual spot of calm amid the chaos, by sitting alone over cold San Miguel beer in a small restaurant.

The day I flew in I hired a jeepney, or rather, had Fil hire a jeepney to drive us down to the southernmost tip of the elongated island. There we had sought out the boy divers who were now all out of work.

Fil provided the free translation as I explained to their fathers and the barrio chiefs that I wasn't taking any sides. It was strictly a human interest story.

The good old Polaroid helped us along, until I brought out the Nikkormat for more professional images this side of posterity.

Indeed awash in human interest were the boys' accounts of their life at sea - packed by the hundreds in a small ship for months on end, diving daily with only makeshift goggles for protection, tugging diligently at the scare lines underwater to ensure a profitable catch of all kinds of reef denizens, at the expense of battered corals.

Short-term gains for everyone, of course. But the perilous work earned the family some credit in the barrio store.

When occasionally a boy of 13 or 15 didn't surface, attacked by sharks, or worse, the bends, then so sorry. One life lost at sea, one mouth less to feed in the poor southern tip of the island. The victim's kin need not mourn over the body. If recovered at all it was buried in some anonymous, far-off isle where luckless divers were destined to spend their eternal summers under a few feet of sand and some tropical shade.

The tapes would have to be transcribed for the next night or so. A simple chore then, a few hours of holding fort in the hotel room. I'd pare down Fil's translations of the boys' stories. Adding no more than a brief intro, I'd let the barrio kids speak for themselves. The cause of ecology would best be served by the voice of the innocents.

For the nonce, languorous time enough to idle at a resto by the quay.

The San Mig isn't quite as chilled as I'd prefer. But my thirst for local color is no sooner provoked than quenched here in this apparent hotbed of cargo cults.

A tuna's jaw is paraded along the row of tables before it's plunked down upon a grill resting on red-hot coals. The instant hiss wafts the call of the sea. Surge of smoke dies back into imminent succulence.

I slide a fork under a cluster of fresh green seaweed swimming in cane vinegar. There it is again, siren song of brine, tart picture of boys diving a hundred feet to pummel the magnificent corals. It's a life. For an American enervated by the afternoon heat, the philosophy of seabreeze is the sole recourse.

Violins with strings made of human hair, Fil had said. Up north, in some obscure settlement no tourists had yet heard of, far from the gleaming white sands of the bewitching coastline.

What is it in these people, I ask myself, that makes light of the uncommon, serves it as fodder to guests of bland interest?

Fil said they saved the tresses of the tribe's departed, twined it round for weeks in a vat filled with tree sap, and pulled on the thickness to create a certain pitch. Then they strung up the instruments, not really violins, said Fil, but similar, without a waist, and no frets, just a small round hole where the bow caressed the belly.

He said he wasn't sure what the bowstring was made of, perhaps some fiber drawn from jungle vine. He hadn't seen the instrument himself, had never heard the tribesman play. But he had gotten word of how they had performed in some barrio in the hinterland, where they had been chanced upon by a musicologist who taught in one of the city's universities. The professor had asked the musicians to give an evening concert for the coming fiesta in the big city.

That wouldn't be until a month. I could go north with Fil as soon as I faxed the follow-up piece on the aborted rape of tropical reefs, answer to another disquieting call of human interest.

This could be bigger game, worthy of Ripley's.

The tuna's jaw is flopped over. Again its juices drip on the live coals and send whiffs of smoke to ride the seawind. Incredibly mouth-watering it is, a hint of Pacific heaven, and certainly worth more than I bargained for when I agreed to go East for the *Examiner*.

Fil arrives in a tricycle. He is all heigh-ho and bluster - a lean, dark man with a grin wider than the tuna's in its grilling throes. He comes lunging towards my table on the balls of his feet.

"Okay, Pardner! We go tomorrow by bus. Leave at nine. Three, four hours' trip. Then we get jeepney from small town. If none, we walk. Only a few hours. Right, Pardner? Ahh, Fil needs beer. Beer and tuna to make Fil and Pardner strong for long trip tomorrow!"

As Fil had warned, the bus ride proved to be an exercise in inertia. We stopped at every barrio to pick up old women and young pigs, baskets of corn and cassava, a couple of soldiers with their M-16s swinging awkwardly to threaten everyone as we creaked and groaned along the winding dirt road.

Soon there was no sight of sea. The rainforest closed in on us, and the implacable jungle stench seemed to quiet even the trussed-up piglets.

Fil and I got off five hours later, way past noon, and headed straight for a small store to pick up some sardine cans. We opened one, dipped some stale buns into the blood-red sauce, and washed it all down with warm Coke.

Between bites and sips, Fil spoke to the pregnant woman tending the store. She sent off a scrawny kid who came back with a fat guy in a greasy undershirt.

I could tell the kind of jeepney the fellow had just by counting the oilstains round his beerbelly, and the way he looked up at the sky and scratched his head as Fil plied him with questions.

In another hour we sputtered off, taking a narrow, overgrown trail up a hill before descending into a small valley. Fording a stream, I asked for a quick stop to fill an empty Coke bottle with cool mountain water. Then we struggled up several steep inclines again, with the jeepney surprisingly coughing up enough power to make it but barely each time.

It was an old logging road, Fil said, now unused. The loggers had moved a number of mountains away. This tribe we're visiting, he said, no one wants to tangle with them. Everyone's afraid his scalp will wind up making strange music. Ha ha ha ha ha, Fil laughed, elbowing the driver's paunch. Ha ha ha ha ha. And the clattering tailpipe laughed along with him.

We stopped at a clearing where the driver said we couldn't go any further. The road didn't end, but he had never made it past that ridge before, he said and Fil translated. We had to walk the rest of the way. The driver would come along, even spend the night with us, for Fil might not make much sense to the tribe, ha ha ha ha ha.

Nonoy the driver was right. The village was just a couple of cigarettes away, off the old logging road and down some damp path through thick jungle. Suddenly we stumbled upon a cluster of huts in a grassy clearing. A good thing it was too, for the mountain dark was fast closing in on us.

The villagers were all excited at the sight of the visitors, especially the white man with the Cokes and cameras. They offered freshly boiled yams I couldn't believe the sweetness of, and sat us by an early fire.

Much of the evening was taken up by Fil's exchanges with the elders, helped along by Nonoy, to much tittering among the women and occasional nodding from the men.

Fil said it was alright to take pictures. I didn't really feel like it but decided to try a new trick by aiming and clicking both cameras simultaneously so they could share the flash. The kids squealed and chattered about how they had gone blind, according to Fil, ha ha ha ha ha.

The squeals grew louder on the part of the women when they saw themselves taking shape and color like slow magic on the white square. Everyone jostled to take a look. One man said that he had lost a snapshot like that taken by a cousin who had worked a year in Saudi Arabia.

For dinner we had salted meat, salted fish, boiled vegetables and crushed corn steamed with rice. Still sitting on our haunches, we shared two bottles of rum and more of Fil's jokes, this time about Japanese tourists flocking to the island's beaches in their floppy hats.

Before we knew it, the band had formed before us, nine men and women fiddling with their bows while smiling shyly to themselves. As we all quieted down, they proceeded to play a tune in unison.

The kids continued to run about and twirl the Coke bottles in the dust. The moon rose above some distant treetops, gibbous and bright orange. The music seemed to rise as well from all the nameless vines and tendrils in the forest.

The tune was rather cloying. The sounds the extraordinary instruments made were terribly scratchy at times, with some of the players frequently sliding up or down into another key. But they were a pretty picture alright, seated on low stools in an irregular row beyond the fire, smiling and laughing at false screeches as they nodded in time over their bows.

The wooden instruments were set on their laps or propped against a hip and strummed downward like a fiddle.

"*Ginse*," an old man said. "*Ginse*," Fil repeated to name the instrument. Its sound was a mite unearthly, incredibly high-pitched, and I couldn't tell if it was the tune that required short stabbing notes or it was just the *ginse*'s limitations, until the musicians fell upon a passage where their bowstrings sawed long and graceful curves to produce extended wails that finally brought the piece to a lugubrious close.

Fil and I clapped loudly and raced one another to the players. A *ginse* was quickly handed over and I plucked innocently at the strings, noting them to be as taut as any bow fiddle's. I slid a thumb upwards and elicited a sharp whine that sent a musician into a mock grimace.

"Is it really human hair?" I asked Fil, still a bit incredulous.

He pressed his own palm up and down the strings before turning to the players to relay my query.

Yes, they all nodded, their faces lighting up with a mischievous glint that seemed to say you don't have to believe it.

An old woman explained in all seriousness how they had made such instruments since as far back as her own mother could remember. The women grew their hair long and had it cut only twice in their lives. The hair was often preserved in separate packets, but sometimes mixed together, until the old men felt it was time to gather the sap of a particular tree, from where the wood for the fiddle's body also came. The hair was boiled in the sap for days, then brought out to cool as thick clumps, pulled in quick jerks and returned to the frothing sap. The process was repeated for weeks.

Fil was getting excited translating what Nonoy said the old woman said, at times heedlessly racing on until Nonoy would shake his head and tug at his arm and correct what he said. A long argument ensued between them over what the old woman had really meant. Then Fil would nod vigorously and so would Nonoy, and they'd agree before Fil turned to me again to alter his initial version, but not beyond a whit.

I asked if it was true that they'd be performing in the city for the fiesta. Yes, they said, it would be the first time they'd face a large crowd. Could you give me the name of the musicologist, and where I can find him in the city? One of the men ran off to his hut and came back waving a calling card.

I copied the name and address, resolving to rely more on the professor's likely notes on the oddity than on Fil's elaborations which I had grown to suspect. I'd take more pictures in the morning, and come up with a story that should titillate the punks in Frisco.

Meanwhile we could sit back around the fire and enjoy the rest of the evening's casual performance. The group continued with their esoteric repertoire long after we ran out of rum.

"It's a pity," one of the women said in the morning, "that Luisito can't come with us to the city. If he did they'd really hear something."

Again Fil and Nonoy had to argue endlessly over the full import of the woman's utterance. She continued to speak to them, and Fil's eyes grew extraordinarily large as he turned around to interpret, then caught himself and questioned the woman further while Nonoy attempted to help.

The story I eventually heard had to do with a boy, not of their tribe, but the son of a mestizo farm owner some hills away. They called him the music child, for he had a truly wondrous voice, the woman said - a boy who never spoke but sang his every phrase, and mimicked to perfection all the birdsounds and jungle calls, the roar of the waterfall by his father's cornfields, the monsoon wind and rustle of stalks.

They had visited the farm some months back, and played before Don Julio on their hair-stringed instruments. He had admired their talent, played along with them on his piano, then introduced his son. The boy couldn't have been more than twelve, but there was no telling for he was probably big for his age, having a large mestizo for a father. Luisito was himself dark-skinned but looked robust. His mother, a native of the place, had died in childbirth.

The father told them the infant had sung, not cried, when held aloft by the midwife upon delivery. His first song had been eerily plaintive, reeking of death, as if he knew, and indeed was describing, his mother's slippage into the afterlife at that very moment.

Don Julio recounted this in near tears before them. He hadn't been too sure if he could share the boy with them that evening, but realized that his son had to meet people who also made music.

The boy was brought out of his room, from where he had obviously been listening. He came out all in smiles, sang his greetings and differences with the purest voice they had ever heard, then launched, with a twinkle in his eyes, into an imitation of their fiddles' sounds. He replicated passages of the music they had played as if he were one of those music boxes the professor had once brought to record their songs.

No, they hadn't told the university man about the boy. They had agreed to honor Don Julio's request to keep him a secret until he grew up.

But since I was of fair skin like the Don, he might not mind, said the woman. He is lonely, she pronounced gravely. He has to share his treasure of a son.

"This isn't just a fancy story?" I kept asking Fil. He turned to the woman again. Some of the other musicians had joined us and now repeated her claims. Never had they heard such a voice, so sweet and powerful, bereft of quaver, and of such assurance and luster that anyone who heard him could not help but gasp. It was effortless singing, they said, as if he were only talking. He had sang with them that night, making up words to fit their music which he was hearing for the first time. But he never fell out of step, predicting correctly where the passage would course even before they strummed the next notes.

Don Julio's eyes were full of joyful tears at the music they made together. And when it was over, he kissed his son and told him to go to bed. The music child sang goodnight and farewell in the most becalming way, using phrases that were a mixture of birdcalls at twilight and certain words from the area's dialect.

They didn't dare ask Don Julio if he would allow the boy to sing with them in the fiesta, not after he had stressed that the boy should remain unknown. He had admitted however that it was just a matter of time before someone breathed a word about the boy to the outside world.

On our return to the city I immediately sought out Dr. Cesar Abellana at a Catholic university.

He proved extremely helpful and articulate, expounding on what he knew of the hair-string fiddlers, as he had chosen to call them. He said he hadn't finished his research on the origin of their uncommon instrument, but had more or less codified the range of its musical capabilities.

91

He rattled off terms that had me scribbling like a freshman in choir school, then allowed as to how he feared that he wasn't doing the right thing, exposing the musicians to possible exploitation by local tourism officials.

He didn't want them to turn into a sideshow, Dr. Abellana said in all earnestness. But he thought that the benefit program would at least make his own students aware of the varieties of musical expression, and of how music was such a crying human need as to defy all convention. Of course the school would also raise funds from the unique attraction of the instruments as much as the cultural fascination with the performers themselves.

I wondered silently how he would react to reports about the music child. The boy had been in my mind for days. The possibility of finding out if what I had heard about him was true had intrigued me no end.

I resolved to finish the transcription of Muro-Ami Part Two, wrap it up and send it off, then go back to the hinterlands with Fil to see what we could come up with on the story of Don Julio and his son.

Fil came to the hotel the next day raring to go. He had taken a lease on an old Willys jeep, four-wheel drive. We could have it for an entire week, he said, although I had only given him enough cash for three days at the normal rate.

Fil always seemed to get everything at a bargain, that much I can say of his aim-to-please attitude. My contact in Manila hadn't fed me a live one when he gave me Fil's address in Cebu. The guy was proving so effectively gung-ho that I could forgive him his rap style.

He did his own research too. We would pick up Nonoy and take a different road to Don Julio's farm. No trekking this time. We could cart in all we wanted of warm Cokes and sardine cans, just in case the music child's recluse of a father proved inhospitable.

Fil had also found out that the Don's farmhands were tribesmen who had only recently been identified by a church group running a linguistics institute.

"What's that? They deal with lingo, huh, Pardner?"

"Yeah, that's what they do alright. You're pretty sharp, Fil. So what are they called, these tribesmen of Don Julio?"

"*Maligta*," he answered quickly. "Aborigines. Short, dark, curly-haired. They go around with spears, bow and arrow... But not to worry, Pardner. Safe, peaceful people. Only problem is, you step on them at nigh. No see them, very small, very dark, ha ha ha ha ha..."

Drove like a laughing demon too, Fil did.

We reached Nonoy's barrio well before noon, and were treated to a sumptuous lunch prepared by his wife - rice and stewed cabbage with sardines.

Fil suggested bringing along a case of beer for the Maligta ("They will like it better than rum, believe you me, Pardner!") and a bottle of local brandy for the Don whom he said was part-Spanish.

The road was carved out of a deeply forested mountainside. Nonoy took over the wheel and kept wheezing as he struggled over the narrow turns and inclines. Fil bounced around on the back seat as he tried to keep a lid on the case of beer and assorted foodstuff.

Almost an hour into the rough, unused road, we were surprised to find it joining a wider track that appeared to have only recently been gouged out of the mountainside. Nonoy screeched to a stop, his brows furrowing.

"Loggers," he said simply.

"They're not supposed to have reached here," said Fil as he craned his neck out one side of the jeep.

Nonoy said something in the dialect as he drove forward and swung the Willys towards the right fork, following the freshly dug-up road marked with heavy truck tires.

"He says it's the new company, Pardner," offered Fil. "They have protection from the soldiers."

In less than another hour, in which we slogged along no more than five miles past a couple of dried-up streambeds, we reached a scenic plateau ringed by low hills. A small road branched off from the loggers' tracks, and Nonoy eased us gently into it. More rolling terrain lay ahead. After a couple of miles we reached the edge of a vast cornfield and knew that we were on Don Julio's land.

Nonoy drove on until we espied a modest cabin that stood on a hillock. Clumps of tall bamboo sheltered it from behind. A solitary figure appeared on the porch. He was a tall man, fair-skinned, bearded. I took him to be Don Julio.

I had earlier thought of presenting myself as a writer concerned with tribal minorities. We would say nothing about the hair-string fiddlers, or of what we had heard from them of Luisito. We would pretend that we were totally unaware of the music child's existence. Our interest had to do with the Maligta.

But upon getting off the jeep and striding purposefully over to the man who stared at us with hard eyes, something told me that we should change our cover.

I said hello and introduced myself, while Fil and Nonoy remained by the jeep. Don Julio didn't say anything. I went on about how we had been travelling in pursuit of reports of illegal logging in the island, and how we had heard of the presence of his farm. I wanted to know if the tribal farmers' existence was now being threatened by the loggers, whom I had heard were in cahoots with the corrupt military.

"You're American," Don Julio said matter-of-factly, while relaxing his stare somewhat.

"Yes," I replied, making a move forward to shake his hand. "I write for *San Francisco Examiner*. I'm here for a series of reports on environmental problems. Perhaps you can help me, sir. This island is obviously experiencing uncontrolled denudation."

He met me halfway and offered his hand. "My name is Julio Cortez."

We shook hands firmly and I repeated my name. "And those guys are my guide and driver, Fil and Nonoy."

"Come in for coffee," he said without acknowledging my companions' presence in the distance.

I hesitated on the porch, wondering whether the invitation had been for myself alone. I decided he couldn't care less if it seemed so, and entered the cabin without any further word. The guys by the jeep would understand. Besides, I figured Don Julio would be more comfortable chatting one-on-one.

It turned out to be a correct assessment. We settled ourselves cozily across one another in low, thickly upholstered armchairs with paisley prints, the kind I had last seen in Aunt Maggie's ranchhouse off San Diego. My host poured steaming coffee into a pair of large ceramic mugs that said "Yo" and "Barcelona" with a red heart between the words.

"Do you play chess?" he asked casually as he gestured at the bowl of brown sugar. I noticed that the square table between us was topped by an intricate chessboard of inlaid mother-of-pearl.

"Haven't played in years," I said truthfully. "But I understand the game, and would be most willing to take it up again with you, sir."

He nodded and took a sip of his dark coffee.

"There's a new logging consortium that's out to terrorize everyone in this part of the island," he said slowly. "We may not be able to stop them, but we will not give up without a fight."

He took a heavier sip, dipped a cigar end into the cup and lit up smoke. He went on to recount his life in brief, quickly leading to recent events that had clearly disturbed his idyll of seclusion. He spoke in measured tones, with a deep melodious voice that betrayed unmistakable good breeding as well as the gravity with which he regarded his current plight.

He had started his farm almost twenty years ago, after tiring of life as a wine importer in Manila. His half-Spanish father and Scottish mother had perished in a fire that struck their ancestral home in a fashionable section of the capital.

He had no other close relations. As a bachelor at 35, he had decided to close down his business, move South, find a large parcel of land and start an orchard. He had sufficient savings for an early retirement. He wanted to be in solitude, away from commerce and civilization. He had no wish to leave the country of his birth, no desire to trace his European roots. Living in the tropics was just fine for him. There was a particular stillness at most hours, if one knew where to go, deep in some mountain where only forest sounds entered one's consciousness.

He had planted mango, banana, and papaya among other indigenous fruit trees. His dream of a self-sustaining orchard was partly realized. But then it meant constant relations with middlemen and a large workforce, something he had increasingly grown averse to.

When the Maligta came to befriend him, he decided they were the only people he wanted to commune with. He had them cultivate fields of corn on his land, and grow tubers and vegetables, enough for them all to live on. The fruit trees were maintained, their bounty gathered every season. But he stopped caring for them as extensively as he had on a commercial basis. The fruits turned sweeter, he noted. They also became less than profitable to truck down to the city markets. The people who tended his land contented themselves with whatever they could gather.

Five years ago they began to have problems with big logging companies. But they had stood their ground and the encroachment stopped. Now it appeared that the new group was determined to have its way. He himself was quite resigned to the thought that their mountains would soon be stripped naked and dry. He had hoped however that his land would not be touched in any way.

But the little people around him were sure to resist the newcomers, and he would have no choice but to help the Maligta. They were peaceable, but turned fierce when fighting for their lives.

It all seemed inevitable now, Don Julio said wearily. Violence had already claimed the lives of his friends who had tried to block the new road with rocks and dead trees.

Accompanied by soldiers, the loggers had exacted swift retribution, stealing into his land a few days ago and shooting down two of the tribesmen. Worse, they had threatened to return to wipe out all resistance.

"You've come at the right time to record all of this," Don Julio said. "We're prepared to do battle. I have an old shotgun that can take a few lives. The little people are fashioning their old weapons. This afternoon they bury their dead, our dead. Your arrival is well-timed. You can take a lot of interesting pictures."

He had settled back on his chair, his eyes resting on the ceiling. It was as if, resigned to the outcome, he had taken to addressing himself, recounting for his own ears what had taken him to this moment.

Once again I wondered whether I had just heard a tall tale. We were nearing the end of the 20th century, after all. Bad guys didn't just show up and kill off recalcitrant natives. It couldn't happen. We were only several hours away from a bustling city. And yet this man before me was painting a scenario of crude confrontation, between two sets of primitives, with himself, surely a civilized man, being drawn into the fray. Did these things still happen?

And he hadn't mentioned his son at all. But before my suspicion grew that I had again been welcomed to the province of fiction, I espied a photograph resting atop the upright piano. It was some distance from where we sat, but I could make out the bright young face of a boy, eyes large and unafraid. He looked about seven or eight years old.

Don Julio seemed to have heard my thoughts, for he suddenly sat upright and took cognizance of my presence.

"My son Luisito is with them now, helping them prepare to bury the dead. You should come with me and meet them. Meet my son, who is ten years old. He is a special child, with a special gift that will amaze you. Perhaps it is time too, for it cannot be helped anymore, that his existence is made known to others. Like yourself."

He lifted his great bulk and waved a hand in my direction.

"Come. They wait for me. We agreed to bury the dead before twilight."

On our way out Don Julio nodded a quiet greeting to Fil and Nonoy who had made themselves comfortable on the porch. Our host maintained his large strides as we followed him up a path towards the jungle beyond the cornfields.

We trudged on silently for a mile, the shadows on the trail deepening with every step. We crossed a stream and hauled ourselves up a ridge. As we broke our run down into another gully, we were greeted by a faint, elegiac tune that was being sung in the distance. It was a young boy's voice, sounding clear and precise as it lured us on.

The words sung in dialect were unintelligible to me, but I noticed wonder and apprehension merging in Nonoy's face. He muttered something to Fil, who quickly apprised me that someone had died. I nodded and ran on after Don Julio, not wanting any other voice to join the marvellous sound I was hearing with increasing clarity at each step.

Soon we burst upon a small glade where close to a hundred dark-skinned men and women had gathered. Pygmies, I thought instantly, noting that their bows stood taller by their sides. They looked at us with hardly any change in their mournful expressions. Some had tears flowing down their cheeks. Beside a deep pit, a couple of bodies lay wrapped in strips of palm leaf and vine. Their faces were uncovered. Above them stood Luisito, singing to his young heart's content, face thrown up to the heavens, eyes virtually closed, phrasing long, curling lines that soared powerfully above the silent group. His features were sharply chiselled, his skin bronzed by the sun. And he was taller than some of the small men standing beside him.

Don Julio walked forward and touched the dead men's faces. When he moved back two women fell forward and cradled the dead men's heads in their arms, rocking them gently in time to Luisito's plaintive singing. Soon they lay the heads down and made way for the men to lift the bodies carefully and pass them on until they rested on the bottom of the pit.

The special child sang on, seemingly oblivious to everything around him. His arms swept up to encompass the sky. Now there was rage in his voice. Then slowly his lament turned into a veritable whisper, still lucid in its lowest registers, as earth was piled upon the bodies and the women wailed softly as one.

I felt no urge to record the scene except with my eyes and ears. But I shall remember with ferocity how the twilight descended slowly upon us while the common grave was levelled, and how the boy fell into mellifluous sobs as he ended his song.

We trooped back in silence to the cabin. A meal was prepared for us. We ate wordlessly, even Fil whose eyes darted constantly about. Until suddenly the boy broke into song again, phrasing lilting questions in the dialect which Don Julio answered in Spanish.

The boy shifted to Spanish himself, then lapsed into a charming, twittering patois that included a few words in English. He turned to me and asked, in a melody I could swear approximated the first bar of the Star-Spangled Banner, whether I was from America. I smiled and said yes. He munched briefly on a corncob, then sputtered into "Oh so proudly we hailed, at the twilight's last gleaming..."

Don Julio smiled appreciatively as the boy burst into full song, ranging lyrically through half of the anthem before breaking into a different melody with unfamiliar but unmistakably English phrases. His father slapped a knee and roared in laughter.

Finally containing himself as his son wove on with his stirring rendition, Don Julio turned to me and explained. "The Flower of Scotland. I sang it once for him and he has never forgotten. I'm afraid he favors it to your own anthem. The Spanish one he doesn't like at all, thinks it's too sentimental. Which I find strange, since he performs with great emotion during wakes and burials."

Don Julio laughed again, mussed the boy's hair as he finished his song, and waved at him to finish his supper.

Later that night Don Julio sat before the piano to showcase his son's admirable gift to the full. Incredibly, Luisito ranged from Manuel de Falla's "Cancion" and "Seguidilla murciana" to Leoncavallo's aria "Una furtiva lagrima" from La Boheme, and then from "Hey Jude" to the lilting folk songs Fil and Nonoy knew and shamelessly hummed along to. He sang "Cu Cu Ru Cu Cu Paloma", which obviously took delight in, embellishing it extensively with his own improvisations in the dialect, and much to his father's resounding approval as manifested by a jazzy thumping of the keyboard. Luisito's "La vie en rose" couldn't have been more sultry or heartfelt, his "Bonnie Banks of Loch Lomond" an unforgettably emotive confluence of garrulousness and poignance. The boy was magnificent, and after a while we tired of applauding him and just sat back to listen in tremulous awe, wondering if there were any limits to his genius.

Don Julio gently ordered him to bed after he finished a sportive medley that married God Save the Queen with La Marseillaise. Then our host led me to the porch while Fil and Nonoy found their bunks for the night.

"My boy hears a tune once and repeats it flawlessly," Don Julio said proudly. "Hearing a passage, he can bring it to its proper conclusion. When I taught him to read words on paper, he was only four, and he lost no time in showing me that he could read notes as well. He would rummage through all the music sheets I kept inside the piano seat, and burst out in Italian, getting the accent right too. He'd turn a score by Wagner upside down and make sport of it, as a boy would the most terrible of toys. It was frightful. It still is."

Bats flapped noisily past the roof and swooshed around the bamboo grove. The night wind lofted across the valley, the cornfields hissing before us.

"Not only is he a great mimic, repeating exactly what he hears. He takes it further where he will, adding his own touches of whimsy, curing it here and there to suit his taste for the game, his own special game. Then too he makes up his own music, chanting epic tales of courage and gallantry, or of how two mountains coupled and gave birth to a new forest. Indeed he was born to sing. Yet never has he sung originally of love. I remember the day his mother dies. The midwife almost dropped him in fright. It was as if he was born to sing of death."

Don Julio drew a long puff from his cigar. Its end glowed like a terribly distant hearth.

"Whatever will I do with them, Senor?"

I couldn't answer. I averted my eyes, and found myself gazing at a low, bright star that was repeatedly erased by a tree branch with each gust of wind. I shivered momentarily at the cruel wonder of it all.

Luisito took me to the waterfall and mocked it with his own song, an echo that drowned its source. He hooted as an owl and clucked as a gecko, then merged these sounds into a playful nocturnal syncopation. He asked me, in his quaint way of trilling melodic refrains, how the birds were in my country. He had heard that they were different, and he had longed to hear birds other than those he had matched notes with in his valley.

I described the largest birds I knew. Even as I was sure that he failed to grasp most of my words, he sensed the shapes and sizes and imagined the sounds they made while soaring high over a great expanse of land. He became the bald eagle and the mighty condor, the buzzard and the whooping crane. He sang the mating dance and the tale of migration. He breathed the flapping of powerful wings and the constant whoosh of wind, before ending his impressions with a sustained, sibilant cry of free fall.

We joined the Maligta in a hunt for monitor lizards and came back with three large specimens of the glistening reptiles. As they were skinned and stewed in vinegar before Don Julio, the dark darling prince of the tribe sang his tribute to their past lives, how they slithered under rotting leaves and fallen branches, how they skulked after rodents and sank their teeth into fowl.

Fil and Nonoy were wordless before him. They could only shake their heads in disbelief as he silenced the treetops with flute-like bubbling trills and prolonged warbling. He would essay the meadow pipit's accelerating sequence of tinkling notes that ended in a high-pitched and far-carrying pee-pee-pee, or the blackbird's staccato dik-dik-dik that wound up in a jarring screech.

Once when we were alone by the porch I brought out the Polaroid and took his portrait. Luisito pressed his face close to the curious blank square. As he saw the colors come into play and his features take shape, he began to sing softly to himself, how Luisito was born one day and said goodbye to his mother, and grew up with his father and his brothers and sisters the little people, how he swung himself down a tree and bathed in the river.

When the print was complete he stared at his face and sang to it repeatedly, Lu-i-si-to, Lu-is-it-o, Lu-iss-ii-ttooo, chanting his name in various modes of self-celebration.

Other than that time I had no urge to photograph him or the Maligta. Or anything else that presented itself before us. We walked around in an apparent daze in the magical valley. But we knew it would not last. It was as if the acknowledgement restrained me from making a serious effort to record any part of the implausible sojourn.

Fil and Nonoy never even asked how long we would stay, or what our next move would be. We shared our supplies with our hosts until we found ourselves relying on the tribesmen's fruits and tubers. We drank brandy with Don Julio and listened to Luisito sing with effortless passion.

On our fourth day at the farm the loggers came back.

They had parked their truck at the edge of Don Julio's land, where the Maligta had narrowed the road and made further passage impossible.

Cries came from the distance when the interlopers were seen marching up the trail.

Don Julio brought out his shotgun and inserted the cartridges without a word. He stepped out calmly into the porch. I followed him, my heart beginning to pound at the thought of fearful consequences.

Shots rang out from beyond the cover of trees. The Maligta were shouting to one another from different directions. Two figures stumbled out of the woods. They were Nonoy and Fil, dragging one another in panic across the field.

Luisito rushed out of the cabin and ran headlong to where more gunfire was erupting. He was bare above the waist, unarmed, bellowing his version of the rifle shots as he hurtled onwards.

His father made no effort to stop him. Don Julio's eyes had turned steely as he stood on the porch gripping his weapon.

Nonoy grabbed the boy as they met, and both fell to the ground. Fil had crumpled down himself, and I realized that he was hurt. As I ran forward I heard Don Julio's imperious cry behind me. "Go! It is not your fight!"

Nonoy grappled with the boy, until Luisito let out an emphatic cry that seemed to propel him out of his pleading captor's grasp. Nonoy fell to his knees again as he reached out desperately. Luisito hurdled the bushes and disappeared into the trees.

I reached Fil as he struggled to crawl away. His thigh was oozing blood. Nonoy helped me right him up and drag him towards the cabin. We must go, we must go, panted Nonoy. To the jeep!

We pushed Fil into the Willys and Nonoy quickly ran around to take the driver's seat, the key shaking in his pudgy hand. I turned and saw Don Julio still motionless on the porch, his face a mask as he peered into the direction of the motley din: running feet, shouts, gunshots, screams of pain - each sound replicated by that familiar wondrous voice that also filled the interim silences with a defiant song.

Nonoy grabbed me from behind and tried to push me into the jeep. I resisted and threw down his thick arm. Fil moaned and writhed in the front seat. Don Julio barked once more: "Go! Get away! It is not your fight!"

Automatic fire burst out in the distance. The fighting had spread and the shrill, chattering voices of the Maligta seemed to cover another hill. Nonoy whimpered, his hands pressing feebly against my chest. I jumped into the backseat and he lost no time in starting the jeep and speeding down the trail towards where the firefight was taking place.

I peered out and saw Luisito running up a bare hillock. He threw his arms up as he reached a mound, and from his throat cascaded what seemed a hymn of fury that soon dissolved into vibrant waves of lament as we sped by.

My hands gripped the restraining bar as I arched halfway out the jeep to see him. More shots were fired and bullets whizzed by. Nonoy whined and crouched low against the wheel as we lurched on.

The boy was still out there atop the bare mound, his arm sweeping across the valley and his head thrown back as he sang. Then I lost sight of him for the final time as we rumbled past the empty truck and into the wider road.

But I could hear his lusty praise for all the bravery taking place around him, and his voice seemed to turn even more luminous as we sped away.

We were all crying in the Willys. Fil sobbed in agony while I tried to make sense of a kerchief and tie it above his ugly wound. Nonoy wailed in gratitude for slipping past unhurt. Tears flowed down my face as I knotted the tourniquet and patted Fil comfortingly on his shoulders.

It seemed a long time before the song of the music child trailed off.

It was hard to tell as we drove on whether it was just the ineradicable memory of his voice that accompanied our flight farther and farther away from all the deaths he celebrated.

ALFRED A. YUSON has published six books to date: two poetry collections, *Sea Serpent* and *Dream of Knives*; a novel, *Great Philippine Jungle Energy Cafe*; a children's story, *The Boy Who Ate Stars* and a collection of fiction, *The Music Child & Other Stories*.

Literary prizes include the SeaWrite (Southeast Asian Writers) Award for 1992 and first prizes for numerous short stories and poetry competitions. He also won the Catholic Mass Media Award and FAMAS Award for feature film screenplay in 1987.

Presently he is a contributing columnist to a national English-language newspaper, *The Manila Chronicle*.

MICHAEL WILDING
The Imagination

When someone rings the doorbell and then hammers the knocker and then beats against the timber itself, or glass or whatever, in this case it was a timber door, and an old iron knocker, and a clockwork bell, all three going together more or less, if you're feeling extroverted and wanting excitement maybe you leap up and answer it to whoever is announcing "Where's the party?" "Come in, my dear, you are the party." Who wouldn't want a leather clad silver studded rapist with a knife climbing in, what an exquisite and so international a literary fantasy. But the leather and stud boys all go across the road and down the steps to the house on the water's edge. Mr Bonmot's, dressed to kill for the weekend, cruising butchers and doctors on their Harley Davisons.

So the threefold knocking at the door is not unfamiliar, it has something of that overdetermination characteristic of certain literary schools and lifestyles. At least the door is closed. I might have left it open and had them just walk in. Sam clutching his bottle of tia maria or ave aquavita, southern comfort or northern desperation, not at all a great western champagne type, within his hand maybe a fish or two, hanging there from a hook like souls being weighed on judgement day, their tails occasionally twitching in some involuntary electric retching orgasm, and in the other hand some chick person clutched by the hobbled anklets or neck feathers, some nubile gesture of asserted heterosexuality though getting on the weird side, approaching the under age size, or maybe it was the short dresses like school tunics, one of those zombie nonpersons he brings round like they've eaten blow fish and are now under his command, buried alive and born again, "Sam, Sam, I am your willing slave, my eyes are dead but my life goes on and as for the imagination, the imagination Sam, imagine the imagination." Sam, Sam, surrender a hand and find us a verb, what are you doing, Sam, out on the doormat where Marcus the mouser deposits disembowelled mouse carcasses?

And it swells there, the great inflation of the imagination, the undirectable dirigible, "Let's go and knock on somebody's door, ring their doorbell, hammer their windows, wood, iron and glass, when shall we three meet again", the imagination is Sam's broomstick, his horse's head handle to prod the lions of deconstruction, his musket to pick up and straddle. "What I like about you is when I come round in the middle of the night and you're pissed off you don't pretend you're not. I go round and see The Egg at three in the morning and he offers me coffee and omelettes, imagine it. Imagine it. And I know he's pissed off. That's why I go round there and get him out of bed." The Egg fingers his moustache and rises tiptoe on his built up heels. Are they angled right for the ascent of Olympus? Will icicles form on the words that will issue from his lips? Sam is impervious. He takes the icicles to pack the fish. He drinks from the built up heels. He would crack alabaster boxes over them if asked, and maybe has. Literature's shoeshine boy. He smiles up at me. Through the window beside the door.

Movie addiction

I don't want to see Sam. And fish. And chick person. I want to watch this trio of horror movies scripted by the man who scripted *Psycho*, I've never seen *Psycho*. I don't like horror movies. I have combed through the television guide and *Movies on TV* to find something there might be a remote reason for watching. Movies consisting of three separate stories, three vaguely related subplots or unrelated variations on a theme, etc., are rarely satisfying, I find. This is all from my perspective. I found. At that point in time. My perspective then. Though my views on those three sectioned movies haven't changed.

Other things have. Changed. Tonight, now, I am not watching a remake of *Invasion of the Body Snatchers* nor a remake of *The Big Sleep*. Though once I might have. The originals, then it might have been different, but it is not the originals, and instead I am recalling this incident of the evening I was watching that Robert Bloch trilogy. Thanks for the counterfeit, ersatz, remade, substitute, food, entertainment, politics, fiction, the less we bother with it. This has some truly revolutionary implications. The negation of the negations.

"No, Sam," I say, "I'm watching a movie, no."

"Why're you watching a movie when you could be talking with a real flesh-and-blood human being?"

Blood has already been inserted into the picture.

"For the reason Americans eat brand-name fast foods," I answer him. "It may not be real food but you know what to expect. Hamburgers and movies for those who want to live safely."

"There's a human being out here."

"Where?"

"I just want to talk to you. Like old friends. Remember about friends. What people used to have. I thought we could be friends. I thought we were friends. We are friends. Aren't we?"

Friendship

Is this what E M Forster was thinking of when he said he hoped he'd have the courage to betray his country rather than his friend? Sam out there, howling protestations of friendship, a greater writer than any of them and probably no worse a friend than Bloomsbury or King's Coll. Cantab. could offer. Friendship, I decide, is a peculiarly bourgeois concept. In the world of work there are mates, comrades, fellows; lovers, partners, in the world of sex. Who are these friends with whom you neither work nor make love? Wasn't Brutus Caesar's friend? An appeal to friendship is not an open sesame round here.

But doesn't Sam know that? Doesn't he know that will keep him on the windswept porch, a beautiful view of the harbour, maybe he could even see the television through the window, but cold out there, as I remember it was cold out there. So he can have the exquisite joy of exclusion, denial, friendship revealed as hollow when it comes to letting him in. Now at his most excluded he most exists and is most present. He rises up at the window like some overbearing djinn. "Go back inside your bottle," I order him. But he's probably swallowed the cork. Now we are stuck with him like a dispersed noxious vapour that has penetrated everything. Asmodeus and the fishy fume. It's not that he's doing a lot of hammering on doors after his first arrival. Nor even being especially vocal. But sitting there. Like Quasimodo without a bell rope. And you know or fear that at any moment he will call out or strike, how can you relax to a horror movie of hands being severed by meat cleavers as they come through walls or electric cables being attached to metal doorhandles ready for visitors, how can you relax and flow into this with Sam at the door?

"What should I do then?" he asks. "Should I phone first?"

"You could try."

"But you never answer it, there's never anyone there when I ring."

"I must be psychic."

"That's cruel," says Sam. "Why are you so cruel? What have I ever done to you?"

We are not going to begin that enumeration. You can't catch old birds with chaff. We are not going to get sucked into an itemised account of all the things Sam has done to me or not, with arguments, variants, extenuating circumstances and maybe even witnesses.

"I brought these for you," he says, holding the fish to the window.

"I don't eat fish, I'm a vegetarian."

"No you're not."

"I'm a Midlander. We never saw fish."

"You never saw lots of things," said Sam. "Here's your chance to see fish."

He presses a fishy eye against the window. Maybe he didn't have fish. Maybe that was another time. Maybe he was just drunk. Maybe he just rang the doorbell and hammered the knocker and banged the door too loud.

"Just open the window," says Sam.

"Why?"

"I want to talk to you. I can't talk with the door shut. I won't try to come in, promise."

Would I have thought he would try to come in if he hadn't said he wouldn't? Yes, I would, that is why it is the window that is at issue, not the door. He doesn't even try about the door. The door will not be opened.

I open the window. Is this remorse at such unfriendliness? Is this weakening, what Sam sees as weakening? I have calculated I can easily push him out before he climbs through, and if he is appropriately positioned a push might send him rolling down the stairs. Even somersaulting. It is these violent fantasies that betray me. I have not calculated that he will simply put his arms through the open window and leave it there, hanging.

"Move it, Sam."

He leaves it there.

"Why do you want your arm there?"

"It's not hurting anything," says Sam. "I'm not breaking in."

"Then take your arm out."

These lines are inevitably perfunctory, since he doesn't, and we both know he won't take the arm out.

"Sam," I say at some point, "if you don't go I'll call the cops." What a bad idea in every regard, it is hardly worth suggesting.

"That would be great," says Sam, Sam the Overjoyed, "they've still got a couple of warrants they've never cancelled out for me, you call the cops and I get taken off to Long Bay and then it's automatic three years for a habitual offender, that would look great, wouldn't it, the man who puts Sam Samson back in gaol, that would look great in the literary histories, wouldn't it?"

It's the bit about the literary histories that makes me feel this is getting out of control. Maybe I should just open the door suddenly and roll him down the stone and concrete steps, about fifteen of them, better heads, or at least other heads, than his have bled on those stone steps, the time when Ms Kiss-me Kate crashed down them and split her head open a bit and demanded we took her, they took her, to her psychiatrist. "Are you sure this is the right sort of head doctor?" Tony Leanto her publisher asking anxiously all the way. But Sam of course might split open too far and who would want to be on a manslaughter charge for Sam, just to watch a horror movie.

Kitchen knives are sawing through wrists, fabric and rubber-insulated wires are stripped back to the gleaming metal ready for insertions too distasteful to look at. I turn back to Sam. Why does he provoke this violence in me, Sam who never strikes a first blow? The master of the provocation. Do you like being punched, Sam, is that your Swinburnian secret, so there is no way of winning with you except by beating you into unconsciousness, which for you is what you want, I fall upon the thorns of life, I bleed, you are not someone who only fights to win and otherwise keeps away, you are as happy to fight to lose, for loss means the exquisite pummelling. Or is this just a psychological profile cunningly circulated so people don't punch you because it seems so obviously not worthwhile. Who can tell the forger from the coin? Sam gives his angelic smile.

The arm still hangs there.

"I'll shut the window on it."

"That's why it's there," says Sam, "so you won't shut the window. I want to talk."

"Talk then, just take your arm out."

He neither talks nor takes his arm out.

It is a sash window. I bring it down on his arm. His arm stays there. I raise the window and bring it down again, harder this time. By the third time I have got the hang of it, got into the swing of things, I've got rhythm. But though the movement is like a guillotine the edge is blunt. The arm remains there, no wrist looped off into the room. There are worse things going on on the television screen, but they are only acted. As far as we know. Maybe much of this is only acted. But I happen to be one of the actors and it is not nice stuff. Not nice to recall, either. Not much to look forward to in return. Sam, we are so aware of your chameleon qualities and your mimetic skills that we assume your manipulations are of flattery for your own ends; but sometimes it seems you let us hold the mirror to our own worse selves, and is this therapeutic, cathartic, is this for us to reform from?

In the end I disgust myself as he knows I will.

I phone La Surreal. "Come and get your rotten husband," I say. Maybe something other than rotten, but after fighting for those freedoms of expression all these years and probably generally losing or only marginally gaining, set back from what we might have gained, anyway, we are back to rotten again.

"I can't," she says, "he's got the car."

"Get a cab," I say.

"We haven't got any money."

"Borrow some from a friend."

"You're our only friend," she says.

I would like to go aaargh and rip out the phone cord from the wall to a rending, blinding flash, yellow on purple background, wham, bam, slam, etc, like comics, like television. The television has people wired up to naked cables. The window frame has Sam leaning through like a chambermaid above a flowerbox of geraniums in La Boheme, a limp arm like a red setter's tongue, spam, pre-tenderized deboned boiled in its own juice ham. Probably whale blubber. The great fat bat of a whale penis. And in the background the harbour, prawn trawlers, cargo ships laden with timber from Borneo, Samarcand, all the ready visual enhancement and exotic associations. In that ugly brick block across the water someone paints jacarandas in bloom. And the bridge grips the two points of land like a tourniquet on a junkie's arm. "Bullshit," Sam would say, would have said, and he should know about that.

Next morning

Next morning the phone rings and it is La Surreal, this early morning cocorico with great red wattles vibrating like they are powered by an electric vibrator, plugged into the mains, all 240 volts aglow. "You must be proud of yourself," she says.

"Oh, I dunno," I say.

"Sam's at the hospital."

"What, the nuthouse?" I say, not my normal parlance but called for at this point, provided, anyway.

"You've broken his arm."

"I hope so."

"It's being x-rayed now."

"Use the x-ray for the cover of his next book," I suggest. They are into snazzy design.

"It's his writing arm."

Bullshit it's his writing arm, he's got an electric typewriter and he types two-handed. A gigantic IBM behind which he shelters like Dr Phibes of Black Mountain, summoning up pterodactyls on the carillon.

"Tell him to use feet. Give up free verse and stick to pentameters."

But what he really wants is a keyboard and synthesiser, like Shelley pouring out his full soul in profuse streams of unpremeditated art, a four track, an eight track, so he could work over it afterwards, something to do at night and keep him off the streets.

110

"What's he going to do now?" asks La Surreal.
"The imagination," I say, "tell him, the imagination."

© Michael Wilding, 1993.

MICHAEL WILDING'S fiction includes the novels *The Paraguayan Experiment* (Penguin), *Living Together* (University of Queensland Press) and *Pacific Highway* (Hale and Iremonger), and the short story collections *Great Climate* (Faber), *The Man of Slow Feeling* (Penguin) and *Under Saturn* (Black Swan). He holds a personal chair in English and Australian Literature at The University of Sydney.

JAN KEMP
Marco of Milano, *a romance*

Marco stood, a still statue in a group of still statues in a lawn of white daisies in the middle of the piazza watching the women come and go to and from the foyer of the Theatre of La Scala. They ducked and dodged the people and the parked buses in the square, hiking their skirts over cobble-stones, stepping over puddles and meeting, losing and re-finding their escorts and friends. Marco's head was cocked and his hat was just so, an arm touched under an elbow on which he leaned and he was smiling to himself.

The patrons of La Scala scurried past the floor-to-ceiling mirrors, interspersed between the grubby, creamy, marble panels. They caught an inadvertent sight of their own glimmering silks and velvets, patted at their hair here, adjusted a waist there, as they waved to friends, way over through the foyer melee or gazed up at the chandeliers which twinkled above them all the while, as they sucked furiously at their long-stemmed cigarettes. *"Bella! Bella!"* they remarked loudly and softly to one another, *"Come sta?"* and *"Come stai?"* admiring each other's costumes, hair-styles and belts and blowing huge puffs of smoke into each other's faces.

Marco watched bemused, his gaze flitting over the patrons, indistinct blurs of colour and movement in and around the marble foyer columns under the clusters of winking lights over-head, then back over the quiet square. He lapsed into meditation.

Just then, a little cloud passed over Marco's statue, so high above the square, if you weren't directly under it, you'd never have noticed. It blocked Marco's view of the night moon, a sight he so loved to look at, when the bustle and buses outside, and all the red plush boxes inside the Theatre of La Scala had died or emptied; his moon that kept him company night after night. The stars would suspend themselves beside this very moon as the year went round and though Marco could not move his head, he remembered his master Leonardo's invention of a swivelling globe made of interlocking strip shapes, that would, if it could have been realised in brass or at worst plastic, clearly have been a mobile representation of the seasonal patterns of the northern hemisphere stars. But now, neither moon nor stars could be seen because of the little cloud.

And then suddenly, it began to rain directly on Marco. He took this as a good omen. He was washed clean of Milano's city grime, for it was good hard rain, rather than the light misty films of early Spring rain to which he was accustomed at that time of year. Besides, it would give the white daisies a good watering. He glanced at the others to see if they too were enjoying the sudden wetness, but no, Leonardo himself was still solemn and central, his genius suggested by his enormous brow, above those wonderfully pendant, bronze eyebrows, and as for the others, Boltraffio, Salaino and Cesare da Sesto, they, as ever they would, flanked Leonardo like the devoted pupils they had been, statuesque and quite dry. Only Marco d'Oggiono himself had been rained upon.

Marco gave an involuntary wriggle to shake the water off his marble skin and to his astonishment he found that his whole body moved as if he, like the patrons of La Scala, were alive. Marco then blinked continuously. His eyelids did open and shut and open again. Then he tried to lift a hand, a foot. They moved too. His beloved moon had granted his long-felt wish and must have sent the cloud to return life to him. But knowing with some vague sixth sense, that he had lived previously and being by nature a thinking sort of fellow, he knew there would be a price for such liberty and that only if he behaved without distraction according to each moment that presented itself to him, would he be sure to discover what the purpose for his new-found freedom was.

It was strange to prance across the little lawn of white daisies and stand with his hands on his hips, like a man in the piazza and look back at his own, now-empty pedestal in the midst of the other pupils, gathered round their adored Leonardo, as so often people had gathered to stand and gaze at them all, as they sauntered by.

Marco gave a little leap of delight, then ran off into the foyer of the Theatre of La Scala, where the patrons who had re-emerged ten minutes previously, had been madly smoking, sipping their drinks and discussing the first act, crying, "*Bella,*

bella! Donizetti!" to each other, ducking and diving around the grubby, creamy pillars until a bell's tinkling had announced the end of the interval and they had begun to hurry back to their seats, past the fifteenth-century-dress-clad ushers with floppy hats, like Marco's own, he noticed, adjusted and rearranging his medallion, so that it too, like theirs, hung down on his chest, clearly visible. Perhaps his presence would not be remarked upon, if he were mistaken as one of them. He stood at the farthest end of his entrance way collecting interval ticket butts, just as the others did.

Then, quickly glancing round, Marco took off his floppy hat and hiding it in his jacket pocket, hurried along behind the last flurry of silk and velvet in front of him, down the tiny passage-way, from where more and tinier passage-ways lead up little staircases to the neatly numbered boxes, that he soon found, as he entered one, lined the whole circular interior of the opera stage and the red-plush seats of the stalls in the middle of the theatre.

Marco couldn't help but utter a gasp of astonishment. The interior was so gracious, like a woman who'd retained her sense of individual style with her years. And so human-sized. Marco leaned forward and put his hands on the chair-back in front of him and then realised another person too was in the box. She turned slowly round to him, a finger to her lips, then indicated an empty chair in the corner of her box and bade him sit as the curtain on stage went up.

* * *

Before he realised what had happened, Marco was following the woman from the box's silk and velvet-costumed figure down the steps of the big, air-conditioned bus where he'd sat with her and forty or so other passengers, as the bus had been driven off into the night from the Theatre of La Scala, after the performance, as if on wings.

Marco had sat down in the bus alongside the woman.

Occasionally, someone else from across the aisle or forward or behind their row leaned over and spoke to her. Then, when she laughed and answered gaily and looked at him and he smiled or nodded and she'd seemed satisfied, he had to admit to himself that he could fathom no correlation between the words he

114

heard all around him and the sounds of his own in his mind, apart from one word alone, *Lugano*. Wasn't that a town somewhere north of his beloved *Milano*? In contrast to these verbal puzzles, his acceptability as unquestionably one of them appeared to be in no doubt. For her part, the woman thought it was a little strange that a La Scala usher should have accompanied her into her box and now back to Lugano on the tour-bus, but she assumed that he was a regular part of the evening's entertainment and belonged to the tour company, so she questioned herself of the matter no further.

It was well past the middle of the night, when, as they disappeared into the dark, first standing in larger, then smaller bunches, then breaking into groups of two or three or here and there a single person, waving and calling farewells, that the party began to break up. Uncertain what to do, Marco kept near his woman from the box and together they strolled to a lakeside, past giant chess pieces on a black and white patchwork chessboard on the pavement of a little park and stood looking through a grove of plane-trees at a fountain two or three metres off-shore, that gave a few hesitant spurts, then, to their delight, a high display, backed by a kaleidoscope of changing colours.

Marco ran the last couple of steps to the water's edge in order to see better. Two white swans floated up towards him out of the dark shadow the nearest plane tree's trunk had cast on the water.

"*I cigni!*" he exclaimed, remembering both life and utterance in a word.

The woman from the box was at his side, equally excited.

"Swans!" she said, exultant.

"Swans?" repeated Marco, tentatively. "*I cigni!*"

"*I cigni?*" the woman said tentatively.

"*I cigni!*" Marco said firmly.

"You, *Italiano?*" she asked, indicating him.

"*Si*, you *Italiano*," Marco said, pointing to himself.

"No, me," she said, pointing to herself. "In *Inglese*, you say me."

"You say me," repeated Marco, indicating himself then her.

"No, no, no, you, me," she replied.

"You, me," This time he got it right.

"Me, you," Then wrong.

She shook her head.

"You, me," she said firmly, lightly tapping his chest, then her own, with her fan.

They both laughed. At least they'd discovered one fulcrum of their difference.

They walked off along the waterfront promenade under the colonnaded plane trees beside the lake. Light from the street lamps shone through the phalanged canopy overhead, making a soft apple-greenness, even in the middle of the night. The tree trunks loomed like black columns out of the dark, suddenly becoming visible as they walked, Marco spirited and excited, the woman attentive. Marco's brown eyes were intense with interest as now and then he turned to her. She realised he was probably explaining the abstractions of an Italian verb, but as there was no referent to which he could point, his finger-wagging lecture soon ended in dissolution, as she playfully shook her head and gesticulated that his words went in one ear and came out amongst the plane trees. Their conversation would necessarily have to be devoted to the world made visible. How then, could he tell her of his moon, his square, La Scala and the white daisies, his Italy? He put on his floppy hat and dandled his medallion. Though she supposed this was his regalia as a La Scala usher, she too decided to play.

"You look like...a Mayor!" she announced.

"*Ah, bene. Molto bene!* You! Mayor!" he repeated.

"No, you're a Mayor," she said, "my name's Mary."

"You, *Maria?*"

"Maria," she acquiesced.

"Me, *Marco*," he said.

"Marco?"

"*Si, Marco, Marco d'Oggiono.*"

Had he ever known quite such delight since unbecoming a statue, Marco wondered as he walked along under the plane-trees. He talked then she, pointing, then rushing up to a flower, a bush, a street sign, the lakeside. The kilometre walk was endless and by the time they reached her hotel, it would be safe to say that each had fallen, in his or her own way, a little in love.

"This is my first ever visit to Italy," she said; and then, as he shook his head, the dark eyes fixed on hers, wanting to know what she'd said, she tried again.

"*Mia, prima* visit *Italia!*" in her best pidgin-Italian. It worked, thank god for Latin.

"*Si?*" he was astonished. Surely everyone knew Italy?

How could she ever have explained to him she came from the Antipodes, from the other hemisphere, one which his map of the stars did not even include, where the Milky Way was visible like a tossed ribbon of white silk and the stars were both huge and tiny against the black sky. How could he ever explain he was a statue, newly-come to life, who couldn't even remember why he had been made a statue in the first place? Frustration mounted in their faces as each, eagerly tried to explain to the other the inexpressible.

Maria leaned her head lightly against Marco's shoulder and they stood for a moment and he almost involuntarily murmured. Perhaps he said, *ah bene!* She heard only the vibration of his voice pass from his into her body and it was quiet and warm and good.

But, suddenly something felt dreadfully wrong. The realisation that he was existing in a time-warp struck home to Marco. This woman he was growing so fond of. What on earth could he do? He couldn't stay with her. He was a statue. He'd have to return to the piazza outside La Scala, for who knew how long he would be free? Who knew if he wouldn't suddenly turn back into stone, far from his pedestal, far from Leonardo and the others?

Whatever was the matter? Marco looked so grave. His eyebrows were furrowed. Maria could see the stubble wanting to bristle out of his chin.

"Marco, what is it?" she asked.

"*Maria, Io, Marco,*" he pointed to himself, "*Andro a Milano.*"

He pronounced the single, separate words carefully, so that she might understand more easily, and nervously dandled his medallion.

"You've got to go back to Milan," Maria responded. So he *was* a La Scala usher and work was calling.

"*Si,*" said Marco.

"*Capisci?*" he asked gently.

Maria understood.

"*Si,*" she smiled, as gaily as she could.

Marco flagged down a neat, green taxi which grew up beside them out of the dark. He talked nervously to the driver; gesturing wildly with his medallion. Then he opened the back door for her to get in.

"You, hotel?" he asked.

"Yes, thank-you."

And five minutes later, outside it, while the taxi-driver waited, bemused, leaning against a wall and smoking a cigarette, they took flash photos of one another with her camera. Her leaning against the taxi and then Marco wearing his floppy hat and standing beside it, leaning with an elbow on the taxi's roof and cocking a foot, so as to rest on the tip of a shoe that he'd tucked in front of the other. Maria had wanted to take the shot length-wise to remember his height. He was a natural before the camera. Just as a mayor should be. How would she herself have been at cutting ribbons, as a mayor's wife, perhaps?

Then, at last he drew her to him and kissed her, both tenta-tively and firmly on the lips, both ways at once, in one kiss, if this is possible.

"You *Antipodes*, me *Milano*," he said, sadly.

"Yes. *Si*," Maria responded. His lips were so warm.

Maria realised she was standing in the car-park at the front of the hotel clutching her camera with one hand, the fingers of her other to her mouth. The taxi had disappeared off into the night.

* * *

Months later, back home in the Antipodes, whenever she felt lonely, she'd look over her photographs, a long view down the colonnaded apple-green trees in the rain, the whimsical shapes of the hills around the lake, the international party on the ferry excursion, and she would always end up, as if transfixed by one picture of a smiling man in a huge, black, floppy hat, who leaned against a neat, green taxi. And surprisingly, one day she noticed something she hadn't yet noticed, she saw in the top corner of the photo, an image of the taxi-driver leaning against a wall, smoking a cigarette and bemusedly smiling. And round his neck, wasn't that Marco's gold medallion glinting out of the darkness?

And the longer she gazed at it, the louder a faint and low vibration came into her body, a voice that said, *ah bene, molto bene*; and, as she gazed still longer, now smiling to herself, glad that life had allowed at least a moment for farewell, for romance does fail, she'd watch at the figure, like a fountain changing its colours, slowly became a still statue with his head cocked to one side, his arm under an elbow on which he leaned and who wore his hat, just so. He stood under a night moon, in a clear sky, on a fixed pedestal in a little lawn of white daisies, in the middle of a piazza. A figure so familiar.

Then Maria, remembered by the past, was herself a flurry of silk and velvet climbing out of a bus and then, ducking and dodging laughing women and their escorts and friends, she found her way around grubby, creamy, marble pillars, past full-length mirrors under chandeliers and out of the foyer of the Theatre of La Scala. And just as she lifted her foot to climb aboard the bus, while at the same time being careful to dodge a puddle, she looked back at the piazza and saw him, standing nonchalantly there, a still statue in a group of still statues surrounding Leonardo. Was Marco smiling at her? Yes, she thought he was. She smiled back, blowing him a kiss. So, she had imagined it. But, no wonder. After all, that night was her first ever visit to Italy.

© Jan Kemp, 1993.

JAN KEMP is a New Zealand writer presently living in Singapore where she teaches English at the National University of Singapore. She holds an M.A. (Hons) degree in English from the University of Auckland. Her third book of poems, *The Other Hemisphere* was published in 1991 by both Three Continents Press, Washington D.C., U.S.A., and by Butterfly Books, N.S.W., Australia. Her first collection of short stories, *The Cook, the Consul & the Crazyman* is due out from Hazard Press, Christchurch, New Zealand, in November, 1993.

119

CHIN WOON PING
After The Phoenix

We passed banana groves, bushy bamboo, willows and casuarinas. Wen Jun pointed out Wutong Shan and Pineapple Hill and then there were white pines and creeping vines over low hills before we saw the first terraces of rice fields. We had arrived at the village.

The entire village was surrounded by a wall with doors and was covered with tiled roofs varying in height and shape, the tallest part at the corners looking like guard towers. Outside this wall at the back entrance was the monstrous, gnarled root section of a fallen tree, to which three water buffaloes were tied. I noticed construction work going on, what looked like the stone frames of two-storied dwellings, and was glad to surmise that the new peasant prosperity one read about in the newspapers had touched this village too.

The first person to greet us was the village leader, the *xiang zhang*. He was apparently related to us and had the same surname as ours. His face beamed welcome. Pretty soon, more people emerged from doorways and alleyways: children, young men, teenagers, women with babies on their hips, nearly twenty to thirty people. Wen Jun seemed to know all of them and introduced me to the older people, using familial terms... This is Ah Nyong...Ah Sook...Ah Sook Por...he said to me.

"Are they all related to us?" I asked.

"Yes," he said. "And all have the same clan name as ours. We are all related."

We headed towards the house in which Wen Jun had grown up with his mother and grandparents. Along the way, I noted that all the houses were built of brick and stone, their white walls smudged with age. All were similarly roofed with grey tiles. On the edge of the side walls of each house, just underneath each curved roof, was painted an abstract, geometrical design in various colors. These houses were narrow and tall, with a finished look, not squat adobes as I'd seen elsewhere but elegant (though patched) structures that to me looked northern in style. Narrow, labyrinthine alleyways and a network of open sewage drains connected the houses. The children ran alongside for a while until we stopped at a house.

Outside the narrow door on the cemented front yard of the house, thatched coops of ducks and geese made noises, probably because their food pans were empty. When we entered the house, it took a few minutes for my eyes to adjust to the darkness. Then I made out the kitchen at the very front, just a stone counter with a round hole for the cooking fire with a black wok over it. The walls of rough cement and exposed brick were grey with smoke. A duster made of rice stalks and a thatched bamboo steamer hung on nails. Beyond the kitchen was a large, long room with two small curtained doors leading to what had to be bedrooms. Wen Jun told my husband and me that Cousin Moi now lived in it with her family.

Our cousin Moi was away, but her husband was in, watching a cartoon program on the television which sat on a rickety formica table. Four children with dirty faces played about, wearing cheap nylon jackets with worn, fake fur collars. In the corner of the room was a large stone mortar for pounding rice and a long wooden pestle attached to it. My cousin's husband jumped up when he saw us and bade us sit down. Then he and the children made much ado of opening biscuit and sweet tins to serve us before he went to boil water for tea.

After some opening remarks, my brother presented Moi's husband with some ginseng root he had gotten during his travels. I asked if I could take a look around, and climbed the ladder that took me to the loft. In it were baskets of hulled rice and a stack of round, dark rice cakes steamed in leaf containers. I recognized the cakes as *nyen gow*, the cake eaten at New Year's (what they called the Spring Festival here), and I remembered that it was barely a few days away. When I came downstairs again, I asked if they still used the stone mortar and pestle and Moi's husband said yes. He and his wife had harvested the rice crop upstairs in the loft.

Wen Jun suggested that we take a walk. Outside, I asked what Moi's husband did. He was an electrician. (He was not Hakka but Cantonese.) Wen Jun then told us about some problems he'd been having with him and our cousin Moi. Though allowed to stay in this house for free for some years, they had turned around

121

and tried to claim another house that Wen Jun and his mother had bought for us many years ago.

For us? You mean, my family? I said.

Yes, said Wen Jun. Mother had some money saved from doing labor elsewhere and she bought this house thinking that there would be a place for Father and all of you should you return here.

Since he said it so matter-of-factly, I did not give it much thought then, but later marvelled to think that his mother, instead of suffering grief and jealousy at the thought of Father marrying again, probably regarded my mother and all of us in the old, traditional way as an extension of the family. She had probably even looked forward to meeting us! What a simple truth, but how it opened my eyes.

Here was a sensitive matter that had always been kept quiet in our household, something Father never talked about and Mother did not like to hear - that in China was his first wife, the first family. What a hard thing it must have been for Mother to live with, even though she had Father all to herself. Here in China, it was a commonly known fact. And for Wen Jun's mother, the knowledge of Father's second family did not bother her, though she did not have him with her. Husbandless after a brief marriage, she lived all her life in lonely celibacy but bearing no grudge towards the woman who had her man, nor to her children. Could I go as far as to conclude that?

I did not recall ever hearing my parents discuss Father's family in China, and certainly none of Mother's relatives ever mentioned them. There was, however, an aunt on Father's side (the wife of his brother who died years ago and was only a name in my childhood) and she told us things about China.

We called this aunt Ah Sim. She struck you upon first meeting with her demeanor of tragedy because half of her mouth hung downwards, twisting her face. I recalled how she and her two daughters had lived with us years and years ago and how I used to fight with the girls.

Ah Sim had married Father's brother in Malaysia when he came to join Father. No one knew or said much about their life together or how they met. She then went to China with him and lived there several years with our grandparents. It was a hard life working in the fields, she told us, and she was not used to it, having been brought up in Malaysia. "Better to be poor in Malaysia than rich in China," she said. (I wonder now if she had come in the 1950's, during the time of scarcity and famine.) After her third child was born, she returned to Malaysia with two of her children. That was when she came to live with us and Father supported their family before they left to live by themselves, Ah Sim apparently in a huff, as I recall. (Did she and my parents quarrel? I don't know. My mother does not discuss these matters.) She took a job as an amah and supported her two daughters thus through Chinese school. For nearly thirty-five years now, Ah Sim had been a servant, cooking and cleaning for others. She had been married less than five years when her husband died, and she never remarried. No wonder she hardly smiled. My sisters and I visited her sometimes and gave her small sums of money when we could.

To hear Ah Sim's story, you would think that Grandmother was the most wicked witch in the world. My mind was stamped with the stories of how Grandmother, fierce as a mother hen, wouldn't let Ah Sim take her youngest daughter with her when she returned to Malaysia, and how she hid Uncle's passport so he couldn't leave with her. Why Ah Sim left, I did not know, but she claimed to have been driven out by Grandmother. Why she had to leave her youngest daughter behind I did not know either, but the version I always had was that Grandmother liked the youngest one so much she wanted to keep her. Ah Sim's husband, my uncle, thus remained behind and took another wife (according to Ah Sim, Grandmother insisted he marry this wife). Then mysteriously, he had died. Ah Sim tried to send for the youngest daughter, but couldn't arrange it for one reason or another, so the years had passed. When she did manage to return to China to visit her youngest daughter, she was an old woman and her daughter had by then grown up. It was this youngest daughter, named Moi, who now lived in our grandparents' house with her husband, the electrician whom I had just met.

I had hoped to meet Moi, but was told that she had gone out for the day. This fact surprised me and I wondered if she had known about our coming.

Wen Jun then told me he was not happy with Moi because of the way she had treated Grandmother. When he and his mother had to leave the village after he was transferred to Canton, Grandmother had stayed behind with Moi. Later, he was shocked to hear from the relatives and neighbors that Moi had bullied Grandmother, browbeating her and refusing to give her food. The neighbors had been appalled to see the old woman eating food put out for the ducks because she was so starved. One day, they found the old woman crying and bleeding in a leg because Moi had beaten her with a stick. This misery Grandmother suffered had something to do with her early death, he suggested.

Wen Jun seemed especially grieved because Moi had been like a sister to him, growing up together. He recounted how his mother had treated her like a daughter, pitying Moi for not having her own.

This story disturbed me, and I tried to connect all those tales I had heard from Ah Sim about wicked Grandmother with this account of a poor, mistreated old woman. Where was the truth of it? If indeed Moi had beaten our grandmother and starved her to death, what prompted her to do so? Did she hate Grandmother for separating her from Ah Sim, her mother? Or was she just a hateful person, since I did not know how true Ah Sim's allegations about Grandmother were? How did she feel growing up without her parents, pining for her mother and sisters far away in Nanyang? In her shoes, how would I have conducted my life?

How much would I ever know, I the "rich cousin" from America dropping into the village for a day? I wondered if Moi was away because she was avoiding me. After all, Wen Jun had sent word days ahead that we were coming - surely she must have known. Perhaps she could not bear to meet the cousin who had it all - Mother, Father, Malaysia, America? Or perhaps she had heard awful things about my family from her Mother? Or perhaps she did not care a hoot? Or perhaps she really hadn't expected me? I would never know.

"Why was Moi left behind by her Mother?" I asked Wen Jun.

"Her mother wanted to go back to Malaysia and her father had to stay. Since she could not manage three children travelling alone, she left the youngest behind. I think he was going to take Moi back to Malaysia and then he died."

"What did Moi's father die of?"

"We don't really know," he replied. "I think he was poisoned, I saw his corpse the day he died - it was all swollen and black. He died from eating dog meat that had been poisoned."

This answer also disturbed me, and I looked at the village from a new light, seeing in its rustic walls and earthy houses hiding places for evil and treachery. Shades of Balinese voodoo and intrigues. I was glad Father had left this place.

Wen Jun added that Grandfather had also died from eating something wrong. He ate glutinous rice and died of indigestion. This fact made Wen Jun realize how both lives could have been saved if someone who knew medicine had been nearby. For that reason, he had urged his daughter to become a doctor and she had recently graduated from medical college.

Back at the house, our cousin's husband had prepared an elaborate meal. A hen had been slaughtered and boiled; there was also fat pork fried with spinach and pork soup. Two other cousins, middle-aged men, were invited to join the table. We all ate quietly, except for the children, who clawed eagerly at the chicken. The youngest was a chubby little boy whose lips were oily with eating and who kept asking for more chicken. It was quite a sight to see, the voracious way he chewed at a leg. Only one and a half years old, he would pause and give me the most mischievous smile. I was enjoying the fresh aroma of the rice we were eating, savoring the fact that it was grown right there, when I felt a sharp pain in my mouth and realized I had bitten down on a stone and cracked one of my molars.

After eating, Wen Jun suggested that I might like to take a piece of village soil with me. It had never occurred to me to do so, but he said that many Overseas Chinese who came carried away a piece of the earth with them as a token. I thought it was a good idea and he produced a red square of silk cloth. As we left for the fields outside, one of the children tagged along, putting her hand in mine.

We walked beyond the wall out to the rice field, a parched landscape of clumps of overturned earth that looked like boulders. Our feet slid over these clumps when we tried to make our way to the center of the field. The two daughters of Moi's showed up, and together we posed for photographs for my husband's camera, squatting among the clods of dirt and dead stalks. Then Wen Jun cupped a handful of dust and put it into the piece of cloth, which I tied by its four corners and knotted.

As we were leaving, we saw a woman walking towards us with a pole over the shoulder from which hung baskets at both ends. Wen Jun recognized her as she drew closer.

"It's Ah Sook Por," he said. I thought we'd already met Ah Sook Por but evidently here was another one. This one, however, was dressed differently. Whereas the other older women wore plain padded cotton jackets and pants, she had a full costume of black and a bright blue apron trimmed with embroidery. Her headdress was similarly ornate and embroidered, and she had on an antique silver bracelet. The whole outfit was perfect, consummate in its simplicity and charm, and I marvelled that it was what she wore to work in. She looked for all the world as if she were heading for one of those ethnic dance shows you saw on the TV in Malaysia.

She seemed excited to see us and called out in a loud voice. It was a strong voice, the diametric opposite of being "giow", a voice for halloing in the fields and calling the geese home. (My mother has a voice like that and we children would tell her to speak softer, embarrassed in public places.) It still surprised me to hear a stranger speak in such familiar language, for one does not hear our kind of Hakka often. (There are so many varieties of Hakka dialect: Moi Yan, Tam Sui, Hoi Luk Fung, Fui Jiu...) I was still not used to having meeting so many new people at once who all spoke my dialect. Somehow, I felt like an anthropologist who had gone to seek out this strange tribe only to find that they were just like her.

"O, so this is your sister!" she exclaimed to Wen Jun. She did not say "half-sister," as the Western term went. (I did not know what the equivalent term was in Chinese, if there was one.) So far, everyone, Wen Jun included, had referred to me as his sister.

We talked for a while about where I came from and my other members of my family. I asked Ah Sook Por if she had known Father.

"Of course I knew your father. I watched him grow up," she said. I was thrilled. Here was a person with another piece of the puzzle.

"Tell me about our Father when he was young. What was he like?"

"Looked just like your brother here," was all she said. She gave me a look as if my question was odd, as if that was no question to ask, or as if Father was standing right there and it was silly to be talking about him like that. I persisted.

"Was he..." I searched my brain for the right Hakka words. "Was he bright...was he unusual...what was his character like?"

"He was a good man, a good man." She was more interested in asking questions about Wen Jun and me. When was Wen Jun coming back to stay? And what about you? she said, turning to me. Would I come and stay here? She urged me in her loud, vigorous voice.

"Come, come and stay here for a while," she said, holding my hand. "Come and live here. Come and live here for a long term." She said it simply and directly, as if all I had to do was put my bags down and move right in.

As we neared Moi's place, another old woman appeared and pulled me by the hand. Wen Jun called her Ah Sook Por - yet another one, I said to myself, no longer surprised. Why don't you come and eat rice at our place? She said. Her son had just married and we had to come. *Loi Sit Fan.* Wen Jun told her we had already eaten, but that we would come visit. He told me that her house was the one in which Father was born. Of course I had to see it, I said.

This was the house, said Wen Jun, for which Father had sent money back to repair. It was not clear to me who owned it now, and if Father had spent money on it, why Wen Jun did not claim it. (I recalled the whisperings in our family how Father was sending all his money back to China to build this big house - we children swore we would never want to go live there with the Communists.) Inside, the structure was almost exactly like the other house my cousin occupied - a long, deep hall with no windows, smoky kitchen in front, curtained bedrooms at the back, storage loft above. There were signs of gaiety and celebration: the far wall was plastered with colorful peasant posters - pictures of the god of longevity, rosy children and beautiful maidens in flowing dresses. On a table was a tangerine (*git zai*) bush loaded with bright fruit, symbol of plenty. The floor was of grimy cement, covered with melon seed husks. Ah Sook Por served glasses of orange crush, we ate melon seeds, and the bride and groom came to join us. The groom, a bony young man with dark complexion, wore a three-piece grey suit, but he had no necktie on and his feet were in vinyl slippers, showing that he was half-relaxed. His wife, a plump Cantonese girl, had on a purple pants-suit and her hair was bouffant with a new perm. Around a formica table we sat, Ah Sook Por cracking jokes and laughing happily.

Come and see the room, said Wen Jun. Ah Sook Por led me into the bedroom at the back - a small space with light coming in from a little square of a window. Most of the room was occupied by an old wooden bed with a brownish mosquito net over it, bedding folded in a corner. I took in the shabby walls and simple fixings: This then, was the scene of nativity, Father a squealing baby, this was his first universe. How far he went. I remembered the family's account of his funeral in Malacca: how the entire community had turned out in a procession led by a brass band, cloth banners hung high on poles, and how the marching schoolchildren dressed in their uniforms stopped in front of our shophouse to pay homage, to this man they did not know themselves but whom the seniors said was a good man who served his people. Even the Malay people who lived behind our house had come bringing cakes they had made, tearfully saying, "Dia orang baik." I had not seen it myself, but the account had stirred me.

And if somewhere along the way Father had returned here, would he not have been out of place? Would he not have said to himself, Yes, this is where I was born, but I have made my home elsewhere. I am a citizen of Malacca. I am a citizen of Malaysia. My life is there.

We left at dusk, escorted to the end by crowds of waving children and the voices of my many Ah Nyong's and Ah Sook Por's calling, Be sure to come back...Come back to see us...

© Chin Woon Ping, 1993

This is an excerpt of Professor Chin's forthcoming book to be published by Times International, Singapore.

CHIN WOON PING is Professor in English at the University of Philadelphia. She was born in Malacca, Malaysia, and received her early education there. She studied at the University of Malaya, where she later became a Tutor, and at Cornell University and the University of Toledo. She was a Reader at Cornell University, and has taught at Drexel University, Haverford College and Bryn Mawr College. She was Senior Fullbright Lecturer in China and Indonesia, Visiting Scholar at Universiti Sains Malaysia, and has been awarded fellowships by the Pennsylvania Council on the Arts and the National Endowment for the Humanities.

Skoob *PACIFICA* will be publishing her book, "Shaman Tales: Jah Hut Myths (with Duncan Holaday and Teoh Boon Seong) & Other Prose & Poems" in Spring/Summer 1994.

ISBN 981-3002-68-9
Paperback   200 pp

Published by:
Landmark Books Pte Ltd
5001 Beach Road,
#02-74/75,
Singapore 0719

Green is the Colour
a novel by
Lloyd Fernando

Nobody could get May sixty-nine right, she thought. It was hopeless to pretend you could be objective about it. Speaking even to someone close to you, you were careful for fear the person might unwittingly quote you to others. If a third person was present, it was worse, you spoke for that person's benefit. If he was a Malay you spoke one way, Chinese another way, Indian another. Even if he wasn't listening. In the end the spun tissue, like an unsightly scab, became your version of what happened: the wound beneath continued to run pus.

PAUL SHARRAD
Introduction to
K.S. Maniam's
IN A FAR COUNTRY

K.S. Maniam's first novel, *The Return*, is a classic account of psychic displacement induced by migration and cultural assimilation under the impact of British colonialism. After some successful plays and a collection of short stories, Maniam here returns to the novel form, investigating the 'far countries' of the mind and dreamed of homelands. The ideal is not recovery of a country of cultural origin, but the discovery of a meaningful connection to the place one inhabits. *In A Far Country* works with similar material: memories of childhood amid the Indian indentured labour of Malaya's rubber plantations, of a dying and bitterly unhinged father and schooling's promise of escape from poverty and meanness of spirit to a bright and increasingly alienated young man. We witness a drama staged inside a man facing the existential void. Achoring private scenes in external 'reality' allows them to be significant for us as well. The narrator's struggle to find a balance between being 'his own man' and being part of the world he finds himself is an old problem, and it is the particular dynamics of the Malaysian context that give it new interest.

Maniam is a Malaysian. His novel is about trying to become a Malaysian. This paradox of being and becoming is expressed throughout the book in philosophical terms, but it also represents a social reality. Mr. Rajan, a successful businessman in a developing country marked by ethnic division, enters a mid-life crisis. Secluded in a room, his thoughts start "straying to avoid the blackness" of his soul and his lack of commitment to the people who have moved through his life: his father, the disillusioned drunk rubber-tapper from India; his obsessive doomed colleague on a jungle development site, Lee Shin; the orphaned vagrant philosopher, Sivasurian; villager Zulkifli, in quest of the spirit of the land; Rajan's wife, Vasanthi, isolated by ingrained patriarchal tradition. The book is Rajan's compendium of notes, letters, memories and meditations: its discursive abstractions tend towards the didactic but are enlivened by dramatic snapshots of memory, jerkily and briefly flashed up, often intense in their imagery.

Most readers today, in this world of shifting populations, will recognise the general problem facing Maniam's protagonist. How does the individual pull up cultural roots and retain a sense of life's significance? How can one *not* divest oneself of a specific group identity in this modern age of levelling multiplicity? Moreover, how do you hold to the supports of ethnic identity while affirming nationality, especially when your nation defines itself officially in terms of another race and culture? *In A Far Country* asks these questions, seeks to bring the far-off ideal into the imaginative country of the here and now. If the quest is broadly familiar, the specifics of this novel's setting may require explanation.

By comparison with India or Africa, Malaya has not loomed large on the popular imagination of the world. Its current national and social formation is the result of colonialism just as much as those other places, but connection to the global network of imperial image-production came relatively late. Also, with the exception of Penang and Singapore, for almost a century Malaya was ruled indirectly through local princes and administered at second hand through India. Kipling and others had said what had to be said; here was merely a repetition of less fabulous proportions which, because of quietly entrenched Islam, denied the West even the vicarious excitement of heroic missionising.

The Malay peninsula and surrounding islands did receive sporadic attention. Clifford tried to evoke the mystery of the jungle, the romance of sorcerers, were-tigers and court intrigues (as in *The Further Side of Silence*). Conrad created moral dramas out of the atmospherics of a brooding tropic coastline in *Almayer's Folly* and *Lord Jim*. Rajah Brooke carved out a personal fiefdom while suppressing piracy and served briefly as a focus for European literary dreams of power and adventure. The region hit its peak in terms of overseas exposure when the rubber boom was on in the twenties and Somerset Maugham captured the sordid 'good life' of planters and civil servants. As his stories make clear, however, plantations were boring places and their managers rather declassé. Despite the historic efforts of a few enthusiasts like Francis Light, Stamford Raffles and Frank Swettenham, Britain remained only half-hearted about this part of the world and let it go quietly to Independence in 1957 after a somewhat shame-faced collapse upon Japanese invasion. When the Commonwealth directly intervened in post-war counter-insurgency measures, literary PR varied from the cynical naturalism befitting guerrilla warfare to the sardonic comic-opera of Burgess's *Malayan Trilogy*.

One lasting effect of Malaysia's desultory but significant colonial history is its multi-racial population and the structuring of it as discrete communities. Malays were left largely to their own cultural devices once they proved amenable to British influence, and when reforms leading to self-government were instituted, it was the Malay elite, both traditional rulers and modern professionals, who took political power, not unnaturally legislating their favoured status as 'sons of the soil' in the new nation. Since most Malays had been rural farmers and fisher-folk, their control of land ownership and the eventual monopoly of the Malay language over national affairs meant that they could continue on unchanged, save by the inevitable impact of modernity.

Through the character of Pak Zul, Maniam gives credence to the Malay villager's strong attachment to the land. One of the most powerful passages in the novel occurs when Zulkifli attempts to bring Rajan into contact with the tiger spirit embo-dying indigenous authenticity. (The compelling treatment of this 'tiger hunt' as a direct counter to colonial fixations on hunting and on Malay 'magic' as colourful 'native superstition'.) The author is careful to resist the appeal of a romanticised induction into this cultural circle. His character, Rajan, can come to learn from his partial encounter with the 'tiger', but he cannot 'convert' totally to that experience: he must accept his other-ness, yet find a way of understanding that is more than merely intellectual assent or visceral repulsion. Maniam also shows that despite privileged national status, the ordinary Malay is as vulnerable as anyone else to cultural alienation. As Pak Zul knows bitterly and Rajan comes to realise, Malay youths like

Zulkifli's son are 'sons of the soil' only as a political slogan. In the modern city it is this identity that leaves them at the bottom of the economic ladder and prey to despair. The son acts out an old colonial stereotype of the Malay who runs amuck, but this time it is not because of the insidious tropics or some supposedly inherent instability, but in response to 'development' - a development that Rajan has played a part in, but which, ironically, has been orchestrated by the Malay political elite.

The novel portrays individuals from other major groups in Malaysia. Chinese had traded for centuries with the Peninsula on a small scale, some having settled in Malacca in the fifteenth century and adapted to local customs. Others were encouraged by the British as traders and were, anyway, already attracted by the money to be made out of tin mining. Since they were organised through Chinese societies and labour bosses and then by special British administrators, and since they had their own schools and remained largely concentrated in towns and mines, they too, were able to remain ethnically autonomous, attuned more to the politics in China than in Malaya. Their almost exclusive involvement in the communist insurgency after the War reflected this as well as their dismay at being squeezed out of the political arena in the emerging nation, but it served to drive a wedge between their people as a whole and the other racial groups of the Federation.

In A Far Country looks for moments in both village and town when inter-racial harmony is attained, but admits that they are both fragile and fleeting. A Chinese shop-keeper is held to be self-interested and stingy, but breaks free of his reputation to support his neighbours, only to enclose himself in the family circle under the stress of Japanese Occupation. Lee Shin, isolated in a forest camp, retreats to a dream of securely stereotypic Chinese traditionalism as an expression of his artistic temperament and a defense against insensitive workmates. In doing so, he counters popular images of Chinese as clannish, family-centred and interested only in money-making. Rajan observes him as a strange species whose music is incomprehensible, but he does manage to establish a rapport on the basis of a common sense of alienation. His attempt to help his colleague by asserting their common manhood on a 'dirty weekend' with some prostitutes downplays ethnic difference and attacks another stereotype of the Chinese male as lusty epicurean. This only drives Lee Shin further into neurosis, but it is his death that eventually forces the narrator to confront his own attitudes to women.

The other major influence on the history of the peninsula was India, whose southern empires in particular wielded immense cultural influence over the ancient kingdoms of South East Asia. Britain brought Indian convict labour to Malaya to build roads and cities, and then indentured large numbers of plantation workers to cultivate coffee, rubber and palm-oil. Again, with a few exceptions who became merchants, police and clerks, these people lived a feudal existence in rural barrack-lines with access mostly only to Indian overseers and a couple of years of Tamil schooling.

The narrator strives to escape this restricted life through a colonial schooling that gives entry to the decultured materialism of the modern professional class. Rajan's sudden sense of rootlessness drives him to remember his father's tormented dreams of ancient Indian trading voyages and then the crowded holds of indentured labour ships. When these prove too disturbing, the son recalls Deepavali celebrations, but that leads to childhood memories of goat slaughter, and so his thoughts break to another temporary escape route. In each flashback there is a passing reference to some ritual suggesting hope of peace or fulfilment. The narrative itself becomes a ritual of "pulling yourself out of passivity and despair by telling a story", even if it puts Rajan in the artist's role of the scapegoat whose sacrifice will keep the nation from complacency.

Segregated communalism was, no doubt, a convenient system for colonial management, but it was hardly a sound basis for nation building; sectional interests and mutual suspicion have continued to strain - sometimes violently - against the otherwise peaceful prosperity of modern Malaysia. The narrator's career in land and housing development reflects both the collective rush towards 'progress' in the early phases of Malayan nationalism and the personal anxiety of a second-generation, upwardly mobile migrant seeking some way of belonging. The novel shows the increasing difficulty of this as communities grow apart under the action of war and independence politics (when "people become peoples").

But if anti-colonial nationalism forces people into ethnic enclaves, it also forces some at least into greater social interaction. Rajan's coffee-shop circle is multi-ethnic and breaks up when he asserts his *individual* opinion. Rajan strives to escape from the stereotypic roles for Malaysian Indians; not only does he move away from a 'coolie' existence, but he constantly alters himself, shifting from a businessman contrasted to the unworldly Sivasurian to someone influenced by his metaphysics. Rajan's existential quest after something deeper than cold rationalism and economic drive implies the nation's need for more than fixed superficial links across class and ethnicity. Maniam's 'far country' is one in which public and private identities are always shifting. The changes occur around given cultural axes, but while these supply frameworks for meaning and direction, they are not themselves immutable. It is this very possibility of painful 'alter-ation' that creates recurrent possibilities for human community.

In A Far Country is remarkable novel for its experiment. It moves beyond early Malayan writing in English which sought to establish a local literary imagination in opposition to an imposed colonial one. It resorted to 'slice-of-life' sketches of a fairly limited world and to the self-conscious introduction of local idiom. Such nationalist realism found its end result in the official assertion that Malay was the only medium for national culture, leaving writing in English marginalised with an increasingly elitist or overseas audience. *In A Far Country* seeks to free itself from this literary ghetto by addressing national issues and departing from realism to do so. Maniam's venture into dreamscapes and metaphysics is important, and, while it works mostly through Hindu-sounding phrases, it offers a point of contact with literature in Malay - the animistic world of Shahnon Ahmad's villagers, for example, or the strong moral tone of Malay poetry. *In A Far Country* builds on the fictional quest after a multicultural national belonging instituted in Lloyd Fernando's *Scorpion Orchid*, but it avoids that book's pessimism partly because it manages not to rely on ethnically representative (potentially stereotypic and therefore imaginatively ghettoised) characters.

The book's texture may suggest the opposite; dreams, recollections, bits of writing and dialogue leap forth and cut off in

135

disconnected fashion. But there is a logic in the narrative that eventually intimates a degree of hopefulness for a more integrated community. Maniam's style relies on 'dead-pan' declarative sentences that seem to imprison the voice in flat objectivity. This is appropriate to Mr. Rajan, the pragmatist who resists enlightenment, but it is set against poetic passages of heightened emotional intensity. Modulation between styles is handled skilfully via shifts in tense that take on a connective rhythm. Another integrating technique is the repetition of rhetorical questions. This can be a dangerous ploy in that we may get tired of the constant deferral of an answer (spiritual truths have a habit of sounding obvious). But religious consolation, whatever its cultural form, does not come easily in real life. The narrator struggles amid separation from his past and his fellows to build a fabric of wisdom, finally learning enough from the wider community to begin improving his own marriage relationship.

A major organisational device is Maniam's use of light and time as motifs that link the 'disjecta membra' of the narrator's memory and connect the character's personal obsessions to general metaphysical questions about truth and appearance, about history as a series of discrete events versus the continuity of experience across everyday action and timeless epiphany. It is this dimension of the book, coupled with a social background carrying legacies of colonialism that suggests comparison with Raja Rao's Indian metaphysical comedy, *The Cat and Shakespeare*, Australian Randolph Stow's *To The Islands*, or, closer to home, the late Lee Kok Liang's ironical *Flowers in the Sky*. K.S. Maniam has given us a challenging new work, solemnly alert to the historical limitations of humanity yet compelled by those dreaming moments when genuine selfhood and community seem possible.

© Paul Sharrad, 1993.

PAUL SHARRAD holds a Ph.D. and teaches post-colonial literatures at Wollongong University, Australia. He has published a book, *Raja Rao and Cultural Tradition*, and co-edits *New Literatures Review*.

K.S. MANIAM
An excerpt of his New Novel
In A Far Country

The protagonist, Rajan, disillusioned with the trappings of silk and satin, reflects on his unrelenting past and old companions. In trying to recant a persona of attachment to material progress, he discovers self-apprehension in an authentic identity.

What was he? The question obsessed me for a long time. But as I went on watching I understood only a little of what he was and wanted to be. He became such a focus of attention for me that I kept, in writing, a study of his movements, behaviour and final developments in his life. I'll reproduce it here so as to see if it can throw any light on my present predicament. The language appears stilted and pseudo-scientific but that was what I was at that time. I've tried to keep myself as much as possible out of the account. Sometimes I've written as I followed his behaviour; sometimes I've written in recollection. This record is extensive in the beginning when we hardly talked; it comes to an abrupt end just before he met his death.

The Lee Shin Study

This study attempts to understand, in detail, Lee Shin's behaviour, thoughts and motivation. While it cannot be exhaustive, it can, nevertheless, be an honest record of what was seen, heard and observed. In this place, after work is done, there is more than enough time for such activities.

Men can be put into two categories: the independent and the dependent. Lee Shin is an independent. The other men here mass together: in the mess, coffeeshops, rest house and the houses of nurses and salesgirls. They clearly belong to the second group. Their code of ethics is based on mutual support. Thus, they support each other's opinions, attitudes, idiosyncracies, actions and the ability to put down those outside their circle.

Lee Shin seems to have come to the settlement with a fierce desire to safeguard his freedom. From the beginning he has kept to himself as if he mistrusted people. It has been more than a month since Lee Shin came under observation but he has not said a word to the observer. As a neighbour, he is uncommunicative and sits by himself in the verandah, late into the evening. Now and then he whistles a tune which has no resemblance to any that the observer has heard. Sometimes the whistling rises to such a pitch as to sound inhuman. Then he breaks off suddenly.

No sound comes from his house throughout the late afternoon. When the observer wakes up from his nap, the house next door is still quiet and looks uninhabited. The observer who has had lunch in town and is preparing to go out for his tea, wonders what Lee Shin has eaten for the afternoon meal.

When the observer returns from his tea, he finds Lee Shin dressed in white shorts and T-shirt. He is out on the slope of grass beside his house ready to begin his exercises. This is the part of Lee Shin's behaviour that the observer finds strange. He never carries out any of the regular exercises young men pick up. Instead, he creates a slow-paced pantomime with his trunk, hands and legs.

Sometimes his movements are so painfully slow that the observer wonders if Lee Shin has entered some sort of a trance. There he stands, within an invisible centre, his body defying gravity and the backbone's flexibility, arms stretched out in a kind of farewell. Then he bends low and holds himself temptingly between sinking down to rest and rising up to fierce combat. But he does neither. He just remains in that position for a long time. He is rivetted to the earth and sky with an invisible bolt. To the casual onlooker he may be a bronze statue balancing itself between life and death.

Perhaps it was that moment that had attracted the observer's attention to this lonely individual. Lee Shin then lifts himself up as if by the hair. The head goes up, followed by his shoulders, waist and thigh, all in slow motion. He does something with his shoulder blades and they spread out like a cobra's hood poised for attack. He dips his head and brings up his hands so that the fingers curve rigidly, as if they were the snake's fangs. He advances slowly, and the fangs come down viciously on some invisible enemy. Lee Shin straightens, relaxes, and resuming his usual slouch, whistles his way to the verandah and sits down on the steps.

The evening is mildly warm and Lee Shin remains seated there for some time, almost immobile. As the day recedes, he acquires the dimension of a granite statue. His body, carved up by shadow and light, appears to be supported by an emaciated purpose. There is dignity in that posture but little else.

When the observer returns from his evening meal, Lee Shin has already bathed and changed. He is once again seated in the verandah, on a chair, and he has started something new. There is a bright object in his hands; he polishes it with a yellow, velvety cloth. Then Lee Shin puts the shiny object to his lips and the sound it emits confuses the observer for a while and then only amuses him. As Lee Shin launches into a full melody, the observer becomes more and more disoriented. He has never heard a harmonica produce such strange strains. 'Yankee Doodle' comes to his mind for that was what was traditionally played on that instrument or it was 'My Bonnie Lies Over the Ocean'.

The days now are a torment for the observer for he does not know how to stop Lee Shin from playing the harmonica. On the silent grounds of the settlement, the music from the harmonica booms like some unearthly sound. What restrains the observer, however, is the objective he chose when he undertook this study. Once he interferes, the subject will be robbed of his peculiar habits and personal circumstances. So the observer has to bear his discomfort and adopt the attitude of a detached recorder.

As the days pass, Lee Shin plays furiously but stops now and then to look in the direction of the observer's house. In the company's offices he casts shy but significant glances at the observer. Is some change imminent in Lee Shin?

The past three days the harmonica has been reedy, desultory and cautious. No blaring, pungent thrusts come to provoke; instead, Lee Shin looks more and more towards the observer's house. The attitude of the other personnel is becoming clearer and is, sometimes, distressing. Obviously, they would like to be elsewhere, in some of the brighter towns but the money here is good. Perhaps this recognition makes them quieter but beneath the calm lies a latent viciousness.

All this makes the observer view Lee Shin differently. He is so self-contained nothing seems to touch him. Can the observer be affected by the observed? It is certainly so in this case: Lee Shin's self-sufficient existence gives the observer a strange sense of confidence. Some of the restlessness the observer felt earlier is gone.

Some weekends Lee Shin tramps off into the jungle nearby, haversack on his back and a butterfly net in his hand. Returning in the evening, he sits in the hall and mounts the specimens. The observer sees him bent over the butterflies, the syringe in his fingers sucking out the insides and, later, pumping in the formaldehyde. What is there about the posture that says neither the activity nor the interest will last? Two or three weeks later Lee Shin has shifted his attention elsewhere. He has taken to pressing leaves, flowers and rare plants. Then he is back at the verandah railing, barehanded and listless.

Then one evening he signals to the observer. It is not so much an invitation as a command, the hand waving imperatively. The observer, taken aback, wonders whether to comply or not. But he is curious and crosses the short distance to Lee Shin's house.

The observer mounts the steps and stands beside Lee Shin. The man makes no move to acknowledge or greet him. Lee Shin's gaze is still turned towards the house down the slope as if the observer has not left it. Then, suddenly, he snaps out of his reverie and looks at the observer.

"The harmonica music has brought you here," Lee Shin says.

"In a way," I say.

The power and necessity to tell a story is the original impulse of any fiction. Rajan, Zulkifli, Lee Shin, Sivasurian and Santhi of different race and religion contribute to the cosmos of this convergent world *In A Far Country*.

© K.S. Maniam, 1993.

This new novel is available from Skoob PACIFICA London. Direct orders Skoob Two, Tel: 071-405 0030 or fax 071-404 4398 GBP £5.99 U.K. post free.

KEE THUAN CHYE
Dilemma of a Dog Barking at a Mountain
Pragmatist-Idealist Dialectic and The Writer in Malaysia

A writer must write with the courage of his conviction. He must brook no compromise and he must not fear the consequence. He must be prepared to sacrifice his own comfort and safety if it is demanded of him.

A writer must be true to his conviction. He must believe in what he is doing to have the strength of spirit to rise above all else. He must believe that what he writes will serve some cause of humanity and be of value to his fellowmen.

A writer must be sensitive to his conscience. If he sees injustice, he cannot turn away. If he knows of corruption, he cannot pretend it does not exist. If he believes that the state abuses its power, he cannot condone it with his silence.

The writer must be a man who stands apart, above political affiliation, having a healthy distrust of authority and a firm commitment to truth. It is his moral responsibility to oppose anything that seeks to oppress, injure, or destroy humanity.

The idealist in me believes in all of the above.

But of late, the pragmatist in me is getting increasingly circumspect and sweaty under the collar.

As such, I have been moved to reassess my position as a writer who desires to write without fear or restraint, and to reassess it in relation to my willingness as a person to accept the consequences of my desire, no matter how adverse these consequences may be. In the process, I find that I am beginning to have suspicions of my validity and self-worth in both capacities.

The pragmatist forces me to consider the harsh realities. Being a writer in a country like Malaysia means being subject to conditions peculiar to its society.

First, we are continually reminded that we are a developing country and certain needs are more important than others. We are also a multi-racial society with its inherent differences and sensitivities. Idealistic notions pertaining to freedom of expression may not have a place in the scheme of things. They may cause dissension and destabilisation, and we can't afford that. What is preferable: freedom or a bowl of rice? What is more desirable: freedom and anarchy or a peaceful and prosperous state?

Our leaders would have us believe that the society is not prepared to see itself for what it is. Their practices tell us that sweeping the dirt under the *mengkuang* mat is the best method to preserve the image that the house is clean. Those who would disturb the dirt are "madmen" or "trouble-makers" whose loyalty to the country can be called into question. And the punishment for that can be detention without trial.

I break out in a sweat when I think of incarceration with no recourse to justice, no appeal to humane consideration, of being totally cut off from loved ones, and being at the mercy of inquisitors. I realise I am vulnerable to the shocks that flesh and mind are heir to.

The pragmatist asks if it is worthwhile to suffer such outrageous fortune, and I actually pause to wonder. Perhaps the impetuosity of youth is no longer one of my traits. Perhaps cowardliness is. Why do examples of sacrifice by writers like Vaclav Havel, W.S. Rendra, Pramoedya Ananta Toer, or, even closer to home, my fellow countryman A. Samad Ismail, seem so distant and intangible?

Have I, like many others in my country, become well and truly frightened into submission after the big swoop of October 1987 when over a hundred "trouble-makers" were detained?

In the face of such a show of power, what resources can the writer draw on to deal with it?, the pragmatist asks. Should the writer then continue to be defiant or should he learn to kowtow? Should he not acquire the virtue of silence and adopt a low profile?

After all, in Malaysia, a writer stands virtually alone. Which, therefore, makes him all the more vulnerable. If he has a following, it consists mainly of the literature-literate, and these are few compared to the masses who read pulp, or don't read at all. Understandably, we do not have as yet a literary culture that counts for much in the larger context. One can be certain there will be no popular uprising or movement to vindicate the writer.

Today, one of our most well-known writers, A. Samad Said, is on a five-year artist's strike to protest against what he calls an insensitive publishing bureaucracy. Four years ago, he was accorded the nation's highest literary award but now, for his action, he has earned more condemnation than sympathy from his peers while the rest of the public does not care. Many don't even know who he is.

How then can the Malaysian writer count on public support to help him withstand the backlash of a powerful establishment?

In the first place, would his voice be heard?

Well, he has much to contend with. The idiot box that sits in the living room of many a Malaysian household spews out glitz and flash that would appeal more readily and immediately than drab, black words on a page. Messages and second messages make easy subliminal contact; they don't even have to reveal themselves as obvious propaganda.

Newspapers are less subtle. Their reflection of ruling-class values and philosophy is not sensed from reading between the lines. Indeed, it is the dissenting newspaper writer who has to resort to such a tactic, but there are not many like him. Generally, newspapers are sunny with positive comments on the health of the state, and often crammed with statements by Cabinet ministers...and Cabinet ministers.

In such a scenario, if the writer challenges the establishment, he is like a dog barking at a mountain. The mountain, on its part, will not be shaken. It controls a mighty media machinery that can easily squelch the poet's whimper by either functioning as a network of disinformation, or by producing - to use a line by Italo Calvino - an "ocean of words, printed or broadcast... (in which) the words of the poet or writer are swallowed up".

Another course of action, and perhaps a more effective one, is to throttle the poet before he can even raise a whimper. In Malaysia, despite the lip service being paid to democratic principles, censorship is still a handy instrument. We are often told that it is necessary in order to safeguard the nation's peace and stability. A few years ago, a 40-minute play about a man recounting the difficulties he underwent to bury his grandfather was construed as a threat to national security. How such a conclusion was arrived at defies logical understanding. Perhaps, unknown to us, burial is regarded as a subversive activity.

After a while, censorship inevitably breeds self-censorship. People become conditioned to saying only what they are allowed to say; what is outside of the permissible is best left unsaid. It is not only newspaper editors second-guessing how their political masters might think, who succumb to self-censorship; even the office worker holds his tongue on certain issues for fear of being overheard. Writers learn quickly what to exclude from their texts if they want their writings published. Playwrights write the kind of plays that they know will be approved for public staging. A playwright who is averse to self-censorship learns bitterly that his play will not be staged for the "sensitive" material it contains. And the people who would deny him his permit after vetting his submitted script would be none other than policemen. They are the ones who decide what is suitable or unsuitable dramatic art.

It is quite obviously for this reason that agitprop has not taken root in Malaysian theatre although it is a form that would be most relevant for examining issues of the times and stimulating reflection and discussion. Agitprop would also be the appropriate alternative to the sedate, mind-numbing dramas on television and, as such, attract people away from their living rooms to the theatre.

But there are other forms that theatre in Malaysia can take; what it has to be most vigilant about now is the phenomenon of reality becoming more and more theatrical and the effect of this on its own position as a medium of expression. Constantly, the ruling class is making use of the media machinery at its disposal to theatricalise reality for its self-aggrandisement. Political events are being turned into staged events; history-making is theatre-making. A ceremony to launch a programme to boost tourism is turned into a spectacle, held in front of a crowd of thousands and telecast 'live', completely stage-managed to make the ruling party look good, such that the tourism programme becomes incidental. Such theatricalisation reminds me of the German playwright Heiner Muller's warning that power "is getting more and more spectacular...and becomes power-play".

As the line between reality and theatre becomes this fine, theatre as we traditionally know it must surely redefine its role.

When the best actors are prime ministers and presidents, and the best directors and stage managers are their PR advisers, what can theatre do to counter that? By the same token, what becomes of the legitimate writer of drama whose role has been somewhat appropriated? Where does he stand as his position is gradually being eroded by the "power-players"?

The theatre must be a marketplace of alternative viewpoints and the writer must protest, says the idealist. But then to protest is to invite trouble. A member of one socially-conscious theatre group was among the unfortunate who were detained in 1987. Its effect on the artistic community was significant.

Nowadays, it seems to be the rule that the more accommodating writers resort to allegory or ambiguity to get around the problem of censorship. The pragmatist in me would tend to go along with that, but the idealist considers it a form of compromise. Thus, the central implication of this inner conflict goes beyond considerations of material and approach; it goes right to the crucial question of whether it is meaningful to write at all.

In debating this, both idealist and pragmatist would, however, agree that there is another problem confronting the Malaysian writer that is more disconcerting than that of censorship because it poses a barrier to communication. That problem is the thorny issue of race.

Race has always been an issue in my country, even before Independence, but never has it been as serious and divisive as it is today. In the last 20 years, race-consciousness has been so institutionalised that it has virtually developed into a Frankenstein. Almost every issue is seen from the perspective of race to the point that it is impossible to obtain a consensus of public opinion on **any** issue.

A writer of any race communicating to such a variegated society is apt to be viewed with misgiving by some quarters. He can hardly take a stand on any issue without drawing ire or suspicion. We do not have as yet a developed Malaysian consciousness to which a writer can address his views with sanguinity; the consciousness of race subverts such a covenant between writer and audience.

What we have is a polarisation of readership or audience that further undermines the extent of the writer's influence.

Under these circumstances, it is virtually impossible to find a Malaysian writer who commands a pan-Malaysian following, even among those who write in the national language. The Truly Malaysian Novel has yet to be written, the Truly Malaysian Film yet to be made. And it may never come about because attendant to the politics of race are the equally passionate politics of language, of culture, and of religion, which create greater schisms of beliefs and values.

Together, they pose formidable and frustrating barriers for the writer whose best intentions can count for nothing in responses coloured by not only racial prejudice but also by cultural or religious prejudice, and sometimes by a crippling combination of all these.

Concomitantly, care has to be taken by the writer not to offend racial, cultural, and religious sensitivities, an observance that seems sensible but at times is open to misinterpretation. Offensive references can be alleged when none was intended because of the arbitrariness of such responses. Furthermore, deference to sensitivities invariably limit the scope of imaginative possibilities; for instance, mores may vary from one persuasion to another but the Malaysian writer who is prudent has to accommodate the mores of **all** persuasions.

Evidently, an environment such as ours is not the kind that encourages a flowering of literature or the arts in general. Too many taboos spoil the art, which explains why the film industry is stagnating and the TV dramas appear so parochial. Indeed, we have become so accustomed to sanitised representations of reality that a recent stage play drew some oohs and ahs in surprised response because its protagonist was a prostitute. When rain appears after a long drought, it is bound to get people excited.

Given the conditions I have detailed above, it would appear that the prospects are bleak for a writer who believes in unfettered expression. The pragmatist believes that it is difficult enough to operate in a society that regards liberal thinking with suspicion; it is practically hopeless when the society is non-homogeneous as well. The writer seeking change will not achieve it with his writing, less so if it challenges authority. The better lot is reserved for the propaganda writer who espouses the official party line. Radical change will only come about either at the initiative of the ruling class or as an outcome of a mass revolution, but since such a revolution is virtually impossible because the masses are polarised, no amount of butting against the pedestal is likely to cause the statue to move.

This, of course, leaves the committed writer in a non-battling position. He can have access to the middle class but the middle class know they have too much to lose if they risk getting involved. They may grumble about the way things are but they are not likely to be stirred to action as long as the economy is not pushed to its limits. In Malaysia, it is very easy to be lured by the temptations of an easy, comfortable, and complacent life and to remain in it. It is easy to place more importance on stock-market prices than the value of personal integrity. A prosperous economy is what guarantees loyalty to comfort and the status quo.

So, how can the writer be a rallying force of change? The ruling class has got it down pat with its practice of divide-and-rule, a colonial legacy, no doubt, but a useful one. Can the courage and conviction of the writer have the power to move mountains? Is it worthwhile for him to risk his safety and comfort for the sake of what appears a practically hopeless cause?

At this point, the pragmatist leans back in his chair, a smug expression of his face, and flexes his fingers in a show of satisfaction. In a measured tone, tasting his words and smacking his lips, he suggests that one can still be a writer writing what one likes without being overtly political, staying "on the borderline between the permissible and the impermissible", to borrow a phrase from the Polish film-maker Andrzej Wajda. One can still feel safe and hope that what one writes can touch some chord in some, if not many, people. Modesty is the best policy.

The idealist is silent for a while, then shoots up on his feet and cries, no compromise! Pacing up and down, he rattles off his objections, spittle spraying from his mouth. How can a writer dishonour his calling? How can he comment on unjust laws being bulldozed through Parliament and not be overtly political? How can he see human rights being trampled on and

147

say it was actually stroked with the feet? He might as well give up being a writer!

And join the middle class, the pragmatist rejoins.

The writer transcends class, the idealist bellows.

And so the debate rages on. But my dilemma is far from being resolved. In this paper, I have raised questions more than provided answers, and I have only another question to add to it: I wonder if something precious is lost when the fire one felt as an angry young man grows weaker as one mellows with age? Would it be a loss when the desire to make a difference is supplanted by indifference? Answering that is probably as difficult as making a choice between writing what is permissible and writing what is not permissible, or even between writing and giving up writing. But at the end of the day, I believe that one has to be accountable to oneself for the things one has done. So I wholeheartedly subscribe to what the actress Cher once said: "I have one fear in life: that I will not live it with guts and integrity, and instead make choices that are safe."

Be that as it may, in 10 years' time, if you hear I've gone into stock-broking or marketing of Proton Sagas, you will know that I'd have completely sold out.

Paper presented at the Fourth Southeast Asian Writers Conference in Manila, February 10-14, 1990.

KEE THUAN CHYE graduated from the Universiti Sains Malaysia as a literature major and also obtained an M.A. in literature (drama) from Essex University. He has been a journalist since 1977 and is presently the Literary Editor of the national newspaper and is actively involved in drama as actor, director and playwright.

Mr Kee's works include plays, *1984 Here and Now* and *The Big Purge,* a biography, *Old Doctors Never Fade,* and a collection of essays *Just in So Many Words* published by Heinemann, Singapore in 1993. He also edited an anthology of short stories *Haunting the Tiger & Other Stories.* **Skoob PACIFICA** London will be publishing a new work in 1994.

SHIRLEY GEOK-LIN LIM

Listening to the Punjabi Singer

Her Urdu voice rises in the performance room.
I could have been married for twenty years
to the man she's singing for - the beloved
who does not return her love and vanishes
forever. Always suffering Asia!

I yearn to be her this evening.
Suffused, securely my own woman,
I play at nostalgia, imagine -
eyes closed - Malaysia now, as if
twenty years have passed and nothing's died.
Not the dream of marriage, of one brown
family and nation. From back-of-the-room
middle age spins fantasy and regret.
Singles the concrete bungalow
in Petaling Jaya, one of thousands

of a race: Malay, Chinese, Indian,
and Eurasian hardened in the same
shelter, if not skin. In front of the white
stone an iron gate, bars, curlicues,
three-inch chain and lock. By the gate

hibiscus, oleander, jacarandas
with dirty plum blossom. Leafage I prune
with words threaten to overtake the evening
just as the singer has overtaken
me - back, in a language I do not know,

to the place of colored doors, the riotous
vegetation, choices, and wild consequences.

Father From Asia

Father, you turn your hands toward me.
Large hollow bowls, they are empty
stigmata of poverty. Light pours
through them, and I back away,
for you are dangerous, father
of poverty, father of ten children,
father of nothing, from whose life
I have learned nothing for myself.
You are the father of childhood,
father from Asia, father of sacrifice.
I renounce you, keep you in my sleep,
keep you two oceans away, ghost
who eats his own children,
Asia who loved his children,
who didn't know abandonment,
father who lived at the center of the world,
whose life I dare not remember,
for memory is a wheel that crushes,
and Asia is dust, is dust.

LATIFF MOHIDIN
midnight lays
Translated from the Malay by Salleh Ben Joned

i

tonight
the moon
has pulled aside
her curtain of gold
the waves'
crimson lips
are parted

moon and waves
meet here
along the lower slopes
of your waist
to witness
                    the dance of your desire
                    the dance of my death

ii

look how i rub
your eyebrows
with honey
a column of ants
in trance
are dancing
a drunken dance
along the crescent
of your eyebrows

iii

from the still depths
of your throat
i hear
        the howling of a wolf
        the neighing of a stallion
        the roar of a lion
        unremitting

and my gullet
vibrates
with ever increasing violence
in answer to the screams
from the depths
of your throat

iv

your thighs:
                sharp scissors
                of thrilling softness

v

seven seas
a lone mountain
of wave
        in the whirling
        heart
        of your belly
a throbbing
in the bowels

of time
is calling
my name
    i climb down the hill
    i leave the vast open field

and crawling
i return
to the dark secret pool
of your being

LATIFF MOHIDIN studied Art in Berlin from 1960-1964, in Paris in 1969 and New York in 1970. He travelled throughout Europe and Asia and produced many fine pieces of work during this period. Latiff has held numerous solo and group exhibitions both in Malaysia and abroad.

His literary contributions include five books of poems in Malay of which four have been translated into English. The fifth, *Garis dari ketitik (Lines from point to point)* has been translated by Adibah Amin and will be published by Dewan Bahasa dan Pustaka in October, 1993. The bilingual edition of his **Selected Poems** is forthcoming **Spring** 1994 by **Skoob PACIFICA,** London.

SALLEH BEN JONED was a lecturer in English Literature at the University of Malaya. He is now a poet and columnist with a newspaper. His first book of poems *Sajak Sajak Saleh: Poems Sacred and Profane* was first published in 1987 and the second edition by Hornbill Publications is due out in October, 1993. His play, **Amok & Other Writings** is forthcoming in **Winter 1993** with **Skoob PACIFICA**, London.

CECIL RAJENDRA
Nite of de Iguana

Kuala Lumpur: The "heroin-filled condoms" doctors removed from the stomach of a man who claimed to have swallowed iguana eggs have been certified as iguana eggs.

City anti-narcotics chief said the chemist's report confirmed the three objects removed from S. Adinarayanan's stomach were iguana eggs.

Doctors who had operated on him after he had complained of stomach pains found three oval-shaped objects which they thought were condoms stuffed with heroin and called the police.

The Star

So one nite
my wife she tole me,
"Ayah, really lah
nowadays you tak guna."
I say, "Wat you mean,
wat you mean, wassamatter?"
She say, "You know lah
dat ting, dat ting ...
no mo fun, too fas lah."

So nex day after work
I go to see dis bomoh
explain my deligate probrem.
He tell me, "Dat kondishun
quite common, no probrem ...
urut also can, but urut
ohnee temporaree solushun.
I have sumtin better
much much better, but will
cos you plenny, plenny dollar."

I say, "Come on, pachee
doan play de fool wit me.
Tell me how much lah?
I no cheepskate wan.
Money no probrem when it
coming to looking after
der wife an der thungachee."

Dis homoh den tell me
"*Bess* cure in town is egg
of iguana se-biji, se-biji
swallowed whole wit honey."
So I gip him pipty dolla
and makan tiga telor iguana.

I go home ready for ackshun
but all I get is plenny
stummach-ake and constipayshun
Adoi, pain terror, brudder;
so much so nex day I
mus go to Hospital Besar.
After X-ray, doktor he say
he mus rightaway operayshun.
So dey put me to sleep
my han hancuff to de bed
and everywhere de mata-mata.

"What's going on, man?"
I ask de fierce sarjan.

Deffler say, "Adinarayan,
you a bad, bad man
to try an smuggle de

dadah in your stummach
bungkus in der condom."

I say, "You crazy or vat?
Dat no dadah, man
dat is egg of iguana!"
An den you know vat
he say, dees crazee sarjan?
Deffler say "Vereee funnee,
Deh Adina, you tink
you can teech your
granmudder to suck eggs, ah?"

So 5-day awreddy I in bed
with hancuff an de sarjan
wile dey send de iguana egg
to testing in Camistry Deparmen.

And den dey fine out
(dees stoopid mata-mata)
wat I dun tell dem all along
dat in my poor stummach
is no topi perancis dadah
but reelly de egg of iguana.

Eye-yo, kadavallay, so much trubble
lah brudder, an all becoz i took
three leetle egg of de iguana
to help, you know lah, tahan lama.

© Cecil Rajendra, 1993.

CECIL RAJENDRA was born in Penang, Malaysia.
He received his formal education in St. Xaviers Institution,

Penang, the University of Singapore and Lincoln's Inn, London where he was admitted as a Barrister-at-Law.

Cecil Rajendra is the author of 13 collections of poems including *Bones & Feathers, Refugees & Other Despairs, Hour of Assassins, Child of the Sun, Dove on Fire, Songs for the Unsung* and Zebrochene Traume (*Debris of Dreams*).

A new collection *Broken Buds* is scheduled for publication in India later this year.

His poems have appeared in over 40 countries and been translated into several languages including German, French, Tagalog, Japanese, Chinese, Urdu, Tamil and Swahili.

Cecil Rajendra practises law in Penang, Malaysia where he devotes the major part of his time co-ordinating free legal aid clinics in the rural areas.

He is married to Rebecca and has 2 children - Yasunari and Shakila.

Rajendra describes himself as a 'radical humanist' totally intolerant of such human indecencies as war, poverty, social injustice and environmental devastation.

Singular Stories
Tales from Singapore, Volume One

Selected by Robert Yeo

Singular Stories presents the finest of these (flowering short fiction in Singapore) efforts, to demonstrate the diversity of themes and styles being employed by Singaporean writers. Volume One looks at the conflict between traditional and modern societies, the role of women, the Japanese occupation, and the lighter side of the Singaporean character; styles range from straight narrative to surreal to experimental.

ISBN 981-00-3939-5
Paperback   152 pp

Yang Publishers,
44 Jalan Sembilang,
Singapore 2057.

LEONG LIEW GEOK

Between Us

Our toes stretch free, their bones
Not bruised or bound for lotus feet;
In different times we grew
To walk the ground with indifferent gait,
A quarter century dividing us
Less than marriage.

I have heard my father-in-law's women
Draw their knives. His mother said
To his wife, her son was young enough
To take another. What other wounds
You've counted, your head
Replaying reel by reel!
I have also seen you bait
Your mother by marriage:
You would not need your children
To feed you in your age.

She's been long dead -
Her knives you've seized to bleed arteries
Still - her death no remedy.
I should be thankful
You throw me no daggers,
But that we both starve
Choking on righteous dust,
You in your past, I in your presence,
Stitched up by gesture and obedience
To hand: two dumb dolls from history's cage.

Must you enter my kitchen
Only to eat and drink?
No more than a house-guest
Seated, to be waited on?
Must your visits be claims
That business calls you here,
For lodging? So you hurry home
Across the Causeway after a night's
Rest, at most two: taking little,
No debts to let go.

For the iron role you've cast,
The fraud I enact
Irons the soul.
The future forbid that I sit,
Dowager to some in-law!
Wooden as a puppet, the past
Its strings. What deadweights we allow
History to haul: the mother-in-law,
Enslaved; her daughter-in-law who plays
The filial knave to majesty.

Must we then, never be friends?
Must distance keep us safe?
Between the elder, and the younger,
Must custom bind and ritual chafe?

Forty Hours

There's an edge to time:
The older one grows, the harder
One falls, feet riding emptiness,
Arms flailing at airy waste.

Or, uncoiled, it whizzes
Past word and deed
To leave slow movers for dead.
Cooking, eating, reading;
Writing, teaching, talking;
Weeding, digging, planting
And making love -

There's time in a lifetime
For few things to be served.
To take the single day's stuff,
Forty hours might just be enough.

© Leong Liew Geok, 1993.

LEONG LIEW GEOK was born in Penang, graduated from La Trobe University and the University of Adelaide. She has a Ph.D. in American Literature from George Washington University and teaches at the National University of Singapore. Her first collection of poems, *Love's Not Enough* was published in 1991 by Times International, Singapore.

LEE TZU PHENG

Revisioning

Five years, my friend, since I overheard
your tears because the universe was silent.
I never went as far as you, not pushed
to desolation's reaches, but the nights
were almost as cold. From the past
a memory of beginnings made me watchful;
taking strange paths under indifferent skies
I longed to recognize the rare, distinctive
kindling in bone - its warmth was human.
If this was what I sought, affirmation,
of life so very nearly lost, it made
the terror of your anguish beautiful;
the chill of a silent God a heavenly fire.

Suffering burns us clean. This baptism we share,
though what in us is deepest seems the hardest
to surrender. And see now where, despite time's
ruthlessness, love reduced to ash may feed new roots.

I live by faith now, as you do discerning
in solitary spaces the freeing of the soul.
We listen still for voices, pay them heed,
but fashion from their words our own responses.
Revisioning is more than finding trails;
it is to move through dead ends to horizons.
It is to see new signs within old lands,
the ancient furrows break like children's smiles.

Excluding Byzantium
on objections to living near a home for the elderly sick

"That is no country for old men."
The aging poet meant another place,
the body contemptible, incompatible
with the passions of the mind:

it is easier, somehow, to bear such ostracism;
art has the compensation of its own realities;
art can mould pain into singing birds,
and scarecrows image saints in holy fires.

Outside of art, what consolations thrive?
Decrepitude may push you to the side of life.
Sickness can make a stranger of the best-loved face.
Mortality's a monster, some think better
relegated to a hidden place.
Hospices and nursing homes may reek
of worse than age; a lingering pall
sour the taste of all human endeavour.
It takes much more than empathy, perhaps,
to receive the aged sick into our midst
without protest, even unvoiced, while
life points us to our expected end.

How many will have art to keep them safe?
How many, art to house our grim reminders?
We know we but banish ourselves to claim
"this is no country for old men".

© Lee Tzu Pheng, 1993.

LEE TZU PHENG is a senior lecturer with the Department of English Language and Literature in the National University of Singapore.

Her published works include a book on reading with pre-schoolers, *Growing Readers* and three collections of poetry: *Prospects of a Drowning* (1980), *Against the Next Wave* (1988) and *Brink of An Amen* (1991). All three collections have been awarded the National Book Development Council of Singapore Book Award for poetry in English.

In 1985 Dr. Lee was awarded the Cultural Medallion for Literature, and in 1987, she received the Southeast Asian Write Award.

KIRPAL SINGH

Mad About Green

they told me to be mad about green
and i became mad about red, yellow, blue, purple, pink
the colours were so right how could i not go mad?

they told me to be mad about green
and i became mad about this brown earth my body
that blue ocean the water of my life
this orange rind of the crust of my seed's fruit
this brilliant black of the night.

go green, they said, go, go, be mad about green
i wrote songs, sang them, danced with my mind
the dance of a million worlds locked in green
a million worlds lost without knowing.

in the mountains of my convulsions
in the valleys of my truncations,
in the rivers of my persuasions
the ecology remained undisturbed, unmined
and they said be mad about green.

i wrote of the whales that disappear
i wrote of the wild dogs who no longer bark
i wrote of the grass which turned into slime
i wrote of the clouds that hung over us.

they told me to be mad about green
being mad they took me aside.

En Route

in the genting cold
your eyes froze the cards
with the heat of passion.

though not the envy of others
our rhythms modulated the curves
while the hills swayed in blessing.

outside the lake was still
and we spoke the language
that has no vocabulary but moods
itself into fusions known.

someday the stars will sing
the sky proclaim
how, warmly, you stole their beauty
returning as gift for compensation
this testimony of a dream.

Empty

and there will be days,
days when, walking expectantly,
you'll find the letter-boxes empty,
and you'll think of words
that meant things before

there will be days, days
when roses, carnations, gifts
that will thaw and thaw
found in your boxes, will ask
questions without words.

and yes, there will be a day
sky blue, earth brown, eye wet,
asking to be chosen, singled out
among alternatives of perception
demanding the silence of touch.

come that day i'll fill the empty
boxes lying in wait for visions
of another merger, this fusion.

D1899/Mag-Empty

DR. KIRPAL SINGH'S poems and stories have been published all over the world and he has been invited to read at Arts Festivals in the U.K., Canada, Australia and Germany. *Catwalking* and *Why Make Love Twice* are his two forthcoming publications. For keeping body and soul together, Kirpal lectures at the Nanyang Technological University, Singapore.

SIEW-YUE KILLINGLEY

Gullprint

Green glass of sea-spun spray
Cleft by the boat into white;
And stretched out far into the sky
Of glassy blue, the taut horizon.
The pure white flight of the seagull
Pulls my deckbound soul in its wake,
Teasing my sight in scales of flight
Musically up to the high blue glass
Of sky then down to mirror of sea.
Self-pouring sprint soaring up, then down,
Up-down-up-down; then a final print
Of motionless bliss on the silent
Sea of my mind as the bright seagull
Hovers still with spread white wings
Below my sight against the green glass
Of sea, white reflecting white of spray.

Autumn Leaves
(Near Barnard Castle)

Sounding amid the sad call of cattle
In the lowering sun, the metal
Leaves drip down, brightly dead,
Falling on an autumn bed,
Covering grass with autumn's sound,
Falling, falling to be ground
Like pages of a remaindered book
Whispering knowledge of life's last look,
Burning amid the lowing of cattle
And the sad fall of sun.

October Moon

The mellow shades of chestnut leaves
In day and evening's light have gone,
Their stacks of colour like autumn sheaves
Muted to shades of gathered corn.

In heavy mist the trees are shadows
Of living red and golden day;
A cold moon flatly overshadows
Their final round of summer's play

Of colours, trodden while still crowned;
The wrinkled leaves of autumn's sound
Are turned while crisply being browned,
Tuned in half tones to winter's round.

Snowfall and Thaw

Silence is suspended
in the old year ended.
White ground of snow
Wraps up earth below.
More white from grey above
Drops gently like a dove
Of prey, on deadened earth.
At last the dripping thaw,
Tree-hung and dropped to earth -

Drip-drop, dropped at birth
From twigs to raw-faced earth
In pock-marks cold and raw.

SIEW-YUE KILLINGLEY was born in December 1940 in Kuala Lumpur. She has been writing poetry since the sixties and her publications include *The Pottery Ring: A Fairy Tale for the Young and Old* and (with Percy Lovell) *Song-pageant from Christmas to Easter, with Two Settings*. She has also published four books on the Cantonese language. Siew-Yue Killingley is now a part-time university lecturer and researcher in Newcastle upon Tyne, England.

ANNE BREWSTER
Two Prayers
(for a.a.)

Kali

At her feet there is an army of horror and despair. An army of ghosts.

Her left foot treads on daisies, the other steps onto Krishna; benignly he offers his chest.

From the severed head blood streams. A hungry dog stands on its hind legs, lapping at it. The cobra raises itself up, puffed up, hunched and beckoning.

Her palms are red. Is this blood or henna? The scimitar drips blood. It is a huge half-moon sweep of dripping blood. She sticks her tongue out, hard, arching downwards. In some pictures her eyes are bright, feverish. She is in a trance like the girls dancing at thaipusam. Her face is wild, carnal, voracious. But this hunger is not niggardly - it is ardent. It is not grasping for but willing gratification.

In two old pictures I have, her body is not the voluptuous, swaying form that mirrors Krishna's cobra, but a stylised and static form: two arms raised aloft with trophies - the grisly head, the scimitar - the other two with palms uplifted, offering. Her body is laden with armour, beaten, ornate; painted red, blue, pink, orange, green and white and decked with heavy necklaces of flowers which hang next to the necklace of severed, bearded heads dripping down her legs, her ankle bracelets of gold and silver, her ringed toes and ten tiny, painted toe nails. On her head too, an elaborate helmet with splayed cobra head, with spirals and twirls, huge circular earrings and here, two rectangular blanks where the eyes should be; one cannot, meet Kali's gaze: to do so would render one incapable of returning to this world.

Kali

what need I say about my despair? You take it and make a sword, a sword for the real world with blood streaming from it.

Kali

the tyrants are beheaded. The foul, ugly faces you have separated from their foul bodies; from their grimaces blood pours like a libation. Their eyes are closed and their mouths are closed. Power and ignorance defeated. The hands of brutality and murder are your belt. They hang round your waist in their hundreds, dead.

Kali

blood flows through the world like it flows through the body. There is energy, coiled and released: the snake, the whip, the sword. The head is silent, finished. I imagine the sweat on your brow, the blood pumping through your arms.

Kali

behind you is war; the ineffectual ghosts in their tens of thousands slaughter each other. How eagerly, how punily they grapple and plunge.

In your arm, in your face is the power to slaughter war, to butcher the butchers. You look straight at me; your face is unflinching and behind you rises the palest of pale pink orbs, a space of no turmoil, a halo that sparkles blind white electricity.

This pink: you have seen it at sunset and sunrise, in the palest of flowers, the quietest of moments. The tenderest of hearts. Drink in this pink now while you can and be healed; tomorrow it will be gone and gore will be all around you again.

* * *

Durga

Durga astride the lion. It rips into a man's flesh, snarling, brow furrowed. She plunges. The man is shocked; flesh hangs off his arm. The lance pierces his breast. He sees his life pass before his eyes; he sees the woman, arms flailing - the conch, the bowl of flame, the spinning disk, the bow, the scimitar dipped in blood and the writhing cobra. He sees the woman as if he suddenly remembered. The man is shocked. His sword, half-raised, will drop. The snake coiling around his neck will finish him if the lion doesn't. Flesh hangs from his arm and his chest is ripped open - his heart pumps blood out over his torso, over the lance that has found its mark. He stares, transfixed.

Durga

lady of the red sari, the small waist; of gold and silver belts, of the golden helmet set with precious stones. Durga of the milk white arms, of bracelets and necklaces, of anklettes and the smooth, white ankle brushing the flank of the lion. Your foot presses, toes splayed, clean and sure. A foothold here between the holy cow - dead, its eyes rolled - the lion unleashed and the man staggering with his wounds. Your ten arms lifted like clockwork, like music; their prizes, their lessons aloft.

Durga

you hold the lance in two arms and plunge. You are intent on this,

I can see. The blood, pouring out around you is the colour of your sari. This makes you strong. The lion's wrath is awful.

Durga

your aim is true. Blood pours out around you. The man, the lion, the terror, the wrath. The helmet blazes and you look straight ahead, aware of all this with only two of your arms. The other eight are arrayed like the passing of time. There is blood, there is fire, there is light, there is violence. You hold that violence and thrusting, return it. Without pause, without blinking. There is fire, there is light. The body poised in action, in stillness. Between bloodshed and meditation. Around you the world erupts. You will take the lance given you. Warrior, yogi. Lady of the blood red sari and blue light.

ANNE BREWSTER teaches creative writing and literature at Curtin University in Perth, Western Australia. She has been anhologised in *The Penguin Book of Australian Women Poets, Wordhord, The Flinders Jubilee Anthology* and *Tuesday Night Live* and is the co-editor of *The Inner Courtyard, Love Poems from South Australia* (Wakefield Press 1990). She is the author of *Towards a Semiotic of Postcolonial Discourse: University Writing in Singapore and Malaysia 1949-1965* (Heinemann Asia) and has two further books in preparation, *Postcolonial Literary Studies* (Melbourne University Press) and *Postcolonial and Ethnic Minority Literatures in Singapore and Malaysia* (Singapore University Press).

MALACHI EDWIN

It Was a Wondrous Sight!

It was a wondrous sight!
A sight for national unity watchers.

He eating fried mee with chopsticks
And she, nasi lemak with fingers.

The young man skilfully
manoeuvred the chopsticks
without letting slip a strand.

The young woman expertly
coordinated her hands and mouth
getting every grain in.

The meal almost over
They make plans to tell their parents.

© Malachi Edwin, 1991.

MALACHI EDWIN is researching his Ph. D. in South East Asian literature at the University of Nottingham.

WONG PHUI NAM
Terminal Ward
(Waking to Prospect of a Dangerous Passage)
"For to be carnally minded is death..."

i

Most will die quickly here. The old,
the young. You amidst them -
breathing faintly, like dropped
foetuses laid out on stained sheets.
You lie here, stripped,
severed from your caul, drugged
that you might sink into your fears
and pain and, in that warm mud,
discard your wet weight of body
to subsist as vestige, as primal ash
and carmine mouth, pulling
the air in lightly in your sleep.
Inside your skin you settle upon
stillness, a stillness which breathes
as mudfish in the hardening earth
waiting out the sun in a dry season.
Others have begun to stir,
feel for limbs yet to be formed,
eating out the old life. They stretch
uneasily at scent of the flesh
failing. There is, for these,
another awakening, another birth,
rupture into dreams that shake loose
from the vitals as they come untied.
A low fire consumes the flesh
till it falls off the bone as mush

to line the loose folds
that hang out from bellies, thighs and chests.

ii

In the filtered dimness of this ward
I sense a queer change hatch
within the sheets. Skins
dry to rough bark, a dead moth-brown.
Eyes, ears dissolve into featureless soft
balls of earth, of vacated faces.
But there is a kind of life, active
in darkness, a disturbance
which unfolds out of stillness -
a stillness concealed, in wait.
They rest here, earth mounds, holding
that life within, dangerous
and enormous, motionless as eggs thrust
up from the alluvium in dried out pits.
They lie encrusted in mud,
with broken twigs and leaves
glued tight together by streaks
of a hardened, profuse, white secretion.
It is a stillness of dying
or that which comes of dying.
Active in darkness... Waiting out the time...

iii

I find you here amidst them...
sinking fast into that loamy blankness
that death first begins to set loose

in the mind. A blackening foetus,
you become more frightful by the hour,
finding another life within,
having waited out your time.
Your mind-out body will let go,
break open to let you forth,
spewing mucus of your dead selves
with tainted waters - of lusts,
of passions, mirage of such parts
of you that you found too fearful
to let go. You will now rise,
transformed, leaving much
that you would love and hold,
oozing now from among
dead bones, dead ligaments, soft
dead webs of flesh - tissue that has
enmeshed you, bound you for so long
to a sick, an unhinged mortality.

iv

I shall not grieve your absence
so much as I shall fear
for your risen state.
I have but sparse, thin words,
threadbare against the touch of ice
and wind, words bereft
of power as charm against
prospect of your travail,
and of your dangerous passage over black gulfs.

Out of mud-encrusted foetuses
only unfinished creatures form,

who drift their way back into a dream
of utter darkness, crying for cold,
crying to be clothed again
in flesh, in body's deformities,
even to be tormented again
with love that sorrows only for itself,
breeding, in the heart, virulent wars
in lust, in fury
against all other flesh,
re-awakened by the smell of blood.

In such a void and desolation
their perverse, savage imaginings
will turn in upon themselves
to ignite sulphurous lakes of fire,
open ravines of grinding ice,
and engender the bodies to know
skin being peeled in flames,
the living bone repeatedly
being melted down as fuel,
or the breath being crushed in
with rib-cage that sticks
through skin, with pierced lungs,
becoming whole to be crushed again,
then compacted, locked into blue
marble sheets of unforgiving ice.

Once out into the void,
they grow large into a life
fed on pain and on terror,
despair that such imaginings will not die.

© Wong Phui Nam, 1993.

JOHN McRAE
Introduction
to
IN THE NAME OF LOVE

What Ramli has done in these three plays is remarkable on several counts. Not only does he reveal a glorious capacity to write touchingly and wittily - which we had no right to expect from South East Asia's greatest dancer and master of physical theatrical expression - but he handles vast themes of love and loss, tradition and art, time and talent in ways that are accessible, original, and entirely true the cultural roots of present-day Malaysia.

Any actress would kill to play these roles: the Western reader might like to imagine an impossible amalgam of Naggie Smith, Dawn French and Alan Bennett in order to capture the spirit, the theatrical vitality and the subversive humour of the plays.

Originally written in Bahasa and performed by Sabera Shaik, the plays met with an ambivalent reaction. When the English version was first performed (by Ramli himself) at Universiti Pertanian Malaysia, the audience's positive response was immediate; the laughter of recognition, involvement with character and emotions, identification with the cultural and emotional issues, and enjoyment of a marvellously idiosyncratic way of rendering the local dialect into the universal language of self-justification.

This is daring theatre taking risks and living dangerously, reviving a spirit that at the same time subverts and affirms the cultural concerns it displays, questioning and challenging, but never losing sight of that essential theatrical quality: entertainment. The plays mark a major contribution to South East Asian theatre, and one which will delight audiences anywhere.

© John McRae, 1993.

RAMLI IBRAHIM
Excerpt from
'Mak Su'

(Mak Su lights another cigarette and at the same time fans herself. She reminisces...)

It's difficult. Difficult Li. Makyong is not easy.

Can't learn Makyong quickly. You can't dance it quickly either. Not only you must know the song, there is also the dance which you must master. Then there is the comedy. If not, Makyong is not complete. No *angin*.

I guess that's the fate of Makyong. If you don't perform - there is no money. And when you perform it, you must be in the right mood. The right *angin*.

When I perform the Makyong, I must have the *angin*. I don't perform just for the money. Oh no!

When we don't have the *angin*, we can't look the audience in the eye. We'd be embarrassed!

We should be above the audience! Then only no room for *malu*[37.] No time to be awkward on stage Li! Means you're not ready!

In my heydays, when I was young, I had that power.

Whenever the audience challenged me - I could rise to the challenge. I could give them double what they asked for!

I had such extraordinary power. I exude inner strength in all my gestures.

---

37 shyness

I could be a mother, when the part requires it
Or convincing enough as a man
When I am child, I feel and behave like one
When sad, I'd grieve
But when angry, watch out - I can be frighteningly so...

You can say I alone could control the mood in that theatre!
(Light slowly dims)

No it's different. I've aged. My memory poor. I've forgotten most of my lines. Forgotten! Of course!

Well! If you don't do things often enough, if you only perform once or twice a year - naturally you start to be out of practice. You get rusty. You forget your songs. You would too! Any artist needs to perform always Li!

Nowadays you can't even perform the real Makyong. Or everything has to be done quickly. People get bored easily. Of course, they'd get bored! Nowadays, nobody knows the story. Not familiar with the melodies. Not like the old days. Nowadays everybody prefers television.

In Kelantan, it's worst. There, it's a different problem!

Like the old saying. Not only you've fallen - but the ladder also crash on you... That's the fate of Makyong now. Don't know. When I die, I guess Makyong will die with me...

Modern Makyong? With modern stories?

Hai, Makyong's about our past, Li! Stories of our Rajas. Their olden courts. *Raja Gondang. Dewa Muda. Anak Raja Tangkai Hati.* Oh, lots more. Can't tell off hand. There're lots more I've forgotten.

From the Makyong story, from the songs, we can have some idea about the ways of our ancient past. Our ancient courts.

For instance, when I sing, I would describe how the Raja would put on his regalia - from his *baju* [38], his trousers, the long cummerbund around his waist, his sash, his traditional headgear - all this I'd recite in the song called *Menghadap Rebab* [39].

Why do I recite these things?

Eh, Makyong is about that time Li!
It is about our ancestors, our Rajas, the court days, ancient times! Makyong times!

(Mak Su recites part of the Menghadap Rebab, demonstrating using solely her selendang, the various gestures of preparation of a Raja that is the essence of this ritualised beginning part of a Makyong performance.)

As the trousers fold up the legs
And the shirt covers the torso
The selendang of a special kind
The keris adorns the side
The cummerbund, the waist around
Three times meeting at the seam
The shoulder, a cloth hangs on
Headress is placed, rightly, above the forehead...

Makyong is out heritage Li!

(Mak Su sighs. She is almost exhausted. Suddenly there is a clap of thunder and lightning. The hot afternoon has brought a brief thunderstorm.)

Fine and hot a minute ago! Now it's raining. Strange weather... Luckily, Abang helped bring in the *sotong*.

It's true. Hasn't rained here for sometime now. Even when it rains, it's just few drops. Nothing serious. I heard that it rains

---

38 jacket
39 to face the Rebab - Malay spiked fiddle

often in Kuala Lumpur, Li. Well, - God's gift! Rain - it always reminds me of the teardrops of Makyong.

RAMLI IBRAHIM is one of the artistic leaders of his generation throughout the ASEAN countries.

Engineer, dancer in three of the world's great disciplines, choreographer, Artistic Director of the dynamic dance-theatre company SUTRA, and of its Annual Festival, which presents the cutting edge of the best of Malaysian creative arts - old and new - Ibrahim has become a hot spokesman for his era on matters artistic.

His university and dance studies took place in Australia; in Perth, in Melbourne (he was a graduate in classical ballet with The Australian Ballet School) and Sydney (a member of the famous Martha Graham-based Sydney Dance Company). For Indian Classical Dance, he went to Madras (Bharata Natyam) and Orissa (Odissi), to study with their leading gurus.

The leading Malaysian newspapers have readily provided him with a platform for raising important issues of Malaysian culture. He is a cogent and articulate writer. He has been forthright in his espousal of Hindu arts, Western arts, and avant garde Malaysian aspirations. A Muslim, he has not been brow-beaten into silence about the future of Malaysian arts by Muslim fundamentalist forces. He is placing the contemporary arts of Malaysia in an international context.

These three plays were written as a vehicle for one of Malaysia's foremost actresses, Sabera Shaik, for performance in one of his vital Festivals, and they delve into the psychic worlds of three aspects of women's love in modern Malaysian society. The regional also becomes the universal and "ballet mummies", "lonely widows" and "ageing artists" everywhere will respond to the sensitivities and sympathy of Ibrahim's view of them.

In the Name of Love represents a new and vital voice in modern Malaysian theatre and is forthcoming in **Winter 1993** with **Skoob PACIFICA**, London.

IN THE NAME OF LOVE
a play in three flushes
Ramli Ibrahim

This range of language and richness of character are the perfect representation of the racial, cultural and historical mix that is present-day Malaysia. Tension is never far below the surface in these plays. There is a range of binaries and dichotomies pulling against one another: present and past, traditional and contemporary, provincial and city, violence and tolerance, insider and outsider.

Prof. John McRae
Introduction to
In the Name of Love

Forthcoming
Winter 1994
Paperback
U.K. Price GBP 6.99

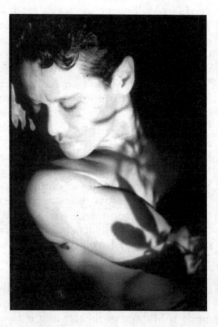

Skoob Books Publishing Ltd, 11A-17 Sicilian Avenue, off Southampton Row and Bloomsbury Square, London WC1A 2QH. Fax: 071 404 8398

PART TWO

Malaysian/Singaporean
Prose in English

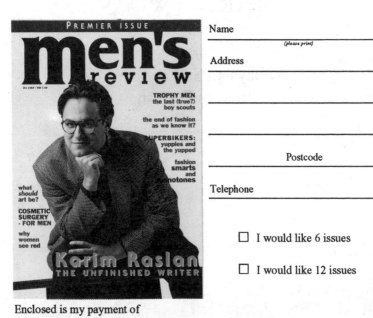

K.S. MANIAM
The Mutes In The Sun *and* Flowers In The Sky:
A Relative View

"...what is man then hating? But the answer admits no doubt; the *decline of his type*. He hates then from out of the profoundest instinct of his species: there is horror, foresight, profundity, far-seeing vision in this hatred - it is the profoundest hatred there is. It is for its sake that art is *profound*..." (Nietzsche, *Twilight of the Idols* and *The Anti-Christ*, Penguin rep. 1975, trans. R.J. Hollingdale, p. 79)

Lee Kok Liang's *The Mutes in the Sun* (first published in 1964, rep. Heinemann, 1974) and *Flowers in the Sky* (Heinemann, 1981) reflect Nietzsche's complex attitude towards creative motivation. Lee Kok Liang deals, basically, with "the decline of his type" in the former, a novella of 18 chapters, and in the latter, a compact, slim novel. The interval of some seventeen years between the two works indicates a significant development in Kok Liang as a Malaysian novelist writing in the English language. To be Malaysian and to write in English can be frustratingly opposing activities. Kok Liang, however, links the two in an imaginative manner. The novella/ novel, until Kok Liang appeared on the Malaysian literary scene, did not attempt to go beneath the tensions of everyday living, banal social encounters, historical impact and intercultural reactions in order to mine a deeper core of experience. In other words, something extraordinary was not made to emerge from the mundane, the ordinary.

The trickle of postwar prose works, between 1945 and 1958, depended on the disruption of daily routines for their impact and thrust. And as the immediacy and interest in the Japanese occupation of the country (1942-1945) receded, these autobiographical/biographical and semifictional works too attracted less and less attention. The works that succeeded them, in the early 60s, had more order or structure, were inventive rather than imaginative, and explored the existing cultural backgrounds, from a need to see richness instead of portraying them from the inside. Kok Liang brought a much needed change to the surface structure of the somewhat descriptive,voyeuristically cultural expose. *The Mutes in the Sun* and *Flowers in the Sky*, hereafter referred to their abbreviated titles *MS* and *FS*, respectively, testifies to an integrated approach towards the materials of fiction. The two are inter-related and an understanding of *MS* leads to a fuller experience of *FS*.

If in *Ms* Kok Liang experiments with a novelist's ability to reach into his materials and fashion a compellingly revealing technique, in *FS* he uses that very skill to fathom hitherto barely approached shades of Malaysian realities. In the former the structure gives the novella a closed-in framework of meaning; in the latter the implications reach beyond the novelistic edifice.

The contents of the story and technique of unfolding it in *MS* suggest a reaching into the stillness of an understanding after a frenzied search for comprehension. The protagonist in *MS*, named once as 'Met', exhibits strange and divergent behaviour. The reader is aware that the protagonist is looking for a moment of revelation that will unlock his personality and also provide the code for understanding life. This emerges only after one has gone through the bewildering and irrational experiences of the protagonist.

The story itself is fairly straightforward. The protagonist is hostile towards his father's plans for him - the reasons are not explicitly presented - but suppresses his reactions most of the time. It is only when the father disrupts the protagonist's friendship with his friend Kee Huat that he openly subverts his father's intentions. The events become increasingly violent and climax in the protagonist killing his father's second wife, Gaik Lang, who is in fact Kee Huat's girl friend. Then after his trial and stay in the Home for Juvenile Delinquents, he renounces his own family and takes to the streets. On one of his excursions into the city entertainment spot he comes upon Kee Huat. The long search for his friend ends. The two, moved by some long submerged motivation, set fire to the protagonist's father's sawmill and stride "up the street like two buccaneers adventuring into the unknown." (*MS*, p. 128).

It is the structure of the novella that yields the writer's objective and the message of the work. Kok Liang's organization of the events, the style, character, portrayal and the use of certain literary motifs give the novella an intensity that become transformed as social comment and psychological insight in *MS*.

The events in this novella fall into two categories. The first consists of episodes and happenings that the protagonist is an unwilling witness to or participator in; the second is made up of those over which he wields some control. Not surprisingly, therefore, the change of pace in the novella occurs when he ceases to be a victim of circumstances and instead becomes responsible for some of them. This happens in the third chapter and Kok Liang subtly destroys the chronological order of events so as to emphasize the psychological thrust of the work. From then on the novella takes on the incisiveness of a scalpel and cuts into the past, personal blindness and social diseases. Such a sentence as, "The road was long and narrow and was pock-marked with two lamps, one at each end" (*MS*, pp. 42/3) takes on added meaning in retrospect.

This significant multiplicity of meaning emerges because, with the destruction of the line between past and present, Kok Liang dramatises thought and emotion even while the experience is only a recollection. Through this technique Kok Liang invests *MS* with a literary lustre so long absent from Malaysian fiction in English. The dramatisation of past experiences that motivate and influence present behaviour is also largely responsible for giving the novella its organic and at the same time a closed-in texture of meaning.

Kok Liang prepares his reader for this approach to the materials and considerations of the novella in the first six paragraphs of the work. The vision presented in these two pages gradually narrows from the extensiveness of a landscape reaching to the horizon down to "the flickering of...children's shadows" (*MS*, p. 44) in a cubicle. The need for such a focus is also justified by the quality of the world-view held by the inhabitants of the dehumanized and dehumanizing, mainly, social environment. Kok Liang works in this implication in the description of the landscape and social mores:

All through the week the vast dark cloud with silvery scalloped edges sat over the city by the sea, slowly showering and depositing particles of heat. The tar on the road burnt the soles of the feet. Sweat lacquered the features of the inhabitants.

The leaves on the trees grew waxy and yellowish and dropped in large indolent spirals. In the evenings when the sun filtered in beneath the edge of the cloud as through the bottom of a closed door, the men drew out their stools and sat in the open, fanning their armpits, like doctors dabbing swabs on an open wound. Faces blank, eyes drooping, they breathed in shallow gasps, waiting for the hot season to end. (*MS*, p. 42).

It is clear that Kok Liang is exploring a sick social and individual landscape. By closely aligning himself with the perceptions of the protagonist, when he appears, Kok Liang, as author, tacitly gives support to his character's attitudes and as yet undiscovered sense of values. In fact, Kok Liang already is beginning to consider, in Nietzsche's phrase, "the decline of his type."

To make this consideration clear and challenging, Kok Liang has chosen a range of characters that immediately draw attention to themselves. Through the protagonist's unpredictable, abnormal behaviour Kok Liang questions the accepted code of ethics. The gap between the protagonist's behaviour and that of his father and other adults further underscores the moralistic implications of the work. Kee Huat and Gaik Lang, the other two juvenile characters (the writer's choice of youths must comment on the demoralizing, corrupt world of the grown-ups), in the conflict-ridden story, are also compelled to deviate from their own personalities and ambitions.

What emerges, by the end of the novella, is that Kok Liang has referred the reader to the corrupt, brutal centre of society. He does this by creating circumstances that force the protagonist, Kee Huat and Gaik Lang to bypass the development of their particular personalities. These characters are seduced, the gentlest form of adult pressure, or simply coerced into satisfying perverted desires. The protagonist's dislike of Gaik Lang is an instinctive disgust of anything that smacks of love. When he kills her it is to wipe out that tarnished image of adult love. The writer hints, and forcefully, that the protagonist harbours resentment towards his father because he, in some manner, abused his mother.

Kok Liang exposes a complex, subconscious world of the individual. He uses a consistently developed technique to bring to the surface the struggles a young man undergoes in order to discover himself and also a set of values that will restore health to life. The bizarre (the protagonist infuriating the gibbons at his father's saw-mill), the down-to-earth (Kee Huat, much older now, sexually assaults beggar women), the repulsive (protagonist cohabits with a crippled woman of indeterminate age in a decrepit house) all fit into the picture of a society denied its healthy existence.

There is little communication between people: father and son, friend and friend, lover and lover. This point is made clear through the letters of Kee Huat and Gaik Lang write to each other and the diary that Gaik Lang records in broken English, in place of a person to person encounter. All these, the letters, the diary, the cardboard cubicles, the prostitute's steaming room, the beggars huddled into their scanty coverlets under the cold night sky, and finally, the large, dilapidated house that the protagonist occupies together with the ageless beggar woman portray a terrifying picture of life without direction, without human warmth, gaps in understanding, social decay, and most of all, lack of coherence.

MS, therefore, is an indictment on society, written from deep within the perceptions of the vagrant, victimised healthy young who are condemned into serving the corrupt morals of the society in which they live. It is not life that they lead but a muddling through a form of existence less than human. That is why the images of people shut in rooms, closed cars, large rotting houses proliferate and gather in anger both in the reader and in the protagonist and lead to an explosion of protest. Man has not been allowed to move towards the freedom that permits the discovery of the dignity of his species. That is why, too, that *MS* can be said to be created out of the profoundest hatred there is, so that there can be that profound beauty, art.

In this short work of Kok Liang's one discerns a built-in system of responses that does not extend beyond the literary structure. At most, it is cathartic, both for the protagonist, who at the close of the novella burns down the saw-mill of his father - a symbol surely of all that is depraved and confining - and through this action, for the reader, *MS* is a dramatised study of abuse, hatred, brutality, callousness and the lack of dignity in man, framed by an almost pure literary structure.

Flowers in the Sky (*FS*), published seventeen years later, retains the fine concern for structure and consciousness for style. But in *FS*, Kok Liang has outgrown a merely literary impression of the work. He functions more as a Malaysian novelist, meaning that he confronts issues that affect the average Malaysian, but at the same time devotes himself to developing a novelistic edifice and texture that possess coherence, integration, and a more lucidly worked out inter-connecting system of literary motifs.

The structure of *FS* opens up several experience, instead of, as observed in *MS*, closing in on one. In *FS*, too, Kok Liang consciously revokes time by, ironically, insisting on chronological demarcation. The entire novel's events occur within a period of six days, each of which is further marked off by an apparently important subdivision in terms of hours. Again Kok Liang obliterates awareness to the passage of time by calling attention to it. The function of such a device is, in keeping with the theme of the novel, to reveal other forms of progress: experiential, reflective or philosophical, and spiritual. The constant intrusion of temporal consciousness is meant to jolt the reader into philosophical and spiritual forms of consciousness. This is one way of affirming that materialistic progress is only the outer shell of our experience of daily life.

In *FS*, Kok Liang attempts to dramatise, ironically, the conflict between materialist and spiritual values. Though he does not successfully resolve this two-way stretch in a man's life, he nevertheless portrays man's attempts to break down the limits imposed on him by society, accepted philosophical attitudes, individual ideas of self-image and spiritual rigidity. From the epigraphs down to the choice of the two principal characters, Mr. K. and Venerable Hung, a doctor and a monk, respectively, there is evidence that Kok Liang sees Malaysian life as bifurcated, fragmented, and sometimes even atomised.

The novel, therefore, tries to provide a coherent picture, artistically structured, of Malaysian society. One of the responses that the reader can make to this work, consequently, is to evolve for himself a fuller, more organic view of struggle and existence in a multi-racial society, in which parochial, communal thinking and feeling may blind one to the more valuable, integrated approach to culture. The novel resonates on a still point of calm yet with vibrant involvement in the daily demands of living in a frustratingly hot country, riddled again by divisive attitudes. This is made clear not so much in the epigraphs as in the opening paragraph of the work:

His eyes watered with softened intensity, between unfocused gaze vagueness gathered an enlarged emptiness, and finally an immobility, the like of which he had sought in vain, washed and caressed every pore and entered and remained in his flesh. (*FS*, p. 1)

This description does not only refer to the effects of anaesthetics on a patient about to lose consciousness but also to that calm point mentioned above, to the synthesis, through a deliberately directed vision, between the materialistic and the spiritual, and the immediate and the eternal. The attempt to understand contrast in life will, it is implied, lead to a transcendence over petty professionalism, communal loyalties, materialistic greed and social conformity.

The objectivity of the dramatic analysis in *MS* is now converted, in *FS*, to an acknowledgement of the real, the socially accepted and the need for a spiritual set of values however abstract. Where in *MS* the objectivity remains as detached incisiveness, in *FS* it is given individual and social backgrounds. Mr. K's and Venerable Hung's thoughts, feelings and desires are recorded in detail down to the last swish of lust (Mr. K had always hankered for large breasts in women).

The movement of the novel, appropriately enough, begins from opposing directions: a monk needs surgical repair, a doctor desires spiritual ballast. The achievements of the doctor reach a materialistic apogee and he inclines now towards some form of philosophical or religious development. The monk's spiritual progress now lands him in the terrain of wealth and personal comfort. With the meeting of the two then, the novelist introduces that hourglass of coincidence necessary, may be even inevitable, for the initiation into new forms of understanding. And because the shape and texture of that awareness is yet inaccessible, the novelist ends on a note of ironic reflection: "And then Mr. K. smiled. He saw that the monk, whom he had discharged that morning, was getting into a Mercedes, helped by a chauffeur. The monk looked tiny beside the car." (*FS*, p. 157) The car's number plate carrying the figures 666 also connotes, in Chinese, triple joy, which for the monk or Mr. K., is not available.

Here in *FS*, then, "the decline of his type" is examined within a socially relevant Malaysian context. While the two-fold direction the novel develops comments on the spiritual progress of man and his development as a member of a complex, multi-racial society, it at the same time maintains that gap between reality and the extensions that men make of it within them-selves. An awareness of this tendency in the writing explains why some characters are not fully entered into, why the sensual aspect of man receives repeated treatment, and why the novel seems to veer from following Venerable Hung's and Mr. K's preoccupations and into the farcical religious incident, the discovery of the Ganesh statue washed up to Mr. K's house facing the sea The diversion is deliberately sketched in to provide a contrast in the quality of different men's approach to fame, success and spiritual satisfaction. In the structure of the novel there has to be a departure from the tenacious following up of a particular development. For is that not the theme of Kok Liang's novel? There are many detours in man's pursuit of the ideal life, many layers of responses to reality and one cannot be sacrificed for another, or allowed to lapse for the sake of another.

Kok Liang has succeeded in shaping a novel, distantly different from his earlier work, *MS*, to elucidate the idea that it is possible to enlarge the dimensions of man's dignity; that everything else, be it political, social, communal, has to give way to the healthy development of an integrated, inclusive mode of perception. Some of the details (Swami Gomez, it is pointed out, cannot be a valid name because Gomez, having a Eurasian ring about it, cannot be a swami, only a padre!) may not have been accurately assimilated but the intention is to show that a breaking down of one's reserves is more important than an in-sistence on formal, exclusive correctness.

He has also harnessed to a style that is at most times skilfully expressive (with some lapses here and there) another element which reflects and synthesizes the several imaginations behind the many languages spoken and written in this country.

Venerable Hung's letter to his Master in China has the formality of carefully practised Chinese calligraphy; the file on Mr. K's patient, Ah Looi, possesses just that number of grammatical errors that reflect present day developments in English in this country. Mrs. K, Inspector Gopal, Inspector Hashim, to mention only a few, speak in a language the nuances of which are affected by their mother tongues, namely, Tamil and Malay.

The resemblances between *The Mutes in the Sun* and *Flowers in the Sky* have been pointed out. But what is more important and significant is the development that is discernible in *Flowers in the Sky*. While the former is iconoclastically literary, the latter is literary, artistically seminal and, in the development of the Malaysian novel in English, a quietly but daringly experimental work. *The Mutes in the Sun* celebrates the energy of man; *Flowers in the Sky* finds ritual passage for the dignity of man in that energy.

© K.S. Maniam, 1993.

K.S. Maniam is associate professor in English at the University of Malaya. He graduated from the University of Malaya in 1973 in English, and received an M.A. in 1979.

His short stories were published in *Commentary, Southeast Asian Review of English, Solidarity* and anthologised in *Malaysian Short Stories* (HEINEMANN ASIA, 1981), *Encounters: Selected Indian and Australian Short Stories* (POINTER PUB., JAIPUR, 1988) and *Rim of Fire: Stories from the Pacific Rim* (VINTAGE, NEW YORK, 1992). His collection *Plot, The Aborting, Parablames and Other Stories* came out in 1989. His play *The Cord*, published in 1983, was staged in Kuala Lumpur in 1984 and Singapore 1986. *The Sandpit: Womensis* was staged in Singapore in 1990 and in Kuala Lumpur 1991. His other two books *The Third Child* and *A Hundred Years After and Other Stories* would be published by TIMES INTN., Singapore at the end of 1993. His first novel *The Return, a Bildungsroman* has been republished by **Skoob PACIFICA, London** in 1993. His new novel, *In A Far Country* has been published recently by **Skoob PACIFICA, London.**

LEE KOK LIANG
Five Fingers
A short story from the collection
The Mutes in the Sun

When I went into the room, he was sitting in his favourite chair, staring at the rows of books lined up in the shelves. He did not turn his head. He was always like that. But I knew he knew I was here.

I walked up, and drawing up a stool, sat opposite him, with the Chinese chessboard between us. We played quietly.

After a while, I said, 'Old Fellow, your mind is keen today. Perhaps that's why you make such a lot of money. You are not a fool like I am. Feeding four children is no fun, even if I have youth on my side. You are a wise chap, Old Fellow. That's why you don't marry. Why don't you marry, Old Fellow.'

As I spoke, he stopped looking at the chessboard. He sat up taut. He looked for a long time at me in silence, hardly breathing at all. With a quick motion he stood up; I thought he was going to strike me. But, instead, he gripped hard at my shirt. Without paying any attention to my protests he dragged me from my seat and pulled me after him with surprising vigour. We half ran through a narrow corridor, and upon coming to a small doorway at the far end, he turned to me.

'Come, don't be surprised, I have something I would like to show you.'

He went in and knelt down, while he fitted a key to a dusty chest in the far corner. He took out a box and handed it to me.

'Look into it, my child. Look.'

It was a beautiful lacquered box, about the size of a small volume, richly embossed with dragons, dark red in colour, with silver strips running along its borders. A bird, finely carved, having small dots of jade where the eyes should have been, perched, wings outstretched, on the top of its cover. I grasped at one of the wings and tilted the cover. I looked inside.

There, lying on the velvet bottom, was a hand. A female hand, embalmed. It was cut off above the wrist where the flesh appeared to be mutilated and dark brown.

'Look, my child, at the fingers. They once belonged to a girl hardly younger than you. The girl lived in a city a hundred and twenty miles from here. She studied at a private school. One day a boy came to the class. The boy was like you. Only younger. He was from a poor family. He loved her. He knew that she loved him too. He felt it. But they did not speak. No, good boys and girls never spoke to each other in those days. So they loved in silence.

'Then one day he found out that they had the same surname, just by chance, when the teacher called out their full names at the annual examination. No, now he could never marry her. Not even hope to. He should not continue to love her. He could not sin. He was not born to sin. But still his heart was hers.

'War started. The city was threatened and all the citizens had to evacuate. Their families moved to a village and happened to stay at the same old house. Their families did not know each other but because of their same surname, they shared the clan house together in time of stress. So they occupied two adjoining rooms, the only ones that did not leak, on the east side. There were no beds, no benches, no mattresses. All had to sleep on the floor. The boy's family took the first room. The second was taken by the girl's family.

'One night, the boy who had been sleeping on the hard floor next to the wall, discovered that some of the bricks at the foot of the wall were loose. He had no pillow. So he cautiously took them out, praying at the same time he might not disturb the spirits of this ancient building, and arranged the bricks so that he would be able to rest his head on them comfortably. The hole made in the wall was about a palm's width. He was about to sleep when he heard a rustling noise among the loose sand in the hole.

'Maybe it was only a rat, he though. He turned over his side and plunged his hand into the hole. He suddenly grasped at a thing. Soft and warm. Five of them. They were all wriggling in his palm. They struggled to escape. Suddenly he knew. He knew and he trembled. The wriggling had stopped; and the imprisoned five, with twitching movements, lay his palm. He slowly pulled the thing out. The wriggling started.

'But when he placed his face against the thing, the wriggling paused, and, somewhat nervously, the thing lay quivering on his

197

face; the five explored. At first, with much hesitation but soon they gained confidence and with feather-duster strokes they played compassionately on his face. They ran over his eyes with cool steps. His eyes full of tears rubbed against them. Like a sponge they sucked up the wetness and bathed his whole face. He felt comfortable and happy. But they would not keep still. The mouth, the ear, the nose. To each one they talked. Sometimes gently, sometimes mischievously, giving hope and sympathy, but always with love.

'Night after night they came. At the approach of dawn they rushed back into cover. He got only a fleeting glimpse of whiteness and shapeliness. He dared not stop them or entrap them, for he knew that they were shy. Any bold move would have frightened them.

'One day the news came that the city had fallen, and the soldiers were fast approaching the village. That night while the boy lay waiting, they crept out of the hole with slow mournful steps. They stood still, glowing at the tips, as the moonlight shone on them. They combed his hair, the five of them, with anxious and reluctant strokes. All of a sudden they pulled hard at his hair. They leapt full upon his cheeks and wrenched the flesh like the teeth of a trap. They went back to his hair. They returned to his face. The movements grew feverish. The boy sensed that all was not well.

'He lay still and listened to what they had to tell him. The message was simple. The soldiers were coming. They must leave him. The soldiers were coming. All this while the movements grew convulsive. He could stand it no more. He put them between his teeth. He bit. The hysterical movements stopped. The five lay quiet and dazed by his violence. He placed his lips against the marks made by the teeth. One by one, his mouth pleaded with them, entreated them to stay longer, even for a night. His mouth pressed reasons and arguments on them.

'The next morning, the boy's mother told him that the family next door would stay for a few days longer than was at first intended. The girl suddenly refused to follow her family. For no reason, she regarded that day as an evil day and would not go. As it was mainly for her safety that the family had evacuated, they had to linger on. Dragging her away would not be possible, as silence and stealth were needed to slip through the sentries. When he heard it, he felt a great happiness.

'Towards evening, as he sat on the floor, he heard the sound of heavy, tramping feet. The soldiers. They knocked down the massive front door. He heard screams, pleading, helpless screams, from the next room. He rushed out; but a soldier smashed him down with the butt of the rifle. When he recovered they had all gone.

'The old house was silent: He went from hall to hall, room to room. There was no one. His mother and father, where were they? And she? He walked painfully across the idol hall to the backyard. And found her. Lifeless. Spattered with blood. It was all his fault. All his. He had to go away. But no. In a daze he went to the kitchen and took from the table a butcher's knife. He returned to her. He held the knife high up. It came down and he laughed.'

LEE KOK LIANG
Ronggeng-Ronggeng
A Short Story from
Death is a Ceremony
and Other Short Stories

KA-TUM-BONG: KA-TUM-BONG: KA-TUM-BONG

Mat beat the small tambourine on his lap.

It was a hot night and when the crowd stirred, puffs of dry dust rose above the heads, gleaming like golden husks of paddy, caught in the slanting shafts of the electric lamps that were strung over the open stage. Seated along the edge on the high cane chairs were the three dancing girls, and below them, at the corner, were the musicians: Mat with his drums and Tok Payah with his fiddle.

The ronggeng was held nightly, except for Fridays, in New World Park, an amusement ground, where one had to pay 10 cents to get in, and where if one was wearing slippers, the sand from the bare earth would get in between one's toes. The stage was in the middle of the park, between the Bangsawan and a Hokkien opera; close by was an open air cinema whose sounds of gunshots from the Westerns would drown the music. All sorts of people came to the park to have fun. It was a place to stroll around and to watch the girls dressed up smartly. And then there were the stalls which sold round ice balls, sticks of pickled mangoes, waterchestnuts, guavas and apples sliced into quar-ters, all heaped neatly on blocks of ice.

Mat looked over the stage at the crowd standing below.

There were the same sort of people. Those Chinese youths, hair smoothed and oiled over, in white starched shirts and trousers, banded together at the back. On the left, a few Indians in shorts. Of course, the familiar Ahmads and Hassans, some with *songkoks*, standing below in the front row, smiling, making coarse jokes and eager for a dance.

Mat shifted the betel cud from one side of the mouth to the other sides and tasted the tang of the lime. Tok Payah, the fiddler, started playing at a fast tempo, sending out thin notes, to indicate the beginning of a new dance. How many times had he warned Tok Payah not to go so fast until towards the very end of the dance. But that man easily forgot and the hotter the night, the faster he would play and then all the girls complain-ed. He beat his tambourine. Some in the crowd made their way to the makeshift box-office to purchase tickets for the dance.

KA-TUM-BONG: KA-TUM-BONG: KA-TUM-BONG

Che Siti, Che Salemah, Che Haminah flopped on the cane chairs, pulled out their handkerchiefs and wiped the sweat off the side of their cheeks, looking at Tok Payah angrily. The fiddler smiled and stopped his fiddling and waited for the first three customers to come up with the tickets.

The girls rose from their cane chairs as the three young Malays stood before them shyly handing out their tickets. Taking them, the girls passed them over to Mat.

Abass, Harun, and Madzir stood breathless and self-conscious after having had to push through the crowds below. Wild taunts and wisecracks came from their friends.

'Go to it Abass.'

'You look like a scrawny cock with a tiny thing motionless between your legs.'

'Madzir, your *songkok* should cover your mouth. It smells.'

'Harun don't put your fingers in your pocket. What are you pinching inside there?'

The crowd roared.

The dancers stood opposite their partners. Che Siti looked at Tok Payah and slightly bent her right leg to relieve the ache in her knee. Mat banged on his tambourine. The dance started. The men, arms akimbo, twisted their shoulders, swaying with the music and came dangerously close to the girls. The girls, as if startled, fluttered backwards, tapping their toes and heels on the wooden boards. The men began to weave round their partners, leaning as close to them without touching, swinging back, darting in and swinging out again.

The fiddler quickened the tempo. Mat followed with reluctance. The dancers went into a rapid motion like palm trees when a strong wind brushed their tops.

Che Siti tapped on her high heels, a bit too softly, Mat thought. She was the most serious girl of the lot and saved most of her earnings. She had the idea that if she tapped lightly her shoes would last twice as long. As though reading his thoughts Che Siti turned round and flashed a quick smile.

Dear Mat, such a good-hearted man. He talked a lot of how he was going to save up to go to Mecca and kiss the Hajr-e Aswad even if it took fifteen years. And how good he could be with the drum, the fingers dancing with the heel of the palm. She must loosen the right shoe strap when the dance was over. How her foot ached. This night was hot. Hardly any rain for two weeks now. Good for ronggeng, but not good for the paddy farmers. From a distance, she heard the cymbals of a Chinese opera faintly drifting towards the stage with a strange pitch; the stage was about 200 feet away and the costumes of the performers sparkled with lights from the sequins sewn into the cloth; peculiar nasal sounds and screams came over. She would never get used to them, even if she lived a thousand years.

What was it that Abass was singing to his partner?

Love is like gold
Tomorrow brings the sun
Tonight brings the fun
Love is like gold.

She loved gold - a beautiful golden anklet on her foot would bring out the texture of her skin. And how the other girls would be so jealous. And the men would look at her foot instead of her breasts. Out of the tail of her eye, she saw Madzir lunging towards her, but with a sudden twist of her waist, she slipped by adroitly, smiling a little, for among all, she liked Madzir the best. He was self-conscious and that reminded her of her younger brother, but he was spending so much money dancing with her so many nights.

She nodded to Che Aminah who smiled and she took up the reply as the girls had considered her having a quicker mind and being so full of cheek as well.

Poor Man always in a hurry
Cooks dried fish and curry
Makes many mistakes
Until he has to jump into a lake.

Madzir danced nearer and stamped hard on the floor. The music quickened and he whirled. She looked at him - he was breathing hard and the mole of his left cheek trembled like a dot of sweat. Only 20 she thought and spending so much money by dancing with her. How could he save and bring up a family? Probably working, by the darkness of his skin and the roughness of his figure, as a street sweeper, and yet so faithful. Never danced with any of the other girls. So shy and not daring to talk to her during the dance as his friends below shouted and made rude suggestions. And then the tempo slowed down and she curtseyed and walked back to her chair. Oh how hot it was. She pulled out her handkerchief and gently wiped both sides of her face, rubbing away some powder. Ah, the strap. Down she bent and loosened it. There. And how fine she felt now.

'Che Siti you danced well. Poor boy, I think he has fallen for you.'

'It's not true, Che Aminah. What a joker you are. I am so much older than he. Look how young he is.'

'Young or not - he buys tickets every night and dances with no one but you. What if that is not love? Marry him lah.'

'What? When I just got divorced. One man is enough for me. Oh how my feet hurt.' Che Siti bent over to touch her heel.

'Get a new shoe, Siti.'

'No, I still can use it. Save money instead buying expensive shoes. And I need the money.'

'But still lah. You have to have new shoes as a dancer. You can't dance barefooted.'

'Oh how hot it is tonight,' Siti changed the subject, 'and there are too many of them tonight, wanting to dance, don't you think so. And I feel as if my period is coming. I wish Mat would let us rest more.'

The drum began.

Che Siti stood up before the Chinese man. He looked crisp in his starched shirt and trousers. When he smiled his gold tooth reflected the lights. He had chosen her. And two Malay men were dancing with the others. Aminah had a fat bloke with a songkok and Salemah, the thin short one who always danced with a handkerchief in his hand.

The Chinese came close to her and he smelt like stale rice. He turned his back and she followed. Then he came up with jiggles and shuddering arm movements. It was hopeless. He did not have definite pattern and the sense of rhythm was not there. It was as if he was trying to learn to swim in strange waters, very clumsily, fighting hard against the waves. The music rose. And the man's arms flailed. She had to be quick to avoid them. It was no use trying to sing anything. He would not understand and even if he did, the fun was not there, as he could not respond. Siti looked at the man closely and she saw that he was young. And he was not so bad-looking at all, despite the gold tooth. He had a high nose, unlike most Chinese, and very kind eyes. They said the Chinese worked hard and saved a lot of money. Was this one rich? Siti could not place the Chinese who came up for a dance. She could spot out the differences when her people came up for a dance. But not the Chinese. But the man was looking at her so boldly that she swung herself away from his gaze and glanced down. Below her, the crowds stood close to the stage, and she noticed Madzir staring very intently at her partner. She smiled at Madzir and at once his friends nudged him on the ribs and they all laughed. The Chinese did not appear to notice that anyone was looking at him with such ferocity and so continued dancing closer.

Ah Peng was his name. He felt good tonight. The crowd guffawed, and he smiled, flashing his gold tooth. Dancing was so good, and much less expensive than trying to find a girl to get married to. He had a crush on the young girl with the strip-tease show in New World Park but he dared not approach her. She was always with the magician of the show and his stupid parrot. Never alone. It was so frustrating, unable to walk up to the girl and talk to her. He was not rich. No rich man ever danced the ronggeng in a public place. And when he danced he imagined he was dancing with his girl. And he would really save up and impress her with expensive watches and shoes. It was so hot tonight and he felt the sweat staining the armpits of his shirt and spreading along his back. Only if the Chinese had rong-geng, he could be dancing with his girl, instead of the Malay girl. She looked all right the Malay girl; but too dark for his taste and she had such strong smell as if she had been bathed in buckets of perfume. But she really could dance and he could not follow her steps. The music stopped and he looked at her. How long the lashes were and how big her eyes were. He wondered what it was like to be married to her. And when he bowed and stumbled down the steps to the howls of his friends.

Che Siti went back to her chair. She took out her hand-kerchief and briskly wiped her throat. This time it was really hot. The music had been too fast. Her feet hurt. A breeze stirred the hem of her sarong and she pulled the sarong across her knees. She stared at the sea of faces below her. Mat was giving them a rest. To her right, across the hawkers stalls, was the new and popular Chinese dance show. They said girls there took off their clothes - shameless, shameless - what a thing to do. But the money was good for them. She would not think of doing such a thing - for all the money in the world. She raised her right hand and brushed the back across her lips, feeling the softness of the touch. She wanted so much a daughter and in her young days, while washing clothes along the river bank, she listened as her grandmother praised her beauty to the other women, and said that she would have many children and that any man would love her. The first child should be a girl, her grandmother smiled, as a daughter would be such a great help when the others came. But that was a long time ago. She had gotten married. Her man had left her for a richer woman. Her father had died and she had had to find work to feed her mother and younger brothers. Mat had taught her the rhythm and steps of the ronggeng. She still had her beauty however and she knew it by the way men glanced at her during the dance.

The fiddler started.

She got up from her chair, lifting up her head at the same time. She was so lost in her daydreaming that she was startled by the first bar of the music. She got up automatically without looking. And when she did, she was surprised to see the huge white soldier standing before her. He was sweating at the armpits and in the front of his khaki shirt, staining down the sides. She dared not look at him closely. Taking the handkerchief in her right hand, she held the other end in her left and started to sway forward towards the man. The white man was so clumsy and slow. His great boots made such a loud noise on the platform and they were so thick that it seemed they would last for years and years. As he lifted his arms, blond hairs stuck out like coconut fibres from his armpits, and he smelt. Are white women like that too? But how could they? They had looked so pretty in the pictures and in their pretty shoes, with such slim straps and very sharp heels, just like the stems of flowers.

As she danced she avoided the soldier. His friends were shouting at him from below the stage. Three of them and by their behaviour, they must have been very drunk. She could only catch the word 'Johnnie! Johnnie!' in their shouts and they waved at him as if asking him to stop dancing and come down. But he ignored them and she had to retreat quickly as he lurched forward. He smelt so much of beer. His great hands were so hairy. She noticed the red blotches on his skin. When she looked up at him, she was surprised. He had such a young face and the eyes were blue and tired-looking. Perhaps he had just come from the jungle, hunting the bandits there. The skin was rough with a growth of beard under the chin and down the throat. He came forward again and she avoided him. He reached out his hand to touch her and his friends shouted out 'Johnnie! Johnnie!', and frantically waved their hands. But the man did not go down. And then the man did a strange thing. He held up two arms in front of him at shoulder height and as if he were holding a chair. He started to reel away from her and going backwards and sliding forwards. Everyone laughed and clapped their hands. She stood still not knowing how to react. Taking advantage of her hesitation, he came forward and suddenly grabbed her round waist and pressed against her body and moved her in one swift rush sidewards. She was startled and gave out a tiny scream. From the corner of her eyes, she saw Madzir and his friends climbing up on the stage.

They came very fast and tore into the white soldier like snapping foxes. Johnnie's friends also came up, just as fast. The two groups met in an explosion of arms and curses. Soon a whistle was blown and the redcap white police officers came. The chairs were thrown off the stage and the girls huddled at a corner - the fiddle was smashed and the drum kicked in. The strap snapped and Che Siti's shoe lay in the centre trampled by the feet of the men and she looked at the wild scene before her. It was like in one of the streets where the men were always fighting, throttling her, punishing her, and opening her up to shameless things.

Mat had jumped off the stage and was helping the girls down, one by one. He had to get them away before the local police came. He had been warned that if there was any trouble he would have to answer for it. Now his drum was broken and the fiddler had walked away. He was left with his girls. He had worked so hard to make his ronggeng troupe the most popular in the State and to make money fast. He was getting old and he wanted to make the pilgrimage when he was still able to walk. What could he do with his girls? The troupe could not go on. There was only one way - and might he be forgiven. Che Siti was no longer as young as when he took her in, finding her crying in a pondok in the rice field at night, and learning that she was abducted by the village ruffians and had bad things done to her.

He would find Che Siti a quick and profitable occupation. With me. Shameless as it was. He did not want to think about it anymore. May he be forgiven. She was always such an obedient woman.

LEE KOK LIANG
An excerpt of
Flowers in the Sky

The Bhiksuni
'Fragrance of the precious lotus',
after receiving the rules of bodhisattva discipline,
fornicated and pretended it was neither killing nor
stealing and was, therefore, not subject to karmic
retribution. As a result, after her genital organ had been
slowly scorched by the flame of passion, she fell into
unintermittent hell.

Matangi (a low caste woman)
succeeded, by means of Kapila magic,
in drawing him close to her sensual body on the mat.

As the needle went in, he felt at peace. A flicker of a thought
crinkled across the surface of his mind; and then, it sank in to
the depths. A million petals radiating, dying away, leaving him
holding an empty stalk. Still the peace lingered for that fraction.
And just before he went blank, a gentle stillness bathed his
senses; his breathing became slow, his limbs hung loosely and
the air was sweet, reaching to the pit of his stomach. His eyes
watered with softened intensity, between his unfocused gaze
vagueness gathered an enlarged emptiness, and finally an immobility, the like of which he had sought for in vain, washed and
caressed every pore and entered and remained in his flesh. And
he remembered, while the layers of sensation wafted away, the
naturalness of walking down the hill in that dream, seeing the
great banks of mauve tree tops across the lake, smelling the
dampness of the morning. Bright red ants criss-crossed the
path, soft with dew. And the air then was good, very good and
clean, and the surface of the lake was as tight as a bolt of blue
silk, and clouds floated like flowers in the sky.

Alone, in his new black canvas shoes, he walked down the
hill, and in a few days would begin his long journey to the
South Seas.

3.00 P.M. WEDNESDAY

Operating Time. Mr. K., the surgeon at the Marvellous Cure Centre, was happy that day. He had done a marvellous round of golf the evening before, and his tax problems were solved by an amazing device set up by his accountants, where his servants were also made directors. He paid them well - the accountants, of course. Never grudge about payments to specialists, he had always told his patients when he carried a small talk with them. He had not grudged when he signed the cheque over to his accountants, the best in the country.

Mr. K. was tall, spare, with a touch of white in his long side-burns which he had recently acquired on his Jubilee jaunt in London. He had felt gawkish, being his first visit after a very long spell of hard work, as he walked down the ramp, neat and short-cropped, into a crowd of long-hairs at Heathrow. Since his return, he had kept his hair long which went very well with his pink-striped shirt and mustard trousers and the great Sam belt.

That day he was really happy and all his staff were grateful. Not to say that he was always grumpy; but Mr. K. did have an acidic manner, and his jokes were cutting, and the way he tapped his forefinger on his gold Rolex could be unnerving. Once his staff remembered how furious he had been when his new Mercedes got banged up two months after he had bought it. He had called in his chauffeur and began gently, in an almost fatherly manner, but within five minutes he was in such a rage that his secretary Miss Kim had had to put off all appointments for the next two hours. Mr. K. then strode out of his consulting room and took a long walk on the beach front. It did not do his blood pressure any good, nor, for all he knew, his digestive tract or gall-bladder either.

That day he was really happy. A touch of everything. Mr. K. went to the sink and scrubbed his large hands, rubbing his spatulate, pale-looking nails and running the stiff brush over his forearms. He loved to rub his arms this way. When he was four he had had his bath in a round wooden tub and the servant girl had bent down to clean him, her large breasts kneading his skinny arms through her coarse dress. He always recalled the sensation whenever he prepared himself over the sink. No point in not admitting it. Admit and be cleansed. All those repressions did no one any good. And when his mother arranged his marriage, his only stipulation was that his bride should have large breasts, the bigger the better. How his mother laughed; she chose for him a girl who not only had large breasts but a very commodious dowry as well.

Pushing the swing doors apart with his left elbow, Mr. K. crossed the antechamber where the nurse held the door to the theatre open for him. Mr. K. gave her a smile and noticed, as he always did, the tiny red mole on the lobe of her right ear. Sexy. Chern Sing had an almost flawless complexion, very smooth around the cheeks, but was on the olive side for a Chinese girl. Probably tanned by generations of tropical sun. It was only in a country like this that one could find Chinese who could not speak Chinese and some who did not even look like Chinese. For that matter, Mr. K. observed, with a detachment which he prided himself on, a Ceylonese Tamil who could not speak Tamil, though, in his case his complexion had not suffered any sun-change. Not to say that the sun could do him any worse. The sun in old Ceylon was just the same as here. Hot and breezy.

Mr. K.'s instructions had been carried out. The patient was already on the table. A white sheet covered the upper torso of the patient. He guessed underneath the sheet, the patient had the singlet on. An extraordinary fellow.

He remembered the fellow's first visit to him. Coming in so quietly with two women behind him. Such a small chap and perching so lightly on the edge of the chair. Pale brown face, not quite olive yet, web-like patches of pink struggling under the smooth skin of the cheeks. A tiny nose and eyes almost child-like, now and then blinking. Wrinkles were beginning to show at the corners of the mouth. Two deep lines, like canals, running from the inner corners of the eyes down the cheeks. A surprisingly smooth forehead and the head itself close shaven, bluish, with the burnt dots of Buddha on the top of the skull.

The fellow had produced a card. Venerable Hung, embossed in black lettering, in English. On the side, the usual Chinese equivalent. The card was edged in gold and some specks had come off on his fingers as he touched it. He recognised the address. A very well-known temple in the City.

The fellow had been sent to him by a G.P. with whom Mr. K. regularly played golf. Mr. K. talked to the fellow while Miss Tang, his nurse, interpreted for him. The symptoms described indicated some obstruction in the intestinal and genital area. Now and then the man held his belly tightly as if to seek some relief from the internal pressure. Well, he had got to be examined.

· Mr. K. pointed to the couch next to the wall. The fellow hesitated, looking at Miss Tang. One of the two women who had accompanied him spoke to Miss Tang and after some exchange, Miss Tang turned to Mr. K., speaking hesitantly.

"She wanted me to leave the room, sir."

"Why?"

"She say all women must leave the room when a monk undress."

"Tell her we have a curtain around the couch."

Miss Tang spoke to the woman and the exchange this time was longer. All this while, the monk sat in the chair, eyes closed, as if he did not want to know what was going on.

And finally it stopped.

"I am sorry, sit," Miss Tang said, "but she say no women allowed in room, even though there are curtains. The atmosphere will be wrong. Like bad air. It would hurt his spirit. I cannot argue her better, sir."

When he was thinking deeply Mr. K. had the habit of putting his palms together and rubbing them hard, listening to their sounds. As he did so, the monk suddenly turned and stared hard. He stopped rubbing. Miss Tang was certainly a poor negotiator in the first place and secondly her spoken English was hopeless. Probably her Chinese too. Falling standards in schools since Independence.

Miss Tang looked as if she was about to cry; the corners of her mouth began to twitch. He did not know what that woman had said to Miss Tang, but she was certainly bruised, the poor girl. Mr. K. liked Miss Tang a lot and took great pleasure in teasing her when he felt like it. He sometimes wondered if she had slept around, what with her big breasts, big for a Chinese girl, that is. She attracted glances. He had caught her talking to another nurse about having a European body and an Oriental face. He had just returned from lunch unexpectedly. But then

210

one could not be sure. Chinese girls could be unpredictably cold and virginal, or worse, lusty and money-minded.

"All right, then. You'd better go with them. Satisfy their silly superstition."

Mr. K. had decided. Getting up from his chair he gestured to the monk to follow him. However, the monk waited till all the women had left the room. Finding that the monk's Malay was not so good, Mr. K. resorted to more gestures to ask the monk to strip.

The monk went about it very neatly. First the heavy gold chain with the tiny Buddha was carefully lowered from the neck; then the long grey tunic was slowly unbuttoned and folded over a chair; the long shapeless grey trousers were loosened and gathered up in the small hands and then placed over the tunic. The monk stood in a cotton singlet and loose underpants. Mr. K. gestured. The monk slowly untied the knot of his underpants and they slid down to his knees. Mr. K. saw at a glance that the hernia was going down to the balls. The monk looked embarrassed. Mr. K. pointed to the couch and when the monk had sat on it, Mr. K. made a sign for him to remove the singlet. The monk was reluctant. But Mr. K. persisted. The sight amazed him. On the chest, above and below both nipples, were marks of the flesh being burnt, some lightly and some deeply leaving irregular weals. The flesh showed up white against these marks. The monk noticed his amazement and then put on the singlet. The sorrow in the monk's eyes put a stop to Mr. K.'s intention of questioning him about these marks.

It took Mr. K. a minute to determine that he must operate on the monk.

Mr. K. signalled to the anaesthetist. As the needles went in, Mr. K. turned to look at the monk. The pupils looked enormous and the expression was one of great doubt and anguish. Mr. K. turned away, annoyed. He had always taken the precaution of not looking into the eyes of those he was about to operate upon. This was a silly lapse.

He pushed the covering of the lower body aside. The gesture startled the nurse who was used to his smooth movements. There was the lower belly below him. Those ugly scars on the chest had been carefully concealed by the tight sheet. It was not

211

surgically correct but he had promised the man that no one would see those scars; however, as a matter of precaution, he had got his secretary to type a letter of indemnity against any mishap which the monk gladly signed. No point in exposing himself to claims.

So, a few days before, Mr. K. had drawn a sketch of the upper garments which he wanted to use during this operation and had them cut out and sewn by the tailor to fit snugly over the monk's body, revealing only the faint outer bluish edges of the scar near the navel. The belly looked white and the skin was surprisingly tight and delicate, almost with the fullness of that of a young girl.

As Mr. K. placed his dark hand against the whiteness of the belly, he remembered the time when, after the Medical Association Annual Dinner, he had gone to a hotel and slept with a Chinese girl, and what had fascinated him was how dark he had suddenly become against the paleness of the girl's body and this had added to his fascination and when his thing came he shouted out the few earthy Tamil words he knew and when it was over, he remembered feeling very sad, very sad at not knowing the language well. In extreme moments of sex, one reverts to one's mother tongue.

And so as Mr. K. placed his dark hand on the white belly, remembering the Chinese girl, remembering his mother tongue, he drew the first incision. The monk had made another request to which Mr. K. had acceded and which he now regretted. The monk had shaved himself with his razor. It was one of those old fashioned type razors with a carved, embossed handle in black mahogany and a blade which was very long. The monk had shown it to him. But the shave had not been clean. Under the bright glare of the lights, the roots of the pubic hair could be seen plainly and what made them more ugly was that the monk had such a sparse growth. Mr. K. cut further into the flesh and there was a gurgling sound as though air were escaping. Mr. K. stopped his thoughts and moved his hands professionally over the belly of the monk.

5.00 A.M. THURSDAY

Namo Tass. Nam Mo Mi. Ommmmmmmmmmmmmmmmm.
The breath left his belly, long and slow, and with a practised

212

movement he joined his palms together, the right below the left. The stillness was leaving him and he concentrated on the spot between his eyes, trying to see into emptiness. When you feel the sounds of the world coming into you - his Master had said - concentrate on the spot, and think of nothing, for there is where we are born and there is where we die. Think of nothing. All form is emptiness and emptiness is form and action stillness, so said Sariputra. *Ommmmmmmmmmmmmmmm*. And he concentrated, but the sounds circled and weaved and impinged and the stillness was broken. He heard the rain against the window pane - the soft wash and the patter of so many tiny bubbles invading and crashing into the stillness he had lost; yes, he had lost the stillness a long time ago.

Venerable Hung slowly turned his head to the window. The street light streaked the glass with reflections of brightness which touched the white sheet of his bed. He felt thirsty and there was a dull ache below his navel and a strange tightness around his balls. So that was it. The doctor had cut him up and he had come through. For that he was grateful to the man. A pleasant person, but the doctor reminded him of the small brook that ran into the ditch water. There was one like that at In Liang Sun, a few hundred yards from the monastery, which skirted the edge of the pine trees as they fell away down the gentle slope. It was a beautiful and clean place. How old was he then? About twelve or thirteen. Always running around the kitchen with the cook monk. How happy he was then. Piling up the firewood and washing the rice and running to the river with a net and coming back wet and tired with the fish. And the games he had played with others of his age. The most daring one was to enter the main hall where, at the west end, was placed a huge Joo Lai, the Laughing Buddha to Come, and surreptitiously to grab a handful of ash from one of the josspots, climb up the altar and rub the ash on the navel of Joo Lai, when the back of the caretaker monk was turned. All the other young ones jumped and clapped their hands when he scooted to safety. After that the Head Monk called all the young ones and punished them. They had to wake up at 3.00 a.m. and meditate in the cold hall until six and no one was to get up even to go to toilet. There was that monk standing guard over them with a bamboo stick, ready to hit them at the slightest movement. But it was fun, and the numbness of the legs and the cold could not dampen their ardour. He would do it again. *Om Na Mo.* He bent his head slightly and bit his lip to stop the laughter growing in him. And then there were so many other escapades in which he led the others to tease the more solemn of the monks, like putting red ants into their underpants or drawing figures of women on the path where they walked during their late afternoon meditation exercises. How he laughed and jumped when they turned their faces away quickly and some even retraced their steps. The younger ones blushed. He hid behind the pines with the others. But his laughter gave him away. He was reported to the Head Monk. Pig Head, the cook monk, was sent to fetch him. Pig Head found him with the others seated on the long wooden bench, memorizing the Diamond Sutra. Pig Head signalled to him. He put down the volume on the bench and followed. He had never been to the quarters of the Head Monk.

They took the path that skirted the dull walls of the monastery going up the slope of pines, for there was where the Head Monk stayed. A very quiet place. About ten minutes climb up the slope. He had seen the small brick building from afar when standing at the edge of the pond trying to net the fish. Washed in yellow amongst the pale green of the pines, like a strange bird, it had caught his imagination. Now his heart was beating strongly as he thought of it. He climbed up the granite steps that were laid on the red earth and followed them round the banks of green ferns and pale golden flowers. It was still in the midst of spring. The air was so clean then. Pig Head was puffing behind him and scraping his rubber shoes on the steps. Pig Head was a silent man. During the one year he was with him in the kitchen, Pig Head had not spoken to him. A man of few words. He sensed that Pig Head was exceedingly anxious to learn the sutras daily, but he had been asked to be the cook of the monastery instead, and this was nearly twenty years ago and now his eyesight was getting bad and his hearing was not so good either. At times, in the evenings, when all the cooking and washing was done, Pig Head would signal to him, and together, they would sit under the eaves of the roof next to the firewood

214

pile and practise meditation. The most he could last would be one hour or so. After that, instead of trying to think of the sutras he had learnt, his mind spun round the day's activities and what he was going to do the next day. On one occasion, when he got up to go, he slowly turned to look at Pig Head. Whether it was the glow cast by the oil lamp or whether it was that he had just rubbed his eyes vigorously, he thought he saw another figure seated by the side of Pig Head, faintly luminescent. Surprised, he looked again but it was not there anymore.

When they reached the top of the steps, the Supervisor Monk, an old man with two front teeth missing, came out of the small doorway leading to the quarters. Pig Head bowed reverently. He did the same. The Supervisor stared at him glumly. He pretended to rub the corner of his left eye with his index finger. The pines grew thickly here. On top of the small hillock they were as straight as the fingers of his hand. The old man shook his head slightly. Apparently, the report was bad, very bad. He grew suddenly frightened.

In the late afternoon, the yellow of the walls surrounding the Head Monk's quarters reminded him of the colour of the scroll that contained the sayings of Dharma which were kept under lock and key in the glass-wall cupboard in the main hall. Pale cross-grained yellow, flecked with dark spots.

He then followed the Supervisor Monk along the path and both entered the side of the building through a wooden doorway. They came to the back courtyard surrounded by high walls. The old man asked him to remain there and went alone through the back door into the main building.

He stood there, feeling uneasy. The courtyard was bare except for a tiny pool which was fed by a trickle from a hollow bamboo stem. The ground was hard, without a trace of sand. He walked over to the pool. It was about four feet long and three feet wide and about two feet deep filled with clear water. Not exactly clear, as some of the algae which clung to its sides, broke off and floated in patches below the surface, but in between these growths the water shone like burnished silver, reflecting the sun.

The walls of the building followed the slope and contours of the land and the sun reached down to the pool where the walls had dipped. The building faced the north where the hill climbed and he now realized why it gave him the impression of a bird in flight, a yellow bird. The main roof humped over the rise of the land and the back of the building trailed downwards into a sort of hollow; a gentle dip at the tail.

He stood looking into the pool. How long, he did not know. He had already scratched the small tuft of hair on his otherwise bald head several time. He did this when he felt he was going to be punished. But no one came. So he stood looking. At first he did not hear the sound but then he heard splashes of the water as it trickled down the bamboo stem, drop by drop. As he started counting the drops he marvelled at the sounds they were making and the beautiful ripples that spread across the pool, one after another, endless; and yet in between was the stillness of the surface as painful as breath held too long in one's lungs. He stopped his scratching. Suddenly his ears caught a different sound coming from the water. A white shape appeared. He did not believe it at first. It was a huge carp. Almost silvery with a red dot on its upper lip. It swung lazily in the pool and the sun etched its brilliant scales, as big as toe nails. The whiskers were long and the tail wide. It seemed to look up at him, sucking the water, so it seemed, with slow movements of the mouth. And when he took a step forward, it turned round and disappeared. It was then that he notices a hole in the edge of the pool below the wall of the main building.

The Supervisor Monk came out. The old man drew a circle on the ground with his staff and pointed at it.

At once he knew what was wanted of him. Looking solemn, he took a step and knelt down in the centre of the circle, his hands behind him, his head bowed slightly. The punishment had begun. The old man, after staring at him and walking about the courtyard, went into the building, but darted out now and then, to see if he was still kneeling. He would be severely whacked with the staff if he was found doing otherwise. What was worse, one of the boys who had been very disobedient had to be sent off and was never seen again. He did not want that to happen to him.

His home had never been pleasant, with his mother grumbling at him the whole day long and frequently hitting him when his younger brother, an idiot, squirted on the household shrine, which the idiot frequently did with great relish. And they said he had to join the order to save his brother. Since he left he had heard that the idiot did not squirt so much, probably because he was not there to be beaten until he cried. He remembered how the idiot had looked at him when he cried - almost reverently. He certainly did not want to be sent home. He had to bear this burden. His father, almost in tears, had said that sometimes one was born to pay the debts owed to others and sometimes one was born to receive the payment of debts. In his case, it was obvious that he had a debt to pay for the sake of his brother. So they had sent him off with a recommendation from his village headman and some gifts to the monastery.

That was about two years ago. Then they shaved his head, leaving a small square tuft of hair right on the top, and put him in the kitchen with Pig Head. On festival days his parents visited him. But the idiot was left at home, as a matter of precaution. He had nothing much to say to them. All agreed that he was behaving nicely. But sometimes he behaved curiously, doing things which normally he would not dream of doing. And they could not understand him at such times. He felt then as if his brother's idiocy had jumped onto his back and however much he fought, it clung to him, and so to get rid of it, he went on such escapades. No one seemed to understand what he was trying to do.

And so he knelt in the circle. The pain and numbness shot into his limbs. His back ached from the shoulders down. The sun had gone, he did not know how long ago. The air had become chilly, and a slight breeze stirred among the pine trees washing them with a dull roaring sound.

He tried to think of the Master to ease the numbness. The Master, the younger monks had said, was a strong fellow and once by himself had lifted a fallen pine which had trapped a rabbit under it. And the Master had a great roar of laughter which could be heard for miles. But the Master laughed rarely. Although eighty, the Master looked like a man of thirty and bathed five times a day, even at two o'clock in the morning, the hour of the tiger. The more he thought about what they had said, the more he felt afraid. The Master would certainly take him and throw him over the wall.

217

It was getting dark. The breeze stirred. Among the pine trees, the waves of sound swept to and fro, high above his head, as if seeking a shore upon which to splash and die away. He could sense the contained strength of the sound, taut and tense, stretched tightly within the confines of the grove as it eddied and rolled towards the crest of the hill, only to curl back in a diminishing, frustrated roar and the beginning of another attempt to hurl itself upwards. The roar travelled closer to his ears. And in the dark of the night, it became very much alive. His sleeves fluttered lightly and fine sand blew into his sandals. He closed his eyes briefly and the sound became persistent, dominating his consciousness, like the unhurried laughter his brother emitted whenever he peed on the top of the altar. Yes, the waves of sound mingled disturbingly with the laughter of his imbecile brother. *Namo tassa. Nam Mo Mi. Ommmmmmm-mmmmmmmmm.* He must concentrate. *Namo. Namo.* Try reasoning to overcome fear, they chanted. If you say Buddha has six supernatural powers, which are beyond description, then all *devas*, ghosts, seers, *asuras* and powerful demons, who also possess supernatural powers, should also be Buddhas. If you say all *arhats* and Bodhisattvas are great people, why should they help you small people to become Buddhas, because if you can be Buddhas you can never be small, and all *arhats* and Bodhisattvas can never be great, but are your equals, which is neither great nor small. Concentrate. Shut your mind against the waves of sound. Shut your mind against the slight annoyances of this life. But open it to the irritations so that your struggle shall cease. Catch a phrase from a sutra, let is hover in your mind, let it sink, let is disappear, know not its meaning, let it be. Catch the sound, let it envelope your mind, let it roar, knocking your mind, let it not escape, hear it and hear it until your mind becomes part of the roar, become the whole roar and everything will be still. The anger is gone. The sound is gone.

For some time he thought he heard the stillness. The numbness had gone from his limbs. His eyes were open, tears streaming down his cheeks, and a lightness touched his body; his breathing was deep. The sweat gathered at his armpits, in the middle of his chest, and at the base of his spine. He farted a long one. And then he heard the drop of water on the pool and then another drop and then one more. The sound was clear and did not shock him. It came to him gently, washing away all his shames. And then he also heard the splash of the carp as it emerged from its hole and swung close to the top of the pool, moved away, coming to the surface and sinking again. It was like awareness swimming in the mind. *Namo Tassa. Nam Mo Mi. Ommmmmmmmmmmmmmm.*

Suddenly he was disturbed by a shaft of light. There was a shadow in the light. Slowly he closed his eyes and gently relaxed his spine waiting for the blood to flow into his limbs and for his breath to quicken.

Then the waves of sound returned, and he heard once more the breeze rushing through the pine trees. He turned his head. Framed in the doorway was the figure of a big man. At a glance he knew it could be no one else but the Master. Quickly he bowed his head. He got whacked between the shoulders. The pain jerked him up and then he was pulled up to his feet with a great deal of force. He saw the Master by the light of the candle burning on a table in the hall of the main building. The Master, as they had said, was a big man. But he had not expected the dark growth of beard and the darkness of the skin.

The Master shook him, saying, "Never bow to me and never bow to any one, not even to Buddha if you can find him. Understand?"

And then the Master released him, observing him fiercely. He stood still, looking at the Master, but not daring to stare.

Dressed simply in grey, with a few torn patches at the knees and elbows, the Master looked like a rough labourer. The Master smiled at him, noting the disbelief in his eyes.

"I do not look like what you think I should look like. It is good. Do you think Buddha looked like the images we have in the monastery? Remember at one time he had to starve - he would have looked like a skeleton then. When he sat under the tree, not moving for years, he was covered with lice and scabies for he has a human body like you and me. Whatever stories they tell you about him, they are pleasant to hear, but do not believe them all, if you want to attain to Buddhahood. Come. This is your first lesson." And the Master, pointing to the pool, said, "I did not come out sooner, until I was sure you'd heard the pool

219

and lost the waves of the sound. But this is the first step and there are so many move; be determined. Now you have to learn to unhear. Come."

The Master led the way into the main hall. Unlike the monastery below, it was bare and simple. The pool extended into the hall, and in the reflected light, looked shallower, its edges serrated with white, sharp-looking chunks of granite, each the size of a man's head. He could see the great white carp lying still in the water, fanning its fins languorously.

At one end of the hall was a raised platform with some rush mats on it. Nowhere could he discover any image of Lord Buddha. A thick red candle stood burning in the middle of a square table a few feet from the pool. Another door could be seen at the corner next to the raised platform. Probably it led to a prayer room. The ceiling was low, uncovered, and great roughly hewn logs held up the roof, dark with age. The floor was uneven, following the contours of the slope and at one corner an outcrop of rocks had forced itself into the hall, or rather the wall had been built around it. Surprisingly, the hall was warm. The breeze did not quite penetrate, though now and then, he heard its roar.

"Here's some water. You must be thirsty after the long sit." The Master scooped the water from the pool with a wooden ladle. He drank it. Sweet and cool.

"Now go and sleep. It's enough for one night." The Master pointed to the platform. He went up and slept on one of the mats. The Master, however, did not come up but went instead to where the rocks were and sat down in a meditative posture facing them.

And when he woke up, the next day, he found the Master still sitting. He left the quarters quietly.

They questioned him. The boys, coming to talk to him, expecting tales. But they found him surprisingly silent. Not quite his usual self. Even Pig Head asked him once or twice, as they sat down under the eaves of the roof for their evening meditation, what it had been like. He simply said it was beautiful.

He was summoned up the hill again and was given duties; cleaning the courtyard and burning the fallen needles of the pine, chopping up wood; he was generally kept busy. He did not see the Master for a long time and thought he would not see him again. But one day, towards evening, the Supervisor asked him to stay back. He remained in the courtyard, waiting. The water in the pool was clearer as he had taken trouble to scoop the algae from its surface and sides. A voice called out to him. He entered and found the Master on the platform. He prostrated himself on the floor before the Master. Suddenly he received a great whack between the shoulders.

The Master held his staff tightly and with angry eyes stared at him. "Have you forgotten what I had told you before?"

With tears streaming down his cheeks, he felt the pain burning across his back; the figure of the Master blurred and became misshapened, even the staff seemed to merge with the body and this image wavered in the reflection of the pool. But it was only for a moment. Then his vision cleared. Without a word the Master left him. He stood there for a long while, not daring to move. Towards morning the Master relented and asked him to sit down. He was so tired. It was after this incident that he sensed that the Master had softened towards him. He began sitting with the Master for short intervals. But it was all done in secret. No one knew about it. Not even the Supervisor. He had to creep up the hill after midnight and come down just before dawn, using the path which was frequented by the public. But he was careful not to boast about these meetings.

However, two years later, when he felt as though he was on the verge, as though he were pushing the doors open, and that he could see what was on the other side, the Master stopped receiving him. And he did not know what he had done wrong. Was it that he tried to talk, to break the silence, now and then? Was it because he showed some anger? Was it because he put his hand into the pool, and gently fondled the carp as he fed it? Was it because he still thought about the face of Lord Buddha and tried hard to know the meaning of certain phrases in the sutras? Or was it because he was still frightened of letting his mind go? But, he remembered once when he had finished his meditation, he found the Master looking at him, and after a while said, a bit sadly, "You cling too much." When he heard this, he tried harder to lose his mind, to swim away from the sea of *samsara*, to search for the quieter shores.

And then the Master stopped receiving him.

But he still remembered the day when the Master went away on his long and final journey. He was then about sixteen. They had brought the Master down from the hill and put him into one of the chambers so that he could receive visitors. The village headman came; the officials, the merchants, the artisans, the heads of families also arrived and even some from hundreds of miles away, so great was the reputation of the Master. The monks held great chanting sessions in the outer halls, and the gongs were struck frequently, and everyone who came, he remembered, never failed to light candles and pray to all the images scattered around the halls, devoutly moving from one to the other, in an ordered sequence. The younger ones even stopped playing practical jokes.

He remembered the strange contraption. It was a picture-taking box. A very big one. Everyone dressed up neatly. The Master refused any help and dressed himself. They all lined up under the pine trees and a picture was taken. And then the day before the Master passed away, he was summoned to the chamber. The Supervisor was there, so was Pig Head, who tried to hold back his tears, and the man with the picture-box. The change in the Master's appearance was so sharp that it startled him. The greatly emaciated figure lay under the covers on the bed. Brilliant eyes, the cheek bones standing out, flecks of white scattered among the hairs, the skin seamed with wrinkles, the flesh over the mouth, tight and pinched, and the breaths coming in shallow and quick gasps. He stood by the side of the bed. The Master reached out and pulled him down.

He bent down to hear what the Master wanted to say to him, smelling the warm musty smell of the dying body. "I am going away. Try hard. Do not fail."

And then the thin hand clutched him tighter, pulling him closer to the top of the bed. He stood still. The picture was taken. The white flash startled him. It lit up the whole chamber. The great white sheet that covered the bed bounced the light and the golden images of Buddhas were exposed in the niches of the wall. In that moment he observed the sudden twitch of the left leg under the covers.

And now, sleeping in the bed under the covers, he gently removed his left leg and watched the mound that was his foot. He did not feel much of a sensation. The surgeon had operated on him well but the tightness around his balls was discomforting.

He wished he had someone like himself to visit him. It was so different in this strange hot land. It was nearly forty-five years since he had arrived. He felt sleepy again. The lights wrinkled in the windows as the soft drizzle sent wavy patterns down the glass. The gentle taps of the drizzle on the glass hushed the sound of the air-conditioner, making it more monotonous than usual.

He could not hear very well these days. One of his ears was continually buzzing. The hot sun did that. And when he sat down to do his meditation, in the hour of the tiger, the right ear opened up another world of sound, not like the waves, not like the tiny drops of water, but something that seemed to catch hold of him and cling to him, ringing and ringing. It had become a part of his existence. This great sound in his ear which came with the hot sun and the roaring rains and the dull yellow streams and the mosquitoes and the unceasing sweat and stench of indolent disciples. If he only could unhear. If he only could. The upper part of his chest itched. And he could do nothing about it but endure. It was so dull now and he closed his eyes as the sedative worked on him.

FLOWERS IN THE SKY
Lee Kok Liang

This compelling first novel, written with an English native-speaker's flair but distinctly Asian voice, joins the local literary scene like a waft of fresh air, a welcome revivification from the puff pieces that abound. Set in an unnamed Malaysian seaside city, the story follows five days in the life of the seemingly quiet, serene monk and lonely, worldly surgeon. As the events unfold, both separately come to terms with their own limitations and strengths.

Federal Publications (S) Pte Ltd, Times Centre, 1 New Industrial Road, Singapore 1953

SHIRLEY GEOK-LIN LIM
Gods Who Fail:
Ancestral Religions in the
New Literatures in English
from Malaysia and Singapore

Reading the opening chapter of Maniam's novel *The Return*, the Malaysian reader is immediately aware that she is in the presence of something at once new and old: a fiction which re-creates the ancient "thick spiritual and domestic air" of some remote district in India in the new "most developed part of Bedong"; a literature in English in which the exhausted post-colonial obsession with adaptations of the master's tongue and master's culture is abandoned for a longer reach into an original racial part. What is the critic to make of a chapter where the land outside and the Malaysian society in which these fictional events are placed are shadowy figures beside that other land "haunted by ghosts, treaded lightly by gods and goddesses" which forms the fiction's true world? If, as H.J. Oliver asserts "(t)he genesis of a local literature in Commonwealth countries has almost always been contemporaneous with the development of a truly national sentiment," in what ways can a critic claim Maniam's book, immersed almost wholly in the interior lives of three generations of one Tamil family and in the spiritual conflicts between a Hindu world-view and the modern English-educated secular world, as a Malaysian text?

These are crucial questions not only to an interpretation of one novel but to an understanding of the new literatures in English from Malaysia/Singapore. For what *The Return* represents is a historical shift in direction for English-language writers from the region which, while perhaps inevitable, offers exciting rich possibilities for the literature and a great many dangers.

Malaysian/Singapore literature in English, since the first undergraduates in the University of Malaya in the 1940's began publishing their attempts, has generally disappointed its public.[1] The chief critic from the region and its most articulate defender,

Edwin Thumboo, has himself expressed doubts over its peripheral status and attempted to explain why although "we have had the language for 150 years" there is so little to show for it. All kinds of reasons are plausible, just as they are plausible for countries such as Nigeria, Kenya, Ghana and the West Indies which have produced worthy contributions to the body of world literature in English. Finally, these reasons do not apply to Malaysia/Singapore, for the region, despite its small size and lack of visibility in world power, is both unique and archetypal in its historic development. [2]

Until very recently, English was the language used by a small Western-educated, middle-class elite, and the literature this elite produced reflected its estrangement from the masses and the radical secularization of its traditional religious/cultural world. An examination of the poetry from the 1940's to the present reveals the growth of the cult of individuality with its emphasis on romantic love and the resulting dissatisfactions and hollowness of narcissism, extreme subjectivity, and social and psychical anomie. Together with this move inward following the loss of native cultural forms is the compensatory move outwards adopting the ideologies of Western civilization: in declarations of political democratic stances and nationalistic sentiments. [3]

Gopal Baratham's *Figments of Experience*, published in 1980, displays these major characteristics. His opening story, "The Welcome," depicts the return of a Singaporean Tamil with his English wife after a stay abroad and ridicules both the cross-cultural difficulties faced by the characters (e.g. the white wife's ludicrous attempt to wear a sari) and the riotous, sentimental behaviour of the Tamil kinsmen. A similar deracination is perceivable in Rebecca Chua's book of short stories, *The Newspaper Editor*. The narrator in "The Washerwoman's Daughter" submits to her working-class fate and abandons her desire for an education and a middle-class life as "useless pipe-dreams." In "Suicide," a group of friends, trapped as social exiles in an oppressive urban world in which the dominant values of material success create intolerable stress, singly kill themselves.

Modernity, the forces of open competition and of atomization, according to Singapore writers such as Baratham, Chua, and Lee Tzu Pheng, results in impotency, an unwise passivity bordering on self-pity, self-hatred, self-induced death. Thus the last page of Chua's book typically offers such indulgent despairing statements as "Nothing is sacred, neither death, nor life itself, because it comes so cheaply;" "We were the last Romantics, too late for knowledge of chemistry, corporations and computers;" and "let me take my last bow and let the curtain fall, *requiescat in pace*." (180) Lee Tzu Pheng's poetry, although more multi-faceted, shows a similar trend of melancholic helplessness in the face of "the megalopolitan appetite." She asks: "Must I like an oyster / repose in the shell, hearing only the dumb / scream of the sea-surge, / moving me against knowledge, / ...(to) new graves?" (*The Second Tongue*, 40) The overwhelming sense of the individual as insignificant before the irresistible force of urban anonymity is again expressed in the poem "Everything is going away" where the poet complains that "coming to life / everything is going away... / to the last futility: / the opening womb, the closing tomb." (159) Although occasionally elegiac when the writer transcends the fragmentary, transitory experience of the multiracial, multilingual city, Singapore writing in English (a language which is rapidly becoming the language of choice for the nation and which is institutionally heavily supported), because it almost always expresses the writers' sense of decadent uprootedness, is almost always homeless. The homeless condition, as local critics have shrewdly noted, accounts for the writers' inability to "come to the people" and consequently, through a spiralling cycle of disownings, in the general social failure to support the writers.

In 1980 also, the Malaysian novel, *The Return* appeared, one of a group of prose works which indicates a move in the region from poetry to fiction. Like Lee Kok Liang's *Flowers in the Sky*, Lloyd Fernando's *Scorpion Orchid*, and Catherine Lim's *The Serpent's Tooth* among others, it seeks to counteract Western-influenced alienation by a return to the moral values encoded originally in the author's native culture. And, in so far as "the religious tradition of a society articulates values more explicitly than any other aspect of the society's general culture," (Verba, 513) these writers, in seeking to discover for their actions a pattern of significance which is other than those deriving from western ideology, in imputing to characters drives and values which are rooted in recognizably religious attitudes, are returning to their ancestral religions.

Maniam's novel demonstrates this move from estrangement to the possibility of renewal of significance through a return to religious values. From that primordial racially integrative society represented by Periathai, the grandmother, and inextricably adhering to the Hindu rituals of purification which she performs and to the reiterated Hindu symbols of the Nataraja and the silver tier lamps, the narrator and main character, Ravi, is ejected into the foreign world of "The English School." Maniam presents two societies as worlds of language. "The lines of curving, intricate Tamil writing unfolded an excitingly unexpected and knowable world." (22) As Derek Walcott forcibly reminds us in his poem "Codicil," "To change your language you must change your life." Miss Nancy is the temptress who teaches the native children English and "transported us into a pleasant, unreachable land." (25) Miss Nancy, through the use of dolls, enacts the English fantasies of Snow White and the Seven Dwarfs and Little Red Riding Hood: "at her altar of miracles, everything or nothing seemed possible." Ravi discovers his individuality through her: "Miss Nancy made me feel I was a discovery in myself." (32) The infancy of Hindu myth and community, symbolized in the Tamil language, gives way to the magic, in the Burkean sense, of the English language: "Magic, verbal coercion, establishment of management by decree, says in effect: 'Let there be...and there was.'" (118) In this sense too, if English is the language of magic (i.e. of mastery of the environment) in the novel, Tamil is the language of religion. (In Burke's formulation, "If magic says, "Let there be such and such," religion says "Please do such and such." The decree of magic, the petition of prayer." (119)

Ravi's educational progress, his scholarship to England and entry into the middle class by way of school-teaching, leaving behind his family's working-class world, all mark in some ways the success of nineteenth-century British liberal positivism and rationalism. But at what cost Maniam is determined to show. More than a foil, Ravi's father appears to take an opposing destiny. At first an economically striving, energetic man, he gradually withdraws from the town of open competition to a house at the fringe of the jungle. Ravi, observing Naina's irrational behaviour, reads it as "immature ambition" against which he weighs his own "comfortable, unthreatened existence," his private world in which one must discover for oneself the "logic and the power that sustains the individual." (147) But Ravi's meditations, the author is careful to show at the novel's conclusion, are partial and incomplete. Naina's death is the sacrifice that resacralizes for Ravi a world which, while private and middle-class, is after all empty and passionless. (163) Ravi's participation in the ritual purifications and burial ceremonies conclude in the narrator's (here almost indistinguishable from the authorial voice) final statement of immature recognition, expressible only in poetry: "Have you been lost / for words?...Words will not serve...You'll be twisted by them... buried in a heart that will not serve." (183)

In contradistinction to those writers whose works passively reflect the dilemma of alienated sensibility, the heart that will not serve, Maniam, in creating the violence of characters who are yet in the grip of powerful religious beliefs, whose actions are motivated by centuries-old attitudes anchored in highly systematized philosophies which dictate the appropriate behaviour of human and divine, creates the possibility of depth in his fiction. The dance of Shiva, the motif of the Tamil image of Nataraja, unites the novel's various sections, paralleling and deepening the meaning of its action. [4] Naina's life becomes meaningful only if it is interpreted through Hindu symbolgy; for example, the conflict with Ayah rests on Naina's defiance of the laws of caste which dictate Naina's lower position as a Vaishya (merchant) to Ayah's superior position as a Kshatriya (warrior). Similarly, his withdrawal from his laundry business follows the classic Hindu pattern of movement from the pursuit of *artha* (wealth) as a valid way of life for the man in the householder stage of life to the stage when he withdraws to seek the ultimate religious goal, *moksha* (release from rebirth).

Lloyd Fernando's *Scorpion Orchid* shows a similar reliance on religious symbols to create violence of meaning where violence of passion and political unrest is treated. The turbulence of racial riots following the British pull-out is given a mythic weight by the introduction of a mystery figure, a holy man, guru, bomoh, or medium, who ironically manifests himself to the major characters as their racial other: to the Chinese/Malay Sally as an Indian priest, to the Indian Santi as a Malay bomoh, to the Malay Sabran as a Chinese medium, and to the Chinese Guan Kheng as a Eurasian, Senor Entalban. The character's search for the mystery figure is also their quest for a key to their future, a quest which must cover self-knowledge and identity. Fernando's opening chapter pointedly demonstrates the inadequacy of traditional religious value systems to see his characters through the "bloody" birth of a new nation. The household altar is stripped and Vishnu, Lakshmi, and Nataraja are packed in a coffin-like box to be shipped back to India with Santi's Indian guardians. Nonetheless, the apocalyptic, prophetic significance in the novel is craftily conveyed in the figure of the holy man in whose racial fusion is symbolized the possibility of a new racial future.

Lee Kok Liang's *Flowers in the Sky* demonstrates the most explicit manipulation of religious materials from the new literature in English from Malaysia. Lee is almost disingenuously open about the motives for his use of these materials. In a letter to Syd Harrex, he admits:

> It is impossible to write honestly in S.E. Asia today without touching a raw nerve now and then: - however, I also found that, one aspect, frequently if not often missing, in the writings of non-Muslim or non-Semitic religions, is the role that religion plays in one's life - by that I mean a vast empyrean of feelings on the question of life and love and how some people are guided. In S.E. Asia again in the meeting and clash of different religions and their resolutions have not yet been worked out and yet every day the nuances are there for all to see.

If we take his admissions seriously, and there is no reason to doubt his statements here, we may very well conclude that Lee's depiction of the relationship between human and sacred is motivated both by his acute perception that "the question of life and love" is still very much guided by religious attitudes in Southeast Asia and also, in a much more complicated manner,

229

that writing on religious matters is (contrary to common assumptions on the sensitivity of the topic) a comparatively "safe" subject, one on which the writer is able "to write honestly...without touching a raw nerve."

The former motive gives the novel its explicit dualistic structure: action is balanced between two male characters, the Venerable Hung representing Buddhist consciousness, other worldly, monastic, celibate, seeking escape from the Karmic world of sensuality through meditation, and the surgeon Mr. K, worldly, a lover of women and material success, a weary, unbelieving Christian. The novel's drama at this level is one of tension between two polarities which, converted into religious terms, becomes a universalistic drama of sinfulness, guilt, and retribution. Lee prepares the reader for this interpretation by opening the novel with two quotations from the Lotus Sutra which directly pertain to a central Buddhist belief that the sin of fornication is subject to karmic retribution. While Lee loosens the novel's form by a non-linear construction (the action moving from Hung to Mr. K to the comic sub-plot, and from present to past to present at will), this apparent openness is tightly controlled by the division of the book into six days, a detail enlarged at the novel's conclusion by the ironic vision of the Venerable Hung leaving the Marvellous Cure Clinic after his surgery in a chauffeur-driven Mercedes carrying the license plate 666. While Mr. K, the subtle, skeptical Christian, is amused by the unwitting allusion to Satan in Chapter 13 of the Book of Revelations, the authorial voice intrudes at this point to remind the reader that 666 in Cantonese approximates to "Joy, Joy, Joy," that is, to beatific vision. (157) In leaving the reader at this conjunction of cultural misinterpretations, the author underscores one of the major themes in his book, the relativism of religious belief.

This relativism, even an ambiguity of valuation, is more than strongly suggested in the portrayal of the monk, the spiritual healer, and the surgeon, the physical healer. For both men, in their separate representations of other-worldly and worldly striving, are two sides of the same coin. Hung's career from a youth in South China to the foremost Temple Abbotship in Penang, the growth of his spiritual self, is vivified by his struggle with his sensual impulses, symbolized in the image of carp which disturbs his meditations as an apprentice and which is recalled later in his sexual attraction to the mute girl, Ah Lan. The novel's sole horrific act, the act of stigmatization when Hung burns charcoal on his chest, is understandable in the light of retribution for his sexuality. (147-8) Lee leaves unsaid whether the act was consummated, but that is hardly relevant for in Buddhist teaching it is desire itself which is evil.

Conversely, K, who "had given up all this rigmarole" of religion (27) and settled for the satisfactions of this earthly paradise, is continuously disturbed by longings for the transcendental. As much as Hung, his greatest consciousness is of what is absent: "The warmth and the tradition seemed to have been sieved off, leaving only struggling maggots of resentment and emptiness where the flesh should have been." (26) While Hung struggles to empty his consciousness of all sensation, K. struggles to keep his sense from ennui, the existential horror of nothingness. As the author remind us, "Yes, (K) had more feeling. But what was the use? Against (his wife) these feelings were nothing." (131)

The novel, at this level of symbolic action, possesses a precision of language and ever-widening network of images which add up to a "piety of style." The graveness of religious concerns here is both self-evident in the authorial tone and in the context of Lee's earlier fictions, his published short stories which show a repeated pattern of obsessive characters ridden by sexual guilt ending in the most violent retribution: mutilation, insanity, murder, patricide. Yet Lee also attempts something else in the novel, and by resorting to a sub-plot which treats religious themes in a facetious manner, he reveals more of his second motive for using religious materials, a motive which approaches religion not for its intrinsic sacramental values but for its sociological content. For, in a country where race has proven an incendiary issue, religion, if treated light-handedly, may be an acceptable substitute for the novelist in portraying multiracial society. The narrative of Inspector Gopal's pursuit of Nila, his Tantric version of Shakti, and of Inspector Hashim' successful control of a near-riot concerning the discovery of a Ganesh statue on the beach, enlarges the novel's social range to include beyond the primary East/West dialectic, seen in Hung and K, the Hindu and Malay aspects of Malaysian society.

While it is unfair to ask that a writer be serious when he means to be comic, nonetheless, it must be said that Lee's depiction of Hindu communal faith in action is shallow, glib, and facile. The comedy here misses the shadow of the possibility of faith which gives the portrayal of K its depth and reverberating significance. Clearly Lee has attempted to write a novel which encompasses the four major racial/cultural groups in Malaysia: the Malay/Islamic, Chinese/Buddhist, Indian/Hindu, and Western/Christian. Like Fernando, he attempts to achieve this economically by creating characters who are also racial types, the Chinese Hung, Sri Lankan K, Indian Gopal, and Malay Hashim. However, the novel shows a radical split, a flaw of conception, when it moves from the interior drama of Buddhist/Christian attitudes, materials into which the author has breathed his own ambivalences and psychic tensions, to the external drama of Hindu action and Malay "crowd-control." The difference between the earnest and the mocking, internality and externality, demonstrates that the author has not been able to actively imagine the experience of cultures foreign to him and his depiction of them therefore remains one-dimensional, without depth.

In the context of Malaysian racial divisions, Lee's attempt to overcome the suspicions and rigidity of one- race-consciousness through a focus on cultural relativism, express in both serious and comic terms, is admirable. Paradoxically, however, writers such as Lee, Fernando, Maniam and Catherine Lim, in their search for renewal of significance in ancestral religious sources, also exemplify a glorification of their racial past as the repository of values, a move which may be perceived as false as much as it is authentic, if it leads to a mystique of a racial past which prevents "the essential movement of human reality toward the future." (Jameson, on Ernst Bloch, 130)

Finally, how are we to understand a socio-literary situation in which writers consciously or unconsciously turn to Hindu and Buddhist/Confucionist values and traditional imagery of the sacred in order to infuse their work with pattern and meaning? In the case of these writers, one explanation for their born-again sensitivity to transcendent themes lies in what their works omit. With the exception of Fernando's novel, none of these fictions deal with the overwhelming question of national identity. In Maniam's novel, all the major and minor characters, with the exception of Miss Nancy who is white, are South Indian. An unknowledgable reader may well believe Malaysia to be, even if pluralistic, an Indian-dominant nation, or at least not a Malay-dominant country. In focussing wholly on the Tamil Hindu community, that is, in choosing to define the novel's conflict as the loss of Hindu spiritual identity in the face of English cultural assimilation, Maniam has also managed to avoid the thorny, politically sensitive issue of race relations, national identity and nationalistic assimilation or non-assimilation which form the chief social realities in Malaysia.

This is not to say that the author should have written a different novel, one more deliberately reflective of the total Malaysian social scene. Still, Maniam's novel of racial identity which draws from his ancestral religion is symptomatic of the response of an emerging group of Malaysian writers who, in the process of nationalism, find themselves doubly dispossessed. For, initially dispossessed by their use of the English language from their native cultures, these writers in English, after the introduction of Bahasa (Malay) as the national language, now find themselves dispossessed a second time in a country in which both their native and adopted cultures have only a minority status.

One way out of this painful position of non-belonging is to avoid the whole issue of national identity which, after all, is the ideology of exclusion, and to seek instead their racial or subjective identities through the resources of religion. But there are dangers intrinsic to any such movement in Malaysia/Singapore, as T. Wignesan aptly indicated:

> While a certain amount of intra-communal rapport permits Malaysians...to co-exist, their religions, by contrast, hermetically seal them off from their separate "home" of lives and from a total acceptance of one another's distinct identities...every retreat into their separate selves turns into

an accentuation of their differing faiths where religion offers a refuge. (71)

In returning to ancestral systems of value, Malaysian writers in English especially and Singapore English-language writers to some extent are turning away from nationality to identity. While their works contain little overt and convert political ideology, this in no way controverts the fact that their expression is just as inevitably a reflection of the social realities which surround their authors. The emergence of these works which return to Buddhist, Hindu, or other Asian religions for a key to an understanding of a transitory society is evidence not so much of an official national culture (in place only since 1957) but of the existence of substantial minority cultures outside the nationalistic one, cultures which although non-dominative are validated by their historical position in the region and by their majority status elsewhere. [Historians tell us that Indian culture was the dominant external influence in Southeast Asia during the first millennium of the Christian era and that Chinese trade in the region was encouraged "by both official policy and official capital during Sung and Yuan time." (*Man, State, and Society*. (433)] In looking to past cultural systems of the sacred to resacralize a potentially meaningless society and to legitimize the individual's position in that society, these writers are recalling for their readers a pluralistic past. In this way, their works should be read as a truly Malaysian literature, for although cultural pluralism may not be the region future, it is indeed the basis for its past.

NOTES

1 See, for example, Jan B. Gordon's one-sided and scathing essay, "The Crisis of Poetic Utterance: The Case of Singapore," where he announces, "There is abundant evidence that new artistic productions of quality are sorely lacking in Singapore, specifically, and in Southeast Asia generally." *Pacific Quarterly Moana*, IV: 1 (Jan. 1979), 9-16.
2 Like the West Indies, Malaysia and Singapore possess large emigrant groups of diverse racial and cultural backgrounds. Unlike the West Indies and more akin to African nations such

as Kenya and Ghana, the region retains also an aboriginal and indigenous society, and the Melanasian stock, recognized by the British as the proper "natives of the soil," after political independence was granted in 1957, has asserted its culture and language (Malay, Islamic, and Bahasa) as the national and politically legitimate one. Malaysia and Singapore share a common history of immigration, British colonialism, and Western acculturation; however, after decades of common rule, in 1967 Malaysia rejected Singapore from the Federation for fear of being overwhelmed by its predominantly Chinese and urban population. While I discuss the region as sharing in common characteristics, it is clear that literary development in both countries is growing markedly disparate. English is very much a minority language in Malaysia, while in Singapore it has grown to be the premier language of commerce, education, politics, and literature.

3 Despite what would appear to be more imposing demands on language and techniques, poetry, until very recently, was the favoured literary genre in the region. *The Second Tongue*, the latest anthology of poetry in English from Malaysia/Singapore, contains the most representative range of poetical attempts which in recent years have led to a number of books of poems disproportionate in the size of the reading public.

4 *Nataraja*, in Maniam's words "the cosmic dancer ringed by a circle of flames," is the motif of the South Indian copper images of the Lord of the Dance. As Ananda Coomaraswamy explains it, it is an iconic figure signifying Shiva as "Lord of Dancers...the manifestation of primal rhythmic energy." The novel's dramatic action parallels the five activities symbolized in Shiva's Dance:

Shrishti - creation; *Sthiti* - preservation;
Samhara - destruction; *Tirobhava* - illusion; and
Anugraha - salvation or the releaser.

BIBLIOGRAPHY

Afendras, E.A. and Kuo, Eddie C.V., editors. *Language and Society in Singapore*. Singapore: Singapore University Press, 1980.

Banks, David J., ed. *Changing Identities in Modern Southeast Asia*. The Hague: Mouton Publishers, 1976.

Baratham, Gopal. *Figments of Experience*. Singapore: Times Books International, 1981.

Burke, Kenneth. *Perspectives By Incongruity* and *Terms For Order*. ed. Stanley E. Hyman. Bloomington: Indiana University Press, 1964.

Burtt, E.A., ed. with commentary. *The Teachings of the Compassionate Buddha*. New York: The New American Library, 1955.

Chua, Rebecca. *The Newspaper Editor and Other Stories*. Singapore: Heinemann Educational Books (Asia) Ltd., 1981.

Coomaraswamy, Ananda K. *The Dance of Shiva*. New York: The Noonday Press, 1957.

Ee Tiang Hong. *Myths for a Wilderness*. Singapore: Heinemann Educational Books (Asia) Ltd., 1976.

Fernando, Lloyd. *Scorpion Orchid*. Kuala Lumpur: Heinemann Educational Books (Asia) Ltd., 1976.

Gordon, Jan B. "The Crisis of Poetic Utterance." *Pacific Quarterly Moana*, IV: 1 (Jan. 1979), 9-11.

Harrex, S.C. "Scapel, Scar, Icon: Lee Kok Liang's *Flowers in the Sky.*" *The Writer's Sense of the Contemporary*. ed. Bruce Bennett, et. al. (University of Western Australia: The Centre for Studies in Australian Literature, 1982), 35-40.

Hunter, Guy. *South-east Asia - Race, Culture, and Nation*. New York: University Press, 1966.

Jameson, Fredric, *Marxism and Form Twentieth Century Dialectical Theories of Literature*. Princeton, New Jersey: Princeton University Press, 1971.

Kirk, James A. *Stories of the Hindus*. New York: Macmillan, 1962.

Lee Kok Liang. *Mutes in the Sun*. Singapore: Heinemann Educational Books (Asia) Ltd., 1974.
Flowers in the Sky. Kuala Lumpur: Heinemann Educational Books (Asia) Ltd., 1981.

Lim, Catherine. *Little Ironies*. Singapore: Heinemann Educational Books (Asia) Ltd., 1978.
Or Else the Lightning God. Kuala Lumpur: Heinemann Educational Books (Asia) Ltd., 1979.
The Serpent's Tooth. Singapore: Times Books International, 1982.

Lim, Shirley. *Crossing the Peninsula and Other Poems*. Kuala Lumpur: Heinemann Educational Books (Asia) Ltd., 1980.
Another Country. Singapore: Times Books International, 1982.

Maniam, K.S. *The Return*. Kuala Lumpur: Heinemann Educational Books (Asia) Ltd., 1981.

McLeod, A.L. *The Commonwealth Pen*. Ithaca, New York: Cornell University Press, 1961.

Pye, Lucian and Verba, Sidney. *Political Culture and Political Development*. Princeton, New Jersey: Princeton University Press, 1965.

Rajendra, Cecil. *Bones and Feathers*. Singapore: Heinemann Educational Books (Asia) Ltd., 1978.

Ruland, Vernon, S.J. *Horizons of Criticism An Assessment of Religious-Literary Options*. Chicago: American Library Association, 1975.

Smith, Donald E. *Religion, Politics, and Social Change in the Third World*. New York: The Free Press, 1971.
Religion and Political Development. Boston: Little, Brown and Co., 1970.

Tan, Nalla, and Nair, Chandran, editors. *The Proceedings of the Seminar on Developing Creative Writing in Singapore*. Singapore: Woodrose Publishers, 1977.

Tennyson, G.B. and Ericson, Edward E., Jr., editors. *Religion and Modern Literature*. Grand Rapids, Michigan: William B. Eerdmans, 1975.

Thumboo, Edwin. *Gods Can Die*. Singapore: Heinemann Educational Books (Asia) Ltd., 1977.
ed. *The Second Tongue*. Singapore: Heinemann Educational Books (Asia) Ltd.

Tilman, Robert, ed. *Man, State, and Society in Contemporary Southeast Asia*. New York: Praeger, 1969.

Walcott, Derek. *The Castaway*. London: Jonathan Cape, 1965.

Wignesan, T. "Religion as Refuge, Or Conflict and Non-Change." *Journal of Commonwealth Literature*. XVI: 1 (August 1981), 76-86.

Wong May. *Superstitions*. New York: Harcourt Brace Jovanovich, 1978.

Yap, Arthur. *Down the Line*. Kuala Lumpur: Heinemann Educational Books (Asia) Ltd., 1980.

Yeo, Robert. *And Napalm Does Not Help*. Singapore: Heinemann Educational Books Ltd., 1977.

Zimmer, Heinrich. *Myths and Symbols in Indian Art and Civilization*. ed. Joseph Campbell, Princeton, New Jersey: Princeton University Press, 1974.

237

DR. C.W. WATSON
Introduction
to
THE RETURN

In a way reminiscent of Camara Laye's classic *L'Enfant Noir*, K.S. Maniam's autobiographical novel *The Return* charts the poignant journey of self-discovery of an Indian boy growing up in Malaya and gradually moving apart from his family and immediate surroundings. In the very movement of separation he is at the same time, through education, assimilating another culture. For the boy, this culture is perceived to be more rewarding and satisfying than the one in which he lives for two related reasons. In the first place the access to a new privileged knowledge which he acquires through his gradual mastery of English enables him to bring into a more objective focus the nature of the social relationships which surround him and which he is thus able to transcend. And second, the literature, and the colonial mythology which comes with it, have at the level of escapism, the capacity to take him out of himself. Thus the education provides for him not only a tool for understanding but also a space for retreat from the world of sordid everyday reality.

The novel can, then, be very easily and enjoyably read at this level, as a *Bildungsroman* detailing the education and intellectual formation of an unusual young man with all the sorrows and triumphs of experience which characterise this genre. In its scope, however, the novel attempts more than just this reconstruction of boyhood, and although additional subjects are not always properly or fully realised they are a significant part of the book. Within the ostensible description of the growth to manhood, for example, three related themes are incorporated; a sense of history, a sense of community and a sense of character. The first of these, history, is conveyed almost imperceptibly. There are no dates, no intrusive indications to the reader that there is some deliberate intention to evoke a time and a place. We are not only occasionally made aware that the period of the narrative falls between 1940 and 1962. The political events, the

Japanese occupation, the Emergency, Independence, are acknowledged, but, for the boy growing up, they lack the significance of
the passing of that other time of social and economic change.
The cinema, the radio, the bicycle and the car are some of the
emblems of that latter change. Most significant of all, however,
is the extension of educational provision, the addition of new
buildings to the school and, for the boy, the movement upwards
from one level of schooling to another, bringing at each stage a
renewed sense of achievement and at the same time a recognition of the increasing distance from the community of origin.

It is indeed this preoccupation with recording the distance
from the community which characterises much of the description within the narrative. It needs to be said that this is not a
romantic and sentimental evocation of community in any way.
On the contrary the representation is starkly realistic. This is a
community of Indian immigrants dependent on a system of
colonial patronage and cowed by the circumstances of the
rubber plantation economy from which they draw their liveli-
hood. It is a community turned in on itself, angry, shrewish,
violent, engaged in unremitting conflict, and dominated by the
seemingly arbitrary viciousness of the menfolk. One has read
descriptions of similar communities in Zola's *Germinal* and in
Lawrence's *Sons and Lovers* or Jasper's *A Hoxton's Childhood*.
The boy recognises himself as part of that way of life, but
gradually, with the growth of wisdom, he sees how he can
detach himself from it. He learns first that even within the
Indian community there are divisions and separations, and that
class and status are demarcated by territorial and social boundaries, which are graphically described in the novel. His first
triumph over the confines of the culture into which he has been
born occurs when a decision is made to stay on at school, thereby
implicitly announcing to the community that he is moving out of
the social status to which he has been ascribed. It is an announcement which, as the narrator describes, the community is
quick to acknowledge through added measures of respect and
deference. Prior to this, his friends had been his neighbours'
children, like Ganesh the boy from next door, but from the time
of secondary school in particular, it is his English speaking

classmates, of different ethnic and social backgrounds who will be his peers.

The community then is recreated in the novel but the distance which the narrator has travelled from it is reflected in the detached way in which its pettiness and misery are recorded. The same detachment is attempted in the description of individuals, but in this case the closeness which the narrator still feels to some of the characters undermines that detachment. Consequently there is a more unrestrained rendering of their extraordinary lives that gives strength to the novel. First appearing, it would seem, as foils to illustrate developments in the growing of self-awareness of the narrator, these individuals quickly acquire a larger stature, first the grandmother, then the eccentric schoolteacher, Miss Nancy, and recurring characters such as the supervisor Menon and Karupi, the boy's stepmother. Above all these, however, looms the character who is for the boy the locus of his own self-appraisal, his father. It is the latter who throughout the narrative implicitly controls the memory of events and determines how they are selected and recorded.

The muted chronicling of changing circumstances, the sober description of a community's style of living and the faithful representation of a set of extraordinary individuals infuse the novel with a textual richness which raises it above the level of a simple account of triumph over adversity. It certainly has its faults, mostly in terms of its stature - a frequent blurring of focus, a lack of balance between sections of the narrative - but the carefully nuanced vivid descriptions, the precise turns of phrase, the snatches of humour and the lyrical but never sentimental prose more than compensate for the imperfections of structure. It is not, ultimately the plot which gives the novel its force but that wonderfully wrought sense of kaleidoscopic life.

One final point, observing the way in which the story shifts between a concentration on the centrality of the narrator and a description of a place, a time and its people, the alert reader might be led to ponder the ambiguity of the title. What is the "Return" which is being celebrated? An answer to the question might be that there are at least three "returns" which we can distinguish: the return of the narrator back to Malaysia and his home after years abroad in England; the return of the autobiographer to the experience of childhood which he reconstructs in the writing; and, finally, the return, in the sense of a gift, a compensation, which the son makes in the form of the published novel presented to the family for them to set against the recorded disappointments and failures along the way. All three "returns" need to be given due weight by the reader.

The growing reputation of *The Return* is much deserved, and its reappearance in this new edition some twelve years after its first publication will allow new readers a rare opportunity to enter imaginatively into a certain kind of Malaysian experience which is, paradoxically perhaps, both highly specific and yet universally representative.

Dr C.W. Watson is a Senior Lecturer at the Department of Social Anthropology, University of Kent at Canterbury.

My other memories were of a lush, green countryside, cloud-striated sky, the cooking place with my mother's glistening face among the pots, and a distant shed, without walls, where my father worked. When my legs were stronger he led me there and allowed me to romp on the rich, thick grass. I moved with the shadow towards the shed until, at midday, I way cowering beside the huge water tub between the thrashing stone and the cauldron. Then my father took me home for lunch.

Left at home, I gave my mother no peace. The house had only two rooms. Half of each room was taken up by a large, wooden, platform. During the day it served as table, sitting dais and a place for resting. At night mats were rolled out, coverlets found and the platforms became sprawling beds. Beneath these trestles, for lack of storing space, were pushed the tins that held rice, chillies, flour, sugar and biscuits. Inside this low, crowded interior, almost tucked away from sight, were garish tin trunks. It was the graying cloth draped over them like a shroud that attracted my attention. At the sound of tins, plates and glass jars tumbling down my mother bawled at me and dragged me out. Finally, I got to the trunks, my mother gone three houses away, and made a fascinating discovery.

Fortunately my mother wasn't within hearing distance. What a solid clatter the contents made! Brass statuettes, bronze lamps, and silver trays came cascading out. I had never seen such lamps before; the squat, kerosine containers, with a wick jutting out, were incomparable to these. Tall, three-tier lamps with multiple spouts, single, hand-worked ones, stand-lamps resembling the globe and the sun! Moulding cardboard pieces held strange patterns; greenish, square and round coins, the Chinese coffee-shop owner beyond the hospital kitchen wouldn't accept, littered the bottom of these tin trunks. My mother's return curtailed further exploration.

I needn't have worried about seeing those lamps again. They appeared all over the house one dark month that year. They flickered in the cooking place, the corners of the house, at the drains beyond and in the centre of the two rooms. Two majestic tier lamps, with a long, tapering stem, burned in the last two places. My mother gave us "palm" cakes. These were sweetened, containing green-pea mash inside and the outside covered with oil. I went from lamp to lamp turning up the wicks, and fell asleep near one of them, keeping vigil.

Later that year I witnessed my first Deepavali. Again lamps played a significant part. Besides the oil lamps already placed in strategic sections of each house, gaslights flooded the long corridor that connected all the cubicle-like houses. Goats that the long-house community had bought and reared for the occasion were slaughtered. The last bleats lingered in my mind as did the red tinge in the sky at sunset. Govindan and Thoplan pumped up the gaslights. The boys brought in the banana leaves and spread them out on the floor. Arokian and Govindan strung the goat carases to the rafter and started skinning them with their short, sharp knives. The air filled with a stench of raw flesh and blood. Boys caught the hunks of meat the two skinners threw at them and plumped them out on the banana leaves.

The feasting began even as the skinners scraped the fat from the meat. Tiny slices of the fat were roasted over coal fires for the very young boys. Older ones singed the goat head, split the skull, gouged out the brain lobes and swallowed them. The goat trotters were burnt over the regular fires and dumped into the soup pot. No one ate rice that night. They spooned trotter soup into their mouths, munching the bones as they watched the mutton being apportioned. The women carried away basins and began the cooking for Deepavali. Entrails were cleaned with hot water, salt rubbed in and a spicy curry made. The unmarried girls (there were a couple to each household), made the thosais on the flat "stone" and families gobbled them throughout the night. Finally the gaslights were put out; people took their rest wherever they were. And at first cockcrow, sitting before the bronze oil lamps or kerosine ones, we were massaged with gingelly oil and sent off in pairs to the cauldron of hot water at the laundry shed. But I only remember the lamps, large, blue-tinged auras on the air, the flames burning steadily.

These festivals, together with *Thaipusam* and *Ponggal*, created a special country for us. We were inhabitants of an invisible landscape tenuously brought into prominence by the lights, mango leaves strung out over the doorways, the pilgrimages to Sri Subramanya temple in Sungai Petani on Thaipusam day, the painting of the bull horns the day after Ponggal and the many taboos that covered our daily lives. We weren't allowed out of the house between midday and two o'clock: the spirits of the dead would be about. Whenever we left for a long trip, we couldn't glance over our shoulders at the house or say, "I'm going". You had to utter: "I'm coming". With these gestures and words you ensured continued existence. One wrong move brought you to the gates of Neraka, hell. Neraka was evoked for us on gramaphone records. Yaman's voice - the man who led us to hell - had a hoarse, frightening tone.

How does one describe the land one lived in but never saw? It was more tangible than the concrete one we flitted through every day. Darkness gave it its true dimensions. Then it vibrated within our hearts. If we saw, perhaps through some quirk of optics, a flame beside the drain, then it was a dead pregnant woman's soul come to haunt the real world; if we heard murmurs, echoed voices among the hills, they were the chanting and tinkling of banana-tree spirits dancing in the courtyard of the night. The quick rush of water in the communal bathshed signified some unappeased soul's feverish bathing. We were hemmed into our rooms, houses, and into our minds. But for all these, there were a lot of colours in our invisible world. The gigantic figures that filled our imagination were turned out in bright togas, arms heavily braceletted, necks studded with gold and heads aureoled by intricate crowns. Fair, gentle men and women (gods and goddesses, I suppose), fought off the more scheming and brutal characters in battles that clashed over our sleeping heads. The tension between good and evil shimmered therefore like an inevitable consciousness within our heads.

We were a gentle people guided and ruled by dreams. Some of these were innocent, others as violent as the thunder and

---

Thaipusam - Hindu festival of repentance.
Ponggal - First day of the first month in the Hindu calendar.

lightning that ripped the sky and destroyed a calm evening. One such bolt fell on me when I had been attending the Tamil school in Bedong for a year. My father suddenly decided to take me out of the school and enrol me in The English School, later renamed Tengku Mahkota, in Sungai Petani. Karupi, my step-mother, was largely responsible for the transfer.

My father had taken Karupi and her sister, Ragini, into the household in an act of kindness. He had promised her dying mother that he would bring them up and marry them off. But when Karupi turned eighteen, ugly rumours circulated among our neighbours. My father took her to the Civil Registry in Sungai Petani to put a stop to all the talk. The submissive, quiet young woman changed into an outgoing, worldly-wise unproclaimed ruler of the household. My mother's voice rose hardly above a whisper, and only in the kitchen.

Karupi related a dream to us one morning:

"You might have heard me shouting in my sleep last night. I had a terrible dream. It's afternoon and we're taking a nap. The house is crowded with all kinds of things: radiogram, ice-box, varnished desk, silver lamps, bedsteads, large mattresses. Ravi, who isn't napping, drinks out of a golden cup in the kitchen.

"Suddenly there's an ear-deafening noise - a cry in a foreign voice. The sleepers all sit up on their comfortable beds. A white man, wearing a coat and tie, rushes at us. There's an axe in his hand. He says terrible things in a language we don't understand. Then he starts hacking away at the things we've just acquired. We try to stop him, talking in our language. But he shakes his head and the axe splinters the beds; the cotton flies and we're almost drowned. Out of this mist the white man's face appears.

"He says, 'Send the boy to English School!'

"He points at Ravi."

I remember my father's laughter. Still chuckling, he returned to sorting the dirty clothes before going to the laundry.

Karupi had spoken one sentence of English.

"Have I used the white man's tongue before?" she said. "Your father thinks the dream is to be laughed at."

She barked at us the whole day. Then she moved from house to house retelling, enlarging and shrilling over the dream. She repeated the English sentence. The neighbours smiled at her contemptuously. Karupi returned, offended and determined. She didn't attend to my father's needs during lunch.

We were familiar with such behaviour. When my father began preparing me for the Tamil school, she had sulked. He went ahead, amused most of the time, irritated occasionally. She wouldn't co-operate. I had already begun helping her with the laundry work. I came to the lunch my mother served drenched by the sun and feeling faint. My mother sometimes went into a huff. Only when she cried to have me beside her was I excused from afternoon chores.

Karupi almost succeeded in blocking my entry into the Tamil school. She would hunt out even the most secret of hiding places where my father put away the money for the initiation ceremony. He finally gave it to Thoplan, the hospital cook and Karupi's enemy, for safe-keeping. Then she turned her attention to the goat being fattened for the occasion.

"Don't let it wander around!" she yelled from the doorway. "It might eat the wrong things and become impure."

When the goat was tethered for the night and if my father wasn't around, she slipped a five-cent coin into my palm and freed the animal.

"Chase it around until it gets tired," she said. "The meat might get fatty if it doesn't get enough exercise."

I would harrass the animal, pushing and poking it on, past the laughing neighbourhood. When my father heard about it he beat me saying I wasn't to torture animals. Karupi didn't talk to him or me for a week. Then she smiled at us in a strange, over-friendly manner.

Basked by his own dreams, my father had enlisted Murugesu's talents. Murugesu had been specially brought out from India for the Tamil school in Riverside Estate. He didn't last for more than three months. Even after two years of disillusionment in Malaysia, he retained that stimulating air of scholarship and imagination. He could make you forget you were listening to a story when he told it. This very ability destroyed his future. Young tapper-girls hung around the classroom, feigning sickness to get out of their daily tapping. The young men ganged up, accused him of seducing these girls, and had him dismissed from his teaching post. Murugesu refused to move out of his estate quarters or to defend himself. He merely went round the Indian homes coaching the children in Tamil.

He shared, wholeheartedly, my father's visions for me. Bathed, and smelling of *sireh* juice, he came punctually to the house. Karupi took an instant dislike to him. She made a clamour in the kitchen or drew away the children with embroidered tales of her hardship. But after the goat incident, she was in the front room almost all the time. Murugesu became immediately inhibited.

"Have a glass of tea, Teacher," Karupi said, ambling in.

Murugesu gazed at the glass as at some defiled object. He shook his head. But Karupi left it on a stool beside him. At the end of the lesson he asked me for a glass of water. When my father returned after delivering clothes, Murugesu hurriedly said goodbye.

Karupi enacted this scene for a whole week.

"Your teacher friend thinks we're unclean," she remarked to my father.

"Leave him alone," my father said.

"He insults our dignity and you turn your face away," Karupi said.

My father laughed.

On Fridays Murugesu made me carry out a *puja* at the house shrine. The Tamil Primer was placed before the picture of Saraswathi, the goddess of learning. The incense-brazier trembled in my hands as I waved it three times round the shrine and the book. Sometimes an abrupt grunt came from Murugesu. I stopped the puja and looked at him. He would nod his head at the doorway. My mother, forgetting I was saying prayers, would have come into the room for a towel or a *vesti*. Murugesu didn't like women in the room while I conducted the puja. Karupi came into the room so often that I couldn't complete the ritual that Friday. Murugesu taught me absent-mindedly and returned home with a distraught face. At last my father had to intervene.

"You take a stranger's side against your own wife?" Karupi said. "How's this boy going to learn the right virtues?"

---

sireh - Leaf chewed with lime and betel nut shavings.
puja - Ritualised prayed.
vesti - White cloth worn by Indian men.

247

My father had to stay home on Friday evenings.

Boys of my age in that hospital compound were mostly attending The English School in Sungai Petani. Their fathers wore *Bose* caps, swaggered aggressively and wanted their children to speak English. They doubted my father's political loyalties, his need to cling to the Tamil tongue and Indian religious practices so tenaciously. They laughed at him; they pointed derisively at our house while buying fish from the Chinese man who cycled in with his tin tub.

The Primer I took off the shelf-shrine every Friday evening, after the puja, had the gloss of a mysterious, rich world. The ornamental oil lamp, with leaf motifs, the back domed, threw a cool band of yellow light on the cover and my hands. The incense filled me with a sense of comfort and wonder. On such nights my voice deepened as I reeled off the alphabet. Murugesu looked like a god himself, pot-bellied, remote and radiating with warmth. The night seemed like a chamber whose walls would suddenly fall apart and reveal a more radiant landscape. I carried some of this light into my excursions into the land beyond the hospital fence, into the hidden kampung huts and the river further on. Everything seemed so clear and plausible.

Karupi had her last laugh on the day of the initiation. A large crowd had gathered in the house. Menon, the Chief Dresser and administrator, had been extended a special invitation. The air flew with speculations about my intelligence, over the incense and camphor smells. Goat *kurma* spiked the conversation and the final preparations for the ceremony. I had faster the whole day and stood in the room, the focus of attention, trembling expectantly.

Trays of bananas, oranges and apples stood on the floor. Another contained a specially decorated coconut, the shell rubbed completely with saffron paste, a cone of husk left intact at the top, and dotted with *kumkum*. On a make shift pedestal was smoothed out a layer of white sand. Menon arrived and, with Murugesu officiating as priest, the ceremony began. The gestures

---

Bose - Patriotic cap worn in honour of Subash Chandra Bose.
kurma - Spicy mutton preparation.
kumkum - Red powder used as decorative dots on an Indian
   woman's forehead.

came from me with a deep sureness. Murugesu's Sanskrit chanting covered me with a vibrant sensitivity. Everything went smoothly until it came to writing the symbol for *Aum* on the white sand. While I was reciting the first few letters of the alphabet, Karupi sniggered. Then the fatal laugh struck. Though I ignored it, I couldn't make the character for "Aum" easily. I succeeded after the third time, but the unexpected disastrous clapping made me shake violently.

The applause spread uncertainly at the beginning, then with the destructive roar of a wave. Karupi had stolen the show once more, clapping as if she were more moved by the spirit of the occasion than I. Late that night she whimpered as my father thrashed her with a rattan cane. But the next morning my father took me on his rickety bicycle to the green building in town.

I had a wonderful time there until Karupi's dream broke into my life. Our neighbours taunted Karupi.

"Send him to English School," they said whenever they passed my house.

My father's face took on a sullen look.

Karupi went on a fast. She was still a healthy, talkative woman ten days later, when my father announced his decision to send me to The English School in Sungai Petani.

The world I had known fell apart. My walk into town - the intolerable year had to be finished - was a nostalgic, upsetting one. The Chinese constable at the railway gates, the sweet, rotting smells from the fruit stalls, the reeking drains at shop corners, all turned foreign. The thought that the sky I had known also domed over other towns, frightened me. I imagined strange assaults of crowds in unfamiliar surroundings. My trips into Sungai Petani had been rare and in my child's eyes the town was a sprawling mass of shops and wide, open fields almost touching the horizon.

Murugesu, drafted into the school begun only that year, had proved to be more than a teacher. I saw him poised and pulling us towards urgent discovery. He added the other familiar dimension to my landscape. The textbooks, specially ordered from India, contained fields, jungles and characters I felt for

---

Aum - The fourth state of supreme consciousness.

and understood. How much of these came from Periathai's own fund of knowledge I can't gauge. Elephants, deer, snakes, mongooses, dogs and cats filled the corners of the house in the hospital compound with frightening and delightful presences. The tortoise made a slow but dignified appearance. The mongoose, though scrawny and smelly, had its attraction: it fought and killed the much-revered cobra that nearly sank its fangs into a sleeping infant. Strict loyalties were undependable, even discouraged. The lines of curving, intricate Tamil writing unfolded an excitingly unexpected and knowable world. Murugesu tied most of these stories to people and incidents we knew. These characters came alive in the shopkeepers, goldsmiths, newspaper-vendor, *chettiar* and labourer we saw daily.

What a wrench it was that first day we rode the bus to The English School! I bounced on the rattan seat all the way. The grinding, rickety red bus, a cream line across its body, disgorged us at the junction. My father hailed a trishaw and the man pedalled us uphill to the school. Under the old, tall *angsana* trees stood the fathers with their sons. The ground, littered with yellow flowers, marked off a new territory. I wandered around, dazed, brushing against the men impeccably dressed in trousers and long-sleeved shirts. Some trishaw riders had brought their sons. They smiled uncomfortably, stiff in their best clothes, beckoning the boys out of the vehicles.

The school, consisting of a single, double-storied block, impressed us with its colonial architecture. A Chinese sat at a large desk on the porch. Dressed in well-pressed pants, a thin, black tie pinned rigidly to the shirt front, he rifled through piles of papers, all the time sternly keeping curious onlookers away. The pairs of huge pillars around the porch rose monumentally towards the roof. A broad staircase led off into a corridor and gloomy, large rooms. The Chinese called, efficiently and at regular intervals, the names of the boys, and the fathers stumbled up the stairs with them.

"Ravi!"

---

chettiar - Commonly known as a money-lender among the Indians in Malaysia.
angsana - Local perennial, broad trunk, yellow flowers.

250

My father flung his black cigar down and, clutching me by the hand, ascended the steps. It seemed hours, my father being directed a few times, before we reached the interviewing panel. The men occupied an oblong room over the porch. My first view of them, against the spreading angsana branches and patches of the blue, morning sky, was astounding. It was truly another sphere altogether. Several men waited, like male nurses, on the white-coated Englishman who occupied a high, rattan chair. A couple of men guided me to another chair opposite his and I gazed at his tomato-hued face across a desert of varnished wood. The Englishman spoke all the time through the upper row of yellow and glistening teeth. Then he shuffled the papers and I was released from the confining chair.

Abruptly I found myself seated in a very silent room, at a desk, facing a square-lined exercise book. Strange, squiggly marks swam on the page. Other boys sat gazing at these same signs. A fair-complexioned woman stood behind a large desk on a platform, the clean blackboard a contrast to her shock of raven hair. She wore a frilled skirt and a starched blouse. We gazed at her as she mimed some incomprehensible activity.

"Write!" she commanded.

We looked at each other, bewildered, one boy whimpering for his father.

"Shut up!"

The voice had a raucous, imperious edge to it and, fumbling, but with one accord, we grasped the pencil on the groove of the desk and bent over the book. I looked at the board and at my exercise book - both contained the same, unfinished creatures and stiff poles. Recalling my first days in the Tamil school, I traced over these shapes. Then, excited by the thickening stumps, curving branches and window frames, I pressed my pencil hard against the picture that formed. Still, it didn't make as much sense as my first lesson at the Tamil school. I looked to my left, beyond the corridor, to the inaccessible trees and hills. The thick jungle infuriated me. Determined to reduce the bloated squiggles to some meaning, I added my own lines. I had accidentally discovered the code - they were really incomplete numbers!

My triumph was short-lived. To my right, boys were moaning under the teacher's slaps!

"Keep your heads down!"

The ripple of panic reached the row beside mine. A big hulk of an Indian boy made the sound that follows a meal of rice and onion curry with plenty of asafoetida in it. For some reason I felt comfortable again. Then the air filled with a damp, pungent smell.

The teacher walked hurriedly to the boy's desk. A spluttering noise greeted her arrival. The boy stood up, his palms spread over his buttocks. Laughter filled the room. The teacher stamped her foot, held her nose and staggered to her desk. Even the offender couldn't held laughing.

"Get him out of here! Clean up the mess!" she yelled before she slumped down on the chair behind the protective desk.

The class tittered and scrambled to help. The boy, Aandy, round-faced, into which were sunk two vacant, blue eyes, smiled as he was led away. Boys surrounded him, as a Roman dignitary would be on his way to the public baths. Those who remained hunted for a pail and mop and swabbed up the splotches.

"Whew! What a smell!" the teacher whined in a high, un-natural voice.

"She no backside ah?" one of the swabbers said in Tamil.

The incident banished the clinical atmosphere from the room. A hilarious note was added to the already rowdy scene when Aandy returned, flapping, in a gardener's oversized shorts. But Miss Nancy, the teacher, had resumed command.

"That'll do," she said sternly.

We were issued glossy books, each page containing a picture, a letter and a word. The pages were splashed with orange, gray and brown, colours that immediately awed and attracted us. They transported us into a pleasant, unreachable land. The ground we walked on was dusty or black or the paths twisted, knobbled here and there with roots. I sometimes led the occasional goat my family reared to very lush, even wild, under-growth. You heard a wet slither through the mottled bushes, a dry snap among the entangled, deep green. I stood, my attention focused by my fright, listening to a hint of creeping, rustling, mysterious life.

"A for apple," we chorused after the teacher.

"B for boy!"

"C for cart!"

"D for Dobbin!"

"E for Ernie!"

That was all we got to that afternoon. But we were already bewildered and fascinated. Dobbin and Ernie absorbed our tiny souls. Dobbin looked like a horse but its knowing eyes disconcerted me. Tufts of fur around the hooves, thick neck and broad, hefty body gave an unpleasant impression of strength. The "boy" had reappeared as "Ernie". I scrutinised him, bending down to the desk. He had tidy, tawny hair, feet sheathed in thick shoes, and he stood gazing at a scatter of yellow flowers. His face was an outline on the page, eyes set marbles of blue. He didn't rise out of the page as Sivam, the village lout, had done in the Tamil Primer.

"Ernie, Ernie, Ernie," I chanted in a whisper all the way back home.

The sound turned on strange lights inside my mind. As the bus bounced me back towards Bedong, the dusk, a heavy mist beyond the windows, caught and echoed the squelch of the tyres. I seemed to be rushed through the cold air into a scentless, nebulous region of swirling, bright colours. The rugged harshness of the rattan seats I had been thrown by in the morning, had disappeared. When I reached home my mother's dark face had a smile I didn't recognise. My body was already encrusted with sleep as she bathed me in warm water, in the communal bathroom, the familiar insect sounds falling away into the distance. Though I had bright dreams that night, some intolerable darkness pinched at my heart.

© K.S. Maniam, 1993.

The Return has been reissued by Skoob *PACIFICA*, London with an Introduction by Dr. C.W. Watson and an Afterword by Dr. Anne Brewster.
Direct orders: SKOOB TWO, Tel: 071-405 0030 or fax 071-404 4398 GBP£5.99 U.K. post free.

OOI BOO ENG
A Note in Preview:
The Return

I have had the pleasure of reading K.S. Maniam's novel *The Return* in manuscript and I should like here to give a preview of it, very brief as it must be since I ought not to pre-empt as much room as a review can more appropriately lay claim to in order to make convincing what there is to be said. Without the space for a patient and self-effacing presentation I will say my piece in general, assertive and personal terms. I had better, then, say right away that I really do believe that *The Return* when published will be a thoroughly respectable item in the steadily lengthening list of Heinemann's Writing in Asia Series.

One way for a reader to try for as much objectivity as can be hoped for in the evaluation of a new work is to have the work under consideration stood up against all other works of the same genre so far published in the series. I have done this a number of times in my mind and I have no doubt that it does stand up well with all the fiction published to date by Malaysian/Singapore authors (and perhaps, too, with the rest by other Asian authors in the series). If *those*, why not *this*? The case, though, is rather stronger than this. It isn't just that *The Return* is no worse than any published Malaysian/Singaporean fiction volume in English one cares to name; in my mind *The Return* bids fair to take a place among the top two or three, whatever these are agreed to be.

The moment I began reading past the first three or four sentences of *The Return* the feeling came, subdued but definite enough, that this was going to be good. That response has a lot to do with something in the quality of the writing and the adjustment of its focus: a style that in terms of diction and phrasing/syntax/movement is almost always lucid and simple - deceptively simple in that (a) it says what is to be said without drawing undue attention to itself and (b) it can at times suggest more than what seems to be said without straining itself to do so; and a focus that can manage factual or concrete observation or description while at the same time making of the observation something that comes with some degree of symbolic overtone to it.

Consider, for example, the beginning of the novel. I can't recall any Malaysian/Singaporean novel which takes off as confidently and simply with the creation of the sense of an opening: 'My grandmother's life and her death, in 1958, made a vivid impression on me. She came, as the stories and anecdotes about her say, suddenly out of the horizon, like a camel, with nothing except some baggage and three boys in tow. And like that animal that survives the most barren of lands, she brooded, humped over her tin trunks, mats, silver lamps and pots, at the junction of the main road and the laterite trail. Later she went up the red, dusty path, into the trees and bushes, the most undeveloped part of Bedong. The people of this small town didn't know how she managed...' It would be a pleasure to go on quoting; this is the kind of writing, not sufficiently common in Malaysian/Singaporean novels, which can bear close, reasoned analysis. Here I have to limit myself to point to a few things impressionistically. Words and phrases are simple but they work with a spot-on effectiveness; 'out of the horizon', for example, is a common phrase but it is just the phrase - as good as any, at any rate, that can be reached for - for creating the impression of a figure nowhere in sight one moment, then very much there the next; 'three boys in tow' is, again, a common phrase but it is idiomatic and registers a subdued humorous attitude to the image of a displaced person determinedly holding on to what she considers essentials, including three boys dragged along with her willy-nilly, nothing unusual about the verb 'brooded' in itself except that it is so much better than 'stood', the verb expected in the context of a phrase like 'at the junction of...' - a verb which would convey the meaning of coming to a pause, a momentary state of inaction, without the suggestion registered in 'brooded' of something like taking thought because of some anxiety or uncertainty; and 'humped' is just the word - it sustains the simile of 'like a camel'. Another aspect inviting comment is that this is a passage of recall, of piecing together anecdotal bits about the grandmother, and the way the passage moves somehow gives the impression of a quietly relaxed concentration given to the recalling. The flow of

255

the syntax of phrasing is smooth without being flaccid or headlong; on the contrary, the easy flow is controlled unobtrusively to bring emphasis to bear where emphasis is needed: the placing of the adverb 'suddenly' *enacts* the meaning of it rather than merely expressing it; and 'brooded' is so placed that the pause induced naturally by the demand of the phrasing gives it a weighted significance - makes 'brooded', in other words, brood. Finally, one of the underlying 'motifs' of the novel as a whole is already there in the passage: the 'motif', that is, of some deeply felt human urge driving a displaced person to strive not just for survival but for a survival that leaves something of the person's past - call it identity or roots (here symbolized in the grandmother's paraphernalia from her past life) - intact.

The point I want to make in going on at such length on a short passage is that here is a Malaysian/Singaporean novelist - Lloyd Fernando is, I think, the only other one - who shows evidence of being able to work into something brief and simple an ample and varied resonance of meaningfulness.

I must say that when K.S. Maniam read the whole opening chapter at a session of 'Readings in Commonwealth Literature' organized by the Malaysian Association for Commonwealth Literature and Language Studies the applause was discreet but far from perfunctory; it was, I thought, spontaneous and sincere - in response, I think, to qualities of the kind pointed to above.

I must also admit to thinking, at one stage of my mulling over the novel, that there was a falling off in quality and presentation through the last quarter or so of it. But on re-reading and re-thinking I began to realize that I had failed to give weight to the possibility that what at first I took to be an inadequacy of perception on the part of the author could be intended as some blindness on the part of the first-person narrator (Ravi) to see and sympathize with the 'dreams' of his father (and grandmother); a refusal almost to see and understand because of too much self-concern. The very end of the novel then takes on the aspect of something deliberately disjunctive - a sort of coda or epilogue which gives notice that with time and brooding insight begins to come and promises to deepen. The first chapter, then, demonstrates the insight achieved which makes it possible for Ravi to give, in a manner marked by both emphatic identification and detached observation, an account of his grandmother who comes across as a person, a character and a force or energy generated by the human need to have a place in the sun in more than the sense of making enough to live on. Seen thus the first chapter falls into place in the design of the novel as a prologue complementing the epilogue referred to above. The epilogue leaves the novel open-ended, allowing for the possiblity of a sequel which could concern itself among other things with imagining through in detail how the insight struggled for and shown implicitly (in the first chapter) to have been achieved is in fact achieved.

Before making a final assertion I ought to say that I hope no expectation has been given of the writing being sustained everywhere at the level of the passage commented on above. Here and there some rephrasing or re-touching may be called for; but there are no abysmal lapses; and it would not take a lot of searching to turn up other stretches in the writing which can stand up well to some such scrutiny as that tried out on the passage quoted.

The Return deserves being seriously reviewed when it comes out, any day now.

© Ooi Boo Eng, 1981.

OOI BOO ENG was formerly Associate Professor in the English Department, University of Malaya and is now in Melbourne.

ISBN 981 01 2061 3 pbk pp184

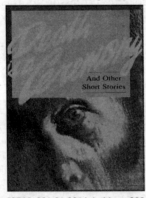

ISBN 981 01 2062 1 pbk pp168

ISBN 981 01 2214 4 pbk pp208

FLOWERS IN THE SKY
Lee Kok Liang

This compelling first novel, written with an English native-speaker's flair but distinctly Asian voice, joins the local literary scene like a waft of fresh air, a welcome revivification from the puff pieces that abound. Set in an unnamed Malaysian seaside city, the story follows five days in the life of the seeminglyquiet, serene monk and lonely, worldly surgeon. As the events unfold, both separately come to terms with their own limitations and strengths.

The Mutes in the Sun
AND OTHER STORIES
Lee Kok Liang

"The author's awareness of his own craftsmanship enables him to write with sureness and with the economy of precision.(In his stories Lee Kok Liang) finds communication between human beings and the outside world even when it is cruel, stupid and non-communicative. He is a poet."

- Times Educational Supplement, London

Death is a Ceremony
AND OTHER SHORT STORIES
Lee Kok Liang

The 12 short stories in this book cover a wide spectrum of human experience: from a writer who is unable to enter the orbit of his Western friends to a young, curious boy who innocently touches his cousin's behind to, still, a successful man who is crippled by the wayward behaviour of his mentally sick wife; and then there are the political prisoner and the Muslim convert, each searching for his peace.

Federal Publications (S) Pte Ltd
1 New Industrial Road, Singapore 1953

PART THREE

Other Literatures
of
the Pacific Rim

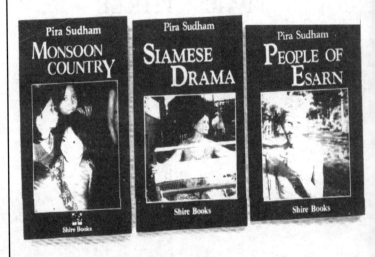

MARCUS RICHARDS
Interview with Pira Sudham
at the Flinders University of S.A.
September 1991

CRNLE: Pira Sudham, you have written perhaps the first English language novels from Thailand. What is the impulse behind your writing?

PS: Social and political changes have taken place in Thailand during the past thirteen years. In my novel *Monsoon Country* I dated each chapter using historical facts more or less chronologically. I am very concerned with what is happening, and what may happen, in the next ten years in Thailand. People ask me whether I would write on my experiences in Australia and Europe, but I consider that that's not the task that I set out to do. A lot of writers can write about these countries but I want to write about the society that I know best. That to me is more worthwhile, because it is very rare that someone from the rice fields of Thailand can be eloquent and write in the English language to tell people around the world about the grass roots of their lives: what is happening there and what has happened. There was a drive in me and I felt this calling very early. I felt it was put to me, by fate, that I could see and be the voice or the eye of the people in my area. Normally our people, the Esarn people of north-eastern Thailand, are very submissive, in very passive communities, and they are not accustomed to making an outcry or making grievances known they are very quiet and they suffer quietly. They have great tolerance for suffering because of the poverty, because of the drought areas and because of the lack of opportunities including education and employment, so I would like to bring these things that I have seen in the past and that I project will happen into a work of art or literature so that what I write may last longer than my own life. I

CRNLE: speak on their behalf on the subjects that people in our society don't discuss or other writers in Thailand don't write about.

CRNLE: How do you see your readership?

PS: In Thailand at the beginning when the books where published, the audience tended to be limited to expatriates or English-speaking communities, but now gradually through their own changing values, Thais, my countrymen, have come to read my books. As bookshop keepers have told me, now Thai people are taking interest. Apart from academics in the university, Thai people are beginning to heed what I am writing about, but that still remains a minority compared to the world-wide audience. My books have been well received in the USA and Europe because publishers in Europe are now producing my books in many languages. I have also sold the rights to a North American publisher.

CRNLE: How common is English language writing in Thailand? Is it a deliberate choice to write in English? Is it the attraction of the language or is it a political mode?

PS: I think it is all of those. I wanted to write when I was quite young. I started writing in Thailand when I was in secondary school, simple stories, about life in villages in Thailand. Then when I was a Commonwealth Plan student in New Zealand I was drawn into the power of literature and was so impressed by people like James Joyce, George Orwell, Emily Bronte and many others of the great English writers. I thought that if I could use them as a frame of reference even though my writing may not be as great, people from outside of Thailand may have read it and then through the power of writing they will come back to Thailand in their thinking. If your country is limited, you move out to England, Africa. I want people to accept their own writing. Another point is the fact that because of my study of English literature my admiration for writers in the English language and the English language is great. If you look at the Thai language we don't have punctuation marks for example. Words are spun together in one line and you can make space between words when you want to start a new line. So it is just like a garland of flowers. You can string them together and then you can make a sentence, so it is quite a loose way of putting words together. It is easier than English and it reflects many things about our mentality. When you compare the English language to French and German, which are very formal and rigid in sentence structure, you can not move, but the English language gives you some flexibility. You can express yourself in a freer form than in German or in French. So to me English is a suitable medium to express myself in but my difficulties lie in the fact that it is not my language; it is a language that I have a good command of and I have spent more than thirty years not only as a linguist but as a writer who wants to use is as a medium of expression.

CRNLE: On the content of the books themselves: your characters are unique and beautifully drawn. Do you have any English language authors as influences?

PS: Yes, definitely. There is George Orwell above all. Essays like those in *Inside the Whale* discuss the way we manipulate language and the way that language reflects our mentality. Orwell stresses the usage of simple over difficult words. He cited how politicians and scientists use words to camouflage, to make murder sound acceptable, to make holocaust sound acceptable. On the other hand, Joyce is also the master of the language. He is such a great artist.

CRNLE: I would have thought that they were rather contrary in their approaches to language, Orwell and Joyce.

PS: They both try to use language to tell you the state of the mind at that moment of consciousness or sub-consciousness.

CRNLE: Would you say your writing is suspended between the conscious and sub-conscious?

PS: My aim is to put simple words together in such a way that poetic truths are suggested.

CRNLE: Your sympathies imply criticism of the Thai system, but you tread a careful line between nuance and outright criticism.

PS: Politically, criticism is a very sensitive thing to write. Just before I left a Thai writer escaped and now lives in Sweden. His name is Sulak Srivalak. He is quite well known, and in a lecture he gave at the University at Bangkok, he criticised the military in the way that an intelligent person would: but in our society we are not allowed to speak out. Therefore he had to leave the country because the military was after him for putting up arguments against the Thai military. Because I don't write in Thai, it appears that I don't address our populace directly. What I talk about is not to be read directly by poor peasants, I don't address the Thai audience directly, and also because I write in the English language, much between the lines and I know how to be careful. I choose to be more subtle.

CRNLE: Would you say that some of your approaches, rather than being confrontationist, show the subtlety of your Buddhist background?

PS: Yes, it may have indirect influence in the way I deal with life and the way I express myself. We were taught to be very tolerant but I tend to leave that behind as a writer. On the other hand, we were brought up as devout Buddhists, and my parents taught me many things about tolerance, about Karma, the vicious circle, that whatever we suffer in this life, our poverty, our shortcomings, our misgivings, are the results of deeds done in a previous lives. Now I was personally brought up by my parents not to make too much noise, not to speak out, not even to *see* what's happening around me, not to speak against the evil and the wrong doers. When I left Thailand to study in overseas cities, I found that, as in your society, you are brought up to speak up, to enjoy literature and to love yourself and to think critically. How can you write an essay about a book if you don't think critically? So in a way I revolted against the way I was brought up. I saw myself as having been thoroughly crippled during my childhood years. I didn't have a mind of my own. I couldn't see the many sides of things.

CRNLE: What you are saying about Buddhism, doesn't come through strongly in your books. Do you feel that you have developed a basic humanitarian approach? Are there other elements that have replaced Buddhism?

PS: My approach comes from my Buddhist background because we were taught to have compassion for other people. I hope this compassion can be seen in my writing; we see the sufferings of the poor as our own. I experienced village poverty in my childhood, and pity and sorrow for the suffering and misery of our people became almost like an energy to me. Somehow I did not accept these sufferings, even though we were taught that we should accept them as our fate. These are human conditions that can be changed. I saw that what happened in France on July 14th over 200 years ago could not happen in Thailand. Buddhism or the belief in Karma becomes like a huge cushion that cushions you against the feeling that it is not your fault, the feeling that you can try to force something to happen and try to improve yourself. So you see in Bangkok, great city of Thailand, the wealthy men riding by in their air-conditioned Mercedes and the poor wait at the bus stop for hours, queueing up and pressing each other forward into the bus. Then I sometimes ask myself, what do they see, what do they feel when they see the rich and the wealthy ones riding by in their Mercedes, or Volvo?

CRNLE: What comes out strongly in, for example, *People in Esarn*, with a portrait of that part of Bangkok, the issues that come up, and the struggles the people go through when they go to Bangkok, are those other images of bargirl and prostitutes. Is that your Bangkok or do you see another side to Bangkok, related to the ancient past and its wisdom?

PS: I wish I could see other sides of Bangkok. To me it draws us vis-à-vis the poor like a magnet. When there's drought, when the land is taken away from them, when there's nowhere for them to go, then they pack themselves into trains that come into the slums of Bangkok. It is chaotic. The traffic and the pollution is so great that it is almost unbearable. It is a place that I never feel at home. If there are beauties at all in the city, it would be in the Buddhist temples. I can see a lot of beauty in the Buddhist temples and life in the street, and amongst the people that you meet. What is impressive to foreigners and visitors are the people, the actual Thai people. They have a charm and friendliness.

CRNLE: The Esarn people in your books, away from Esarn, fear the use of the lower language, which is such an integral part of their culture. Do you ever feel like writing in the lower language?

PS: We were not taught to write in our dialect because the government would broadcast the news over loudspeakers in the villages, and it was broadcast in Thai. The radios that used to play our music and dialect have disappeared so now everything is in Thai, Thai, Thai. Therefore, we were not taught to write, I don't even know how to write in Thai, so in Esarn, that part of the north-east, in Esarn, we can speak the language, but we don't know how to write it.

CRNLE: So you see traditional culture as being under real threat?

PS: Very much so, because our people from Esarn are ashamed of their own language. It is the poorest region of Thailand, and so when they come to look for employment, they are looked down on because they are people from Esarn. Many chapters in my books deal with this, the people being ashamed of their origins.

CRNLE: A particularly interesting feature of these stories is that part of them is written in the voice of a woman, rather than using the first person.

PS: Yes, that is my technique. I know that in their normal life they are not speaking, but I give them the voice... a deep slow voice of one person who has fought centuries, who cannot speak. You begin to know this voice. Most of the people share this same slow, gentle voice, that comes out, not their own voice, but the voice that I have given them, without any contrived manners, without any hatred.

CRNLE: Another theme in several stories concerns Vietnam, Kampuchea and Cambodia. Are you going to expand on the influences of, say, the Vietnam war, or is that too political?

PS: The Vietnam war played a major role in our society. I didn't include it in the novels because the north-east of Esarn had three major American air bases. These air bases became "America in Thailand"; village girls never had a chance. I have seen two girls from my village marry American men from the bases and now they become American citizens. They forgot completely about their family. The bases are no longer there but have left a lot of marks and dents in our society.

CRNLE: Thailand has a distinction that it is the only South-East Asian country that has not been colonized. Do you think there are advantages or disadvantages in the fact that Thailand wasn't colonized by Europe?

PS: I'll talk about disadvantages first - that we cannot speak or write English fluently, like Singapore, Malaysia and Hong Kong. That's why I had a lot of problems learning this language at the beginning. There is a lack of discipline I think. For example, Singapore has more discipline, because English laws somehow expose corruption and create conscience. The advantages are that we do not hold grudges against people. We don't feel that we have been oppressed or exploited. Hence we feel that foreigners are there as our guests, as our visitors. We trade

267

freely with them. We don't look at Europeans as being former enemies in our colony.

CRNLE: What experience of English did you have as a school-child in Thailand?

PS: When I was in my village, at the age of six, a missionary entered our village. He stopped he car in the middle of the village and took out a little piano, and I remember being so amazed at this. I heard them speak in a foreign language so I asked my father "What's that?" and he said "English." I said "What's English like?" and he said "It's full of sssssssssssssss."

When I came to Bangkok, I went to secondary school, and later went to Melbourne for Honours and I was attracted immediately to the language. I don't know why. Now the Thai people say "Oh, it must be your past life."

CRNLE: Did you read Shakespeare at school?

PS: Not in Thailand but I mentioned earlier that the first impression I had of English literature was that written by James Joyce, Emily Bronte, George Orwell, Patrick White...these four writers are great masters.

CRNLE: Did you have a special interest in rural Australia because of your life in Esarn?

PS: Yes, there is so much land outside your cities. You drive out of Adelaide, and find so many areas that are burnt, dry and desolate, just like Esarn. I feel very at home in the outback. Patrick White catches this well in *The Tree of Man*. He shows inner Australia, the physical side against the spiritual side, the wealth and richness of the mind.

CRNLE: Pira, thank you.

© Marcus Richards, 1992.

With the kind permission of *CRNLE Reviews Journal 1992, No. 1.*, Flinders University of South Australia.

MARCUS RICHARDS teaches at the Flinders University of South Australia.

PIRA SUDHAM
Rains

"Why do the grown-ups do things like that?" Dan asked, moving closer to his friend, Kum, who was still panting because they had been running along the hot sandy path.

Dan wanted to repeat the question but then Kum sat down on his heels, arms akimbo. Dan did so too, keeping close to his friend. Their elbows touched but the meager shade of the mango tree could not give them much comfort.

Kum's silence compelled Dan to be quiet. So Dan turned to the group of monks and the laymen of the village as they sat in the glaring sun. The monks were chanting in unison, with their hands cupped in the manner of praying and their eyes closed while the villagers crouched in concentration.

Why must they perform such a ritual in the terribly hot sun? Dan wanted to ask but then he dared not disturb the solemnity of the gathering. In front of everyone there was a toad tied to a stake. The animal was trying vainly to free itself, mortified by the human din and the exposure.

Dan was perplexed, his eyebrows curved into a silent question. Shifting uncomfortably, he once more searched Kum's face for explanation. Kum remained serious and mottled. The light and shade made an interplay on the boyish face.

"Why?" Dan tried to whisper, nudging his friend with his elbow.

Kum made a low grunting sound, then lapsed into his seriousness once more, staring intently at the monks and old men and women as if he was being stupefied by the awesome rite.

Dan's own grandmother and Kum's grandmother were among the people who were submitting themselves to the ritual. Missing were the school teacher and the Chinese shopkeeper. The latter had already packed up his shop and moved elsewhere since there was no more money to be made from the drought-stricken peasants.

Under this burning sun you could cook an egg in the sand, Dan was thinking, and why? Why do they make themselves so pitiful? The boy was moved by the sight of his grandmother as she swayed her perspiring, emaciated body to the rhythm of helplessness. Dan recalled what she had said to the members of the family, that if the monsoon did not come soon, it would mean famine. Her prophesy fell on all ears for it was what everyone was concerned about, in dread of. However, nobody commented or acknowledged her despair. So the old wizened woman lamented further, saying that in her life she had never been through any year as bad as this.

The wind from the burning rice fields seared hot and dry, carrying dust of two successive years of drought, breeding sorrow and fear, hunger and sickness.

The streams and the dams and wells were dry, and the earth cracked in millions of fissures. In the aridity of the wind there seemed to be mockery from the supernatural on the dignity and the significance of mankind. What could villagers do then but torment themselves and the toad so that the supernatural, the spirits good or evil, would take pity on them and so give them rain.

The rain-begging rite was their last hope when human resources failed. But Dan, being only six years old, did not understand the meaning of it. Nevertheless, he had been taught to respect the solemnity of the monks and the old people. He too sensed the despair prevailing in the sweltering air.

As if he could not bear the ceremony any longer, Kum gave up his serious pose. Taking Dan by the hand, he led the way, walking off, yet still in awe and silence. They went along the track where they had come, walking away disheartened, seeking comfort from each other by holding hands.

Hunger drove them from the emptiness of the fields into the woods to hunt for lizards. When they had caught a few of these reptiles, Kum made a fire and cooked their catch. After the scanty meal had been wordlessly eaten, Kum stopped being sulky. The heat waves rose high from the plain of salt pans and grey scrub and endless mirages. Dan coughed the dust out of his parched throat.

Lying under the shade of the tamarind tree, Kum said:

"They tried to beg for rain from the lords, the spirits."

"Will it rain then?" Dan asked.

"It might," Kum said ruefully.

Dan scanned the skies for clouds which would give rise to their hope.

"Maybe in the evening," Dan hoped.

It was also Dan's attempt to comfort his friend. But Kum took on that expression of seriousness again, staring at the grey infinity distorted by the heat haze. He did not seem to mind the flies covering the wound on his left knee.

"The drought might be so bad that we don't have to go to school," Dan ventured after a long pause.

Could Kum be comforted by not having to attend the village school under the gruelling supervision of the teacher who would flog children when they could not learn sums? So Dan's idea of going to school to face the teacher seemed more frigh-tening than the famine.

"Aw, it's bad enough now," Kum groaned. "We've nothing to eat and my father is going to give me away."

Dan became tongue-tied with this information, at the thought that Kum would be taken away from the village by strangers whom one must call Dad and Mum. When Dan could speak, he said meekly:

"Maybe you could live with us."

Kum could not believe that was possible. "You don't know what the grown-ups would do," he said.

Then they left it at that, having touched on the gate of their own despair.

Days passed but no rain came. There was not even a faint thunder or the sight of rain-bearing clouds to raise hope.

Meanwhile, several families left the village for elsewhere, where ponds and streams and rivers held water most times of the year and where the monsoon was regular and the earth yielded.

Rumours of those going to leave next spread fast; people called to one another saying goodbye. Ox-carts laden with sad-eyed peasants and their children and possessions rolled away, leaving dust and memories behind.

The village mourned its departed inhabitants. The soil turned sour. Loneliness and despair tinged the sounds of goodbye. In leaving, people reminded one another of the centuries of filial ties and kinship. The trembling voice of the aged sang back across the gulf of hopelessness. Would we ever see you again? they cried.

Meanwhile, the adults talked of rites and sacrifices to gain mercy from the spirits.

For rain, life, the normal turn of the seasons.

Dan would rather suffer in place of his grandmother or of most of the old men and women, for he felt sorry for them.

Perhaps they might let him join in some of the rites and make him a sacrifice. His suffering might help them to succeed and so prevent Kum from being taken away by strangers to a far-off place.

But Dan had not been included in the adults' suffering and responsibilities. He could only watch how the men killed an ox, a buffalo, a pig for their blood and flesh as the votive offering to the spirits at the village spirit house.

The rituals took on a more macabre air as the people became more desperate. The fatal twist of the knives, the mortal wounds, the deadly cries of the animals, and the flow of blood pointed to one thing: the men appeared despairingly savage.

But to no avail, except that the hearts were relieved by the primeval savagery and cruelty.

One day, Dan went off by himself.

The vastness of the arid landscape made the tiny boy more minute and alone.

Without Kum by his side, he began to be afraid of the solitude and the great expanse of the desiccated plain. He halted several times, looking back towards the village.

Where Dan chose to sit was unprotected by any vegetation. Sitting cross-legged under the excruciating sun, he tried to pray, but since he had not been taught the art, his was only an imitation, following the manner of monks and old people he had observed. Closing his eyes, Dan swayed a little.

"Pity me. Oh spirits," Dan prayed.

The experience was both enthralling and fearful. For he, so insignificant and small, dared put himself up against the powerful.

Silence, which seemed to weigh heavily on him, became a threat. The sun whipped him so mercilessly that his head throbbed, and the perspiration ran down his face and torso.

"Pity me. Oh lords."

Gradually courage came back to him and helped him expand wider. In departing from himself, Dan saw in his mind eye the face of Kum, a face of seriousness and fear. Must Kum be taken away by strangers? Dan saw also himself coming home from the fields, hallooing and laughing, riding a water buffalo. The image of the old grandmother loomed: it was a picture of happiness when she turned to smile broadly at him while ploughing the paddies in a good year. Old as she was, she worked unabatedly provided that there was water enough to grow rice.

"Oh lords, have pity on Kum and Grandma. Be merciful," Dan raised his voice.

The blazing sun kept beating on him, yet he prayed on. "Oh lords have mercy on Grandma and all the old people. Grandma eats nothing; she is so old and bony. Her clothes are also old and tattered. Have pity on old people for they cannot dig for yams and taro or chase grasshoppers and catch lizards for food."

His endurance was that of a child's. Curiosity forced him to open his eyes to see the effect of his rite. But to his dismay the skies remained cloudless; there was no cool breeze to herald the approach of rain.

Heavy with disappointment, the boy sighed and shifted. Perhaps his suffering was seen as a child's fancy, a mockery of the solemn and sacred rite reserved for monks and old men.

"My lords," Dan made another attempt, but no more words came.

The dehydrating heat of the sun was immense. He trembled at the thought that he would be consequently punished by the spirits for his fanciful action.

There seemed to be so much of the cynicism in life, the universal suffering, sorrow, the primeval bitterness and the futility of all things.

Now it was his own seriousness that frightened him so that he shuddered. But there was no way out now except to prove his sacrifice to the lords.

He must offer his blood to the lords.

The knife taken from his father's toolbox flashed in the noon sun.

273

Only then was he convinced that he would not fail, for the sacrifice would be so immense that the lords would take pity on him and so yield rain.

But the sharp metal opened the wound deeper than intended on his wrist.

Dan winced with pain, throwing the instrument away. The flow of blood made him giddy. Still he lifted the wounded hand towards the sun for the lords to see, till he fell.

Lying flat on his back, Dan tried to call out for help but could not. His throat was so dry, and he trembled, seeing that darkness was descending quickly on him.

Yet he strained in sheer effort to hear any rumble of thunder that would mean rain.

PIRA SUDHAM
A voice from the grassroots of Thailand

When I went to Bangkok for the first time, I realised I came from the poorest region of the Kingdom. Some Bangkok Thais who wanted to show their contempt said that I was not Thai, but a Lao from Esarn, a water buffalo or a peasant fit only for hard labour. Many of us, who try to make a success of our lives in Thailand's large cities, become coolies, tuk-tuk drivers, taxi drivers, workers in factories, servants and prostitutes. Some luckier ones are champion boxers or employees in offices. Some try to hide from their new friends and colleagues that they are from Esarn, being ashamed of their humble origins. A large number of us in exile do not want to return home.

Poverty, drought, debt, land becoming more barren or damaged by brine from salt mining, land loss through debt, gambling or forced 'relocation' to make way for planting the fast-growing eucalyptus to enable investors to establish pulp and paper industries, drive the people of Esarn away from their villages. Unfortunate children are sold by their parents to buyers from Bangkok and other cities to become child labourers in factories or prisoners in brothels. I, too, was 'given away' to

274

a Buddhist monk who took me from the village to serve him as a 'Dek Wat' or a servant in a city temple.

Here it dawned on me that as a temple boy I had very little chance to improve myself. Fortunately I was allowed to attend a school in the temple, for I could see that without some level of education it would be difficult to be somebody in a money-conscious society. During the stay, I sold coconut juice in the streets of Bangkok and later I moved to Wat Po to sell souvenir items to tourists to see myself through the secondary school and high school. I was in the second year in the Faculty of Arts of Chulalongkorn University when I won a New Zealand government scholarship to study English literature at Victoria University, Wellington, where I had a wonderful chance to learn not by rote but by thinking, discussing, and asking questions. I also learned a process of reasoning. I wonder why, as a child and as a student in Thailand, I had to be quiet, blindly obedient, not speak out and not be inquisitive. Perhaps if I had learned how to think, and think critically, I might have become wise, but discontented with my lot in life. I might have had a mind of my own and been branded 'Kon Hua Kaeng' (hard-headed man), posing a threat to some corrupt leaders.

After New Zealand, I lived for three years in Australia, from 1969 to 1971. I used the Fisher library at the University of Sydney to read Australian literature. At night I wrote my novel and short stories. From 1975 to 1978 I stayed in Europe, saving myself and my manuscripts from the political changes in Thailand.

In New Zealand, Australia, England, France and Germany I experienced the Western way of life. I wanted to have an enquiring mind, which is scarce in Thai society. I grew up mentally in foreign countries, and I am grateful for that, for not remaining childish, or a child in an adult body like many of our politicians and leaders. However, parts of my mind had already been crippled, maimed for life, during the formative years in Thailand. I wished to make up for the crippled parts by fully developing those which had escaped maiming. I tried to stay as long as possible in London and in many European countries to learn more, to think, to reflect from afar and to finish my novel, *Monsoon Country*.

After so many years abroad, the call of Napo could not be resisted. I came home eventually. A team of local carpenters built me a modest wooden house on the land where I was born, among bamboo thickets, mango trees and jungles of bananas, left untended after my father dismantled our old house and rebuilt it on another plot of land in the heart of the village. Our land reminded me so much of my childhood. Here, grandparents told us tales and folklore, of hunting in jungles which no longer exist today, of their journeys to some unknown regions in search of new lands.

Here, lodged deeply in my head, are memories of love, birth, death, the age-old suffering, anger, bitterness and the faces of beautiful young girls who stayed a few years with us to learn by heart ballads and songs my father composed for them so they could become 'Mohlam', Esarn folk singers.

Because I am the oldest son, I observe the unwritten law of our land and assume the responsibility of taking care of our parents and relatives. Instead of devoting all my time to writing, I have also to work for commercial companies, saving some money to provide for the welfare of my parents and my brothers and their wives and children. When there is money to spare, it goes to poor villagers who are sick.

Apart from providing fish fry to be farmed in village ponds and young fruit trees for the village, in 1991 I donated several buffaloes to rice farmers. Many boys and girls of poor families receive money, clothes, books and occasionally food from my kitchen. In Bangkok, I am not ashamed to beg from rich Thai families or from expatriates for old clothes, for which the people of Napo are grateful.

On a personal level, I manage to achieve a balance between a working life and the life of a writer. But the sadness, happiness and anger I experienced in childhood did not leave me. Embedded deeply within me, they became an impetus, a force and source of energy. The irony of it is that my childhood sentiments are being experienced all over again, in rural Thailand, today.

For now the Masters have increased in number and proportion. They are far more gigantic and powerful than those I recognised in my childhood and portrayed in *Monsoon County*:

276

corrupt, tyrannical officials, shopkeepers, rice traders and middlemen who swindled illiterate peasants, and the local money lenders and gangs of gamblers who induced villagers to gamble away their money and their lands. These are pale and diminutive compared to new Masters some of whom become extremely rich through bribery and accepting bribes, acquire public lands and forests through corruption and by force, plunder the country, enslave the farmers by the so-called 'Contract Farming', destroy the forests by logging and then claim them for private commercial purposes, damage the environment and make the soil, canals and rivers saline and polluted with chemical waste and effluent released from factories. They are bigger and greedier, with international networks and high power.

I observe how the villagers are totally defenceless against the new omnipotent Masters. The lions and tigers are devouring their prey. By destroying for their own immediate gain they do harm to their own children and grandchildren and great-grandchildren, for generations to come, due to their greed and short-sightedness.

© Pira Sudham, 1993.

PIRA SUDHAM studied at the Faculty of Arts of Chulalongkorn University and later won a New Zealand government scholarship to study English literature at Victoria University, Wellington.

His literary works include *Monsoon Country*, *Siamese Drama* and *People of Esarn* all published by Shire Books.

The Pira Sudham Estate earns income from Pira Sudham's properties, copyright, and royalties. It is grateful to contributors and over one million readers of *Monsoon Country*, *People of Esarn*, *Siamese Drama* and *Pira Sudham's Best*. For enquiries, please contact: The Pira Sudham Estate, 105 Moo 13, Napo, Burirum 31230, Thailand. International Tel & Fax: (662) 2581975.

From Chairil Anwar (1922-1949)

i

Headstone
(For Grandmother)

It is not that death
has really found you out
but that you knew acceptance,
transcending all.
Out of the ashes and the pain
of your mortality
you are risen, sovereign
and boundless in your freedom.

ii

Spirit Rampant

When the hour comes
there shall be
no redeeming word, no help,
not even from you.

Done with mourning,

I shall take on,
with all its unreason,
the blind unregeneracy

of the beast
forced in upon itself
and rage, though guns
may open great wounds in my sides,
rage against dying.

Bearing all wounds, all infections,
I shall press on

till past pain,
past mere mortality,
I seize an inward freedom,
will to live
yet another thousand years.

iii

At the Mosque

I shouted to Him
till He came.

We clashed, bearing head-on,
face to face.

He glowed, a live flame
in the heart -
and would not be put out.

In great drops of sweat
I wrestled Him,
I would not
that I be broken to another's will.

In one single space,
in close confines,
I took my war to Him.

Seeking each the other
to annihilate,
one became consumed with curses,
the other, mad.

iv

I Will Have You Back

If you should want it,
I will have you back -
with my whole heart.

I am yet alone.

You know you are not
as you have been before,
a flower others have looked at.

Do not look down.
Face me with your eyes, boldly.

If you should want it,
I will have you back -
wholly to myself.

Not even with the mirror
would I want you shared.

v

Garden

This is our garden,
garden that holds
you,
me
is room enough,
so small,
in it, one
will not lose
the other;
garden sufficient
to us
though the flowers
will not break out
in a multitude
of surprising colours,
and the grass
is not spread out
like a carpet
firm, yet soft
to the touch of feet.
This is for us
no great matter,
as, in our garden, garden that holds
you,
me,
you are the flower
and I, the bee
I am the bee
and, you, the flower.

Small and close, full of the mild sun,
this garden is place
sequestered,
far from the press,
far from the noise
of the common, intruding world.

vi

As You Gently...

As you gently
bite me
on the mouth,
you touch off
hate; erupting,
it wells over.
Why did I not
strangle you, who
by your excess
of tenderness
cut into me
as into a wound?

© Wong Phui Nam, 1993.

WONG PHUI NAM graduated from the University of Malaya
(then in Singapore) in Economics and has since worked manily
in development finance and merchant banking.

Most of the poems he wrote during the Sixties first appeared
in *Bunga Mas*, an anthology of Malaysian Writing published in

the United Kingdom in 1963. They were subsequently collected in book form and published as *How the Hills Are Distant* in 1968 (*Tenggara* Supplement) by the Department of English, University of Malaya. In 1989 his second volume *Remembering Grandma and Other Rumours* was published by the English Department, National University of Singapore.

Mr Wong's poems have also appeared in *Seven Poets, The Second Tongue, The Flowering Tree, Young Commonwealth Poets '65, Poems from India, Sri Lanka, Singapore and Malaya*. He was also published by literary journals like *Tenggara, Tumasek, South East Asian Review of English* and *Westerly*. His latest book *Ways of Exile: Poems from the First Decade* has been published by **Skoob PACIFICA, London** in 1993. He also writes a poetry column for a newspaper.

ALAN DURANT
Afterword to
Wong Phui Nam's "WAYS OF EXILE"
'Making One's Language as One goes Along'

In his foreword to this collection, K.S. Maniam draws attention
to how Wong Phui Nam ended his own Introduction to the first
edition of 'How the Hills are Distant' in the 1960s with an
especially suggestive remark about the central role played in his
work by a *creative* use of poetic language:

> On looking back I realise I have written these poems for those
> who truly understand what it means to have to make one's own
> language as one goes along. [1]

In a precise sense, of course, the situation Wong alludes to is
rarely literally true. Language is almost by definition something
which pre-exists the individual user; and so 'making one's own
language as one goes along' - no matter how extensive the process may seem to someone engaged in it - it almost always a
process of only marginal modifications, revision or coinage.
Essentially conventional and social characteristics are what
most clearly distinguish a genuinely living language from a
made-up, personal or private 'language'. In this sense, Wong's
English (as he recognized when he indicates that he is, at least
partly, an 'heir to the tradition of Shakespeare and Milton' [2] is in
important ways an already-established - if nonetheless problematic - social and historical construct.

In a less literal sense, however, Wong Phui Nam's statement
signals an important dimension of the poet's work. Writing
poetry not only draws on existing linguistic and cultural codes,
but also transforms given materials so that they can articulate, in
a texture of often unresolved connections, new and unique
perceptions and social experience. In the case of English writing
in Malaysia, this individually creative, rather than conventional
or formulaic aspect of poetic writing is amplified by two specific
factors. The multilingual situation of the country, in which
English occupies a marginal and unstable position alongside
Malay, Chinese, Tamil and other languages, means that writing

in English already represents a very significant choice - a choice made all the more problematic by a current divergence, in attitudes towards English, between traditions carried over from its earlier colonial impo-sition on the one hand, and its siren, contemporary role as threshold to an international world of technology and commerce on the other. Writing in English in Malaysia in these circum-stances represents a marked cultural choice - a choice no doubt overdetermined by responses to a range of issues concerning personal and national identity, foreseen local and foreign readerships, and attitudes towards culture and colonialism.

Having selected English as the preferred medium of public expression, at a practical level the Malaysian poet is obliged to mould existing usage of the language to the task of describing emotional attitudes, thought processes and experience for which its history has not directly suited it. The scale of this task - and accomplishment in it - would be self-evident, if 'making one's own language as one goes along' were achieved through neologism, dense use of dialect markers or thickness of local cultural allusion; but the achievement is equivalent even where newness lies in nuance, in implied connections between concepts or images, or in local rhythmic patterns or speech conventions. Commenting on such formal aspects of his work, Wong Phui Nam describes what he sees as a need to 'clean out' words of their traditional English connotations whenever these intrude into the texture of the writing, and so to forge new possibilities for them. [3] It is in this sense - of subtle nuance, as English is redirected towards new, specifically Malaysian purposes - that the poetry in this collection constitutes, beyond its clear importance within the national literature of Malaysia, a signi-ficant innovation within English expression internationally, and occupies an important (and unduly neglected) position within the emergent New Literatures in English.

II

In order to appreciate the urgency with which Wong Phui Nam's poetry tackles the question of a newly-made language, however, we should consider further the sense of necessity conveyed by the words 'have to' in Wong's formulation. What is it he assumes is lacking? As Wong puts it in the brief reflective essay, 'Out of the Stony Rubbish' (included in this volume), there is for the Malaysian poet writing in English no common body of cultural assumptions or traditions on which to draw. The poet writing in English in Malaysia, he argues, therefore 'becomes painfully conscious of a special kind of poverty that comes from being almost entirely bereft of an identity that finds its confirmation in a community of belief and tradition - and in the use of a received language whose origins may be traced back to common ancestral beginnings.'[4] Emphasising further the deprivation he considers a consequence of this situation, Wong continues, 'Without access to a meaningful tradition or claim to even a disintegrating one, the Malaysian writer in English brings, as it were, to his work a naked and orphaned psyche.'[5]

The circumstances Wong Phui Nam alludes to here are specific and historical, rather than permanent or essential; they form part of the colonial, and more recently post-colonial, history of Malaysia rather than a general South East Asian or even Third World artistic consciousness or sensibility. At the time of Wong's early writing, in the late 1950s, Malaysia was entering a major phase in its shift - during a period of rapid global decolonisation - from colonial rule towards government by an emergent Malay ruling class, following the defeat of revolutionary communist forces. What is significant about this period as regards writing in particular is that by this time earlier, colonial literary aspirations were already largely discredited (partly as a result of arguments taking place elsewhere about Indian and African writing in English), but new directions for Commonwealth Literature which were gradually being defined in a number of post-colonial situations were as yet not being self-confidently or accessibly promulgated in Malaysia itself.

As part of a generation of Chinese Malaysians born in the 1930s, Wong came to maturity and studied at a university with a marked European cultural bias at the end of the 1950s, within an active, indigenous intellectual culture whose links to arguments being debated by intelligentsias in other, comparable situations were nevertheless restricted by political conditions. It is true that, following its establishment in Singapore at the end of the 1940s, the University of Malaya acted as a centre for literary discussion and composition. But the influence of the so-called 'Pioneer poets' (Lim Thean Soo, Beda Lim, Goh Sin Tub) had passed its immediate peak, and the work of writers such as Muhammad Haji Salleh, Omar Mohd, Pretam Kaur and Shirley Geok-lin Lim was still to come. Bridging the divide between colonized and post colonial formations - and paving the way for this later generation of writers - the 'university poets' (Edwin Thumboo, Wong and Ee Tiang Hong, first gathered together in the collection Litmus One: Selected University Verse, 1949-1957) experimented to an unprecedented degree, while remaining in some ways within a formative, Western literary-cultural paradigm shaped by Modernist writers such as T.S. Eliot. [6]

In the context of these broad circumstances and influences, the sense Wong Phui Nam forms during this period of what he calls a 'cultural wasteland' takes on a clearer shape. But that sense has several further, interlocking historical causes which are also worth noting.

First, there is the much earlier formation in Malaysia of a Chinese diaspora, following extensive but piecemeal immigration. Wong himself reports that the Chinese migrants from whom he is descended were deprived, by class position, from access to much of the Chinese culture they otherwise might have brought with them; and since they arrived in small groups rather than as a single community (unified as colonisers, soldiers, or evangelists, for instance) they could not easily establish a common set of roots from which later cultural forms might grow in any kind of continuous descent.

Second, a high degree of cultural separation between Malays, Chinese and Indians has retarded in Malaysia the process of formation of a new, common (and necessarily hybrid) cultural tradition which might have been expected to result from extensive social contact and intermarriage between communities, and from multilingualism and translation between languages. Such ethnic, cultural and religious separation, which has occasionally fuelled mutual suspicion between the respective communities, has inhibited the emergence of a distinctively new syntax of Malaysian multicultural identity that might be reflected in literary and other forms.

287

Third, as regards English in particular, language policies since Independence (unlike those adopted by many other formerly colonized, Anglophone countries) have resulted in a lack of institutions or outlets for writing; and more generally, Wong notes, one 'external aspect of the Malaysian poetic wasteland is the lack of, for want of a better word, an infrastructure for the support of its propagation and growth'. [7] Nationalist reaction against English in the 1960s and 1970s significantly reduced the potential national audience for English writing, and appears to have implied on some occasions that English writing involves a form of cultural dissent.

Fourthly, and relatedly, relative isolation of individual writers from one another has resulted in a shortage of opportunities for discussion or for informal critical comment and review. Contemplating this isolation, Wong has said that the Malaysian writer accordingly as 'much in the situation of, perhaps, the mythical shipwrecked sailor who casts messages in sealed bottles into the sea, relegating them to the wind and tide to carry themselves wherever they ill.'

Considered together, these four factors produce for Malaysian writing in English a distinctive dynamic within the global development of post-colonial literatures. The unique configuration of ethnic, economic, religious and other factors should, of course, preclude generalized response to Malaysian writing as being somehow representative of 'Third World literature' (eg. on the basis of an assumption that individual works should be consistently read as 'allegories of national experience' [8], and so should guarantee an international hearing for works by Wong Phui Nam and other important Malaysian writers. At the same time, however, to the extent that little of the writing in English produced in Malaysia has dealt with cultural or political struggle, or been aligned with perceived socially progressive forces within the society - the two main factors which typically recommend non-European writing to the attentions of a metropolitan Western readership - Malaysian writing remains neglected by comparison with works from (for example) the Philippines, the Indian sub continent, or Southern Africa. For his part, nevertheless, Wong dismisses politically partisan writing, on the basis that,

Ultimately, artistic work for the national cause (at least this is made patently clear to writers in English in Malaysia) will be doomed to failure. [9]

III

If we are to read Wong Phui Nam's poetry closely, within these larger coordinates of the changing literary geography of English, it is important briefly to consider two consequences described above, as regards what Wong chooses to write about and how his writing is presented: first, the generic or formal conventions Wong chooses to follow; and second, what might be called the poetry's patterns of repetition, contrast and transformation between themes and topics.

The collection 'Ways of Exile' is made up of four sections, each a sequence of short lyrics: 'How the Hills are Distant', in which 'Nocturnes and Bagatelles' convey a sense of loneliness and separation accentuated for the poet by being awake during the night; 'For a Local Osiris', which depicts a resurrected, mythical Osiris seeking to redeem an evil world for civilization; 'What Are the Roots...', which contains English version of Taoist poems and writings by Tu Fu, evidently as a quest to constitute or restore an absent poetic tradition; and 'Rumours of Exits', which presents a range of images of death, as well as modes of access to a transcendental, other world. [10]

Throughout, these sequences reflect in their modes of composition a set of constraints Wong feels exist on writing English poetry in Malaysia. For example, he discusses difficulties presented by certain English verse forms, such as the sonnet or ballad, arguing that these appear inappropriate to a culture with a largely agrarian history; Wong prefers short lyrical forms arranged in loose sequences to such closely-structured idioms. Noting, too, the suggestiveness of precise details of register, Wong negotiates issues of mode of address and sense of occasion by opting for an introspective lyrical subjectivity rather than any suggestion of public declaration. And in 'What are the Roots...', translation plays an important role in creating a specifically Chinese Malaysian poetic voice. Rejecting the idea of scholarly, word-for-word translation, as well as such terms as 'imitations' or 'interpretations', Wong argues rather that,

'Because of the differences between the languages, I feel the best strategy for rendering an English version of a Chinese text is to write it as if it is an original poem in English' [11]; and pointing to the cultural purpose of translation - perhaps especially resonant in the Tu Fu sequence - he suggests that translation makes possible 'putting poems into English, and saying, in the process, something about the Malaysian condition in ways I could not manage in my own verse'. [12]

It is less, however, this ability of translation to symbolise contemporary cultural conditions than more local symbolic patterns which has given rise to descriptions of Wong Phui Nam's work as especially rich in symbolic qualities. Much of his reputation follows from the observation that a focus for many of the poems is provided by two recurrent symbols - the body and the landscape - woven together into a symbolic texture which is well illustrated by the following lines from poem (vi) in the 'Hills' sequence:

> I feel out of the verges of the swamps
> in the body's tides, out of the bones
> of an ancient misery,
> the dead stir with this advent of rain;
> and in a landscape too long
> in the contours of a personal anguish,
> assume its presences: hedges and barb-wire,
> trees in the numbness of the field;
> and, moving in the dark between the houses,
> conjure the heart
> to breed upon the hint of a primal terror. [13]

In other poems in the sequence (where more conventional contrasts are also drawn between city corruption and escape into the natural world), landscape is presented in an extension from established pastoral conventions as a representation simultaneously of physical, mental and social structure; and Wong depicts the death of the individual, anatomically and graphically, both to record individual pain and to symbolise more general forms of cultural death (perhaps most effectively in the poem 'For my old amah'). Working through patterns of symbolic equivalence, contrast and transformation, Wong develops personal, contemplative lyrics into larger-scale, social and philosophical comment.

But if such descriptions suggest that 'Ways of Exile' is concerned only with decay, pain, and death, it should be emphasised that a way out of 'the desert', and out of 'primal terror', lies for Wong in what he calls the 'transcendent' [14]. A symbolic pattern suggestive of this 'transcendent' presence is developed, for example, in Wong's translation 'A Mountain Visit', where the poet's efforts and labour in ascent (searching, significantly, for 'an ancient trail') are contrasted with the tranquility, plenitude and knowledge offered on arrival by the poet's conversation with a figure ('the master') whom the poet has clambered up to consult. Here are the opening lines:

> The mountains here dissolve into the one blue
> of the sky - into silence - towards a stillness
> beyond the bounds of time. I grope my way up them
> through descending banks of cloud, feel
> for traces of an ancient trail.

But the temporary stasis and plenitude enjoyed by the poet is quickly displaced; and the poem ends with the poet symbolically returned to his 'ways of exile':

> I find the master in. Our conversation fades
> with the light which turns rivers into slow veins
> blackening on the far plains at the approach of night.
> Alone, I stumble my way down into biting cold and
> fog. [15]

IV

In citing the title of the collection here, however, we should pause to consider what 'exile' means in this context. The term has gained such currency in recent cultural analysis that its meanings are complex, ranging from a literal sense of political expulsion to figurative description of a universal, ontological condition of general 'uprootedness' [16]; and a convergence between these two senses - brought about partly by intellectuals from post-colonial countries now resident in the West, and combining in some instances political engagement with post-structuralist theory - has helped in efforts to include New Literatures within university and school curricula. Wong's own use of the term - unlike Ee Tiang Hong, Wong has continued to live in Malaysia - brings together a sense of present cultural marginalisation with a more abstract sense of historica displacement influenced (like many writers and teachers of the period) by T.S. Eliot's belief in the essential value of cultural tradition. Set alongside the palliative of transcendent forces invoked in Wong's poetry, 'exile' also implies exclusion from a paradise which cultural belonging might have provided.

Wong's most interesting insights combine the influence from Eliot, however, with acute observations about the situation of the Malaysian writer, as in this striking passage from the 'Stony Rubbish' essay, which is worth quoting at length:

> The non-English writer who writes in English and has no similar recourse to his own language is thus, in allowing English to take over his affective faculties, in a very deep sense a miscegenated being, very much and yet not an heir to the tradition of Shakespeare and Milton. The language he uses to name, organise and express his experience of the life around him removes him from that life and, whether he is aware of it or not, he becomes a stranger cut off and always looking in as an outsider into that life. In that sense, the more facility he has with the adopted language, the more authentic he becomes. Culturally, and so spiritually, he is induced to place himself in exile from England and be cast out of an imagined Eden. [17]

The parallels with Eliot are evident, stylistically as well as conceptually (for example, in such words and phrases as 'heir to the tradition' and 'unauthentic', or in the essay title itself, 'Out of the Stony Rubbish' - as elsewhere in Wong's idea of a 'cultural wasteland', the 'impossibility of meaning', or the 'primal terror'). But the argument has gained a vital new dimension, by focusing on how the cultural incongruity of the colonial language interrupts perceptions which might connect the poet more closely with his or her immediate social surroundings, while, implicitly, a combination of Malay hegemony and the earlier, intellectual formation of the poet block off the otherwise obvious nationalist, vernacular alternatives.

It is this cluster of concerns with language and social belonging which most distinguish and inspire Wong Phui Nam's writing; at the same time, forms of repetition or closure in the treatment of these concerns signify the formative conditions of his work. Wong's term 'miscegenation', for instance, has increasingly been re-cast in post-colonial writing as a phenomenon of 'cultural hybridisation' (in which experimentation in local or 'nativized' dialects of English plays an important part [18]; and much contemporary argument over post-colonial literatures takes *as one of its starting-points* a presumption that English is no longer the property of native speakers, given a shifting global balance between monolingual and bilingual uses of the language. Despite risks of being lumped together in a simplistic unity of 'oppositionality' and otherness - especially in the hands of Western reviewers and critics - post-colonial writers and critics have increasingly explored comparisons between respective national experiences, and developed supportive connections with each other (including with writers literally in exile).

Such descriptions can easily seem idealistic or pious, however; and Wong Phui Nam himself remained silent through the 1970s and most of the 1980s, returning to public prominence again with 'Remembering Grandma and other Rumours' in 1989. Rather than contributing to a global dialogue ironically facilitated by the colonial imposition of English, in fact, contemporary Malaysian writing in English may merely 'die out like dinosaurs' (as Wong himself suggests [19]). But if this happens, then readers and writers alike will have failed fully to appreciate the insights into linguistic and cultural identity presented so vividly in this collection of Wong Phui Nam's work.

NOTES

1. See Wong Phui Nam's, *Ways of Exile* (1993 **Skoob PACIFICA** London) p. 3.
2. p. 140.
3. p. 141.
4. p. 133.

5. p. 133.
6. For more detailed discussion, see, Anne Brewster, 'The Sense of place in Singaporean and Malaysian poetry in English with special reference to Wong Phui Nam and Arthur Yap', in, Peggy Nightingale (ed), *A Sense of Place in the New Literatures in English* (St. Lucia: University of Queensland Press, 1986), pp. 132-42. For a longer critical history of writing in English in Malaysia, see, Lloyd Fernando, *Cultures in Conflict: Essays on Literature and the English Language in South East Asia*, esp. pp. 128-49.
7. p. 143..
8. For a detailed argument along these lines, see, Fredric Jameson, 'Third World LIterature in the Era of Multinational Capital', *Social* Text, Fall (1986), 65-88. A range of perspectives on the degree of generalization, based on 'common denominators', that is reasonable with regard to regional or otherwise marginal 'minority' discourses can be found in Abdul R. Janmohamed and David Lloyd (eds), *The Nature and Context of Minority Discourse* (Oxford: OUP, 1990).
9. p. 138.
10. For further commentary, see Anne Brewster, op. cit.
11. p. 87.
12. p. 86.
13. p. 11.
14. p. 139.
15. p. 84.
16. For an exemplary discussion of the development of post-colonial literatures (and reactions to them) which investigates in detail relationship between writing, intellectuals, and political circumstances, see Aljaz Ahmad, *In Theory: Classes, Nations, Literatures* (London: Verso, 1992).
17. p. 140.
18. For discussion of creative uses of English in New Literatures in English, see, for example, Braj Kachru, *The Other Tongue: English Across Cultures* (Oxford: Pergamon Press, 1982); and for more general background to the emergence of the New Englishes, see, John Pride, *New*

Englishes (Rowley, Mass: Newbury House, 1982), or Robert McCrum, William Cran and Robert MacNeil, *The Story of English* (London: Faber, 1986). Some relevant theoretical perspectives are offered in, Chinweizu, Ouwuchekwa Jemie and Ihechukwu Madubuike, *Toward the Decolonization of African Literature: African fiction and poetry and their critics* (London: KPI, 1980); Randolph Quirk and H.G. Widdowson (eds), *English in the World: teaching and learning the language and Literatures* (Cambridge: CUP, 1985); Homi Bhabha (ed), *Nation and Narration* (London: Routledge, 1990); Gayatri Chakravorty Spivak, *The Post-colonial Critic: Interviews, Strategies, Dialogues* (London: Routledge, 1990); and Edward W. Said, *Culture and Imperialism* (London: Chatto and Windus, 1993).

19. p. 144.

ALAN DURANT is Professor and Head of the School of English, Cultural and Communication Studies, Middlesex University London, and was previously Professor and Head of English, Goldsmiths' College, University of London. He is the author of *Ezra Pound, Identity in Crisis* (1981), *Conditions of Music* (1984), *Literary Studies in Action* (with Nigel Fabb, 1990), *Ways of Reading: Advanced Reading Skills for Students of Literature* (with Martin Montgomery et al., 1992), and *How to Write Essays, Dissertations and Theses in Literary Studies* (with Nigel Fabb, 1993), as well as co-editor, with Nigel Fabb and others, of *The Linguistics of Writing: Arguments between Language and Literature* (1987). He has lectured extensively in more than twenty countries around the world on the teaching of English language and literature.

CRITICISM

From Commonwealth to Post-Colonial

Editor: Anna Rutherford

New thoughts about new writing. These thirty-seven essays subject the body of literature from the Commonwealth countries to fresh critical interpretations. Metropolitan literary theories like post-modernism are tested in the crucible of post-colonial social formation, and the new awareness gives rise to an altered and specific post-colonial view.

Contributors: Christopher Balme, Elleke Boehmer, Carolyn Cooper, T.J.Cribb, Robin Dizard, Pauline Dodgson, Simon Gikandi, D.C.R.A. Goonetilleke, Veronica M. Greg, Gareth Griffiths, Wilson Harris, Dorothy Jones, Ketu H. Katrak, Bruce King, Viney Kirpal, Koh Tai Ann, Roger Langen, Shirley Geok-lin Lim, Ishrat Lindblad, Chandani Lokugé, Oliver Lovesey, Amin Malak, Russell McDougall, Ganeswar Mishra, Emmanuel S. Nelson, Oyekan Owomoyela, Rajeev S. Patke, Velma Pollard, David Richards, Anna Rutherford, Nayantara Sahgal, Edward W. Said, Paul Sharrad, Beheroze F. Shroff, Carol Sicherman, Kirpal Singh, Helen Tiffin, Kathrin M. Wagner, Anne Walmsley.

ANNA RUTHERFORD, Chair of ACLALS, is Professor in English, Aarhus University, Denmark.

ISBN 1 87049 42 3
464pp
GBP 14.95

DANGAROO PRESS:
P.O. Box 20, Hebden Bridge, West Yorkshire HX7 5UZ, UK
Pinds Hus, Geding Søvej 21, 8381 Mundelstrup, Denmark
G.P.O. Box 1209, Sydney, NSW 2001, Australia

PART FOUR

The Nobel Laureates

Skoob *PACIFICA* Anthology No: 2
THE PEN IS MIGHTIER THAN THE SWORD
Forthcoming Winter 1993

Part One
New Writings of the Pacific Rim

Part Two
Malaysian/Singaporean Prose in English:
Main feature: The books of **Chin Kee Onn**.

Part Three
Other literatures of the Pacific Rim:
Ashcroft, Griffiths & Tiffin: *Post-colonial reconstructions: Literature, Meaning and Value and Post-colonialism as a Reading Strategy* (excerpts from *The Empire Writes Back, Theory and Practice in Post-colonial Literatures*)
and **other studies** of Southeast Asian literatures.

Part Four
The Nobel Laureates:
Josef Brodsky * **Czeslaw Milosz** (with the *Witness of Poetry : The Charles Eliot Norton Lectures 1981-2*)
Jean-Paul Sartre (*The Writer and His Language* and Citation, Address and Refusal)
Nadine Gordimer * **Naguib Mahfouz**
Gabriel Marquez * **Octavio Paz**.

Part Five
Literary Features:
Vikram Seth's Journey Continues:
Chapter 2 *Heaven Lake* and Chapter 3 *An Eastward Loop* (excerpts from *From Heaven Lake, Travels through Sinkiang and Tibet*)
V.S. Naipaul's Travels through Malaysia:
First Conversations With Shafi: The Journey Out of Paradise. (excerpts from *Among the Believers: An Islamic Journey*)

ON DEREK WALCOTT:
1992 Nobel Prize for Literature
by
Annie Greet

In selecting Derek Walcott, 62-year-old West Indian poet and playwright, as this year's recipient of the prestigious Nobel Prize for Literature, the Swedish Academy has continued to acknowledge the leading role played by writers from places once designated as being "outside the metropolis". Simultaneously, in drawing world attention to the oft-misrepresented West Indies, the Academy has been instrumental in offering access to them as reflected in the words of a master poet and dramatist. The award is also a tribute to a virile, vital Caribbean literature, the English-language multi-island tradition of which consists of such powerful figures as C.L.R. James, Jean Rhys, V.S. Naipaul, Wilson Harris, Louise Bennett, George Lamming, Roger Mais, John Hearne, Olive Senior, Sam Selvon, Jamaica Kincaid...and so many others.

Derek Alton Walcott was born on the island of St. Lucia, two hundred kilometres north of Trinidad. As a young man, he studied for an arts degree in Jamaica, and taught in St. Lucia, Jamaica and Grenada. His mother, a school teacher, helped finance the publishing of a small book of his poems when he was eighteen, and ten years later, in 1958, he was awarded a Rockefeller Foundation Fellowship to study theatre in the United States of America. The following year he went to Trinidad and founded the Little Carib Theatre Workshop, later the Trinidad Theatre Workshop, in Port of Spain, and between 1960 and 1968, produced regular columns on art, theatre and literature for *The Trinidad Guardian*.

Walcott remained director of TTW until 1976, and was this year the recipient of a special citizen's award for his service to the arts in Trinidad. His writing for the theatre is particularly acknowledged in Trinidad and in the United States, where he has collaborated for many years with his friend Galt Mac Dermot, composer of the score for the musical *Hair*. Since 1981, Walcott has taught creative writing at Boston University in Massachusetts, returning to the Caribbean during the non-academic year.

Walcott's childhood ambition was to follow his father, a talented amateur artist who died when Walcott was a year old, in capturing the world with paint and sketchbook. He had prominent West Indian artist and local eccentric Harold Simmons as his master, but eventually found that he could not express the nuances of life he saw around him - "the crystal of ambiguities" as he called them - on canvas. So he came to recognise metaphor as his natural medium, and, in love with both the English language of the literature he devoured and the creole rhythms and structures of the local patois, he set himself to become a poet. He is also recognised as a competent water-colourist, and his work has been displayed in galleries throughout the West Indies.

For a small island, St. Lucia bears a weight of history, and Walcott grew up with an imaginative awareness of imperialism, surrounded as he was by the paraphernalia of its heritage. He was also mesmerised by the natural beauty of his island, by the fecundity and richness as yet unspoken in literature. The Caribbean constantly washed the seams of his imagination, and images of the "chiton-fluted sea" were to become a dominant presence in his writing. Moreover, he and his friend Dunstan St. Omer (who went on to become a successful painter on St. Lucia) set about "naming", in their paintings and poems, what they saw as the unnamed, unknown Eden they lived in. They saw themselves as having "Adam's task": now, forty years on, Eden's other names are taking their place around the world.

But Walcott has done more for the West Indies. Speaking for but not down to them, as he pointed out in an interview recently, he gives a voice to the real people, the fishermen and taxi drivers, the cane workers and rum shop owners, the old women who heal - "that alphabet of the emaciated...the stars of my mythology", he calls them in his superb book-length autobiographical poem, *Another Life*. For Walcott is, above all, a compassionate man, a humanist. His deep love for the people of these islands is an undertow in all his writing, and makes him accessible to readers in Third and Western Worlds alike.

From his humanism springs political acerbity, and a third achievement of his writings - apart from naming his world (as

Wordsworth did the Lakes District) and giving his people dignity and identity - has been nothing less than the rewriting of Caribbean history. Taught history from the imperialist perspective of glorious conquest and the amassing of wealth, the history he records so forcefully in his poems and plays reveals the other side of the coin. Walcott's writing painfully constructs a present and a presence for his people, in the West Indies and in the world, a writing which exploits the dramatic powers of patois and standard languages with equal facility and brilliance.

His first poems were published in 1948, when Walcott was eighteen years old. He has since brought out eleven volumes of poems, including *Another Life* (1973), *Midsummer* (1984), *Collected Poems, 1948-84* and *Omeros* (1991), and eighteen or more plays. Amongst the notable essays he has written are "The Muse of History" (in *Is Massa Day Done?* ed. Orde Coombs, 1974) and "What the Twilight Says: an Overture" (in *Dream on Monkey Mountain and Other Plays*, 1980).

In 1962, Walcott's Trinidadian compatriot and friend, renowned writer V.S. Naipaul, wrote, "History is built around achievement and creation; and nothing was created in the West Indies." Today, thanks to the Academy, that statement can be buried in the past, and Walcott is rightly acknowledged for his vision and artistry in setting the record straight.

© Annie Greet, 1992.

With the kind permission of C.R.N.L.E. *Reviews Journal 1992, No.2.*

THE ANTILLES: FRAGMENTS OF EPIC MEMORY

Felicity is a village in Trinidad on the edge of the Caroni plain, the wide central plain that still grows sugar and to which indentured cane cutters were brought after emancipation, so the small population of Felicity is East Indian, and on the afternoon that I visited it with friends from America, all the faces along its road were Indian, which, as I hope to show, was a moving, beautiful thing, because this Saturday afternoon *Ramleela*, the epic dramatization of the Hindu epic the *Ramayana*, was going to be performed, and the costumed actors from the village were assembling on a field strung with different-coloured flags, like a new gas station, and beautiful Indian boys in red and black were aiming arrows haphazardly into the afternoon light. Low blue mountains on the horizon, bright grass, clouds that would gather colour before the light went. Felicity! What a gentle Anglo-Saxon name for an epical memory.

Under an open shed on the edge of the field, there were two huge armatures of bamboo that looked like immense cages. They were parts of the body of a god, his calves or thighs, which, fitted and reared, would make a gigantic effigy. This effigy would be burnt as a conclusion to the epic. The cane structures flashed a predictable parallel: Shelley's sonnet on the fallen statue of Ozymandias and his empire, that "colossal wreck" in its empty desert.

Drummers had lit a fire in the shed and they eased the skins of their tablas nearer the flames to tighten them. The saffron flames, the bright grass, and the hand-woven armatures of the fragmented god who would be burnt were not in any desert where imperial power had finally toppled but were part of a ritual, evergreen season that, like the cane-burning harvest, is annually repeated, the point of such sacrifice being its repetition, the point of the destruction being renewal through fire.

302

Deities were entering the field. What we generally call "Indian music" was blaring from the open platformed shed from which the epic would be narrated. Costumed actors were arriving. Princes and gods, I supposed. What an unfortunate confession! "Gods, I suppose" is the shrug that embodies our African and Asian diasporas. I had often thought of but never seen *Ramleela*, and had never seen this theatre, an open field, with village children as warriors, princes, and gods. I had no idea what the epic story was, who its hero was, what enemies he fought, yet I had recently adapted the *Odyssey* for a theatre in England, presuming that the audience knew the trials of Odysseus, hero of another Asia Minor epic, while nobody in Trinidad knew any more than I did about Rama, Kali, Shiva, Vishnu, apart from the Indians, a phrase I use pervertedly because that is the kind of remark you can still hear in Trinidad: "apart from the Indians".

It was as if, on the edge of the Central Plain, there was another plateau, a raft on which the *Ramayana* would be poorly performed in this ocean of cane, but that was my writer's view of things, and it is wrong. I was seeing the *Ramleela* at Felicity as theatre when it was faith.

Multiply that moment of self-conviction when an actor, made-up and costumed, nods to his mirror before stopping onstage in the belief that he is a reality entering an illusion and you would have what I presumed was happening to the actors of this epic. But they were not actors. They had been chosen; or they themselves had chosen their roles in this sacred story that would go on for nine afternoons over a two-hour period till the sun set. They were not amateurs but believers. There was no theatrical term to define them. They did not have to psych themselves up to play their roles. Their acting would probably be as buoyant and as natural as those bamboo arrows crisscrossing the afternoon pasture. They believed in what they were playing, in the sacredness of the text, the validity of India, while I, out of the writer's habit, searched for some sense of elegy, of loss, even of degenerative mimicry in the happy faces of the boy-warriors or the heraldic profiles of the village princes. I was polluting the afternoon with doubt and with the patronage of admiration. I misread the event through a visual echo of

History - the cane fields, indenture, the evocation of vanished armies, temples, and trumpeting elephants - when all around me there was quite the opposite: elation, delight in the boys' screams, in the sweets-stalls, in more and more costumed characters appearing; a delight of conviction, not loss. The name Felicity made sense.

Consider the scale of Asia reduced to these fragments: the small white exclamations of minarets or the stone halls of temples in the cane fields, and one can understand the self-mockery and embarrassment of those who see these rites as parodic, even degenerate. These purists look on such ceremonies as grammarians look at a dialect, as cities look on provinces and empires on their colonies. Memory that yearns to join the centre, a limb remembering the body from which it has been severed, like those bamboo thighs of the god. In other words, the way that the Caribbean is still looked at, illegitimate, rootless, mongrelized. "No people there", to quote Trollope, "in the true sense of the word". No people. Fragments and echoes of real people, unoriginal and broken.

The performance was like a dialect, a branch of its original language, an abridgement of it, but not a distortion or even a reduction of its epic scale. Here in Trinidad I had discovered that one of the greatest epics of the world was seasonally performed, not with that desperate resignation of preserving a culture, but with an openness of belief that was as steady as the wind bending the cane lances of the Caroni plain. We had to leave before the play began to go through the creeks of the Caroni Swamp, to catch the scarlet ibises coming home at dusk. In a performance as natural as those of the actors of the *Ramleela*, we watched the flocks come in as bright as the scarlet of the boy archers, as the red flags, and cover an islet until it turned into a flowering tree, an anchored immortelle. The sigh of History meant nothing here. These two visions, the *Ramleela* and the arrowing flocks of scarlet ibises, blent into a single gasp of gratitude. Visual surprise is natural in the Caribbean; it comes with the landscape, and faced with its beauty, the sigh of History dissolves.

We make too much of that long groan which underlines the past. I felt privileged to discover the ibises as well as the scarlet archers of Felicity.

The sigh of History rises over ruins, not over landscapes, and in the Antilles there are few ruins to sigh over, apart from the ruins of sugar estates and abandoned forts. Looking around slowly, as a camera would, taking in the low blue hills over Port of Spain, the village road and houses, the warrior-archers, the god-actors and their handlers, and music already on the sound track, I wanted to make a film that would be a long-drawn sigh over Felicity. I was filtering the afternoon with evocations of a lost India, but why "evocations"? Why not "celebrations of a real presence"? Why should India be "lost" when none of these villagers ever really knew it, and why not "continuing", why not the perpetuation of joy in Felicity and in all the other towns of the Central Plain: Couva, Chaguanas, Charley Village? Why was I not letting my pleasure open its windows wide? I was entitled like any Trinidadian to the ecstasies of their claim, because ecstasy was the pitch of the sinuous drumming in the loudspeakers. I was entitled to the feast of Husein, to the mirrors and crêpe-paper temples of the Muslim epic, to the Chinese Dragon Dance, to the rites of that Sephardic Jewish synagogue that was once on Something Street. I am only one-eighth the writer I might have been had I contained all the fragmented languages of Trinidad.

Break a vase, and the love that resembles the fragments is stronger than that love which took its symmetry for granted when it was whole. The glue that fits the pieces is the sealing of its original shape. It is such a love that resembles our African and Asiatic fragments, the cracked heirlooms whose restoration shows its white scars. This gathering of broken pieces is the care and pain of the Antilles, and if the pieces are disparate, ill-fitting, they contain more pain than their original sculpture, those icons and sacred vessels taken for granted in their ancestral places. Antillean art is this restoration of our shattered histories, our shards of vocabulary, our archipelago becoming a synonym for pieces broken off from the original continent.

And this is the exact process of the making of poetry, or what should be called not its "making" but its remaking, the fragmented memory, the armature that frames the god, even the rite that surrenders it to a final pyre; the god assembled cane by cane, reed by weaving reed, line by plaited line, as the artisans of Felicity would erect his holy echo.

Poetry, which is perfection's sweat but which must seem as fresh as the raindrops on a statue's brow, combines the natural and the marmoreal; it conjugates both tenses simultaneously: the past and the present, if the past is the sculpture and the present the beads of dew or rain on the forehead of the past. There is the buried language and there is the individual vocabulary, and the process of poetry is one of excavation and of self-discovery. Tonally the individual voice is a dialect; it shapes its own accent, its own vocabulary and melody in defiance of an imperial concept of language, the language of Ozymandias, libraries and dictionaries, law courts and critics, and churches, universities, political dogma, the diction of institutions. Poetry is an island that breaks away from the main. The dialects of my archipelago seem as fresh to me as those raindrops on the statue's forehead, not the sweat made from the classic exertion of frowning marble, but the condensations of a refreshing element, rain and salt.

Deprived of their original language, the captured and indentured tribes create their own, accreting and secreting fragments of an old, an epic vocabulary, from Asia and from Africa, but to an ancestral, an ecstatic rhythm in the blood that cannot be subdued by slavery or indenture, while towns are renamed and the given names of places accepted like Felicity village or Choiseul. The original language dissolves from the exhaustion of distance like fog trying to cross an ocean, but this process of renaming, of finding new metaphors, is the same process that the poet faces every morning of his working day, making his own tools like Crusoe, assembling nouns from necessity, from Felicity, even renaming himself. The stripped man is driven back to that self-astonishing, elemental force, his mind. That is the basis of the Antillean experience, this shipwreck of fragments, these echoes, these shards of a huge tribal vocabulary, these partially remembered customs, and they are not decayed but strong. They survived the Middle Passage and the *Fatel Rozack*, the ship that carried the first indentured Indians from the port of Madras to the cane fields of Felicity, that carried the chained Cromwellian convict and the Sephardic Jew, the Chinese grocer and the Lebanese merchant selling cloth samples on his bicycle.

And here they are, all in a single Caribbean city, Port of Spain, the sum of history, Trollope's "non-people". A downtown babel of shop signs and streets, mongrelized, polyglot, a ferment without a history, like heaven. Because that is what such a city is, in the New World, a writer's heaven.

A culture, we all know, is made by its cities.

Another first morning home, impatient for the sunrise - a broken sleep. Darkness at five, and the drapes not worth opening; then, in the sudden light, a cream-walled, brown-roofed police station bordered with short royal palms, in the colonial style, back of it frothing trees and taller palms, a pigeon fluttering into the cover of an eave, a rain-stained block of once-modern apartments, the morning side road into the station without traffic. All part of a surprising peace. This quiet happens with every visit to a city that has deepened itself in me. The flowers and the hills are easy, affection for them predictable; it is the architecture that, for the first morning, disorients. A return from American seductions used to make the traveller feel that something was missing, something was trying to complete itself, like the stained concrete apartments. Pan left along the window and the excrescences rear - a city trying to soar, trying to be brutal, like an American city in silhouette, stamped from the same mould as Columbus or Des Moines. An assertion of power, its decor bland, its air conditioning pitched to the point where its secretarial and executive staff sport competing cardigans; the colder the offices the more important, an imitation of another climate. A longing, even an envy of feeling cold.

In serious cities, in grey, militant winter with its short afternoons, the days seem to pass by in buttoned overcoats, every building appears as a barracks with lights on in its windows, and when snow comes, one has the illusion of living in a Russian novel, in the nineteenth century, because of the literature of winter. So visitors to the Caribbean must feel that they are inhabiting a succession of postcards. Both climates are shaped by what we have read of them. For tourists, the sunshine cannot be serious. Winter adds depth and darkness to life as well as to literature, and in the unending summer of the tropics not even poverty or poetry (in the Antilles poverty is poetry with a V, *une vie*, a condition of life as well as of imagination) seems capable of being profound because the nature around it is so exultant, so resolutely ecstatic, like its music. A culture based on joy is bound to be shallow. Sadly, to sell itself, the Caribbean encourages the delights of mindlessness, of brilliant vacuity, as a place to flee not only winter but that seriousness that comes only out of culture with four seasons. So how can there be a people there, in the true sense of the word?

They know nothing about seasons in which leaves let go of the year, in which spires fade in blizzards and streets whiten, of the erasures of whole cities by fog, of reflection in fireplaces; instead, they inhabit a geography whose rhythm, like their music, is limited to two stresses: hot and wet, sun and rain, light and shadow, day and night, the limitations of an incomplete metre, and are therefore a people incapable of the subtleties of contradiction, of imaginative complexity. So be it. We cannot change contempt.

Ours are not cities in the accepted sense, but no one wants them to be. They dictate their own proportions, their own definitions in particular places and in a prose equal to that of their detractors, so that now it is not just St. James but the streets and yards that Naipaul commemorates, its lanes as short and brilliant as his sentences; not just the noise and jostle of Tunapuna but the origins of C.L.R. James's *Beyond a Boundary*, not just Felicity village on the Caroni plain, but Selvon Country, and that is the way it goes up the islands now: the old Dominica of Jean Rhys still very much the way she wrote of it; and the Martinique of the early Césaire; Perse's Guadeloupe, even without the pith helmets and the mules; and what delight and privilege there was in watching a literature - one literature in several imperial languages, French, English, Spanish - bud and open island after island in the early morning of a culture, not timid, not derivative, any more than the hard white petals of the frangipani are derivative and timid. This is not a belligerent boast but a simple celebration of inevitability: that this flowering had to come.

On a heat-stoned afternoon in Port of Spain, some alley white with glare, with love vine spilling over a fence, palms and a hazed mountain appear around a corner to the evocation of Vaughn or Herbert's "that shady city of palm-trees", or to the memory of a Hammond organ from a wooden chapel in Castries, where the congregation sang "Jerusalem, the Golden".

It is hard for me to see such emptiness as desolation. It is that patience that is the width of Antillean life, and the secret is not to ask the wrong thing of it, not to demand of it an ambition it has no interest in. The traveller reads this as lethargy, as torpor.

Here there are not enough books, one says, no theatres, no museums, simply not enough to do. Yet, deprived of books, a man must fall back on thought, and out of thought, if he can learn to order it, will come the urge to record, and in extremity, if he has no means of recording, recitation, the ordering of memory which leads to metre, to commemoration. There can be virtues in deprivation, and certainly one virtue is salvation from a cascade of high mediocrity, since books are now not so much created as remade. Cities create a culture, and all we have are these magnified market towns, so what are the proportions of the ideal Caribbean city? A surrounding, accessible countryside with leafy suburbs, and if the city is lucky, behind it, spacious plains. Behind it, fine mountains; before it, an indigo sea. Spires would pin its centre and around them would be leafy, shadowy parks. Pigeons would cross its sky in alphabetical patterns, carrying with them memories of a belief in augury, and at the heart of the city there would be horses, yes, horses, those animals last seen at the end of the nineteenth century drawing broughams and carriages with top-hatted citizens, horses that live in the present tense without elegiac echoes from their hooves, emerging from paddocks at the Queen's Park Savannah at sunrise, when mist is unthreading from the cool mountains above the roofs, and at the centre of the city seasonally there would be races, so that citizens could roar at the speed and grace of these nineteenth-century animals. Its docks, not obscured by smoke or deafened by too much machinery, and above all, it would be so racially various that the cultures of the world - the Asiatic, the Mediterranean, the European, the African - would be represented in it, its human variety more exciting than Joyce's Dublin. Its citizens would intermarry as they chose, from instinct, not tradition, until their children find it increasingly futile to trace their genealogy. It would not have too many avenues difficult or dangerous for pedestrians, its mercantile area would be a cacophony of accents, fragments of the old language that would be silenced immediately at five o'clock, its docks resolutely vacant on Sundays.

This is Port of Spain to me, a city ideal in its commercial and human proportions, where a citizen is a walker and not a pedestrian, and this is how Athens may have been before it became a cultural echo.

The finest silhouettes of Port of Spain are idealizations of the craftsman's handiwork, not of concrete and glass, but of baroque woodwork, each fantasy looking more like an involved drawing of itself than the actual building. Behind the city is the Caroni plain, with its villages, Indian prayer flags, and fruit vendors' stalls along the highway over which ibises come like floating flags. Photogenic poverty! Postcard sadnesses! I am not re-creating Eden; I mean, by "the Antilles", the reality of light, of work, of survival. I mean a house on the side of a country road, I mean the Caribbean Sea, whose smell is the smell of refreshing possibility as well as survival. Survival is the triumph of stubbornness, and spiritual stubbornness, a sublime stupidity, is what makes the occupant of poetry endure, when there are so many things that should make it futile. Those things added together can go under one collective noun: "the world".

This is the visible poetry of the Antilles, then. Survival.

If you wish to understand that consoling pity with which the islands were regarded, look at the tinted engravings of Antillean forests, with their proper palm trees, ferns, and waterfalls. They have a civilizing decency, like Botanical Gardens, as if the sky were a glass ceiling under which a colonized vegetation is arranged for quiet walks and carriage rides. Those views are incised with a pathos that guides the engraver's tool and the topographer's pencil, and it is this pathos which, tenderly ironic, gave villages names like Felicity. A century looked at a landscape furious with vegetation in the wrong light and with the wrong eye. It is such pictures that are saddening rather than the tropics itself. These delicate engravings of sugar mills and harbours, of native women in costume, are seen as a part of History, that History which looked over the shoulder of the engraver and, later, the photographer. History can alter the eye and the moving hand to conform a view of itself; it can rename places for the nostalgia in an echo; it can temper the glare of tropical light to elegiac monotony in prose, the tone of judgement in Conrad, in the travel journals of Trollope.

These travellers carried with them the infection of their own malaise, and their prose reduced even the landscape to melancholia and self-contempt. Every endeavor is belittled as imitation, from architecture to music. There was this conviction in Trollope that since History is based on achievement, and since the history of the Antilles was so genetically corrupt, so depressing in its cycles of massacres, slavery, and indenture, a culture was inconceivable and nothing could ever be created in those ramshackle ports, those monotonously feudal sugar estates. Not only the light and salt of Antillean mountains defied this, but the demotic vigour and variety of their inhabitants. Stand close to a waterfall and you will stop hearing its roar. To be still in the nineteenth century, like horses, as Brodsky has written, may not be such a bad deal, and much of our life in the Antilles still seems to be in the rhythm of the last century, like the West Indian novel.

By writers even as refreshing as Graham Greene, the Caribbean is looked at with elegiac pathos, a prolonged sadness to which Lévi-Strauss has supplied an epigraph: *Tristes Tropiques*. Their *tristesse* derives from an attitude to the Caribbean dusk, to rain, to uncontrollable vegetation, to the provincial ambition of Caribbean cities where brutal replicas of modern architecture dwarf the small houses and streets. The mood is understandable, the melancholy as contagious as the fever of a sunset, like the gold fronds of diseased coconut palms, but there is something alien and ultimately wrong in the way such a sadness, even a morbidity, is described by English, French, or some of our exiled writers. It relates to a misunderstanding of the light and the people on whom the light falls.

These writers describe the ambitions of our unfinished cities, their unrealized, homiletic conclusion, but the Caribbean city may conclude just at that point where it is satisfied with its own scale, just as Caribbean culture is not evolving but already shaped. Its proportions are not to be measured by the traveller or the exile, but by its own citizenry and architecture. To be told you are not yet a city or a culture requires this response. I am not your city or your culture. There might be less of *Tristes Tropiques* after that.

Here, on the raft of this dais, there is the sound of the applauding surf: our landscape, our history recognized, "at last". *At Last* is one of the first Caribbean books. It was written by the Victorian traveller Charles Kingsley. It is one of the early books to admit the Antillean landscape and its figures into English literature. I have never read it but gather that its tone is benign. The Antillean archipelago was there to be written about, not to write itself, by Trollope, by Patrick Leigh-Fermor, in the very tone in which I almost wrote about the village spectacle at Felicity, as a compassionate and beguiled outsider, distancing myself from Felicity village even while I was enjoying it. What is hidden cannot be loved. The traveller cannot love, since love is stasis and travel is motion. If he returns to what he loved in a landscape and stays there, he is no longer a traveller but in stasis and concentration, the lover of that particular part of earth, a native. So many people say they "love the Caribbean", meaning that someday they plan to return for a visit but could never live there, the usual benign insult of the traveller, the tourist. These travellers, at their kindest, were devoted to the same patronage, the islands passing in profile, their vegetal luxury, their backwardness and poverty. Victorian prose dignified them. They passed by in beautiful profiles and were forgotten, like a vacation.

Alexis Saint-Léger Léger, whose writer's name is Saint-John Perse, was the first Antillean to win this prize for poetry. He was born in Guadeloupe and wrote in French, but before him, there was nothing as fresh and clear in feeling as those poems of his childhood, that of a privileged white child on an Antillean plantation, "*Pour Fêter une Enfance*", "*Éloges*", and later "*Images à Crusoe*". At last, the first breeze on the page, salt-edged and self-renewing as the trade winds, the sound of pages and palm trees turning as "the odour of coffee ascents the stairs".

Caribbean genius is condemned to contradict himself. To celebrate Perse, we might be told, is to celebrate the old plantation system, to celebrate the *bequé*, or plantation rider, verandahs and mulatto servants, a white French language in a white pith helmet, to celebrate a rhetoric of patronage and hauteur; and even if Perse denied his origins, great writers often have this folly of trying to smother their source, we cannot deny

312

him any more than we can the African Aimé Césaire. This is not accommodation, this is the ironic republic that is poetry, since, when I see cabbage palms moving their fronds at sunrise, I think they are reciting Perse.

The fragrant and privileged poetry that Perse composed to celebrate his white childhood and the recorded Indian music behind the brown young archers of Felicity, with the same cabbage palms against the same Antillean sky, pierce me equally. I feel the same poignancy of pride in the poems as in the faces. Why, given the history of the Antilles, should this be remarkable? The history of the world, by which of course we mean Europe, is a record of intertribal lacerations, of ethnic cleansings. At last, islands not written about but writing themselves! The palms and the Muslim minarets are Antillean exclamations. At last! the royal palms of Guadeloupe recite "*Éloges*" by heart.

Later, in "*Anabase*", Perse assembled fragments of an imaginary epic, with the clicking teeth of frontier gates, barren wadis with the froth of poisonous lakes, horsemen burnoosed in sandstorms, the opposite of cool Caribbean mornings, yet not necessarily a contrast any more than some young brown archer at Felicity, hearing the sacred text blared across the flagged field, with its battles and elephants and monkey-gods, in a contrast to the white child in Guadeloupe assembling fragments of his own epic from the lances of the cane fields, the estate carts and oxens, and the calligraphy of bamboo leaves from the ancient languages, Hindi, Chinese, and Arabic, on the Antillean sky. From the *Ramayana* to Anabasis, from Guadeloupe to Trinidad, all that archaeology of fragments lying around, from the broken African kingdoms, from the crevasses of Canton, from Syria and Lebanon, vibrating not under the earth but in our raucous, demotic streets.

A boy with weak eyes skims a flat stone across the flat water of an Aegean inlet, and that ordinary action with the scything elbow contains the skipping lines of the *Iliad* and the *Odyssey*, and another child aims a bamboo arrow at a village festival, another hears the rustling march of cabbage palms in a Caribbean sunrise, and from that sound, with its fragments of tribal myth, the compact expedition of Perse's epic is launched,

313

centuries and archipelagos apart. For every poet it is always morning in the world. History a forgotten, insomniac night; History and elemental awe are always our early beginnings, because the fate of poetry is to fall in love with the world, in spite of History.

There is a force of exultation, a celebration of luck, when a writer finds himself a witness to the early morning of a culture that is defining itself, branch by branch, leaf by leaf, in that self-defining dawn, which is why, especially at the edge of the sea, it is good to make a ritual of the sunrise. Then the noun, the "Antilles" ripples like brightening water, and the sounds of leaves, palm fronds, and birds are the sounds of a fresh dialect, the native tongue. The personal vocabulary, the individual melody whose metre is one's biography, joins in that sound, with any luck, and the body moves like a walking, waking island.

This is the benediction that is celebrated, a fresh language and a fresh people, and this is the frightening duty owed.

I stand here in their name, if not their image - but also in the name of the dialect they exchange like the leaves of the trees whose names are suppler, greener, more morning-stirred than English - *laurier canelles, bois-flot, bois-canot* - or the valleys the trees mention - *Fond St. Jacques, Mabonya, Forestièr, Roseau, Mahaut* - or the empty beaches - *L'Anse Ivrogne, Case en Bas, Paradis* - all songs and histories in themselves, pronounced not in French - but in patois.

One rose hearing two languages, one of the trees, one of school-children reciting in English:

> I am monarch of all I survey,
> My right there is none to dispute;
> From the centre all round to the sea
> I am lord of the fowl and the brute.
> Oh, solitude! where are the charms
> That sages have seen in thy face?
> Better dwell in the midst of alarms,
> Than reign in this horrible place -

While in the country to the same metre, but to organic instruments, hand-made violin, chac-chac, and goatskin drum, a girl named Sesenne singing:

Si mwen di 'ous' ça fait mwen la peine
'Ous kai dire ça vrai.
(If I told you that caused me pain
You'll say, "It's true".)
Si mwen di 'ous' ça pentetrait mwen
'Ous peut dire ça vrai
(If I told you you pierced my heart
You'd say, "It's true".)
Ces mamailles actuellement
Pas ka faire l'amour z'autres pour un rien.
(Children nowadays
Don't make love for nothing.)

It is not that History is obliterated by this sunrise. It is there in Antillean geography, in the vegetation itself. The sea sighs with the drowned from the Middle Passage, the butchery of its aborigines, Carib and Aruac and Taino, bleeds in the scarlet of the immortelle, and even the actions of surf on sand cannot erase the African memory, or the lances of cane as a green prison where indentured Asians, the ancestors of Felicity, are still serving time.

That is what I have read around me from boyhood, from the beginnings of poetry, the grace of effort. In the hard mahogany of woodcutters: faces, resinous men, charcoal burners; in a man with a cutlass cradled across his forearm, who stands on the verge with the usual anonymous khaki dog; in the extra clothes he put on this morning, when it was cold when he rose in the thinning dark to go and make his garden in the heights - the heights, the garden, being miles away from his house, but that is where he has his land - not to mention the fishermen, the footmen on trucks, groaning up mornes, all fragments of Africa originally but shaped and hardened and rooted now in the island's life, illiterate in the way leaves are illiterate; they do not read, they are there to be read, and if they are properly read, they create their own literature.

But in our tourist brochures the Caribbean is a blue pool into which the republic dangles the extended foot of Florida as inflated rubber islands bob and drinks with umbrellas float towards her on a raft. This is how the islands from the shame of necessity sell themselves; this is the seasonal erosion of their identity, that high-pitched repetition of the same images of service that cannot distinguish one island from the other, with a future of polluted marinas, land deals negotiated by ministers, and all of this conducted to the music of Happy Hour and the rictus of a smile. What is the earthly paradise for our visitors? Two weeks without rain and a mahogany tan, and, at sunset, local troubadours in straw hats and floral shirts beating "Yellow Bird" and "Banana Boat Song" to death. There is a territory wider than this - wider than the limits made by the map of an island - which is the illimitable sea and what it remembers.

All of the Antilles, every island, is an effort of memory; every mind, every racial biography culminating in amnesia and fog. Pieces of sunlight through the fog and sudden rainbows, *arcs-enciel*. That is the effort, the labour of the Antillean imagination, rebuilding its gods from bamboo frames, phrase by phrase.

Decimation from the Aruac downwards is the blasted root of Antillean history, and the benign blight that is tourism can infect all of those island nations, not gradually, but with imperceptible speed, until each rock is whitened by the guano of white-winged hotels, the arc and descent of progress.

Before it is all gone, before only a few valleys are left, pockets of an older life, before development turns every artist into an anthropologist or folklorist, there are still cherishable places, little valleys that do not echo with ideas, a simplicity of rebeginnings, not yet corrupted by the dangers of change. Not nostalgic sites but occluded sanctities as common and simple as their sunlight. Places as threatened by this prose as a headland is by the bull-dozer or a sea almond grove by the surveyor's string, or from blight, the mountain laurel.

One last epiphany: A basic stone church in a thick valley outside Soufrière, the hills almost shoving the houses around into a brown river, a sunlight that looks oily on the leaves, a backward place, unimportant, and one now being corrupted into significance by this prose. The idea is not to hallow or invest the place with anything, not even memory. African children in Sunday frocks come down the ordinary concrete steps into the church, banana leaves hang and glisten, a truck is parked in a yard, and old women totter towards the entrance. Here is where a real fresco should be painted, one without importance, but one with real faith, mapless, Historyless.

316

How quickly it could all disappear! And how it is beginning to drive us further into where we hope are impenetrable places, green secrets at the end of bad roads, headlands where the next view is not of a hotel but of some long beach without a figure and the hanging question of some fisherman's smoke at its far end. The Caribbean is not an idyll, not to its natives. They draw their working strength from it organically, like trees, like the sea almond or the spice laurel of the heights, Its peasantry and its fishermen are not there to be loved or even photographed; they are trees who sweat, and whose bark is filmed with salt, but every day on some island, rootless trees in suits are signing favourable tax breaks with entrepreneurs, poisoning the sea almond and the spice laurel of the mountains to their roots. A morning could come in which governments might ask what happened not merely to the forests and the bays but to a whole people.

They are here again, they recur, the faces, corruptible angels, smooth black skins and white eyes huge with an alarming joy, like those of the Asian children of Felicity at *Ramleela*; two different religions, two different continents, both filling the heart with the pain that is joy.

But what is joy without fear? The fear of selfishness that, here on this podium with the world paying attention not to them but to me, I should like to keep these simple joys inviolate, not because they are innocent, but because they are true. They are as true as when, in the grace of this gift, Perse heard the fragments of his own epic of Asia Minor in the rustling of cabbage palms, that inner Asia of the soul through which imagination wanders, if there is such a thing as imagination as opposed to the collective memory of our entire race, as true as the delight of that warrior-child who flew a bamboo arrow over the flags in the field at Felicity; and now as grateful a joy and a blessed fear as when a boy opened an exercise book and, within the discipline of its margins, framed stanzas that might contain the light of the hills on an island blest by obscurity, cherishing our insignificance.

1986 Nobel Prizewinner for Literature

Speech by Professor LARS GYLLENSTEN of the Swedish Academy.
Translation from the Swedish text

Your Majesties, Your Royal Highnesses, Ladies and Gentlemen,

Wole Soyinka, born in Nigeria in 1934, writes in English and is chiefly recognized as a dramatist. His many-sided and vital literary works also include some important collections of poems and novels, an interesting autobiography and a large number of articles and essays. He has been, and is, very active as a man of the theatre and has staged his own plays in England and Nigeria. He has himself taken part as an actor and energetically joined in theatrical debates and theatre policies. During the civil war in Nigeria in the middle of the 1960s he was drawn into the struggle for liberty because of his opposition to violence and terror. He was imprisoned under brutal and illegal forms in 1967 and was released over two years later - an experience that drastically affected his outlook on life and literary work.

Soyinka has depicted his childhood in a little African village. His father was a teacher, his mother a social worker - both Christian. But in the preceding generation there were medicine men and others who believed firmly in spirits, magic, and rites of anything but a Christian kind. We encounter a world in which tree spirits, ghosts, sorcerer and primitive African traditions were living realities. We also come face to face with a more complicated world of myth, which has its roots far back in an African culture handed down by word of mouth. This account of childhood gives a background to Soyinka's literary works - a self-experienced, close connection with a rich and complex African heritage.

Soyinka made an early appearance as a dramatist. It was natural for him to seek this art form, which is closely linked with the African material and with African forms of linguistic and mime creation. His plays make frequent and skilful use of many elements belonging to stage art and which also have genuine roots in African culture - dance and rites, masques and pantomime, rhythm and music, declamation, theatre within the theatre etc. His first dramas are lighter and more playful than the later ones - pranks, ironical and satirical scenes, pictures of everyday life with telling and witty dialogue, often with a tragi-comical or grotesque sense of life as keynote. Among these early plays can be mentioned *A Dance of the Forests* - a kind of African "Midsummer Night's Dream", with dryads, ghosts, spirits, and gods or demi-gods. It is about creativeness and sacrifice, with the god or hero Ogun as one of the performers. This Ogun is a Prometheus-like figure - the demi-god of iron and artistic skill but also of war and battle, a double figure combining both creation and destruction in his being. Soyinka has often reverted to him.

Soyinka's dramas are deeply rooted in an African world and culture. But he is also a widely read, not to say learned writer and dramatist. He is familiar with western literature, from the Greek tragedies to Beckett and Brecht. Also outside the field of drama he is well versed in the great European literature. A writer like James Joyce, for instance, has left traces in his novels. Soyinka is an author who writes with great deliberation, and especially in his novels and poems he can be avant-gardistically sophisticated.

During the war years, his time in prison and afterwards, his writing takes on a more tragic character. The psychological, moral and social conflicts appear more and more complex and menacing. The book-keeping of good and evil, of destructive and constructive forces, becomes increasingly ambiguous. His dramas become equivocal - dramas which in the shape of allegory or satire take up moral, social, and political matters for mythical-dramatic creation. The dialogue is sharpened, the characters become more expressive, often exaggerated to the point of caricature, demanding dénouement - the dramatic temperature is raised. The vitality is no less than in the first works - on the contrary: the satire, the humour, the elements of grotesquery and comedy, and the mythical fable-making come vividly to life. The way in which Soyinka makes use of the mythical material,

319

the African, and the literary schooling, the European, is very independent. He says he uses the myths as "the aesthetic matrix" for his writing. It is thus not a question of a folkloristic reproduction, a kind of exoticism, but an independent and co-operative work. The myths, traditions, and rites are integrated as nourishment for his writing, not a masquerade costume. He has called his wide reading and literary awareness a "selective eclecticism"- i.e. purposeful and sovereign choice. Among the later dramas special mention can be made of *Death and the King's Horseman* - a genuinely, dramatically convincing work full of many ideas and meanings, of poetry, satire, surprise, cruelty, and lust. Superficially it is about a conflict between western morals and convention on the one hand, and African culture and tradition on the other. The theme moves around a ritual or cultic human sacrifice. The drama goes so deeply into human and superhuman conditions that it cannot be reduced to something that teaches us about breaches between different civilizations. Soyinka himself prefers to see it as a metaphysical and religious drama of fate. It is about the conditions of the human identity and realization, the mythical pact of life and death, and the possibilities of the unborn.

To Soyinka's non-dramatic works belong the autobiographically inspired accounts *The Man Died*, from his time in prison, and the novel *The Interpreters*, from intellectual circles in Nigeria. The novel *Season of Anomy* is an allegory with the Orpheus and Eurydice myth as framework, a somewhat complicated, symbolic-expressionistic story with a background in brutal social and political conditions of oppression and corruption. Outstanding among the poems are collections with motifs from his time in prison, some of them written during his imprisonment as a kind of mental exercise to help the author survive with dignity and fortitude. The imagery in these poems is compact and rather hard to penetrate, sometimes, however, with a laconic or ascetic concentration. It take some time to get to know them intimately, but they can then yield a strange emanation that gives evidence of their background and role in a harsh, difficult period in the poet's life - moving testimony to courage and artistic strength.

As already mentioned, it is chiefly the dramas that stand out as Wole Soyinka's most significant achievement. They are of course made to be acted on the stage, with dance, music, masques, and mime as essential components. But his plays can also be read as important and fascinating literary works from a richly endowed writer's experience and imagination - and with roots in a composite culture with a wealth of living and artistically inspiring traditions.

Dear Mr. Soyinka,

In your versatile writings you have been able to synthesize a very rich heritage from your own country, ancient myths and old traditions, with literary legacies and traditions of European culture. There is a third component, a most important component in what you have thus achieved - your own genuine and impressive creativity as an artist, a master of language, and your commitment as a dramatist and writer of poetry and prose to problems of general and deep significance for man, modern or ancient. It is my privilege to convey to you the warm congratulations of the Swedish Academy and to ask you to receive this year's Nobel prize for literature from the hand of His Majesty the King.

DISCOURS DES LAURÉATS

Wole Soyinka

Your Majesties, Ladies and Gentlemen,

It was inevitable that the Nordic world and the African, especially that part of it which constitutes the Yoruba world - should meet at the crossroads of Sweden. That I am the agent of such a symbolic encounter is due very simply to that my creative Muse is Ogun, the god of creativity and destruction, of the lyric and metallurgy. This deity anticipated your scientist Alfred Nobel at the very beginning of time by clearing a path through primordial chaos, dynamiting his way through the core of earth to open a route for his fellow deities who sought to be reunited with us, mortals. I covered that event for my publishers - well, taking a few poetic licences, naturally - under the title IDANRE. You may have run into that reportage which has been translated into

321

Swedish under the title, OGUN SKUGGA. If you have not, I recommend that you proceed to the nearest bookseller for this piece of pre-history which makes Ogun, very definitively, the progenitor of your great inventor, Alfred Nobel.

I urge this especially because, if you happened to take a casual walk through the streets, or peer into the hotel lobbies of Stockholm, you might get the impression that my nation, Nigeria, has tried to solve some of its many problems by shifting half its population surreptitiously to Sweden. I assure you, however, that they have merely come to satisfy a natural curiosity about the true nationality of this inventor. For they cannot understand why their Ogun should have transferred such a potent secret to a Swede rather than to his Yoruba descendants. The mountains of Sweden are a tempting habitat for this deity, we know, but the Swedish winter and long midnights are hardly congenial to his temperament. And while the local acqua-vitae might help to infuse some warmth into his tropical joints, we do know that he tends to stick to his favourite palm wine.

Some day, I suppose, we will unravel this mystery. In the meantime, however, we will content ourselves with saluting the vision which made our presence here today a positive event, since it was Alfred Nobel's hope that the humanistic conversion, even of the most terrible knowledge, can improve the quality of life for mankind. That also is the lesson of Ogun, that essence of the warring duality of human nature. And we join in the endeavour that the lyric face of that demiurge will triumph in our time, snaring for all time that elusive bird - peace - on our planet earth.

WOLE SOYINKA

Soyinka was born on 13 July 1934 at Abeokuta, near Ibadan in western Nigeria. After preparatory university studies in 1954 at Government College in Ibadan, he continued at the University of Leeds, where later, in 1973, he took his doctorate. During the six years spent in England, he was a dramaturgist at the Royal Court Theatre in London 1958-59. In 1960, he was awarded a Rockefeller bursary and returned to Nigeria to study African drama. At the same time, he taught drama and literature at various universities, at Ibadan, Lagos, and Ife, where, since 1975, he has been professor of comparative literature. In 1960, he founded the theatre group "The 1960 Masks" and in 1964, the "Orisun Theatre Company", in which he has produced his own plays and taken part as actor. He has periodically been visiting professor at the universities of Cambridge, Sheffield, and Yale.

During the civil war in Nigeria, Soyinka appealed in an article for cease-fire. For this he was arrested in 1967, accused of conspiring with the Biafra rebels, and was held as a political prisoner for 22 months until 1969.

Soyinka has published about 20 works - drama, novels and poetry. He writes in English, and his literary language is marked by great scope and richness of words.

As dramatist Soyinka has been influenced by, among others, the Irish writer J.M. Synge but links up with the traditional popular African theatre with its combination of dance, music, and action. He bases his writing on the mythology of his own tribe - the Yoruba - with Ogun, the god of iron and war, at the centre. He wrote his first plays during his time in London - *The Swamp Dwellers* and *The Lion and the Jewel* (a light comedy), which were performed at Ibadan in 1958 and 1959 and were published in 1963. Later satirical comedies are *The Trial of Brother Jero* (performed in 1960, publ. 1963) with its sequel *Jero's Metamorphosis* (publ. 1973, performed 1974), *A Dance of the Forests* (performed 1960, publ. 1963), *Kongi's Harvest* (performed 1965, publ. 1967) and *Madmen and Specialists* (performed 1970, publ. 1971). Among Soyinka's serious philosophic plays are (apart from "The Swamp Dweller") *The Strong Breed* (publ. 1963, performed 1966), *The Road* (1965) and *Death and the King's Horseman* (publ. 1975, performed 1976). In *The Bacchae of Euripides* (1973) he has rewritten the Bacchae for the African stage and in *Opera Wonyosi* (performed 1977, publ. 1981) bases himself on John Gay's *Beggar's Opera* and Brecht's *The Threepenny Opera*. Soyinka's latest dramatic works are *A Play of Giants* (1984) and *Requiem for a Futurologist* (1985).

Soyinka has written two novels, *The Interpreters* (1965), narratively a complicated work which has been compared to Joyce's and Faulkner's, in which six Nigerian intellectuals discuss and interpret their African experiences, and *Season of Anomy*

(1973), which is based on the writer's thoughts during his imprisonment and confronts the Orpheus and Euridice myth with the mythology of the Yoruba. Purely autobiographical are *The Man Died: Prison Notes* (1972) and the account of his childhood *Aké* (1981), in which the parents' warmth and interest in their son are prominent. Literary essays are collected in, among others, *Myth, Literature and the African World* (1975).

Soyinka's poems, which show a close connection to his plays, are collected in *Idanre, and Other Poems* (1967), *Poems from Prison* (1969), *A Shuttle in the Crypt* (1972) and in the long poem *Ogun Abibiman* (1976).

THIS PAST MUST ADDRESS ITS PRESENT
Nobel lecture, December 8, 1986
by
WOLE SOYINKA
*Institut International du Théâtre,
1, rue Miollis, F-75015 Paris, France.*

A rather curious scene, unscripted, once took place in the wings of a London theatre at the same time as the scheduled performance was being presented on the actual stage, before an audience. What happened was this: an actor refused to come on stage for his allocated role. Action was suspended. A fellow actor tried to persuade him to emerge, but he stubbornly shook his head. Then a struggle ensued. The second actor had hoped that, by suddenly exposing the reluctant actor to the audience in full glare of the spotlight, he would have no choice but to rejoin the cast. And so he tried to take the delinquent actor by surprise, pulling him suddenly towards the stage. He did not fully succeed, so a brief but untidy struggle began. The unwilling actor was completely taken aback and deeply embarrassed - some of that tussle was quite visible to a part of the audience.

The performance itself, it should be explained, was an improvisation around an incident. This meant that the actors were free, within the convention of the performance - to stop, re-work any part they wished, invite members of the audience on stage, assign roles and change costumes in full view of the audience. They therefore could also dramatize their wish to have that unco-operative actor join them - which they did with gusto. That actor had indeed left the stage before the contentious scene began. He had served notice during rehearsals that he would not partici-pate in it. In the end, he had his way, but the incident proved very troubling to him for weeks afterwards. He found himself compelled to puzzle out this clash in attitudes between himself and his fellow writers and performers. He experienced, on the one hand, an intense rage that he had been made to appear incapable of confronting a stark reality, made to appear to suffer from interpretative coyness, to seem inhibited by a cruel reality or perhaps to carry his emotional involvement with an event so far as to interfere with this professional will. Of course, he knew that it was none of these things. The truth was far simpler. Unlike his colleagues together with whom he shared, unques-tionably, the same political attitude towards the event which was being represented, he found the mode of presentation at war with the ugliness it tried to convey, creating an intense disquiet about his very presence on that stage, in that place, before an audience whom he considered collectively responsible for that dehuman-izing actuality.

And now let us remove some of the mystery and make that incident a little more concrete. The scene was the Royal Court Theatre, London, 1958. It was one of those Sunday nights which were given to experimentation, an innovation of that remark-able theatre manager-director, George Devine, whose creative nurturing radicalised British theatre of that period and produced later icons like John Osborne, N.F. Simpson, Edward Bond, Arnold Wesker, Harold Pinter, John Arden, etc., and even forced the then conservative British palate to sample stylistic and ideological pariahs like Samuel Beckett and Bertold Brecht. On this particular occasion, the evening was devoted to a form of "living" theatre, and the main fare was titled ELEVEN MEN DEAD AT HOLA. The actors were not all professional actors; indeed they were mostly writers who jointly created and performed these dramatic pieces. Those with a long political memory may recall what took place at Hola Camp, Kenya, during the Mau-Mau Liberation struggle. The British Colonial

325

power believed that the Mau-Mau could be smashed by herding Kenyans into special camps, trying to separate the hard cases, the mere suspects and the potential recruits - oh, they had it all neatly worked out. One such camp was Hola Camp and the incident involved the death of eleven of the detainees who were simply beaten to death by camp officers and warders. The usual enquiry set up, and it was indeed the Report which provided the main text on which the performance was based.

We need now only identify the reluctant actor and, if you have not guessed that by now - it was none other than this speaker. I recall the occasion as vividly as actors are wont to recollect for ever and ever the frightening moment of a blackout, when the lines are not only forgotten but even the moment in the play. The role which I had been assigned was that of a camp guard, one of the killers. We were equipped with huge night-sticks and, while a narrator read the testimony of one of the guards, our task was to raise the cudgels slowly and, almost ritualistically, bring them down on the necks and shoulders of the prisoners, under orders of the white camp officers. A surreal scene. Even in rehearsals, it was clear that the end product would be a surrealist tableau. The Narrator at a lectern under a spot; a dispassionate reading, deliberately clinical, letting the stark facts reveal the states of mind of torturers and victims. A small ring of white officers, armed. One seizes a cudgel from one of the warders to demonstrate how to beat a human being without leaving visible marks. Then the innermost clump of detainees, their only weapon - non-violence. They had taken their decision to go on strike, refused to go to work unless they obtained better camp conditions. So they squatted on the ground and refused to move, locked their hands behind their knees in silent defiance. Orders were given. The inner ring of guards, the blacks, moved in, lifted the bodies by hooking their hands underneath the armpits of the detainees, carried them like toads in a state of petrification to one side, divided them in groups.

The faces of the victims are impassive; they are resolved to offer no resistance. The beatings begin: one to the left side, then the back, the arms - right, left, front, back. Rhythmically. The cudgels swing in unison. The faces of the white guards glow with professional satisfaction, their arms gesture languidly from time to time, suggesting it is time to shift to the next batch, or beat a little more severely on the neglected side. In terms of images, a fluid, near balletic scene.

Then the contrast, the earlier official version, enacting how the prisoners were supposed to have died. This claimed that the prisoners had collapsed, that they died after drinking from a poisoned water supply. So we staged that also. The prisoners filed to the water wagons, gasping with thirst. After the first two or three had drunk and commenced writhing with pain, these humane guards rushed to stop the others but no, they were already wild with thirst, fought their way past salvation and drank greedily the same source. The groans spread from one to the other, the writhing, the collapse - then agonized deaths. That was the version of the camp governors.

The motif was simple enough, the theatrical format a tried and tested one, faithful to a particular convention. What then was the problem? It was one, I believe, that affects most writers. When is playacting rebuked by reality? When is fictionalizing presumptuous? What happens after playacting? One of the remarkable properties of the particular theatrical convention I have just described is that it gives off a strong odour of perenniality, that feeling of "I have been here before". "I have been witness to this." "The past enacts its presence." In such an instance, that sense of perenniality can serve both as exorcism, a certificate of release or indeed - especially for the audience, a soporific. We must bear in mind that at the time of presentation, and to the major part of that audience, every death of a freedom fighter was a notch on a gun, the death of a fiend, an animal, a bestial mutant, not the martyrdom of a patriot.

We know also, however, that such efforts can provoke changes, that an actualization of the statistical, journalistic footnote can arouse revulsion in the complacent mind, leading to the beginning of a commitment to change, redress. And on this occasion, angry questions had been raised in the Houses of Parliament. Liberals, humanitarians and reformists had taken up the cause of justice for the victims. Some had even travelled to Kenya to obtain details which exposed the official lie. This profound unease which paralysed my creative will, therefore reached beyond the audience and, finally, I traced its roots to my own feelings of assaulted humanity, and its clamour for a different form of response. It provoked a feeling of indecency about that presentation, rather like the deformed arm of a leper which is thrust at the healthy to provoke a charitable sentiment. This, I believe, was the cause of that intangible, but totally visceral rejection which thwarted the demands of my calling, rendered it inadequate and mocked the empathy of my colleagues. It was as if the inhuman totality, of which that scene was a mere fragment, was saying to us: Kindly keep your comfortable sentiment to yourselves.

Of course, I utilize that episode only as illustration of the far deeper internalised processes of the creative mind, a process that endangers the writer in two ways: he either freezes up completely, or he abandons the pen for far more direct means of contesting unacceptable reality. And again, Hola Camp provides a convenient means of approaching that aspect of my continent's reality which, for us whom it directly affronts, constitutes the greatest threat to global peace in our actual existence. For there is a gruesome appropriateness in the fact that an African, a black man should stand here today, in the same year that the progressive Prime Minister of this host country was murdered, in the same year as Samora Machel was brought down on the territory of the desperate last-ditch guardians of the theory of racial superiority which has brought so much misery to our common humanity. Whatever the facts are about Olaf Palme's death, there can be no question about his life. To the racial oppression of a large sector of humanity, Olaf Palme pronounced, and acted, a decisive No! Perhaps it was those who were outraged by this act of racial "treachery" who were myopic enough to imagine that the death of an individual would arrest the march of his convictions; perhaps it was simply yet another instance of the Terror Epidemic that feeds today on shock, not reason. It does not matter; an authentic conscience of the white tribe has been stilled, and the loss is both yours and mine. Samora Machel, the leader who once placed his country on a war footing against South Africa went down in as yet mysterious circumstances. True, we are all still haunted by the Nkomati Accord which negated that earlier triumphant moment on the African collective will; nevertheless, his foes across the border have good reason to rejoice over his demise and, in that sense, his death is, ironically, a form of triumph for the black race.

Is that perhaps too stark a paradox? Then let me take you back to Hola Camp. It is cattle which are objects of the stick, or whip. So are horses, goats, donkeys etc. Their definition therefore involves being occasionally beaten to death. If, thirty years after Hola Camp, it is at all thinkable that it takes the ingenuity of the most sophisticated electronic interference to kill an African resistance fighter, the champions of racism are already admitting to themselves what they continue to deny to the world: that they, white supremacist breed, have indeed come a long way in their definition of their chosen enemy since Hola Camp. They have come an incredibly long way since Sharpeville when they shot unarmed, fleeing Africans in the back. They have come very far since 1930 when, at the first organized incident of the burning of passes, the South African blacks decided to turn Dingaan's Day, named for the defeat of the Zulu leader Dingaan, into a symbol of affirmative resistance by publicly destroying their obnoxious passes. In response to those thousands of passes burnt on Cartright Flats, the Durban police descended on the unarmed protesters killing some half dozen and wounding hundreds. They backed it up with scorched earth campaign which dispersed thousands of Africans from their normal environment, victims of imprisonments and deportation. And even that 1930 repression was a quantum leap from that earlier, spontaneous protest against the Native Pass law in 1919, when the police merely rode down the protesters on horseback, whipped and sjamboked them, chased and harried them, like stray goats and wayward cattle, from street corner to shanty lodge. Every act of racial terror, with its vastly increasing sophistication of style and escalation in human loss, is itself an acknowledgement of improved knowledge and respect for the potential of what is feared, an acknowledgement of the sharpening tempo of triumph by the victimized.

For there was this aspect which struck me most forcibly in that attempt to recreate the crime at Hola Camp: in the various testimonies of the white officers, it stuck out, whether overtly stated or simply through their efficient detachment from the on-

329

going massacre. It was this: at no time did these white overseers actually experience the human "otherness" of their victims. They clearly did not experience the reality of the victims as human beings. Animals perhaps, a noxious form of vegetable life maybe, but certainly not human. I do not speak here of their colonial overlords, the ones who formulated and sustained the policy of settler colonialism, the ones who dispatched the Maxim guns and tuned the imperial bugle. They knew very well that empires existed which had to be broken, that civilizations had endured for centuries which had to be destroyed. The "sub-human" denigration for which their "civilizing mission" became the altruistic remedy, was the mere rationalizing icing on the cake of imperial greed. But yes indeed, there were the agents, those who carried out orders (like Eichmann, to draw parallels from the white continent); they - whether as bureaucrats, tech-nicians or camp governors had no conceptual space in their heads which could be filled - except very rarely and exceptionally - by "the black as *also* human". It would be correct to say that this has remained the pathology of the average South African white since the turn of the last century to this moment. Here, for example is one frank admission by an enlightened, even radical mind of that country:

> "It was not until my last year in school that it had occurred to me that these black people, these voteless masses, were in any way concerned with the socialism which I professed or that they had any role to play in the great social revolution which in these days seemed to be imminent. The 'workers' who were destined to inherit the new world were naturally the white carpenters and bricklayers, the tramworkers and miners who were organized in their trade unions and who voted for the Labour Party. I would no more have thought of discussing politics with a native youth than of inviting him home to play with me or to a meal or asking him to join the Carnarvon Football Club. The African was on a different plane, hardly human, part of the scene as were dogs and trees and, more remotely, cows, I had no special feelings about him, not interest nor hate nor love. He just did not come into my social picture. So completely had I accepted the traditional attitudes of the time."

Yes, I believe that this self-analysis by Eddie Roux, the Afrikaaner political rebel and scientist, remains today the flat, unvarnished truth for the majority of Afrikaaners. "No special feelings, not interest nor hate nor love", the result of a complete acceptance of "traditional attitudes". That passage captures a mind's racial tabula rasa, if you like - in the first decade of this century - about the time, in short, when the Nobel series of prizes was inaugurated. But a slate, no matter how clean, cannot avoid receiving impressions once it is exposed to air - fresh or polluted. And we are now in the year 1986, that is after an entire century of direct, intimate exposure, since that confrontation, that first rejection of the dehumanizing label implicit in the Native Pass Laws.

Eddie Roux, like hundreds, even thousands of his country-men, soon made rapid strides. His race has produced its list of martyrs in the cause of non-racialism - one remembers, still with a tinge of pain, Ruth First, destroyed by a letter bomb delivered by the long arm of Apartheid. There are others - André Brink, Abram Fischer, Helen Suzman, Breyten Breytenbach - with the scars of martyrdom still seared into their souls. Intellectuals, writers, scientists, plain working men, politicians - they come to that point where a social reality can no longer be observed as a culture on a slide beneath the microscope, nor turned into aesthetic variations on pages, canvas or the stage. The blacks of course are locked into an unambiguous condition: on this occasion I do not need to address *us*. We know, and we embrace our mission. It is the *other* that this precedent seizes the opportunity to address, and not merely those who are trapped within the confines of that doomed camp, but those who live outside, on the fringes of conscience. Those specifically, who with shame-less smugness invent arcane moral propositions that enable them to plead inaction in a language of unparalleled political flatulence: "Personally, I find sanctions morally repugnant". Or what shall we say of another leader for whom economic sanc-tions which work against an Eastern European country will not work in the Apartheid enclave of South Africa, that master of histrionics who takes to the world's airwaves to sing: "Let Poland be", but turns off his hearing aid when the world shouts: "Let Nicaragua be". But enough of these world leaders of double-talk and multiple moralities.

It is baffling to any mind that pretends to the slightest claim to rationality, it is truly and formidably baffling. Can the same terrain of phenomenal assimilation - that is, one which produced evidence of a capacity to translate empirical observations into implications of rational human conduct - can this same terrain which, over half a century ago, fifty entire years, two, three generations ago produced the Buntings, the Roux, the Douglas Woltons, Solly Sachs, the Gideon Bothas - can that same terrain, fifty, sixty, even seventy years later, be peopled by a species of humanity so ahistorical that the declaration, so clearly spelt out in 1919 at the burning of the passes, remains only a troublesome event of no enduring significance?

Some atavistic bug is at work here which defies all scientific explanation, an arrest in time within the evolutionary mandate of nature, which puts all human experience of learning to serious question! We have to ask ourselves then, what event can speak to such a breed of people? How do we reactivate that petrified cell which houses historic apprehension and development? Is it possible, perhaps, that events, gatherings such as this might help? Dare we skirt the edge of hubris and say to them: Take a good look. Provide your response. In your anxiety to prove that this moment is not possible, you had killed, maimed, silenced, tortured, exiled, debased and dehumanized hundreds of thousands encased in this very skin, crowned with such hair, proudly content with their very being. How many political partners in the science of heart transplant have you wasted? How do we know how many black South African scientists and writers would have stood here, by now, if you had had the vision to educate the rest of the world in the value of a great multi-racial society?

Jack Cope surely sums it up in his Foreword to THE ADVERSARY WITHIN, a study of dissidence in Afrikaaner literature when he states:

"Looking back from the perspective of the present, I think it can justly be said that, at the core of the matter, the Afrikaaner leaders in 1924 took the wrong turning. Themselves the victims of imperialism in its most evil aspect, all their sufferings and enormous loss of life nevertheless failed to convey to them the obvious historical lesson. They became themselves the new imperialists. They took over from Britain the mantle of empire and colonialism. They could well have set their faces against annexation, aggression, colonial exploitation, and oppression, racial arrogance and barefaced hypocrisy, of which they had been themselves the victims. They could have opened the doors to humane ideas and civilizing processes and transformed the great territory with its incalculable resources into another New World.

Indeed they deliberately set the clock back wherever they could. Taking over ten million indigenous subjects from British colonial rule, they stripped them of what limited rights they had gained over a century and tightened the screws on their subjection."

Well, perhaps the wars against Chaka and Dingaan and Diginswayo, even the Great Trek were then too fresh in your *laager memory*. But we are saying that over a century has passed since then, a century in which the world has leapt, in comparative tempo with the past, at least three centuries. And we have seen the potential of man and woman - of all races - contend with the most jealously guarded sovereignty of Nature and the Cosmos. In every field, both in the Humanities and Sciences, we have seen that human creativity has confronted and tempered the hostility of his environment, adapting, moderating, converting, harmonizing, and even subjugating. Triumphing over errors and resuming the surrendered fields, when man has had time to lick his wounds and listen again to the urgings of his spirit. History - distorted, opportunistic renderings of history have been cleansed and restored to truthful reality, because the traducers of the history of others have discovered that the further they advanced, the more their very progress was checked and vitiated by the lacunae they had purposefully inserted in the history of others. Self-interest dictated yet another round of revisionism - slight, niggardly concessions to begin with. But a breach had been made in the dam and an avalanche proved the logical progression. From the heart of jungles, even before the aid of high-precision cameras mounted on orbiting satellites, civilizations have resurrected, documenting their own existence with unassailable iconography and art. More amazing still, the records of the ancient voyagers, the merchant adventurers of the age when Europe did not yet require to dominate territories in order to feed its industrial mills - those objective recitals of mariners and adventurers from antiquity confirmed what the archeological remains affirmed so loudly. They spoke of living communities which regulated their own lives, which had evolved a working relationship with Nature, which ministered to their own wants and secured their future with their own genius. These narratives, uncluttered by the impure motives which needed to mystify the plain self-serving rush to dismantle independent societies for easy plundering - pointed accusing fingers unerringly in the direction of European savants, philosophers, scientists, and theorists of human evolution. Gobineau is a notorious name, but how many students of European thought today, even among us Africans, recall that several of the most revered names in European philosophy - Hegel, Locke, Montesquieu, Hume, Voltaire - an endless list - were unabashed theorists of racial superiority and denigrators of the African history and being? As for the more prominent names among the theorists of revolution and class struggle - we will draw the curtain of extenuation on their own intellectual aberration, forgiving them a little for their vision of an end to human exploitation.

In any case, the purpose is not really to indict the past, but to summon it to the attention of a suicidal, anachronistic present. To say to that mutant present: you are a child of those centuries of lies, distortion and opportunism in high places, even among the holy of holies of intellectual objectivity. But the world is growing up, while you wilfully remain child, a stubborn, self-destructive child, with certain destructive powers, but a child nevertheless. And to say to the world, to call attention to its own historic passage of lies - as yet unabandoned by some - which sustains the evil precosity of this child. Wherein then lies the surprise that we, the victims of that intellectual dishonesty of others, demand from that world that is finally coming to itself, a measure of expiation? Demand that it rescues itself, by concrete acts, from the stigma of being the wilful parent of a monstrosity, especially as that monstrous child still draws material nourishment, breath, and human recognition from the strengths and devices of that world, with an umbilical cord which stretches across oceans, even across the cosmos via so-called programmes of technological co-operation. We are saying very simply but urgently: Sever that cord. By any name, be it Total Sanction, Boycott, Disinvestment, or whatever, sever this umbilical cord and leave this monster of a birth to atrophy and die or to re-build itself on long-denied humane foundations. Let it collapse, shorn of its external sustenance, let it collapse of its own social disequilibrium, its economic lopsidedness, its war of attrition on its most productive labour. Let it wither like an aborted foetus of the human family if it persists in smothering the minds and sinews which constitute its authentic being.

This pariah society that is Apartheid South Africa plays many games on human intelligence. Listen to this for example. When the whole world escalated its appeal for the release of Nelson Mandela, the South African Government blandly declared that it continued to hold Nelson Mandela for the same reasons that the Allied powers continued to hold Rudolf Hess! Now a statement like that is an obvious appeal to the love of the ridi-culous in everyone. Certainly it wrung a kind of satiric poem out of me - Rudolf Hess as Nelson Mandela in blackface! What else can a writer do to protect his humanity against such egregious assaults! But yet again to equate Nelson Mandela to the arch-criminal Rudolf Hess is a macabre improvement on the attitude of regarding him as sub-human. It belongs on that same scale of Apartheid's self-improvement as the ratio between Sharpeville and Von Brandis Square, that near-kind, near-considerate, almost benevolent dispersal of the first Native Press rebellion.

That world which is so conveniently traduced by Apartheid thought is of course that which I so wholeheartedly embrace - and this is my choice - among several options - of the significance of my presence here. It is a world that nourishes my being, one which is so self-sufficient, so replete in all aspects of its productivity, so confident in itself and in its destiny that it experiences no fear in reaching out to others and in responding to the reach of others. It is the heartstone of our creative exis-tence. It constitutes the prism of our world perception and this means that our sight need not be and has never been permanently turned inwards. If it were, we could not so easily understand the enemy on our doorstep, nor understand how to obtain the means to disarm it. When this society which is Apartheid South Africa indulges from time to time in appeals to the outside world that it represents the last bastion of civilization against the hordes of barbarism from its North, we can even afford an indulgent smile. It is sufficient, imagines this state, to raise the spectre of a few renegade African leaders, psychopaths and robber barons who we ourselves are victims of - whom we denounce before the world and overthrow when we are able - this Apartheid society insists to the world that its picture of the future is the reality which only its policies can erase. This is a continent which only destroys, it proclaims, it is peopled by a race which has never contributed anything positive to the world's pool of knowledge. A vacuum that will suck into its insatiable maw the entire fruits of centuries of European civilization, then spew out the resulting mush with contempt. How strange that a society which claims to represent this endangered face of progress should itself be locked in centuries-old fantasies, blithely unaware of, or indifferent to the fact that it is the last, institutionally functioning product of archaic articles of faith in Euro-Judaic thought.

Take God and law for example, especially the former. The black race has more than sufficient historic justification to be a little paranoid about the intrusion of alien deities into its destiny. For even today, Apartheid's mentality of the pre-ordained rests - according to its own unabashed claims, on what I can only describe as incidents in a testamentary Godism - I dare not call it Christianity. The sons of Ham on the one hand; the descendants of Shem on the other. The once pronounced, utterly immutable curse. As for Law, these supremacists base their refusal to concede the right of equal political participation to blacks on a claim that Africans have neither respect for, nor the slightest proclivity for Law - that is, for any arbitrating concept between the individual and the collective.

Even the mildest, liberal, somewhat regretful but contented apologists for Apartheid, for at least some form of Apartheid which is not Apartheid but ensures the *status quo* - even this ambivalent breed bases its case on this lack of the idea of Law in the black mind. I need only refer to a recent contribution to this literature in the form of an autobiography by a famous heart transplant surgeon, one who in his own scientific right has probably been a candidate for a Nobel Prize in the Sciences. Despite constant intellectual encounters on diverse levels, the sad phenomenon persists of Afrikaaner minds which, in the words of Eddie Roux, is a product of that complete acceptance of the "traditional attitudes of the time".

They have, as already acknowledged, quite "respectable" intellectual ancestors. Friedrich Wilhelm Hegel, to cite just my favourite example, found it convenient to pretend that the African had not yet developed to the level where he

> "attained that realization of any substantial objective existence - as for example, God, or Law - in which the interest of man's volition is involved and in which he realizes his own being".

He continues:

> "This distinction between himself as an individual and the universality of his essential being, the African in the uniform, undeveloped oneness of his existence, has not yet attained: so that the knowledge of absolute Being, an Other and a Higher than his individual self, is entirely wanting".

Futile to waste a moment refuting the banal untruthfulness of this claim, I content myself with extracting from it only a lesson which escapes, even today, those who insist that the pinnacle of man's intellectual thirst is the capacity to project this universality in the direction of a Super-Other. There is, I believe a very healthy school of thought which not only opposes this materially, but has produced effectively structured societies which operate independently of this seductive, even productively, inspiring but extravagant fable.

Once we thus overcome the temptation to contest the denial of this feat of imaginative projection to the African, we find ourselves left only with the dispassionate exercise of examining in what areas we encounter differences between the histories of societies which, according to Hegel and company, never conceived of this Omnipotent Extrusion into Infinite Space, and those who did - be these differences in the areas of economic or artistic life, social relations or scientific attainment - in short, in all those activities which are empirically verifiable, quite different from the racial consequences of imprecations arising from that post Adam-and-Eve nudist escapade in the Old Testament.

When we do this, we come upon a curious fact. The pre-colonial history of African stories - and I refer to both Euro-Christian and Arab-Islamic colonization - indicates very clearly that African societies never at any time of their existence went to war with another over the issue of *their* religion. That is, at no time did the black race attempt to subjugate or forcibly convert others with any holier-than-thou evangelizing zeal. Economic and political motives, yes. But not religion. Perhaps this unnatural fact was responsible for the conclusions of Hegel - we do not know. Certainly, the bloody histories of the world's major religions, localized skirmishes of which extend even to the present, lead to a sneaking suspicion that religion, as defined by these eminent philosophers, comes to self-knowledge only through the activity of war.

When, therefore, towards the close of the twentieth century, that is, centuries after the Crusades and Jihads that laid waste other and one another's civilizations, fragmented ancient cohesive social relations and trampled upon the spirituality of entire peoples, smashing their cultures in obedience to the strictures of unseen gods, when today, we encounter nations whose social reasoning is guided by canonical, theological claims, we believe, on our part, that the era of darkness has never truly left the world. A state whose justification for the continuing suppression of its indigenes, indigenes who constitute the majority on that land, rests on claims to divine selection is a menace to secure global relationship in a world that thrives on nationalism as common denominator. Such a society does not, in other words, belong in this modern world. We also have our myths, but we have never employed them as a base for the subjugation of others. We also inhabit a realistic world, however, and, for the recovery of the fullness of that world, the black race has no choice but to prepare itself and volunteer the supreme sacrifice.

In speaking of that world - both myth and reality - it is our duty, perhaps our very last peaceful duty to a doomed enemy - to remind it, and its supporters outside its boundaries, that the phenomenon of ambivalence induced by the African world has

338

a very long history, but that most proponents of the slanderous aspects have long ago learnt to abandon the untenable. Indeed it is probably even more pertinent to remind this racist society that our African world, its cultural hoards and philosophical thought, have had concrete impacts on the racists' own forebears, have proved seminal to a number of movements and even created tributaries, both pure and polluted, among the white indigenes in their own homelands.

Such a variety of encounters and responses have been due, naturally, to profound searches for new directions in their cultural adventures, seeking solaces to counter the remorseless mechanization of their existence, indeed seeking new meanings for the mystery of life and attempting to overcome the social malaise created by the very triumphs of their own civilization. It has led to a profound respect for the African contribution to world knowledge, which did not, however, end the habitual denigration of the African world. It has created in places a near-deification of the African person - that phase in which every African had to be a prince - which yet again, was coupled with a primitive fear and loathing for the person of the African. To these paradoxical responses, the essentiality of our black being remains untouched. For the black race knows, and is content simply to know, itself. It is the European world that has sought, with the utmost zeal, to re-define itself through these encounters, even when it does appear that he is endeavouring to grant meaning to an experience of the African world.

We can make use of the example of that period of European Expressionism, a movement which saw African art, music, and dramatic rituals share the same sphere of influence as the most disparate, astonishingly incompatible collection of ideas, ideologies, and social tendencies - Freud, Karl Marx, Bakunin, Nietzsche, cocaine, and free love. What wonder then, that the spiritual and plastic presences of the Bakota, Nimba, the Yoruba, Dogon, Dan etc., should *find themselves at once the inspiration* and the anathematized of a delirium that was most peculiarly European, mostly Teutonic and Gallic, spanning at least four decades across the last and the present centuries. Yet the vibrant goal remained the complete liberation of man, that freeing of his yet untapped potential that would carve marble blocks for

the constructing of a new world, debourgeoisify existing con-
strictions of European thought and light the flame to forge a
new fraternity throughout this brave new world. Yes, within
this single movement that covered the vast spectrum of outright
fascism, anarchism, and revolutionary communism, the reality
that was Africa was as always, sniffed at, delicately tested,
swallowed entire, regurgitated, appropriated, extolled, and
damned in the revelatory frenzy of a continent's recreative
energies.

Oscar Kokoschka for instance: for this dramatist and painter
African ritualism led mainly in the direction of sadism, sexual
perversion, general self-gratification. It flowed naturally into a
Nietzschean apocalyptic summons, full of self-induced, ecstatic
rage against society, indeed, against the world. Vassily Kadinsky
on his part, responded to the principles of African art by
foreseeing:

> "a science of art erected on a broad foundation which must be
> international in character".

insisting that

> "it is interesting, but certainly not sufficient, to create an
> exclusively European art theory".

The science of art would then lead, according to him, to

> "a comprehensive synthesis which will extend far beyond the
> confines of art into the realm of the oneness of the human
> and the 'divine'".

This same movement, whose centenary will be due for celebrations in European artistic capitals in the next decade or two -
among several paradoxes the phenomenon of European artists
of later acknowledged giant stature - Modigliani, Matisse,
Gauguin, Picasso, Brancusi etc. worshipping with varying degrees
of fervour, at the shrine of African and Polynesian artistic
revelations, even as Johannes Becher, in his Expressionist
delirium, swore to build a new world on the eradication of all
plagues, including -

340

"Negro tribes, fever, tuberculosis, venereal epidemics, intellectual psychic defects - I'll fight them, vanquish them."

And was it by coincidence that contemporaneously with this
stirring manifesto, yet another German enthusiast, Leo Frobenius
- with no claims whatever to being part of, or indeed having the
least interest in the Expressionist movement, was able to visit
Ile-Ife, the heartland and cradle of the Yoruba race and be
profoundly stirred by an object of beauty, the product of the
Yoruba mind and hand, a classic expression of that serene
portion of the world resolution of that race, in his own words:

> "Before us stood a head of marvellous beauty, wonderfully
> cast in antique bronze, true to life, incrusted with a patina of
> glorious dark green. This was, in very deed, the Olokun,
> Atlantic Africa's Poseidon."

Yet listen to what he had to write about the very people whose
handiwork had lifted him into these realms of universal
sublimity:

> "Profoundly stirred, I stood for many minutes before the
> remnant of the erstwhile Lord and Ruler of the Empire of
> Atlantis. My companions were no less astounded. As though
> we have agreed to do so, we held our peace. Then I looked
> around and saw - the blacks - the circle of the sons of the
> 'venerable priest', his Holiness the Oni's friends, and his
> intelligent officials. I was moved to silent melancholy at the
> thought that this assembly of degenerate and feeble-minded
> posterity should be the legitimate guardians of so much
> loveliness."

A direct invitation to a free-for-all race for dispossession,
justified on the grounds of the keeper's unworthiness, it recalls
other schizophrenic conditions which are mother to, for instance,
the far more lethal, dark mythopoeia of Van Lvyck Louw, For
though this erstwhile Nazi sympathizer would later rain
maledictions on the heads of the more extreme racists of his
countrymen:

> "Lord, teach us to think what 'own' is, Lord let us think! and
> then: over hate against blacks, browns, whites: over this and
> its cause, I dare to call down judgement."

341

Van Lvyck's powerful epic RAKA was guaranteed to churn up the white cesspools of these primordial fears. A work of searing, visceral impact operating on racial memory, it would feed the Afrikaaner Credo on the looming spectre of a universal barbaric recession, bearing southwards on the cloven hooves of the Fifth Horseman of the Apocalypse, the black.

There is a deep lesson for the world in the black races' capacity to forgive, one which, I often think, has much to do with ethical precepts which spring from their world view and authentic religions, none of which is ever totally eradicated by the accretions of foreign faiths and their implicit ethnocentricism. For, not content with being a racial slanderer, one who did not hesitate to denigrate, in such uncompromisingly nihilistic terms, the ancestral fount of the black races - a belief which this ethnologist himself observed - Frobenius was also a notorious plunderer, one of a long line of European archeological raiders. The museums of Europe testify to this insatiable lust of Europe; the frustrations of the Ministries of Culture of the Third World and of organizations like UNESCO are a continuing testimony to the tenacity, even recidivist nature of your routine receiver of stolen goods. Yet, is it not amazing that Frobenius is today still honoured by black institutions, black leaders, and scholars? That his anniversaries provide ready excuse for intellectual gatherings and symposia on the black continent, *that his racist condescensions, assaults* have not been permitted to obscure his contribution to their knowledge of Africa, or the role which he has played in the understanding of the phenomenon of human culture and society, even in spite of the frequent patchiness of his scholarship?

It is the same largeness of spirit which has informed the relationship today of erstwhile colonial nations, some of whom have undergone the most cruel forms of settler or plantation colonialism, where the human degradation that goes with greed and exploitation attained such levels of perversion that human ears, hands, and noses served to atone for failures in production quota. Nations which underwent the agony of wars of liberation, whose earth freshly teems with the bodies of innocent victims and unsung martyrs, live side by side today with their recent enslavers, even sharing the control of their destiny with those

342

who, barely four or five years ago, compelled them to witness the massacre of their kith and kin. Over and above Christian charity, they are content to rebuild, and share. This spirit of collaboration is easy to dismiss as the treacherous ploy of that special breed of leaders who settle for early compromises in order to safeguard, for their own use, the polished shoes of the departing oppressors. In many cases, the truth of this must be conceded. But we also have examples of regimes, allied to the aspirations of their masses on the black continent, which have adopted this same political philosophy. And, in any case, the final arbiters are the people themselves, from whose relationships any observations such as this obtain any validity. Let us simply content ourselves with remarking that it is a phenomenon worthy of note. There are, after all, European nations today whose memory of domination by other races remains so vivid more than two centuries after liberation, that a terrible vengeance culturally, socially, and politically is still exacted, even at this very moment, from the descendants of those erstwhile conquerors. I have visited such nations whose cruel histories under foreign domination are enshrined as icons to daily consciousness in monuments, parks, in museums and churches, in documentation, woodcuts, and photogravures displayed under bullet-proof glass-cases but, most telling of all, in the reduction of the remnants of the conquering hordes to the degraded status of aliens on sufferance, with reduced civic rights, privileges, and social status, a barely tolerable marginality that expresses itself in the pathos of downcast faces, dropped shoulders, and apologetic encounters in those rare times when intercourse with the latterly assertive race is unavoidable. Yes, all this I have seen, and much of it has been written about and debated in international gatherings. And even while acknowledging the poetic justice of it in the abstract, one cannot help but wonder if a physical pound of flesh, excised at birth, is not a kinder act than a lifelong visitation of the sins of the father on the sons even to the tenth and twelfth generations.

Confronted with such traditions of attenuating the racial and cultural pride of these marginalized or minority peoples, the mind travels back to our own societies where such causative histories are far fresher in the memory, where the ruins of formerly thriving communities still speak eloquent accusations and the fumes still rise from the scorched earth strategies of colonial and racist myopia. Yet the streets bear the names of former oppressors, their statues and other symbols of subjugation are left to decorate their squares, the consciousness of a fully confident people having relegated them to mere decorations and roosting-places for bats and pigeons. And the libraries remain unpurged, so that new generations freely browse through the works of Frobenius, of Hume, Hegel, or Montesquieu and others without first encountering, freshly stamped on the fly-leaf: WARNING! THIS WORK IS DANGEROUS FOR YOUR RACIAL SELF-ESTEEM.

Yet these proofs of accommodation, on the grand or minuscule scale, collective, institutional, or individual, must not be taken as proof of an infinite, uncritical capacity of black patience. They constitute in their own nature, a body of tests, an accumulation of debt, an implicit offer that must be matched by concrete returns. They are the blocks in a suspended bridge begun from one end of a chasm which, whether the builders will it or not, must obey the law of matter and crash down beyond a certain point, settling definitively into the widening chasm of suspicion, frustration, and redoubled hate. On that testing ground which, for us, is Southern Africa, that medieval camp of biblical terrors, primitive suspicions, a choice must be made by all lovers of peace: either to bring it into the modern world, into a rational state of being within that spirit of human partnership, a capacity for which has been so amply demonstrated by every liberated black nation on our continent, or - to bring it abjectly to its knees by ejecting it, in every aspect, from humane recognition, so that it caves in internally, through the strategies of its embattled majority. Whatever the choice, this inhuman affront cannot be allowed to pursue our twentieth century conscience into the twenty-first, that symbolic coming-of-age which peoples of all cultures appear to celebrate with rites of passage. That calendar, we know, is not universal, but time is, and so are the imperatives of time. And of those imperatives that challenge our being, our presence, and humane definition at this time, none can be considered more pervasive than the end of racism, the eradication of human inequality, and the dismantling of all their structures.

The Prize is the consequent enthronement of its complement:
universal suffrage, and peace.

© THE NOBEL FOUNDATION 1986
With the kind permission of the Nobel Foundation.

WOLE SOYINKA
Myth, Literature & the African World

Preface

In 1973, unable to assume my position at the University of Ife,
Nigeria, I accepted a year's appointment as Fellow of Churchill
College, Cambridge. I was simultaneously Visiting Professor at
Sheffield University, at which institution I came directly into the
Department of English which boasts a full African Literature
programme, including a course leading to a post-graduate degree.
Cambridge was somewhat more circumspect. On the initiative
of the Department of Social Anthropology, a series of lectures
on Literature and Society was proposed in which the Department
of English was, naturally, to participate. The idea turned out to
be not so natural. The lectures were duly given, but they took
place entirely in the Department of Social Anthropology. Casual
probing after it was all over indicated that the Department of
English (or perhaps some key individual) did not believe in any
such mythical beast as 'African Literature'. A student of mine
whose post-graduate project was centred on mythopoeia in
black literature had apparently undergone a similar experience
before the approval of his subject. If I had not, providentially,
been available as his tutor, it seemed likely that the lack of
adequate supervision would have become a key argument in the
rejection of his proposed programme.

I was, paradoxically, quite sympathetic to the dilemma of the
English Literature traditionalists. They at least have not gone so
far as to deny the existence of an African world - only its
literature and, perhaps, its civilisation. Many African universities
have begun to reconsider the once convenient location of

contemporary African literature as an appendage of English literature. A few have sensibly substituted the title Department of (Comparative) Literature for the orthodox Department of English. Others have, not so unsatisfactorily, brought the study of African literature under a Department of African Studies. Important as it sounds, however, the problem of nomenclature is ultimately secondary, the motivation being everything. Today this goes beyond the standard anti-colonial purge of learning and education and embraces the apprehension of a culture whose reference points are taken from within the culture itself. The themes which were selected for these lectures are a reflection of this positive apprehension.

It is often difficult to convey, both to aliens and to the alienated within one's society, the replete reality of this self-apprehension. Social emancipation, cultural liberation, cultural revolution are easier but deflective approaches, for they all retain external reference points against which a progression in thinking can be measured. The expression of a true self-apprehension is itself still most accessible today in the active language of cultural liberation etc.; that is, in order to transmit the self-apprehension of a race, a culture, it is sometimes necessary to liberate from, and relate this collective awareness to, the values of others. The misunderstanding of this merely expedient process is what in African academia has created a deified aura around what is falsely called intellectualism (= knowledge and exposition of the reference points of colonial cultures). To the truly self-apprehending entity within the African world reality, this amounts to intellectual bondage and self-betrayal.

Having contested the claims of Negritude since my earliest contact with its exegetes, a position which is still affirmed in the trend of these lectures, a contradiction may appear in their emphasis, which is one of eliciting the African self-apprehended world in myth and literature. These positions are, I hope, clarified in the lectures and demonstrated to be not only mutually compatible but consistently so. The choice of the theme is of course not fortuitous. I have long been preoccupied with the process of apprehending my own world in its full complexity, also through its contemporary progression and distortions - evidence of this is present both in my creative work and in one of

346

my earliest essays, *The Fourth Stage*, included in this collection as an appendix. The persistent thread in the more recent lectures stems from this earliest effort to encapsulate my understanding of this metaphysical world and its reflection in Yoruba contemporary social psyche. *The Fourth Stage* was in fact published in its first and only draft - I was arrested and became incommunicado soon after I sent it to the editor, requesting him to pass it on to G. Wilson Knight, my former Professor at Leeds, for his comments. I have tried now to reduce what a student of mine complained of as 'elliptical' obstacles to its comprehension. There were in addition a number of printing (or typing) errors which further obstructed clarity - these have been removed. The essays on drama will be seen as more recent elaborations of this central concern to transmit through analysis of myth and ritual the self-apprehension of the African world.

There has however developed in recent years (especially in the last four or five) a political reason for this increased obsession with the particular theme. From a well-publicised position as an anti-Negritudinist (if only one knew in advance what would make one statement more memorable than the next!) it has been with an increasing sense of alarm and even betrayal that we have watched our position distorted and exploited to embrace a 'sophisticated' school of thought which (for ideological reasons) actually repudiates the existence of an African world! Both in cultural and political publications, and at such encounters as the UNESCO Conference on the Influence of Colonialism on African Culture, Dar es Salaam 1972, the 6th Pan-African Congress, Dar es Salaam 1974, the pre-Colloque of the Black Arts Festival, Dakar 1974 etc., etc., we black Africans have been blandly invited to submit ourselves to a second epoch of colonisation - this time by a universal-humanoid abstraction defined and conducted by individuals whose theories and prescriptions are derived from the apprehension of *their* world and *their* history, *their* social neuroses and *their* value systems. It is time, clearly, to respond to this new threat, each in his own field. The whoring profession which the practice of literary criticism sometimes suggests will hopefully play its part in this contest whose timing, when we recall that we are at a definitive stage of African self-liberation, is particularly crucial. For after (or simultaneously with) an externally-directed and conclusive

347

confrontation on the continent must come a reinstatement of the values authentic to that society, modified only by the demands of a contemporary world. This appears an obvious enough process in the schemata of interrupted histories. Could this be why of late we Africans have been encountering a concerted assault, decked in ideological respectability, on every attempt to re-state the authentic world of the African peoples and ensure its contemporary apprehension through appropriate structures? In vain we conjure with the names of Mbiti, Bolaji Idowu, Ogotommeli, Kagame, Willie Abrahams, Cheik Anta Diop, and foreign triers like Father Tempels, Pierre Verger, Herskovits etc. For the new breed of deniers they have never existed nor written a line, nor provided one clue that fleshes out, at the very least, a composite image of the African world.

The Yoruba have a proverb for it: its wit is unfortunately lost in translation, being based on a pun on *'ni tan* (related to each other) and *n'ítan* (at the thigh): *A ò lè b'ára 'ni tan, k'á f'ara wa n'ítan ya.* A free translation would read: Kinship does not insist that, because we are entwined, we thereby rip off each other's thigh. The man who, because of ideological kinship tries to sever my being from its self-apprehension is not merely culturally but politically hostile. (Trotsky understood this only too well, so did Amilcar Cabral.) When ideological relations begin to deny, both theoretically and in action, the reality of a cultural entity which we define as the African world while asserting theirs even to the extent of inviting the African world to sublimate its existence in theirs, we must begin to look seriously into their political motivation. This volume does not however concern itself with that. It is engaged in what should be the simultaneous act of eliciting from history, mythology and literature, for the benefit of both genuine aliens and alienated Africans, a continuing process of self-apprehension whose temporary dislocation appears to have persuaded many of its non-existence or its irrelevance (= retrogression, reactionarism, racism, etc.) in contemporary world reality.

Some of the literature discussed in these lectures has a note of stridency; this in itself is an index of the sudden awakening of a new generation of writers to threats to their self-apprehension. Such writers are, without exception, those who have responded with boredom and indifference to the romanticised rhetoric of

Negritude. The stridency in their voices is a predictable reaction to the experience of being stabbed in the back, and from totally unexpected quarters. To refuse to participate in the creation of a new cult of the self's daily apprehended reality is one thing; to have that reality contemptuously denied or undermined by other cultic adherents is far more dangerous and arouses extreme reactions. The solution, for the moment, appears to be a continuing objective re-statement of that self-apprehension, to call attention to it in living works of the imagination, placing them in the context of primal systems of apprehension of the race.

Nothing in these essays suggests a detailed uniqueness of the African world. Man exists, however, in a comprehensive world of myth, history and mores; in such a total context, the African world, like any other 'world' is unique. It possesses, however, in common with other cultures, the virtues of complementarity. To ignore this simple route to a common humanity and pursue the alternative route of negation i   for whatever motives, an attempt to perpetuate the external subjugation of the black continent. There is nothing to choose ultimately between the colonial mentality of an Ajayi Crowther, West Africa's first black bishop, who grovelled before his white missionary superiors in a plea for patience and understanding of his 'backward, heathen, brutish' brothers, and the new black ideologues who are embarrassed by statements of self-apprehension by the new 'ideologically backward' African. Both suffer from externally induced fantasies of redemptive transformation in the image of alien masters. Both are victims of the doctrine of self-negation, the first requirement for a transcendentalist (political or religious) fulfilment. Like his religious counterpart, the new ideologue has never stopped to consider whether or not the universal verities of his new doctrine are already contained in, or can be elicited from the world-view and social structures of his own people. The study of much contemporary African writing reveals that they can: this group of literature I have described as the literature of a secular social vision. It marks the beginning of a prescriptive validation of an African self-apprehension.

W.S.

Accra
September 1975

349

The Religious Factor
of
Ideology and the Social Vision

Asked recently whether or not I accepted the necessity for a literary ideology, I found myself predictably examining the problem from the inside, that is, from within the consciousness of the artist in the process of creating. It was a familiar question, one which always reappears in multiple guises. My response was - a social vision, yes, but not a literary ideology. Generally the question reflects the preoccupation, neither of the traditional nor the contemporary writer in African society but of the analyst after the event, the critic. An examination of the works of most contemporary writers confirms this. But then, it would be equally false to suggest that contemporary African literature is not consciously formulated around certain frameworks of ideological intent. The problem is partly one of terminology and the associations of literary history, mostly European. The danger which a literary ideology poses is the act of consecration - and of course excommunication. Thanks to the tendency of the modern consumer-mind to facilitate digestion by putting in strict categories what are essentially fluid operations of the creative mind upon social and natural phenomena, the formulation of a literary ideology tends to congeal sooner or later into instant capsules which, administered also to the writer, may end by asphyxiating the creative process. Such a methodology of assessment does not permit a non-prejudicial probing of the capsule itself, at least not by the literature which brings it into being or which it later brings into being. Probing, if there is any, is an incestuous activity on its own, at least until the fabrication of a rival concept. It is easy to see that this process can only develop into that in-breeding which offers little objective enlightenment about its nature, since its idiom and concepts are not freed from the ideology itself. When the reigning ideology fails finally to retain its false comprehensive adequacy, it is discarded. A new set, inviolable mould is fabricated to contain the current body of literature or to stimulate the next along predetermined patterns.

There may appear to be contrary instances to invalidate the suggestion that literary ideologies are really the conscious formulation of the critic, not the artist. But this contradiction exists only when we take as our frame of reference - which regrettably still seems the automatic thing to do - European literary experience. The idea of literature as an objective existence in itself is a very European idea, and ideologies are very much systems of thought or speculative goals considered desirable for the health of existing institutions (society, ecology, economic life etc.) which are, or have come to be regarded as, ends in themselves. Take the French Surrealist movement: even while paying lip-service to the claims of literature as an expression of an end (the infinity of human experience), the Surrealists laboured, by their obsessive concentration on the ontology of a creative medium (in their case literature) to set the medium apart as an autogenous phenomenon, so cutting it off from the human phenomenon which it is supposed to reflect, or on behalf of which it is supposed to speculate. Perhaps it came from taking far too literally the annunciation of the Gospel - In the beginning was the *Word*. Similar claims for the objective existence of the medium are even more overtly stated in the other arts, painting especially. Since we have no experience of such distortions of objective relationships in African society, it is reasonable to claim that a literary ideology traditionally has had little to do with the actual process of creating that literature. In contemporary times there has been one important exception to this pattern, apart from lesser related efforts which periodically attempt to bring the direction of African writing under a fiat of instant-assimilation poetics.

Some literary ideologies take private hallucinatory forms. Samuel Beckett, for instance, gropes incessantly towards the theatrical statement that can be made in one word, a not-too-distant blood-relation of the chimeric obsessions of the Surrealists. If we leave the lunatic fringe of the literary Unilateral Declaration of Independence, however, we discover that despite its tendency towards narrow schematism, a literary ideology does occasionally achieve coincidence - and so a value expansion - with a social vision. From merely turning the mechanics of creativity into a wilful self-regulating domain, irrespective of the burden of statement, it elevates its sights to a regenerative social goal which makes continuing demands on the nature of that ideological medium and prevents its smug stagnation. Brecht's ideology of theatre and dramatic literature is the most successful example. A not-so-successful instance was the French neo-fiction movement of the Fifties which rejected metaphorical language for a bare diction of objective reality, this being for its practitioners a necessary aid to the conditioning of a social consciousness. Alas, the energy and passion of social revolution appears perversely to quarry into the metaphorical resources of language in order to brand its message deeper in the heart of humanity: the products of that movement now largely belong to the literary museum. It was, however, a far cry from the purely stylistic and intellectual preoccupations of its distant forerunner, the eighteenth-century European Enlightenment, whose ideology of literature all but re-defined poetry and tragic drama out of imaginative existence. In Africa, Negritude remains the only claimant to this fruitful coincidence. The concept of a socio-racial direction governed a whole literary ideology and gave it its choice of mode of expression and thematic emphasis. Both for Africans on the mother-continent and for the black societies of the diaspora, Negritude provided both a life-line along which the dissociated individual could be pulled back to the source of his matrical essence, and offered a prospect for the coming-into-being of new black social entities. In the process it enmeshed itself unnecessarily in negative contradictory definitions. We shall deal more fully with the phenomenon of Negritude in our encounter with the development of a secular social vision.

I have said already that all this must not be taken to mean that contemporary literature in Africa is not consciously guided by concepts of an ideological nature. But the writer is far more preoccupied with visionary projection of society than with speculative projections of the nature of literature, or of any other medium of expression. The ontology of the idiom is subservient to the burden of its concerns; yet there is no record of periods of total literary atrophy in societies that boast a recognisable literary tradition. This is because, in reality, the umbilical chord between experience and form has never been severed, no matter how tautly stretched. But the reflection of experience is only one of the functions of literature; there is also its extension. And when that experience is social we move into areas of ideological projections, the social vision. It is this latter form of literature that holds the most promise for the strengthening of the bond between experience and medium since it prevents the entrenchment of the habitual, the petrification of the imaginative function by that past or present reality upon which it reflects. Literature of a social vision is not a perfect expression for this dimension of creative writing but it will serve for the moment, for want of a better. Yambo Oulouguem's *Le Devoir de Violence* is one paradoxical example of such a literature; it is purposely introduced at this stage in order to crystallise through its example that most important function of the genre, the decongealment of the imaginative function by past or present reality, even in the process of reflecting upon them. The claims of a literary ideology are related but the practical effects on the creative process lead to predictability, imaginative constraint, and thematic excisions.

It will be necessary also to suspend our habitual prejudices in our approach to this literature. The expression 'social vision' is chosen as a convenient delimitation for certain types of literature to be discussed, not as an elevated concept of the type. 'Vision' is a word which has strong connotations of the lofty and the profound, and this tends to rub off on literature which lays claim to it. This, of course, is not necessarily the case. A novelette like Alex la Guma's *A Walk in the Night* (Mbari Publications, 1964) makes no social visionary claims but restricts itself to a near obsessive delineation of the physical, particularised reality of a South African ghetto existence. Yet its total statement both about the reality of that situation and on the innate regressive capacity of man in a dehumanised social condition provides a more profound and disturbing insight into humanity than we find in the visionary piety of his fellow country man Alan Paton or the multi-racial visionary of Peter Abrahams. A demand which I once made in a paper that the writer in our modern African society needs to be a visionary in his own times has, I find, been often interpreted as a declaration that this is the highest possible function for the contemporary African writer. The misunderstanding has to do with the elevated status which the European mind inclines to give to work of a mystical or visionary persuasion - witness the way in which the dotty excursions of W.B. Yeats into a private never-never land are reverently exegetised! Let it be noted that in a culture where the mystical and the visionary are merely areas of reality like any other, the use of such expression does not connote a higher perception of the imaginative faculty.

A creative concern which conceptualises or extends actuality beyond the purely narrative, making it reveal realities beyond the immediately attainable, a concern which upsets orthodox acceptances in an effort to free society of historical or other superstitutions, these are qualities possessed by literature of a social vision. Revolutionary writing is generally of this kind, though whether or not much of the writing which aspires to the label is always literature is another question. Sembene Ousmane's *God's Bits of Wood* leaves one in no doubt about its literary qualities, and combines revolutionary fervour with a distinctly humanist vision. The intellectual and imaginative impulse to a re-examination of the propositions on which man, nature and society are posited or interpreted at any point in history; the effort to expand such propositions, or to contest and replace them with others more in tune with the writer's own idealistic disposition or his pragmatic, resolving genius; this impulse and its integrative role in the ordering of experience and events leads to a work of social vision. A literary ideology and social vision may meet in particular modes of creative expression - they do, certainly, in the literature of Negritude, in Brecht's epic theatre and (with the usual reservations) in the dramatic literature of European Expressionism. (The amorphous, even contradictory and unruly nature of some products of the conscious marriage of ideology and form can be seen in this last example. Not many analysts of that Expressionist ferment will disagree with Gorelik, who said: '...just what Expressionism meant was rather puzzling to its reviewers at the time and in fact is not entirely clear to this day.') With such occasional productive concurrence of a literary ideology and a social vision in mind, it is possible to claim that the lack of excessive stylistic contrivance in modern African literature is due to the refusal of the artist to respond to the blandishments of literary ideology-manifesto art. Much African

354

writing is still rooted in the concept of literature as part of the normal social activity of man, but one which is nonetheless individual in its expression and its choice of areas of concern. That writing which claims for itself, subtly or stridently, the poet's famous province - unacknowledged legislators of mankind - with or without the poetry or the poetic insight, is always socially significant. For it gives clues to mental conditioning by previous history or colonial culture; or conversely shows the will to break free of such incubi in its projection of a future society. The literature which devotes itself to this area is a revelation both of the individual sensibility of the writers and of the traditional and colonial background of Africa's contemporary reality.

© Cambridge University Press 1976.

Chapter 3 of *Myth, Literature and the African World*.
With the permission of Cambridge University Press.

Wasafiri

CARIBBEAN, AFRICAN, ASIAN AND ASSOCIATED LITERATURES IN ENGLISH
Literary criticism
Imaginative writing
The journal appears twice annually in Spring and Autumn
ANNUAL SUBSCRIPTION (2 ISSUES)

	UK	Overseas
Institutions	GBP14	GBP18
Individuals	GBP10	GBP14

Cheques for subscription should be made payable to *Wasafiri* (ATCAL) and sent to The Editor, *Wasafiri*, P.O. Box 195, Canterbury, Kent CT2 7XB, U.K.

YASUNARI KAWABATA
1968 Nobel Prizewinner for Literature

*"For his narrative mastery which with great sensibility
expresses the essence of the Japanese mind"*

Speech by Anders Österling, Ph.D., of the Swedish Academy
Translation

The recipient of this year's Nobel Prize for Literature, the
Japanese Yasunari Kawabata, was born in 1899 in the big
industrial town of Osaka, where his father was a highly cultured
doctor with literary interests. At an early age, however, he was
deprived of this favorable growing-up environment on the
sudden death of his parents and, as an only child, was sent to
his blind and ailing grandfather in a remote part of the country.
These tragic losses, doubly significant in view of the Japanese
people's intense feeling for blood ties, have undoubtedly
affected Kawabata's whole outlook on life and been one of the
reasons for his later study of Buddhist philosophy.

As a student at the imperial university in Tokyo he decided
early on a writing career, and he is an example of the kind of
restless absorption that is always a condition of the literary
calling. In a youthful short story, which first drew attention to
him at the age of twenty-seven, he tells of a student who, during
lonely autumn walks on the peninsula of Izu, comes across a
poor, despised dancing girl, with whom he has a touching love
affair; she opens her pure heart and shows the young man a
way to deep and genuine feeling. Like a sad refrain in a folk-
song the theme recurs with many variations in his following
works; he presents his own scale of values and with the years
he has won renown far beyond the borders of Japan. True, of
his production only three novels and a few short stories have so
far been translated into different languages, evidently because
translation in this case offers especially great difficulties and is
apt to be far too coarse a filter, in which many finer shades of
meaning in his richly expressive language must be lost. But the

translated works do give us a sufficiently representative picture of his personality.

In common with his older countryman Tanizaki, now deceased, he has admittedly been influenced by modern Western realism, but at the same time he has, with greater fidelity, retained his footing in Japan's classical literature and therefore represents a clear tendency to cherish and preserve a genuinely national tradition of style. In Kawabata's narrative art it is still possible to find a sensitively shaded situation poetry which traces its origin back to Murasaki's vast canvas of life and manners in Japan about the year 1000.

Kawabata has been especially praised as a subtle psychologist of women. He has shown his mastery as such in the two short novels "The Snow Kingdom" and "A Thousand Cranes", to use the Swedish titles. In these we see a brilliant capacity to illuminate the erotic episode, an exquisite keenness of observation, a whole network of small, mysterious values, which often put the European narrative technique in the shade. Kawabata's writing is reminiscent of Japanese painting; he is a worshipper of the fragile beauty and melancholy picture language of existence in the life of nature and in man's destiny. If the transience of all outward action can be likened to drifting tufts of grass on the surface of the water, then it is the genuinely Japanese miniature art of haiku poetry which is reflected in Kawabata's prose style.

Even if we feel excluded, as it were, from his writing by a root-system, more or less foreign to us, of ancient Japanese ideas and instincts, we may find it tempting in Kawabata to notice certain similarities of temperament with European writers from our own time. Turgeniev is the first to spring to mind, he too a deeply sensitive story-teller and a broadminded painter of the social scene, with pessimistically coloured sympathies within a time of transition between old and new.

Kawabata's most recent work is also his most outstanding, the novel "Kyoto" completed six years ago and now available in Swedish translation. The story is about the young girl Chiëko, a foundling exposed by her poverty-stricken parents and adopted into the house of the merchant Takichiro, where she is brought up according to old Japanese principles. She is a sensitive, loyal being, who only in secret broods on the riddle of her origin. Popular Japanese belief has it that an exposed child is afflicted with a lifelong curse, in addition to which the condition of being a twin, according to the strange Japanese viewpoint, bears the stigma of shame. One day it happens that she meets a pretty young working girl from a cedar forest near the city and finds that she is her twin sister. They are intimately united beyond the social pale of class - the robust, work-hardened Naëko and the delicate, anxiously guarded Chiëko, but their bewildering likeness soon gives rise to complications and confusion. The whole story is set against the background of the religious festival year in Kyoto, from the cherry-blossom spring to the snow-glittering winter.

The city itself is really the leading character, the capital of the old kingdom, once the seat of the mikado and his court, still a romantic sanctuary after a thousand years, the home of the fine arts and elegant handicraft, nowadays exploited by tourism but still a beloved place of pilgrimage. With its Shinto and Buddha temples, its old artisan quarters and botanical gardens, the place possesses a poetry which Kawabata expresses in a tender, courteous manner, with no sentimental overtones, but naturally, as a moving appeal. He has experienced his country's crushing defeat and no doubt realizes what the future demands in the way of industrial go-ahead spirit, tempo and vitality. But in the postwar wave of violent Americanization his novel is a gentle reminder of the necessity of trying to save something of the old Japan's beauty and individuality for the new. He describes the religious ceremonies in Kyoto with the same meticulous care as he does the textile trade's choice of patterns in the traditional sashes belonging to the women's dresses. These aspects of the novel may have their documentary worth, but the reader prefers to dwell on such a deeply characteristic passage as when the party of middle-class people from the city visits the botanical garden - which has been closed for a long time because the American occupation troops have had their barracks there - in order to see whether the lovely avenue of camphor trees is still intact and able to delight the connoisseur's eye.

With Kawabata, Japan enters the circle of literary Nobel prizewinners for the first time. Essential to the forming of the decision is the fact that as a writer he imparts a moral-esthetic cultural awareness with unique artistry, thereby in his way contributing to the spiritual bridge-building between East and West.

Mr Kawabata,
The citation speaks of your narrative mastery, which with great sensibility expresses the essence of the Japanese mind. With great satisfaction we greet you here in our midst today, an honoured guest from afar on this platform. On behalf of the Swedish Academy I beg to express our hearty congratulations, and at the same time ask you now to receive this year's Nobel Prize for literature from the hands of His Majesty the King.

RÉPONSES DES LAURÉATS
M. Kawabata:

Your Majesty, Your Royal Highnesses, Your Excellencies the President and the Trustees of the Nobel Foundation, Members of the Royal Swedish Academy, Excellencies, Ladies and Gentlemen:
It is the great honor of my life to have been proposed by the Swedish Academy for the Nobel Prize for Literature for 1968 and to have received the award at Your Majesty's own hands.
The reason for the supreme brilliance of the history of this award is that it is also given to foreigners. It has, so to speak, the breadth of a world award. Two Japanese, Drs. Yukawa and Tomonaga, have in recent years become Nobel Laureates in physics. Alfred Nobel wrote poetry and prose in several languages, and in that spirit the prize for literature has gone to writers in numbers of countries. It is now fifty-five years since it last went to an Oriental, Rabindranath Tagore. In view of the complexities presented by differences in language, and in view of the fact that my works, no doubt more than those of others, have had to be perused in translation, I must indicate my deep and undying gratitude and respect for the resolve shown by Your Excellencies of the Academy. This first award to an Oriental in fifty-five years has I believe made a deep impression upon Japan, and perhaps upon the other countries of Asia as well, and upon

all countries whose languages are little known internationally. I do not look upon my happiness and good fortune in having received the award as mine alone. My emotions are yet deeper at the thought that it perhaps has a new and broad significance for the literature of the world.

Such are my feelings, indeed, honored with my fellow laureates by Your Excellencies of the Nobel Foundation upon this grand occasion, and granted the further honor of offering a few words of thanks, that I almost think we have here a symbol of understanding and friendship between East and West, of literature moving from today into tomorrow. I thank you.

YASUNARI KAWABATA

Yasunari Kawabata, son of a highly cultivated physician, was born in 1899 in Osaka. After the early death of his parents he was educated in the country by his maternal grandfather. From 1920 to 1924 Kawabata studied at the Royal University of Tokyo, where he received his degree. He was one of the founders of the publication "Bungai Jidai", the medium of a new movement in modern Japanese literature. Kawabata made his début as a writer with the short story "Izu dancer", published in 1927. After several distinguished works, the novel "Snow country" in 1937 secured Kawabata's position as one of the leading authors in Japan. In 1949 the publication of the serials "Thousand cranes" and "Sound of mountain" was commenced. He became a member of the Art Academy of Japan in 1953 and four years later he was appointed chairman of the P.E.N. club of Japan. At several international congresses Kawabata was the Japanese delegate for this club. "The lake" (1955) "The sleeping beauty" (1960) and "Kyoto" (1962) belong to his later works and of these novels, "Kyoto" is the one that made the deepest impression in the author's native country and abroad. In 1959 Kawabata received the Goethe-medal in Frankfurt.

Japan, the Beautiful and Myself
Nobel lecture December 12, 1968
by
YASUNARI KAWABATA

"In the spring, cherry blossoms, in the summer the cuckoo.
In autumn the moon, and in winter the snow, clear, cold."

"The winter moon comes from the clouds to keep me company.
The wind is piercing, the snow is cold."

The first of these poems is by the priest Dōgen (1200-1253)
and bears the title "Innate Spirit". The second is by the priest
Myōe (1173-1232). When I am asked for specimens of calligraphy, it is these poems that I often choose.

The second poem bears an unusually detailed account of its
origins, such as to be an explanation of the heart of its meaning:
"On the night of the twelfth day of the twelfth month of the
year 1224, the moon was behind clouds. I sat in Zen meditation
in the Kakyu Hall. When the hour of the midnight vigil came, I
ceased meditation and descended from the hall on the peak to
the lower quarters, and as I did so the moon came from the
clouds and set the snow to glowing. The moon was my companion, and not even the wolf howling in the valley brought fear.
When, presently, I came out of the lower quarters again, the
moon was again behind clouds. As the bell was signalling the
late-night vigil, I made my way once more to the peak, and the
moon saw me on the way. I entered the meditation hall, and the
moon, chasing the clouds, was about to sink behind the peak
beyond, and it seemed to me that it was keeping me secret
company."

There follows the poem I have quoted, and with the explanation that it was composed as Myōe entered the meditation hall
after seeing the moon behind the mountain, there comes yet
another poem:

"I shall go behind the mountain. Go there too, O moon.
Night after night we shall keep each other company."

Here is the setting for another poem, after Myõe had spent the rest of the night in the meditation hall, or perhaps gone there again before dawn:

"Opening my eyes from my meditation, I saw the moon in the dawn, lighting the window. In a dark place myself, I felt as if my own heart were glowing with light which seemed to be that of the moon:

'My heart shines, a pure expanse of light;
And no doubt the moon will think the light its own.'"

Because of such a spontaneous and innocent stringing together of mere ejaculations as the following, Myõe has been called the poet of the moon:

"Bright, bright, and bright, bright, bright, and bright, bright. Bright and bright, bright, and bright, bright moon."

In his three poems on the winter moon, from late night into the dawn, Myõe follows entirely the bent of Saigyõ, another poet-priest, who lived from 1118 to 1190: "Though I compose poetry, I do not think of it as composed poetry." The thirty-one syllables of each poem, honest and straightforward as if he were addressing the moon, are not merely to "the moon as my companion". Seeing the moon, he becomes the moon, the moon seen by him becomes him. He sinks into nature, becomes one with nature. The light of the "clear heart" of the priest, seated in the meditation hall in the darkness before the dawn, becomes for the dawn moon its own light.

As we see from the long introduction to the first of Myõe's poems quoted above, in which the winter moon becomes a companion, the heart of the priest, sunk in meditation upon religion and philosophy, there in the mountain hall, is engaged in a delicate interplay and exchange with the moon; and it is this of which the poet sings. My reason for choosing that first poem when asked for a specimen of my calligraphy has to do with its remarkable gentleness and compassion. Winter moon, going behind the clouds and coming forth again, making bright my footsteps as I go to the meditation hall and descend again, making me unafraid of the wolf: does not the wind sink into you, does not the snow, are you not cold? I choose the poem as a poem of warm, deep, delicate compassion, a poem that has in it the deep quiet of the Japanese spirit. Dr. Yashiro Yukio, internationally known as a scholar of Botticelli, a man of great learning in the art of the past and the present, of the East and the West, has summed up one of the special characteristics of Japanese art in a single poetic sentence: "The time of the snows, of the moon, of the blossoms...then more than ever we think of our comrades." When we see the beauty of the snow, when we see the beauty of the full moon, when we see the beauty of the cherries in bloom, when in short we brush against and are awakened by the beauty of the four seasons, it is then that we think most of those close to us, and want them to share the pleasure. The excitement of beauty calls forth strong fellow feelings, yearnings for companionship, and the word "comrade" can be taken to mean "human being". The snow, the moon, the blossoms, words expressive of the seasons as they move one into another, include in the Japanese tradition the beauty of mountains and rivers and grasses and trees, of all the myriad manifestations of nature, of human feelings as well.

That spirit, that feeling for one's comrades in the snow, the moonlight, under the blossoms, is also basic to the tea ceremony. A tea ceremony is a coming together in feeling, a meeting of good comrades in a good season. I may say in passing, that to see my novel *Thousand Cranes* as an evocation of the formal and spiritual beauty of the tea ceremony is a misreading. It is a negative work, and expression of doubt about and warning against the vulgarity into which the tea ceremony has fallen.

"In the spring, cherry blossoms, in the summer the cuckoo.
In autumn the full moon, in winter the snow, clear, cold."

One can, if one chooses, see in Dōgen's poem about the beauty of the four seasons no more than a conventional, ordinary, mediocre stringing together, in a most awkward form of representative images from the four seasons. One can see it as a poem that is not really a poem at all. And yet very similar is the deathbed poem of the priest Ryōkan (1758-1831):

"What shall be my legacy? The blossoms of spring,
The cuckoo in the hills, the leaves of autumn."

In this poem, as in Dōgen's, the commonest of figures and the commonest of words are strung together without hesitation... no, to particular effect, rather...and so they transmit the very essence of Japan. And it is Ryōkan's last poem that I have quoted.

"A long, misty day in spring:
I saw it to a close, playing ball with the children."

"The breeze is fresh, the moon is clear.
Together let us dance the night away, in what is left of old
   age."

"It is not that I wish to have none of the world,
It is that I am better at the pleasure enjoyed alone."

Ryōkan, who shook off the modern vulgarity of his day, who was immersed in the elegance of earlier centuries, and whose poetry and calligraphy are much admired in Japan today...he lived in the spirit of these poems a wanderer down country paths, a grass hut for shelter, rags for clothes, farmers to talk to. The profundity of religion and literature was not, for him, in the abstruse. He rather pursued literature and belief in the benign spirit summarized in the Buddhist phrase "a smiling face and gentle words." In his last poem he offered nothing as a legacy. He but hoped that after his death nature would remain beautiful. That could be his bequest. One feels in the poem the emotions of old Japan, and the heart of a religious faith as well.

"I wondered and wondered when she would come.
And now we are together. What thoughts need I have?"

Ryōkan wrote love poetry too. This is an example of which I am fond. An old man of sixty-nine (I might point out that at the same age I am the recipient of the Nobel Prize), Ryōkan met a twenty-nine-year old nun named Teishin, and was blessed with love. The poem can be seen as one of happiness at having met the ageless woman, of happiness at having met the one for whom the wait was so long. The last line is simplicity itself.

Ryōkan died at the age of seventy-three. He was born in the province of Echigo, the present Niigata Prefecture and the setting of my novel *Snow Country*, a northerly region on what is known as the reverse side of Japan, where cold winds come down across the Japan Sea from Siberia. He lived his whole life in the snow country, and to his "eyes in their last extremity", when he was old and tired and knew that death was near, and had attained enlightenment, the snow country, as we see in his last poem, was yet more beautiful, I should imagine. I have an essay with the title "Eyes in their Last Extremity."

The title comes from the suicide note of the short-story writer Akutagawa Ryunosuke (1892-1927). It is the phrase that pulls at me with the greatest strength. Akutagawa said that he seemed to be gradually losing the animal something known as the strength to live, and continued:

"I am living in a world of morbid nerves, clear and cold as ice...I do not know when I will summon up the resolve to kill myself. But nature is for me more beautiful than it has ever been before. I have no doubt that you will laugh at the contradiction, for here I love nature even when I am contemplating suicide. But nature is beautiful because it comes to my eyes in their last extremity".

Akutagawa committed suicide in 1927, at the age of thirty-five.

In my essay "Eyes in their Last Extremity", I had to say: "How ever alienated one may be from the world, suicide is not a form of enlightenment. However admirable he may be, the man who commits suicide is far from the realm of the saint." I neither admire nor am in sympathy with suicide. I had another friend who died young, as avant-garde painter. He too thought of suicide over the years, and of him I wrote in this same essay: "He seems to have said over and over that there is no art superior to death, that to die is to live," I could see, however, that for him, born in a Buddhist temple and educated in a Buddhist school, the concept of death was very different from that in the West. "Among those who give thoughts to things, is there one who does not think of suicide?" With me was the knowledge that that fellow Ikkyu (1394-1481) twice contemplated suicide. I have "that fellow", because the priest Ikkyu is known even to children as a most amusing person, and because anecdotes about his limitlessly eccentric behavior have come down to us in ample numbers. It is said of him that children climbed his knee to stroke his beard, that wild birds took feed from his hand. It would seem from all this that he was the ultimate in mindlessness, that he was an approachable and gentle sort of priest. As a matter of fact he was the most severe and profound of Zen priests. Said to have been the son of an emperor, he entered a temple at the age of six, and early showed his genius as a poetic prodigy. At the same time he was troubled with the deepest of doubts about religion and life. "If there is a god, let him help me. If there is none, let me throw myself to the bottom of the lake and become food for fishes." Leaving behind these words he sought to throw himself into a lake, but was held back. On another occasion, numbers of his fellows were incriminated when a priest in his Daitokuji Temple committed suicide. Ikkyu went back to the temple, "the burden heavy on my shoulders," and sought to starve himself to death. He gave his collected poetry the title "Collection of the Roiling Clouds", and himself used the expression "Roiling Clouds" as a pen name. In this collection and its successor are poems quite without parallel in the Chinese and especially the Zen poetry of the Japanese middle ages, erotic poems and poems about the secrets of the bedchamber that leave one in utter astonishment. He sought, by eating fish and drinking spirits and having commerce with women, to go beyond the rules and proscriptions of the Zen of his day, and to seek liberation from them, and thus turning against established religious forms, he sought in the pursuit of Zen the revival and affirmation of the essence of life, of human existence, in a day of civil war and moral collapse.

His temple, the Daitokuji at Murasakino in Kyoto, remains a centre of the tea ceremony, and specimens of his calligraphy are greatly admired as hangings in alcoves of tea rooms.

I myself have two specimens of Ikkyu's calligraphy. One of them is a single line: "It is easy to enter the world of the Buddha, it is hard to enter the world of the devil." Much drawn to these words, I frequently make use of them when asked for a specimen of my own calligraphy. They can be read in any number of ways, as difficult as one chooses, but in that world of the devil added to the world of the Buddha, Ikkyu of Zen comes home to me with great immediacy. The fact that for an artist, seeking truth, good, and beauty, the fear and petition even as a prayer in those words about the world of the devil...the fact that it should be there apparent on the surface, hidden behind, perhaps speaks with the inevitability of fate. There can be no world of the Buddha without the world of the devil. And the world of the devil is the world difficult of entry. It is not for the weak of heart.

"If you meet a Buddha, kill him. If you meet a patriarch of the law, kill him."

This is a well-known Zen motto. If Buddhism is divided generally into the sects that believe in salvation by faith and those that believe in salvation by one's own efforts, then of course there must be such violent utterances in Zen, which insists upon salvation by one's own efforts. On the other side, the side of salvation by faith, Shinran (1173-1262), the founder of the Shin sect, once said: "The good shall be reborn in paradise, and how much more shall it be so with the bad." This view of things has something in common with Ikkyu's world of the Buddha and world of the devil, and yet at heart the two have their different inclinations. Shinran also said: "I shall take not a single disciple."

"If you meet a Buddha, kill him. If you meet a patriarch of the law, kill him." "I shall not take a single disciple." In these two statements, perhaps, is the rigorous fate of art.

In Zen there is no worship of images. Zen does have images, but in the hall where the regimen of meditation is pursued, there are neither images nor pictures of Buddhas, nor are there scriptures. The Zen disciple sits for long hours silent and motionless, with his eyes closed. Presently he enters a state of impassivity, free from all ideas and all thoughts. He departs from the self and enters the realm of nothingness. This is not the nothingness or the emptiness of the West. It is rather the reverse, a universe of the spirit in which everything communicates freely with everything, transcending bounds, limitless. There are of course masters of Zen, and the disciple is brought toward enlightenment by exchanging questions and answers with his master, and he studies the scriptures. The disciple must, however, always be lord of his own thoughts, and must attain enlightenment through his own efforts. And the emphasis is less upon reason and argument than upon intuition, immediate feeling. Enlightenment comes not from teaching but through the eye awakened inwardly. Truth is in "the

discarding of words", it lies "outside words". And so we have
the extreme of "silence like thunder", in the Vimalakirti Nirdesa
Sutra. Tradition has it that Bodhidharma, a southern Indian
prince who lived in about the sixth century and was the founder
of Zen in China, sat for nine years in silence facing the wall of
a cave, and finally attained enlightenment. The Zen practice of
silent meditation in a seated posture derives from Bodhidharma.

Here are two religious poems by Ikkyu:

"Then I ask you answer. When I do not you do not.
What is there then on your heart, O Lord Bodhidharma?"

"And what is it, the heart?
It is the sound of the pine breeze in the ink painting."

Here we have the spirit of Zen in Oriental painting. The heart
of the ink painting is in space, abbreviation, what is left undrawn.
In the words of the Chinese painter Chin Nung: "You paint the
branch well, and you hear the sound of the wind." And the priest
Dōgen once more: "Are there not these cases? Enlightenment in
the voice of the bamboo. Radiance of heart in the peach
blossom."

Ikenobō Sen'ō, a master of flower arranging, once said (the
remark is to be found in his Sayings): "With a spray of flowers,
a bit of water, one evokes the vastness of rivers and mountains."
The Japanese garden too, of course symbolizes the vastness of
nature. The Western garden tends to be asymmetrical, the
Japanese garden asymmetrical, and this is because the asymmetrical has the greater power to symbolize multiplicity and
vastness. The asymmetry, of course, rests upon a balance imposed by delicate sensibilities. Nothing is more complicated,
varied, attentive to detail, than the Japanese art of landscape
gardening. Thus there is the form called the dry landscape,
composed entirely of rocks, in which the arrangement of stones
gives expression to mountains and rivers that are not present,
and even suggests the waves of the great ocean breaking in upon
cliffs. Compressed to the ultimate, the Japanese garden becomes
the *bonsai* dwarf garden, or the *bonseki*, its dry version.

In the Oriental word for landscape, literally "mountain-
water", with its related implications in landscape painting and

landscape gardening, there is contained the concept of the sere and wasted, and even of the sad and the threadbare. Yet in the sad, austere, autumnal qualities so valued by the tea ceremony, itself summarized in the expression "gently respectful, cleanly quiet", there lies concealed a great richness of spirit; and the tea room, so rigidly confined and simple, contains boundless space and unlimited elegance. The single flower contains more brightness than a hundred flowers. The great sixteenth-century master of the tea ceremony and flower arranging, Rikyu, taught that it was wrong to use fully opened flowers. Even in the tea ceremony today the general practice is to have in the alcove of the tea room but a single flower, and that a flower in bud. In winter a special flower of winter, let us say a camellia, bearing some such name as White Jewel or Wabisuke, which might be translated literally as "Helpmate in Solitude", is chosen, a camellia remarkable among camellias for its whiteness and the smallness of its blossoms; and but a single bud is set out in the alcove. White is the cleanest of colors, it contains in itself all the other colors. And there must always be dew on the bud. The bud is moistened with a few drops of water. The most splendid of arrangements for the tea ceremony comes in May, when a peony is put out in celadon vase; but here again there is but a single bud, always with dew upon it. Not only are there drops of water upon the flower, the vase too is frequently moistured.

Among flower vases, the ware that is given the highest rank is old Iga, from the sixteenth and seventeenth centuries, and it commands the highest price. When old Iga has been dampened, its colors and its glow take on a beauty such as to awaken on afresh. Iga was fired at very high temperatures. The straw ash and the smoke from the fuel fell and flowed against the surface, and as the temperature dropped, became a sort of glaze. Because the colors were not fabricated but were rather the result of nature at work in the kiln, color patterns emerged in such varieties as to be called quirks and freaks of the kiln. The rough austere, strong surfaces of old Iga take on a voluptuous glow when dampened. It breathes to the rhythm of the dew of the flowers.

The taste of the tea ceremony also asks that the tea bowl be moistened before using, to give it its own soft glow.

Ikenobō Sen'ō remarked on another occasion (this too is in his *Sayings*) that "the mountains and strands should appear in their own forms." Bringing a new spirit into his school of flower arranging, therefore, he found "flowers" in broken vessels and withered branches, and in them too the enlightenment that comes from flowers. "The ancients arranged flowers and pursued enlightenment". Here we see how awakening to the heart of the Japanese spirit, under the influence of Zen. And in it too, perhaps, is the heart of a man living in the devastation of long civil wars.

The Tales of Ise, compiled in the tenth century, is the oldest Japanese collection of lyrical episodes, numbers of which might be called short stories. In one of them we learn that the poet Ariwara no Yukihira, having invited guests, put in flowers:

"Being a man of feeling, he had in a large jar a most unusual wistaria. The trailing spray of flowers was upwards of three and a half feet long."

A spray of wistaria of such length is indeed so unusual as to make one have doubts about the credibility of the writer; and yet I can feel in this great spray a symbol of Heian culture. The wistaria is a very Japanese flower, and it has a feminine elegance. Wistaria sprays, as they trail in the breeze, suggest softness, gentleness, reticence. Disappearing and then appearing again in the early summer greenery, they have in them that feeling for the poignant beauty of things long characterized by the Japanese as *mono no aware*. No doubt there was a particular splendor in that spray upwards of three and a half feet long. The splendors of Heian culture a millennium ago and the emergence of a peculiarly Japanese beauty were as wondrous as this "most unusual wistaria", for the culture of T'ang China had at length been absorbed and Japanized. In poetry there came, early in the tenth century, the first of the imperially commissioned anthologies, the *Kokinshu*, and in fiction the *Tales of Ise*, followed by the supreme masterpieces of classical Japanese prose, the *Tale of Genji* of Lady Murasaki and the *Pillow Book* of Sei Shōnagon, both of whom lived from the late tenth century into the early eleventh. So were established a tradition which influenced and even controlled Japanese literature for eight hundred years. The *Tale of Genji* in particular is the highest pinnacle of Japanese literature. Even down to our day there has not been a piece of fiction to compare with it. That such a modern work should have been written in the eleventh century is a miracle, and as a miracle the work is widely known abroad. Although my grasp of classical Japanese was uncertain, the Heian classics were my principal boyhood reading, and it is the *Genji* I think , that has meant the most to me. For centuries after it was written, fascination with the *Genji* persisted, and imitations and re-workings did homage to it. The *Genji* was a wide and deep source of nourishment for poetry, of course, and for the fine arts and handicrafts as well, and even for landscape gardening.

Murasaki and Sei Shōnagon, and such famous poets as Izumi Shikibu, who probably died early in the eleventh century, and Akazome Emon, who probably died in the mid eleventh century, were all ladies-in-waiting in the imperial court. Japanese culture was court culture, and court culture was feminine. The day of the *Genji* and the *Pillow Book* was its finest, when ripeness was moving into decay. One feels in it the sadness at the end of glory, the high tide of Japanese court culture. The court went into its decline, power moved from the court nobility to the military aristocracy, in whose hands it remained through almost seven centuries from the founding of the Kamakura Shogunate in 1192 to the Meiji Restoration in 1867 and 1868. It is not to be thought, however, that either the imperial institution or court culture vanished. In the eighth of the imperial anthologies, the *Shinkokinshu* of the early thirteenth century, the technical dexterity of the *Kokinshu* was pushed yet a step further, and sometimes fell into mere verbal dalliance; but there were added elements of the mysterious, the suggestive, the evocative and inferential elements of sensuous fantasy that have something in common with modern symbolist poetry. Saigyō, who has been mentioned earlier, was a representative poet spanning the two ages, Heian and Kamakura.

"I dreamt of him because I was thinking of him.
Had I known it was a dream, I should not have wished to
  awaken."

"In my dreams I go to him each night without fail.
But this is less than a single glimpse in the waking."

These are by Ono no Komachi, the leading poetess of the *Kokinshu*, who sings of dreams, even, with a straightforward realism. But when we come to the following poems of the Empress Eifuku, who lived at about the same time as Ikkyu, in the Muromachi Period, somewhat later than the *Shinkokinshu*, we have a subtle realism that becomes a melancholy symbolism, delicately Japanese, and seems to me more modern:

"Shining upon the bamboo thicket where the sparrows twitter,
The sunlight takes on the color of the autumn."

"The autumn wind, scattering the bush clover in the garden,
   sinks into one's bones.
Upon the wall, the evening sun disappears."

Dōgen, whose poem about the clear, cold snow I have gusted and Myōe, who wrote of the winter moon as his companion, were of generally the Shinkokinshu period. Myōe exchanged poems with Saigyō and the two discussed poetry together. The following is from the biography of Myōe by his disciple Kikai:

"Saigyō frequently came and talked of poetry. His own attitude towards poetry, he said, was far from the ordinary. Cherry blossoms, the cuckoo, the moon, snow: confronted with all the manifold forms of nature, his eyes and his ears were filled with emptiness. And were not all the words that came forth true words? When he sang of the blossoms the blossoms were not on his mind, when he sang of the moon he did not think of the moon. As the occasion presented itself, as the urge arose, he wrote poetry. The red rainbow across the sky was the sky taking on color. The white sunlight was as the sky growing bright. Yet the empty sky, by its nature, was not something to become bright. It was not something to take on color. With a spirit like the empty sky he gives color to all the manifold scenes but not a trace remained. In such poetry was the Buddha, the manifestation of the ultimate truth."

Here we have the emptiness, the nothingness, of the Orient. My own works have been described as works of emptiness, but it is not to be taken for the nihilism of the West. The spiritual foundation would seem to be quite different. Dōgen entitled his

poem about the seasons "Innate Reality", and even as he sang
of the beauty of the seasons he was deeply immersed in Zen.

© THE NOBEL FOUNDATION 1968.

With the kind permission of the Nobel Foundation.

Izu no Odoriko

The Izu Dancer was first published in 1925 and established
Yasunari Kawabata. Following is a partial translation in English
of an unfinished work. Set in the Izu peninsula, south of Tokyo,
it is about a high-school student's encounter with a troupe of
touring performers and his attraction to the pubescent dancer,
in the period of his despondency. This semi-autobiographical
classic is not as melancholic as his other stories and affirms the
possibility of love. Yukio Mishima's theory is that the young
virgin is the epitome of the unattainable. On attainment, she
becomes the object of the yearning. In the last sentence, the word
"nothing" is a translator's compromise. In the Nobel lecture,
Kawabata has expressed that the nothingness or emptiness in
the East differs from the bleak nihilism of the West. There is
positivity in the sadness, to be sought after, an enlightenment
not to be avoided.

Ike Ong

YASUNARI KAWABATA
Translated by EDWARD G. SEIDENSTICKER
The Izu Dancer
(Izu no Odoriko)

I

A shower swept toward me from the foot of the mountain,
touching the cedar forests white, as the road began to wind up
into the pass. I was nineteen and traveling alone through the Izu
Peninsula. My clothes were of the sort students wear, dark

kimono, high wooden sandals, a school cap, a book sack over my shoulder. I had spent three nights at hot springs near the center of the peninsula, and now, my fourth day out of Tokyo, I was climbing toward Amagi Pass and South Izu. The autumn scenery was pleasant enough, mountains rising one on another, open forests, deep valleys, but I was excited less by the scenery than by a certain hope. Large drops of rain began to fall. I ran on up the road, now steep and winding, and at the mouth of the pass I came to a tea-house. I stopped short in the doorway. It was almost too lucky: the dancers were resting inside.

The little dancing girl turned over the cushion she had been sitting on and pushed it politely toward me.

"Yes," I murmured stupidly, and sat down. Surprised and out of breath, I could think of nothing more appropriate to say.

She sat near me, we were facing each other. I fumbled for tobacco and she handed me the ash tray in front of one of the other women. Still I said nothing.

She was perhaps sixteen. Her hair was swept up in mounds after an old style I hardly know what to call. Her solemn, oval face was dwarfed under it, and yet the face and the hair went well together, rather as in the pictures one sees of ancient beauties with their exaggerated rolls of hair. Two other young women were with her, and a man of twenty-four or twenty-five. A stern-looking woman of about forty presided over the group.

I had seen the little dancer twice before. Once I passed her and the other two young women on a long bridge half way down the peninsula. She was carrying a big drum. I looked back and looked back again, congratulating myself that here finally I had the flavour of travel. And then my third night at the inn I saw her dance. She danced just inside the entrance, and I sat on the stairs enraptured. On the bridge then, here tonight, I had said to myself: tomorrow over the pass to Yugano, and surely somewhere along those fifteen miles I will meet them - that was the hope that had sent me hurrying up the mountain road. But the meeting at the tea-house was too sudden. I was taken quite off balance.

A few minutes later the old woman who kept the tea-house led me to another room, one apparently not much used. It was open to a valley so deep that the bottom was out of sight. My teeth were chattering and my arms were covered with goose flesh.

I was a little cold, I said to the old woman when she came back with tea.

"But you're soaked. Come in here and dry yourself." She led me to her living room.

The heat from the open fire struck me as she opened the door. I went inside and sat back behind the fire. Steam rose from my kimono, and the fire was so warm that my head began to ache.

The old woman went out to talk to the dancers. "Well, now. So this is the little girl you had with you before, so big already. Why, she's practically a grown woman. Isn't that nice. And so pretty, too. Girls do grow up in a hurry, don't they?"

Perhaps an hour later I heard them getting ready to leave. My heart pounded and my chest was tight, and yet I could not find the courage to get up and go off with them. I fretted on beside the fire. But they were women, after all; granted that they were used to walking, I ought to have no trouble overtaking them even if I fell a half mile or a mile behind. My mind danced off after them as though their departure had given it license.

"Where will they stay tonight?" I asked the woman when she came back.

"People like that, how can you tell where they'll stay? If they find someone who will pay them, that's where it will be. Do you think they know ahead of time?"

Her open contempt excited me. If she is right, I said to myself, then the dancing girl will stay in my room tonight.

The rain quieted to a sprinkle, the sky over the pass cleared. I felt I could wait no longer, though the woman assured me that the sun would be out in another ten minutes.

"Young man, young man." The woman ran up the road after me. "This is too much. I really can't take it." She clutched at my book sack and held me back, trying to return the money I had given her, and when I refused it she hobbled along after me. She must at least see me off up the road, she insisted. "It's really too much. I did nothing for you - but I'll remember, and I'll have something for you when you come this way again. You will come again, won't you? I won't forget."

So much gratitude for one fifty-sen piece was rather touching. I was in a fever to overtake the little dancer, and her hobbling only held me back. When we came to the tunnel I finally shook her off.

Lined on one side by a white fence, the road twisted down from the mouth of the tunnel like a streak of lightning. Near the bottom of the jagged figure were the dancer and her companion. Another half mile and I had overtaken them. Since it hardly seemed graceful to slow down at once to their pace, however, I moved on past the women with a show of coolness. The man, walking some ten yards ahead of them, turned as he heard me come up.

"You're quite a walker...Isn't it lucky the rain has stopped."

Rescued, I walked on beside him. He began asking questions, and the women, seeing that we had struck up a conversation, came tripping up behind us. The man had a large wicker trunk strapped to his back. The older woman held a puppy in her arms, the two young women carried bundles, and the girl had her drum and its frame. The older woman presently joined in the conversation.

"He's a highschool boy," one of the young women whispered to the little dancer, giggling as I glanced back.

"Really, even I know that much," the girl retorted. "Students come to the island often."

They were from Oshima in the Ieu Islands, the man told me. In the spring they left to wander over the peninsula, but now it was getting cold and they had no winter clothes with them. After ten days or so at Shimoda in the south they would sail back to the islands. I glanced again at those rich mounds of hair, at the little figure all the more romantic now for being from Oshima. I questioned them about the islands.

"Students come to Oshima to swim, you know," the girl remarked to the young woman beside her.

"In the summer, I suppose." I looked back.

She was flustered. "In the winter too," she answered in an almost inaudible little voice.

"Even in the winter?"

She looked at the other women and laughed uncertainly.

"Do they swim even in the winter?" I asked again.

She flushed and nodded very slightly, a serious expression on her face.

"The child is crazy," the older woman laughed.

From six or seven miles above Yugano the road followed a river. The mountains had taken on the look of the South from the moment we descended the pass. The man and I became firm friends, and as the thatched roofs of Yugano came in sight below us I announced that I would like to go on to Shimoda with them. He seemed delighted.

In front of a shabby old inn the older woman glanced tentatively at me as if to take her leave. "But this gentleman would like to go on with us," the man said.

"Oh, would he?" she answered with simple warmth. "'On the road a companion, in life sympathy,' they say. I suppose even poor things like us can liven up a trip. Do come in - we'll have a cup of tea and rest ourselves."

We went up to the second floor and laid down our baggage. The straw carpeting and the doors were worn and dirty. The little dancer brought up tea from below. As she came to me the teacup clattered in its saucer. She set it down sharply in an effort to save herself, but she succeeded only in spilling it. I was hardly prepared for confusion so extreme.

"Dear me. The child's come to a dangerous age," the older woman said, arching her eyebrows as she tossed over a cloth. The girl wiped tensely at the tea.

The remark somehow startled me. I felt the excitement aroused by the old woman at the tea-house begin to mount.

An hour or so later the man took me to another inn. I had thought till then that I was to stay with them. We climbed down over rocks and stone steps a hundred yards or so from the road. There was a public hot spring in the river bed, and just beyond it a bridge led to the garden of the inn.

We went together for a bath. He was twenty-three, he told me, and his wife had had two miscarriages. He seemed not unintelligent. I had assumed that he had come along for the walk - perhaps like me to be near the dancer.

A heavy rain began to fall about sunset. The mountains, gray and white, flattened to two dimensions, and the river grew yellower and muddier by the minute. I felt sure that the dancers would not be out on a night like this, and yet I could not sit still. Two and three times I went down to the bath, and came restlessly back to my room again.

Then, distant in the rain, I heard the slow beating of a drum. I tore open the shutters as if to wrench them from their grooves and leaned out the window. The drum beat seemed to be coming nearer. The rain, driven by a strong wind, lashed at my head. I closed my eyes and tried to concentrate on the drum, on where it might be, whether it could be coming this way. Presently I heard a *samisen*, and now and then a woman's voice calling to someone, a loud burst of laughter. The dancers had been called to a party in the restaurant across from their inn, it seemed. I could distinguish two or three women's voices and three or four men's voices. Soon they will be finished there, I told myself, and they will come here. The party seemed to go beyond the harmlessly gay and to approach the rowdy. A shrill woman's voice came across the darkness like the crack of a whip. I sat rigid, more and more on edge, staring out through the open shutters. At each drum beat I felt a surge of relief. "Ah, she's still there. Still there and playing the drum." And each time the beating stopped the silence seemed intolerable. It was as though I were being borne under by the driving rain.

For a time there was a confusion of footsteps - were they playing tag, were they dancing? And then complete silence. I glared into the darkness. What would she be doing, who would be with her the rest of the night?

I closed the shutters and got into bed. My chest was painfully tight. I went down to the bath again and splashed about violently. The rain stopped, the moon came out; the autumn sky, washed by the rain, shone crystalline into the distance. I thought for a moment of running out barefoot to look for her. It was after two.

III

The man came by my inn at nine the next morning. I had just gotten up, and I invited him along for a bath. Below the bathhouse the river, high from the rain, flowed warm in the South Izu autumn sun. My anguish of last night no longer seemed very real. I wanted even so to hear what had happened.

"That was a lively party you had last night."

"You could hear us?"

"I certainly could."

"Natives. They make a lot of noise, but there's not much to them really."

He seemed to consider the event quite routine, and I said no more.

"Look. They've come for a bath, over there across the river. Damned if they haven't seen us. Look at them laugh." He pointed over at the public bath, where six or seven naked figures showed through the steam.

One small figure ran out into the sunlight and stood for a moment at the edge of the platform calling something to us, arms raised as though for a plunge into the river. It was the little dancer. I looked at her, at the young legs, at the sculptured white body, and suddenly a draught of fresh water seemed to wash over my heart. I laughed happily. She was a child, a mere child, a child who could run out naked into the sun and stand there on her tiptoes in her delight at seeing a friend. I laughed on, a soft, happy laugh. It was as though a layer of dust had been cleared from my head. And I laughed on and on. It was because of her too-rich hair that she had seemed older, and because she was dressed like a girl of fifteen or sixteen. I had made an extraordinary mistake indeed.

We were back in my room when the older of the two young women came to look at the flowers in the garden. The little dancer followed her halfway across the bridge. The old woman came out of the bath frowning. The dancer shrugged her shoulders and ran back, laughing as if to say that she would be scolded if she came any nearer. The older young woman came up to the bridge.

"Come on over," she called to me.

"Come on over," the younger woman echoed, and the two of them turned back toward their inn.

The man stayed on in my room till evening.

I was playing chess with a traveling salesman that night when I heard the drum in the garden. I started to go out to the veranda.

"How about another?" asked the salesman. "Let's have another game." But I laughed evasively and after a time he gave up and left the room.

Soon the younger women and the man came in.

"Do you have somewhere else to go tonight?" I asked.

"We couldn't find any customers if we tried."

They stayed on till past midnight, playing away at checkers. I felt clear-headed and alive when they had gone. I would not be able to sleep, I knew. From the hall I called in to the salesman.

"Fine, fine." He hurried out ready for battle.

"It's an all-night match tonight. We'll play all night." I felt invincible.

We were to leave Yugano at eight the next morning. I poked my school cap into my book sack, put on a hunting cap I had bought in a shop not far from the public bath, and went up to the inn by the highway. I walked confidently upstairs - the shutters on the second floor were open - but I stopped short in the hall. They were still in bed.

The dancing girl lay almost at my feet, beside the youngest of the women. She flushed deeply and pressed her hands to her face with a quick flutter. Traces of make-up were left from the evening before, rouge on her lips and dots of rouge at the corners of her eyes. A thoroughly appealing little figure. I felt a bright surge of happiness as I looked down at her. Abruptly, still hiding her face, she rolled over, slipped out of bed, and bowed low before me in the hall. I stood dumbly wondering what to do.

The man and the older of the young women were sleeping together. They must be married - I had not thought of it before.

"You will have to forgive us," the older woman said, sitting up in bed. "We mean to leave today, but it seems there is to be a party tonight, and we thought we'd see what could be done with it. If you really must go, perhaps you can meet us in Shimoda. We always stay at the Koshuya Inn - you should have no trouble finding it."

I felt deserted.

"Or maybe you could wait till tomorrow," the man suggested. "She says we have to stay today...But it's good to have someone to talk to on the road. Let's go together tomorrow."

"A splendid idea," the woman agreed. "It seems a shame, now that we've gotten to know you...and tomorrow we start out no matter what happens. Day after tomorrow it will be forty-nine days since the baby died. We've meant all along to have a service in Shimoda to show that we at least remember, and we've been hurrying to get there in time. It would really be very kind of you...I can't help thinking there's a reason for it all, our getting to be friends this way."

I agreed to wait another day, and went back down to my inn. I sat in the dirty little office talking to the manager while I waited for them to dress. Presently the man came by and we walked out to a pleasant bridge not far from town. He leaned against the railing and talked about himself. He had for a long time belonged to a theater company in Tokyo. Even now he sometimes acted in plays in Oshima, while at parties on the road he could do imitations of actors if called upon to. The strange, leglike bulge in one of the bundles was a stage sword, he explained, and the wicker trunk held both household goods and costumes.

"I made a mistake and ruined myself. My brother has taken over for the family in Kofu and I'm really not much use there."

"I thought you came from the inn at Nagaoka."

"I'm afraid not. That's my wife, the older of the two women. She's a year younger than you. She lost her second baby on the road this summer - it only lived a week - and she isn't really well yet. The old woman is her mother, and the girl is my sister."

"You said you had a sister thirteen?"

"That's the one. I've tried to think of ways of keeping her out of this business, but there were all sorts of reasons why it couldn't be helped."

He said his own name was Eikichi, his wife was Chiyoko, the dancer, his sister, was Kaoru. The other girl, Yuriko, was a sort of maid. She was sixteen, and the only one among them who was really from Oshima. Eikichi became very sentimental. He gazed down at the river, and for a time I thought he was about to weep.

IV

On the way back, just off the road, we saw the little dancer petting a dog. She had washed away her make-up.

"Come on over to the inn," I called as we passed.

"I couldn't very well by myself."

"Bring your brother."

"Thank you. I'll be right over."

A short time later Eikichi appeared.

"Where are the others?"

"They couldn't get away from mother."

But the three of them came clattering across the bridge and up the stairs while we were playing checkers. After elaborate bows they waited hesitantly in the hall.

Chiyoko came in first. "Please, please," she called gaily to the others. "You needn't stand on formality in *my* room."

An hour or so later they all went down for a bath. I must come along, they insisted; but the idea of a bath with three young women was somewhat overwhelming, and I said I would go in later. In a moment the little dancer came back upstairs.

"Chiyoko says she'll wash your back for your if you come down now."

Instead she stayed with me, and the two of us played checkers. She was surprisingly good at it. I am better than most and had little trouble with Eikichi and the others, but she came very near beating me. It was a relief not to have to play a deliberately bad game. A model of propriety at first, sitting bold upright and stretching out her hand to make a play, she soon forgot herself and was leaning intently over the board. Her hair, so rich it seemed unreal, almost brushed against my chest. Suddenly she flushed crimson.

"Excuse me. I'll be scolded for this," she exclaimed, and ran out with the game half finished. The older woman was standing beside the public bath across the river. Chiyoko and Yuriko clattered out of the bath downstairs at almost the same moment and retreated across the bridge without bothering to say goodby.

Eikichi spent the day at my inn again, though the manager's wife, a solicitous sort of woman, had pointed out that it was a waste of good food to invite such people in for meals.

The dancer was practicing the *samisen* when I went up to the inn by the highway that evening. She put it down when she saw me, but at the older woman's order, took it up again.

Eikichi seemed to be reciting something on the second floor of the restaurant across the street, where we could see a party in progress.

"What in the world is that?"

"That? He's reading a *Noh* play."

"An odd sort of thing to be doing."

"He has as many wares as a dime store. You can never guess what he'll do next."

The girl shyly asked me to read her a piece from a storyteller's collection. I took up the book happily, a certain hope in my mind. Her head was almost at my shoulder as I started to read, and she looked up at me with a serious, intent expression, her eyes bright and unblinking. Her large eyes, almost black, were easily her best feature. The lines of the heavy lids were indescribably graceful. And her laugh was like a flower's laugh. A flower's laugh - the expression does not seem strained when I think of her.

I had read only a few minutes when the maid from the restaurant across the street came for her. "I'll be right back," she said as she smoothed out her clothes. "Don't go away. I want to hear the rest."

She knelt in the hall to take her leave formally.

We could see the girl as though in the next room. She knelt beside the drum, her back towards us. The slow rhythm filled me with a clean excitement.

"A party always picks up speed when the drum begins," the woman said.

Chiyoko and Yuriko went over to the restaurant a little later, and in an hour or so the four of them came back.

"This is all they gave us." The dancer casually dropped fifty sen from her clenched fist into the older woman's hand. I read more of the story, and they talked of the baby that had died.

I was not held to them by curiosity, and I felt no condescension toward them. Indeed I was no longer conscious that they belonged to that low order, traveling performers. They seemed to know it and to be moved by it. Before long they decided that I must visit them on Oshima.

"We can put him in the old man's house." They planned everything out. "That should be big enough, and if we move the old man out it will be quiet enough for him to study as long as he can stay."

"We have two little houses, and the one on the mountain we can give to you."

383

It was decided, too, that I should help with a play they would give on Oshima for the New Year.

I came to see that the life of the traveling performer was not the forbidding one I had imagined. Rather it was easy-going, relaxed, carrying with it the scent of meadows and mountains. Then too this troupe was held together by close family affection. Only Yuriko, the hired girl - perhaps she was at a shy age - seemed uncomfortable before me.

It was after midnight when I left their inn. The girls saw me to the door, and the little dancer turned my sandals so that I could step into them without twisting. She leaned out and gazed up at the clear sky. "Ah, the moon is up. And tomorrow we'll be in Shimoda. I love Shimoda. We'll say prayers for the baby, and mother will buy me the comb she promised, and there are all sorts of things we can do after that. Will you take me to a movie?"

Something about Shimoda seems to have made it a home along the road for performers who wander the region of the Izu and Sagami hot springs.

V

The baggage was distributed as on the day we came over Amagi Pass. The puppy, cool as a seasoned traveler, lay with its fore-paws on the older woman's arms. From Yagano we entered the mountains again. We looked out over the sea at the morning sun, warming our mountain valley. At the mouth of the river a beach opened wide and white.

"That's Oshima."

"So big! You really will come, won't you?" the dancer said.

For some reason - was it the clearness of the autumn sky that made it seem so? - the sea where the sun rose over it was veiled in a springlike mist. It was some ten miles to Shimoda. For a time the mountains hid the sea. Chiyoko hummed a song, softly, lazily.

The road forked. One way was a little steep, but it was more than a mile shorter than the other. Would I have the short, steep way, or the long, easy way? I took the short way.

The road wound up through a forest, so steep now that climbing it was like climbing hand-over-hand up a wall. Dead leaves laid it over with a slippery coating. As my breathing became more painful I felt a perverse recklessness, and I pushed on faster and faster, pressing my knee down with my fist at each step. The others fell behind, until presently I could only hear their voices through the trees; but the dancer, skirts tucked high, came after me with tiny little steps. She stayed always a couple of yards behind, neither trying to come nearer nor letting herself fall farther back. Sometimes I would speak to her, and she would stop and answer with a startled little smile. And when she spoke I would pause, hoping that she would come up even with me, but always she waited until I had started out again, and followed the same two yards behind. The road grew steeper and more twisted. I pushed myself on faster, and on she came, two yards behind, climbing earnestly and intently. The mountains were quiet. I could no longer hear the voice of the others.

"Where do you live in Tokyo?"

"In a dormitory. I don't really live in Tokyo."

"I've been in Tokyo. I went there once to dance, when the cherries were in bloom. I was very little, though, and I don't remember anything about it."

"Are your parents living?" she would take up again, or, "Have you ever been to Kofu?" She talked of the movies in Shimoda, of the dead baby.

We came to the summit. Laying her drum on a bench among the dead autumn weeds, she wiped her face with a handkerchief. After that she turned her attention to her feet, then changed her mind and bend down instead to dust off the skirt of my kimono. I drew back surprised, and she fell to one knee. When she had brushed me off front and back, bent low before me, she stood up to lower her skirts - they were still tucked up for walking. I was breathing heavily. She invited me to sit down.

A flock of small birds flew up beside the bench. The dead leaves rustled as they landed, so quiet was the air. I tapped the drum a couple of times with my finger, and the birds started up in alarm.

"I'm thirsty."

"Shall I see if I can find you some water?" But a few minutes later she came back empty-handed through the yellowing trees.

"What do you do with yourself on Oshima?"

She mentioned two or three girls' names that meant nothing to me, and rambled on with a string of reminiscences. She was talking not of Oshima but of Kofu, apparently, of a grammar school she had been in for the first and second grades. She talked artlessly on as the memories of her friends came back to her.

The two younger women and Eikichi came up about ten minutes later, and the older woman ten minutes later still. On the way down I purposely stayed behind talking to Eikichi, but after two hundred yards or so the little dancer came running back up. "There's a spring below. They're waiting for you to drink first."

I ran down with her. The water bubbled clear and clean from shady rocks. The women were standing around it. "Have a drink. We waited for you. We didn't think you would want to drink after we had stirred it up."

I drank from my cupped hands. The women were slow to leave. They wet their handkerchiefs and washed the perspiration from their faces.

At the foot of the slope we came out on the Shimoda highway. Down the highway, sending up columns of smoke here and there, were the fires of the charcoal-makers. We stopped to rest on a pile of wood. The dancing girl began to curry the puppy's shaggy coat with a pinkish comb.

"You'll break the teeth," the older woman warned.

"That's all right. I'm getting a new one in Shimoda."

It was the comb she wore in her hair, and even back in Yugano I had planned to ask for it when we got to Shimoda. I was a little upset to find her combing the dog with it.

"But all he would have to do would be to get a gold tooth. Then you'd never notice," the dancer's voice came to me suddenly. I looked back.

They were obviously talking about my crooked teeth. Chiyoko must have brought the matter up, and the little dancer suggested a gold tooth for me. I felt no resentment at being talked about and no particular need to hear more. The conversation was subdued for a time.

"He's nice, isn't he," the girl's voice came again.

"He seems to be very nice."

"He really is nice. I like having someone so nice."

She had an open way of speaking, a youthful, honest way of saying exactly what came to her, that made it possible for me to think of myself as, frankly, "nice." I looked up anew at the mountains, so bright that they made my eyes ache a little. I had come at nineteen to think of myself as a misanthrope, a lonely misfit, and it was my depression at the thought that had driven me to this Izu trip. And now I was able to look upon myself as "a nice person" in the everyday sense of the expression. I find no way to describe what this meant to me. The mountains grew brighter - we were getting near Shimoda and the sea.

Now and then, on the outskirts of a village, we would see a sign: "Vagrant performers keep out."

The Koshuya was a cheap inn at the northern edge of Shimoda. I went up behind the rest to an attic-like room on the second floor. There was no ceiling, and the roof sloped down so sharply that as the window overlooking the street one could not sit comfortably upright.

"Your shoulder isn't stiff?" The older woman was fussing over the girl. "Your hands aren't sore?"

The girl went through the graceful motions of beating a drum. "They're not sore. I won't have any trouble. They're not sore at all."

"Good. I was worried."

I lifted the drum. "Heavy!"

"It's heavier than you'd think," she laughed. "It's heavier than that pack of yours."

They exchanged greetings with the other guests. The hotel was full of peddlers and wandering performers - Shimoda seemed to be a migrants' nest. The dancer handed out pennies to the inn children, who darted in and out. When I started to leave she ran to arrange my sandals for me in the doorway.

"You will take me to a movie, won't you?" she whispered, almost to herself.

Eikichi and I, guided part of the way by a rather disreputable-looking man from the Koshuya, went on to an inn said to belong to an ex-mayor. We had a bath together and lunch, fish new from the sea.

I handed him a little money as he left. "Buy some flowers for the services tomorrow," I said. I had explained that I would have to go back to Tokyo on the morning boat. I was, as a matter of fact, out of money, but told them I had to be back in school.

"Well, we'll see you this winter in any case," the older women said. "We'll all come down to the boat to meet you. You must let us know when you're coming. You're to stay with us - we couldn't think of letting you go to a hotel. We're expecting you, remember, and we'll all be down at the boat."

When the others had left the room I asked Chiyoko and Yuriko to go to a movie with me. Chiyoko, pale and tired, lay with her hands pressed to her abdomen. "I couldn't, thank you. I'm simply not up to so much walking."

Yuriko stared stiffly at the floor.

The little dancer was downstairs playing with the inn children. When she saw me come down she ran off and began wheedling the older woman for permission to go to the movies. She came back looking distant and crestfallen.

"I don't see anything wrong. Why can't she go with him by herself?" Eikichi argued. I found it hard to understand myself, but the woman was unbending. The dancer sat out in the hall petting a dog when I left the inn. I could not bring myself to speak to her, so chilling was this new formality, and she seemed not to have the strength to look up.

I went to the movies alone. A woman read the dialogue by a small flashlight. I left almost immediately and went back to my inn. For a long time I sat looking out, my elbows on the window sill. The town was dark. I thought I could hear a drum in the distance. For no very good reason I found myself weeping.

VI

Eikichi called up from the street while I was eating breakfast at seven the next morning. He had on a formal kimono, in my honor it seemed. The women were not with him. I was suddenly lonesome.

"They all wanted to see you off," he explained when he came up to my room, "but we were out so late last night that they couldn't get themselves out of bed. They said to apologize and tell you they'd be waiting for you this winter."

An autumn wind blew cold through the town. On the way to the ship he bought me fruit and tobacco and a bottle of a cologne called "Kaoru." "Because her name's Kaoru," he smiled. "Oranges are bad on a ship, but persimmons you can eat. They help seasickness."

"Why don't I give you this?" I put my hunting cap on his head, pulled my school cap out of my pack, and tried to smooth away a few of the wrinkles. We both laughed.

As we came to the pier I saw with a quick jump of the heart that the little dancer was sitting at the water's edge. She did not move as we came up, only nodded a silent greeting. On her face were the traces of make-up I found so engaging, and the rather angry red at the corners of her eyes seemed to give her a fresh young dignity.

"Are the others coming?" Eikichi asked.

She shook her head.

"They're still in bed?"

She nodded.

Eikichi went to buy ship and lighter tickets. I tried to make conversation, but she only stared silently at the point where the canal ran into the harbor. Now and then she would nod a quick little nod, always before I had finished speaking.

The lighter pitched violently. The dancer stared fixedly ahead, her lips pressed tight together. As I started up the rope ladder to the ship I looked back. I wanted to say good-by, but I only nodded again. The lighter pulled off. Eikichi waved the hunting cap, and as the town retreated into the distance the girl began to wave something white.

I leaned against the railing and gazed out at Oshima until the southern tip of the Izu Peninsula was out of sight. It seemed a long while before that I had said good-by to the little dancer. I went inside and on to my stateroom. The sea was so rough that it was hard even to sit up. A crewman came around to pass out metal basins for the seasick. I lay down with my book sack for a pillow, my mind clear and empty. I was no longer conscious of the passage of time. I wept silently, and when my cheek began to feel chilly I turned my book sack over. A young boy lay beside me. He was the son of an Izu factory owner, he explained, and he was going to Tokyo to get ready for high-school entrance examinations. My school cap had attracted him.

"Is something wrong?" he asked after a time.

"No, I've just said good-by to someone." I saw no need to disguise the truth, and I was quite unashamed of my tears. I thought of nothing. It was as though I were slumbering in a sort of quiet fulfillment. I did not know when evening came, but there were lights on when we passed Atami. I was hungry and a little chilly. The boy opened his lunch and I ate as though it were mine. Afterwards I covered myself with part of his cape. I floated in a beautiful emptiness, and it seemed natural that I should take advantage of his kindness. Everything sank into an enfolding harmony.

The lights went out, the smell of the sea and of the fish in the hold grew stronger. In the darkness, warmed by the boy beside me, I gave myself up to my tears. It was as though my head had turned to clear water, it was falling pleasantly away drop by drop; soon nothing would remain.

PART FIVE

Literary Features

YUKIO MISHIMA
Fountains in the Rain
From the book
ACTS OF WORSHIP,
seven stories translated by John Bester

The boy was tired of walking in the rain dragging the girl, heavy as a sandbag and weeping continually, around with him.

A short while ago, in a tea shop in the Marunouchi Building, he had told her he was leaving her.

The first time in his life that he'd broken with a woman!

It was something he had long dreamed of; it had at last become a reality.

It was for this alone that he had loved her, or pretended to love her; for this alone he had assiduously undermined her defenses; for this alone he'd furiously sought the chance to sleep with her, slept with her - till lo, the preparations were complete and it only remained to pronounce the phrase he had longed just once to pronounce with his own lips, with due authority, like the edict of a king:

"It's time to break it off!"

Those words, the mere enunciation of which would be enough to rend the sky asunder...Those words that he had cherished so passionately even while half-resigned to the impossibility of the fact...That phrase, more heroic, more glorious than any other in the world, which would fly in a straight line through the heavens like an arrow released from its bow...That spell which only the most human of humans, the most manly of men, might utter...In short:

"It's time to break it off!"

All the same, Akio felt a lingering regret that he'd been obliged to say it with such a deplorable lack of clarity, with a rattling noise in the throat, like an asthmatic with a throatful of phlegm, which even a preliminary draft of soda pop through his straw had failed to avert.

At the time, his chief fear had been that the words might not have been heard. He'd have died sooner than be asked what he'd said and have to repeat it. After all, if a goose that for years had longed to lay a golden egg had found it smashed before anyone could see it, would it promptly have laid another?

Fortunately, however, she had heard. She'd heard, and he hadn't had to repeat it, which was a splendid piece of luck. Under his own steam, Akio had crossed the pass over the mountains that he'd gazed at for so long in the distance.

Sure proof that she'd heard had been vouchsafed in a flash, like chewing gum ejected from a vending machine.

The windows were closed because of the rain, so that the voices of the customers talking around them, the clatter of dishes, the ping of the cash register clashed with each other all the more violently, rebounding subtly off the clammy condensation on the inside of the panes to create a single, mind-fuddling commotion.

Akio's muffled words had no sooner reached Masako's ears through the general uproar than her eyes - wide, staring eyes that seemed to be trying to shove her surroundings away from her thin, unprepossessing features - opened still wider. They were no longer eyes so much as an embodiment of disaster, irretrievable disaster. And then, all at once, the tears had burst forth.

There was no business of breaking into sobs; nor did she bawl her head off: the tears simply gushed, expressing nothing, and with a most impressive force.

Akio naturally assumed that waters of such pressure and flow would soon cease. And he marvelled at the peppermint freshness of mind with which he contemplated the phenomenon. This was precisely what he had planned, worked to encompass, and brought to reality: a splendid achievement, though admittedly somewhat mechanical.

It was to witness this, he told himself again, that he had made love to Masako: he, who had always been free from the dominance of desire.

And the tearful face of the woman now in front of him - this was reality! A genuine forsaken woman - forsaken by himself, Akio!

Even so, Masako's tears went on for so long with no sign of abating that the boy began to worry about the people around them.

393

Masako, still wearing her light-colored raincoat, was sitting upright in her chair. The collar of a red blouse showed at the neck of the coat. She looked as though set in her present position, with her hands pressed down on the edge of the table, a tremen-dous force in both of them.

She stared straight ahead, letting the tears flow unchecked. She made no move to take out a handkerchief to wipe them. Her breath, catching in her thin throat, gave out a regular wheeze like new shoes, and the mouth that with student perverseness she refused to paint turned up disconsolately, quivering continually.

The older customers were looking at them curiously, with stares of a kind calculated to disturb Akio's newfound sense of maturity.

The abundance of Masako's tears was a genuine cause for astonishment. Not for a moment did their volume diminish. Tired of watching, Akio dropped his gaze and looked at the tip of the umbrella he had stood against a chair. The raindrops running from it had formed a small, darkish puddle on the old-fashioned, tile mosaic floor. Even the puddle began to look like Masako's tears to him.

Abruptly, he grabbed the bill and stood up.

The June rains had been falling steadily for three days. As he left the Marunouchi Building and unfurled his umbrella, the girl came silently after him. Since she had no umbrella herself, he had no choice but to let her share his. It reminded him of the way older people, for the benefit of the outside world, went on pre-tending even after they'd stopped feeling anything. Now he too had acquired the same habit; to share an umbrella with a girl once you'd made the move to break with her was just a gesture for other people's benefit. It was simply being cut-and-dried about things. Yes: to be cut-and-dried (even when it took such subtle forms) suited Akio's nature...

As they wandered along the broad sidewalk in the direction of the Imperial Palace, the problem foremost in his mind was finding somewhere to dump this tearbag he was saddled with.

I wonder - he thought vaguely to himself - if the fountains work even when it's raining?

Why should the idea of fountains have occurred to him? Another few paces, and he realized the physical pun in his own train of thought.

The girl's wet raincoat, which he was touching - remotely, of course, and unfeelingly - in the cramped space beneath the umbrella, had the texture of a reptile. But he bore with it, forcing his mind to follow the pun to its logical conclusion.

Yes: fountains in the rain. He'd bring the fountains and Masako's tears into confrontation. Even Masako would surely find her match there. For one thing, the fountains were the type that used the same water over and over again, so the girl, whose tears all ran to waste could hardly compete with them. A human being was scarcely a match for a reflex fountain; almost certainly, she'd give up and stop crying. Then he'd be able somehow to get rid of this unwanted baggage. The only question was whether the fountains would be working as usual in the rain.

Akio walked in silence. Masako, still weeping, followed doggedly under the same umbrella. Thus, while it was difficult to shake her off, it was easy to drag her along where he wanted.

What with the rain and the tears, Akio felt as if his whole body was getting wet. It was all right for Masako in her white boots, but his own socks, inside his loafers, felt like thick, wet seaweed around his feet.

There was some time still before the office workers came out, and the sidewalk was deserted. Traversing a pedestrian crossing, they made their way toward Wadakura Bridge, which crossed the palace moat. When they reached the end of the bridge with its old-fashioned wooden railings topped by pointed knobs, they could see on their left a swan floating on the moat in the rain and, to the right, on the other side of the moat, the white table-cloths and red chairs of a hotel dining room, dimly visible through rain-blurred glass. They crossed the bridge. Passing between high stone ramparts, they turned left and emerged in the small garden with the fountains.

Masako, as ever, was crying soundlessly.

Just inside the garden was a large Western-style summer-house. The benches under its roof, which consisted of a kind of blind of fine reeds were protected to some extent from the rain, so Akio sat down with his umbrella still up and Masako sat down next to him, at an angle, so that all he could see, right in front of his nose, was a shoulder of her white raincoat and her wet hair. The rain on the hair, repelled by the oil on it, looked like a scattering of fine white dew. Still crying, with her eyes wide open, she might almost have been in some kind of coma, and Akio felt an urge to give the hair a tug, to bring her out of it.

She went on crying, endlessly. It was perfectly clear that she was waiting for him to say something, which made it impossible, as a matter of pride, for him to break the silence. It occurred to him that since that one momentous sentence he hadn't spoken a single word.

Not far away, the fountains were throwing up their waters in profusion, but Masako showed no inclination to look at them.

Seen from here, head on, the three fountains, two small and one large, were lined up one behind the other, and the sound, blotted out by the rain, was distant and faint, but the fact that their blurring of spray was not visible at a distance gave the lines of water, dividing up in various directions, a clearly defined look like curved glass tubes.

Not a soul was in sight anywhere. The lawn on this side of the fountains and the low ornamental hedge were a brilliant green in the rain.

Beyond the garden, though, there was a constant procession of wet truck hoods and bus roofs in red, white, or yellow; the red light of a signal at a crossing was clearly visible, but when it changed to the lower green, the light disappeared in a cloud of spray from the fountains.

The act of sitting down and remaining still and silent aroused an indefinable anger in the boy. With it, amusement at his little joke of a while ago disappeared.

He couldn't have said what he was angry about. Not long before, he had been on a kind of high, but now, suddenly, he was beset with an obscure sense of dissatisfaction. Nor was his inability to dispose of the forever crying Masako the whole extent of the frustration.

Her? I could easily deal with *her* if I cared to, he told himself. I could just shove her in the fountain and do a bunk - and that would be the end of it. The thought restored his earlier elation.

396

No, the only trouble was the absolute frustration he felt at the rain, the tears, the leaden sky that hung like a barrier before him. They pressed down on him on all sides, reducing his freedom to a kind of damp rag.

Angry, the boy gave in to a simple desire to hurt. Nothing would satisfy him now till he had got Masako thoroughly soaked in the rain and given her a good eyeful of the fountains.

Getting up suddenly, he set off running without so much as a glance back; raced on along the gravel path that encircled the fountains outside and a few steps higher than the walk around the fountains themselves; reached a spot that gave a full view of them; and came to a halt.

The girl came running through the rain. Checking herself just as she was about to collide with him she took a firm grip of the umbrella he was holding up. Damp with tears and rain, her face was pale.

"Where are you going?" she said through her gasps.

Akio was not supposed to reply, yet found himself talking as effortlessly as though he'd been waiting for her to ask this very thing.

"Just look at the fountains. Look! You can cry as much as you like, but you're no match for them."

And the two of them tilted the umbrella and, freed from the need to keep their eyes on each other, stared for a while at the three fountains: the central one imposing, the other two slighter, like attendants flanking it on both sides.

Amidst the constant turmoil of the fountains and the pool around them, the streaks of rain falling into the water were almost indistinguishable. Paradoxically, the only sound that struck the ear was the fitful drone of distant cars; the noise of the fountains wove itself so closely into the surrounding air that unless you made an effort to hear you seemed to be enclosed in perfect silence.

First, the water at the bottom bounced in isolated drops off the huge shallow basin of black granite, then ran in a continual drizzle over the black rim.

Another six jets of water, describing far-flung radiating arcs in the air, stood guard around the main column that shot upward from the center of each basin.

This column, if you watched carefully, did not always achieve the same height. In the almost complete absence of a breeze, the water spouted vertically and undisturbed toward the gray, rainy sky, varying from time to time in the height of its summit. Occasionally, ragged water would be flung up to an astonishing height before finally dispersing into droplets and floating to earth again.

The water near the summit, shadowed by the clouds that were visible through it was gray with an admixture of chalky white, almost too powdery-looking for real water, and a misty spray clung about it, while around the column played a mass of foam in large white flakes mingling like snow with the rain.

But Akio was less taken with the three main columns of water than with the water that shot out in radiating curves all around.

The jets from the big central fountain in particular leaped far above the marble rim flinging up their white manes only to dash themselves gallantly down again onto the surface of the pool. The sight of their untiring rushing to the four quarters threatened to usurp his attention. Almost before he knew it, his mind, which till now had been with him in this place, was being taken over by the water, carried away on its rushing, cast far away...

It was the same when he watched the central column.

At first glance, it seemed as neat, as motionless, as a sculpture fashioned out of water. Yet watching closely he could see a transparent ghost of movement moving upward from bottom to top. With furious speed it climbed, steadily filling a slender cylinder of space from base to summit, replacing each moment what had been lost the moment before, in a kind of perpetual replenishment. It was plain that at heaven's height it would be finally frustrated; yet the unwanting power that supported unceasing failure was magnificent.

The fountains he had brought the girl to see had ended by completely fascinating the boy himself. He was still dwelling on their virtues when his gaze, lifted higher, met the sky from which the all-enveloping rain was falling.

He got rain on his eyelashes.

The sky, hemmed in by dense clouds, hung low over his head; the rain fell copiously and without cease. The whole scene was filled with rain. The rain descending on his face was exactly the same as that falling on the roofs of the red-brick buildings and hotel in the distance. His own almost beardless face, smooth and shiny, and the rough concrete that floored the deserted roof of one of those building, were no more than two surfaces exposed, unresisting, to the same rain. From the rain's point of view, his cheeks and the dirty concrete roof were quite identical.

Immediately, the image of the fountains there before his eyes was wiped from his mind. Quite suddenly, fountains in the rain seemed to represent no more than the endless repetition of a stupid and pointless process.

Before long, he had forgotten both his joke of a while ago and the anger that had followed it, and felt his mind steadily becoming empty.

Empty, save for the falling rain...

Aimlessly, the boy started walking.

"Where are you going?" She fell into step with him as she spoke, this time keeping a firm hold on the handle of the umbrella.

"Where? That's my business, isn't it? Told you quite plainly some time ago, didn't I?"

"What did you tell me?"

He gazed at her in horror, but the rain had washed away the traces of tears from the drenched face, and although the damp, reddened eyes still showed the aftermath of weeping, the voice in which she spoke was no longer shaky.

"What do you mean, 'what'? I told you a while back, didn't I? - that we'd better split up."

Just then, the boy spotted, beyond her profile as it moved through the rain, some crimson azalea bushes blooming, small and grudgingly, here and there on the lawn.

"Really? Did you say that? I didn't hear you." Her voice was normal.

Almost bowled over by shock, the boy managed a few steps further before an answer finally came and he stammered:

"But - in that case, what did you cry for? I don't get it."

She didn't reply immediately. Her wet little hand was still firmly attached to the umbrella handle.

"The tears just came. There wasn't any special reason."

Furious, he wanted to shout something at her, but at the crucial moment it came out as an enormous sneeze.

If I'm not careful I'm going to get a cold, he thought.

YUKIO MISHIMA died in November 1970. He was only 45, yet he had written 40 novels, including *The Sound of Waves* and *Confessions of Mask*, eighteen plays and twenty volumes of short stories, and had been nominated three times for the Nobel Prize.

JOHN BESTER, born and educated in England, is one of the foremost translators of Japanese literature, including Mishima's autobiographical *Sun and Steel*. He was awarded the 1990 NOMA Award for the translation of Japanese literature.

With the permission of Harper Collins Publishers Ltd., London.

VIKRAM SETH
From Heaven Lake
Travels Through Sinkiang and Tibet

Introduction

I am Indian, and lived in China as a student at Nanjing University
from 1980-82. In the summer of 1981 I returned home to Delhi
via Tibet and Nepal.

The land route - for this was a hitch-hiking journey - from
the oases of northwest China to the Himalayas crosses four
Chinese provinces: Xinjiang (Sinkiang) and Gansu in the north-
western desert; then the basin and plateau of Qinghai; and finally
Tibet. This book is based on the journal I kept and the photographs I took while I was on the road.

1
Turfan:
July in the desert

The flies have entered the bus, and their buzzing adds to the
overwhelming sense of heat. We drive through the town first: a
few two-storey buildings of depressing concrete, housing
government offices or large shops - foodstores, clothing, hard-
ware. Small street stalls, too, with their wares displayed on the
pavement and vendors selling refreshments - glasses of bilious
yellow and red liquids, looking increasingly attractive as our
thirst builds. Donkey-carts pulled by tired-looking donkeys,
pestered by flies and enervated by the dry, breezeless heat, some
ridden by young boys with white skull-caps, others standing
beside piles of watermelons. Even when they flick their tails, they
do so listlessly. It is not long past dawn, and already the heat
has struck. And the light, shining on walls and signs - in Chinese,
Latin and Arabic scripts - has a painful brilliance.

Turfan; July. The combination is not a happy one, even for
someone accustomed to the oven of Delhi as the summer heat
builds up over northern India. The only way to remain even
tolerably cool in Turfan is to pour cold water on your head and

let your hair dry in the air. This happens in minutes and the process can then be repeated.

Turfan lies in a depression in Xinjiang (Sinkiang), the extreme northwest province of China bordering on the Soviet Union. In summer it bakes and in winter it freezes. It is an oasis town, and its agriculture depends on subterranean water-sources under the inclined plains south of a distant range - just visible to us, purple on the horizon. But since everything evaporates so alarmingly fast at the time that irrigation is most needed, an ingenious system has been constructed for the preservation and transportation of this water. We are to see this later today.

As for Xinjiang itself, it is a curious province. The name means 'New Borderland', but the 'new' is as appropriate a modifier as in the 'New Forest'. The area, populated mainly by people quite different from the Hans (who make up more than nine-tenths of China's population), was first 'pacified' by the Chinese some two thousand years ago. Since then it has been an area of Chinese interest dotted with military outposts and, in different periods, tenuously or closely connected with China: sometimes independent, sometimes semi-independent, and sometimes (as now) an integral province of the country. Strictly speaking, it is not a 'province'. The Chinese call it an 'autonomous region'. This is the name for administrative entities of provincial size which are populated largely by minorities, i.e. non-Hans. (Tibet is another such region.) But effective power is entirely in Beijing's hands.

Xinjiang is a desert province, with the huge Tarim Basin at its heart. When it came to this basin, the ancient Silk Route from China to the Mediterranean bifurcated into the northern and southern Silk Routes. These skirted the periphery of the Tarim, to join again at its western end and continue the long traffic from Changan to Antioch. Along these routes - sometimes desert tracks, sometimes not tracks at all but wastes marked by a beacon or tower - lay the green nodes of oasis-towns. Here imperial officials, or whoever happened to hold the region at the time, would examine the visas of merchants and travellers, verify their credentials, provide them with permission to hire or buy fresh mounts (usually camels), and allow them to proceed. Along the southern route lie such towns as Yarkand and Khotan. Along the northern lie Turfan and Urumqi. The routes rejoin at Kashgar, in western Xinjiang.

402

But Kashgar is out of bounds for foreign travellers. Any area too close to the Soviet 'social imperialists' is, and the green-uniformed People's Liberation Army is everywhere in evidence. The treaties of the two imperial, not to say imperialist, powers have left the boundary in some dispute, and their two socialist successors have fought bloodily over it. Furthermore, each side has a 'minority problem' in the area, for the Uighurs and Kazakhs who live in this historical no-man's-land of Central Asia and whose far-ranging communities, settled or nomadic, are scattered on both sides of a border negotiated or contended over by others, feel little sense of allegiance to the Russians who dominate the USSR or the Hans who dominate China.

They are Muslim in culture and religion; cultures based on the Orthodox Church or on Confucianism are equally alien to them. The script of the Uighur language is Arabic. The dress of the people on the streets outside is colourful, unlike the drab ubiquitous blue of eastern China. Their features are more marked, eyes larger, skin browner: they are in fact racially more akin to the Turks than to the Chinese. But China is a multi-national state, and sixty per cent of its area is peopled by the six per cent of its minorities. Beijing is not unalive to the reality of minority disaffection and the need to appease or crush it.

One feature apparently shared by the Uighurs and the Hans is the passion for walls. We have passed out of the town centre and are in the residential outskirts. Small mud houses with walled compounds go past, a grape trellis flung over a courtyard, an occasional tall sunflower raising its head over the wall. Claire cuts a Hami melon. It is not sweet, unlike the watermelons and grapes we have been eating ever since we arrived in Turfan. But it is cool, and we are now in the desert again. The minibus (organised for the Foreign Students Office of Nanjing University by the Foreign Affairs Office of Turfan) pants courageously along the straight metalled road, aimed for another oasis in the distance. This lies close to the old capital city of a local kingdom, whose vast ruins of clay wall and clay edifice continue till today to crumble and survive.

A wall, miles long, circles the ruins. There are towers and domes and palaces and ramparts, and a heat and dryness that are breathtaking. Our guide gives us names and dates and they go straight out of my head - evaporate. I walk away by myself, and climb a flight of collapsing steps to the top of a high wall. From here I watch a donkey-cart with a load of grass - green! green! - trundle through the baked ruins to a market in the small settlement beyond. Every few minutes I take a swig from my waterbottle. I am trying to recall how 'Ozymandias' goes when the bus horn reminds me that the group is about to leave. I scramble down, notice I have left my lens-cap at the top of the wall, scramble up - the honking of the horn has become frantic - rush down again and arrive breathless and heat-dazed at the bus.

The ruins we have just visited are described as follows in a pictorial guide to Turfan:

The most famous place is Ko Chang Old City. The City is in the south-east of Turpan and is said to be built in 1 B.C. It is lasted until the 14th. Century. In other words, the City has a long history of about 1500 years.

In the ancient time, Ko Chang City acted as an important political, economical and cultural centre. It was also a city along the Silk Route. The City was ruined during a fierce battle which fighting cause is religion.

Before the Muslim invasion and conversion, the area around Turfan was Buddhist. We are now to be taken to some Buddhist temples and monasteries that lie - also in ruins - on the other side of Turfan. When we arrive I look for lizards in the cracked clay crevices, but can see none. The heat is stifling and there is no vegetation except for the sporadic thorny scrub. The buildings are domed, of uncoloured clay, preserved to some extent through dryness, but damaged, I imagine, by the expansion of freezing moisture during cooler months: the clear skies make for a large daily swing in temperature. This site is a long plateau, islanded between the fork and rejoin of a stream far below. Its edges are precipitous, and the braiding stream so far down feeds a brilliant band of green growth. It must have been an enormous task supplying the monastery and temples with water, and I wonder if this place, like Fatehpur Sikri, died for lack of it. I should ask, I suppose; but it will mean a walk back to the guide; and the heat is so intense that I decide to sit in ignorance in the shadow of a wall and stare at a stone.

I am the last one on the bus. 'You are late as usual,' says the guide, an amiable Uighur official who is keener to get us from one tourist attraction to another an hour away than to allow us twenty minutes at the places themselves. He looks at his watch and sucks in his breath. There is a hurried consultation with the driver, after which we descend from the plateau to find ourselves in the desert again.

The three week tour we are on has been organised by Nanjing University for its foreign students: a mixed bunch, though largely from the richer countries, with Japan and the US predominating. During the one or two years we are at Nanjing we study or research our subjects - ranging from philosophy to Chinese literature, from economics to history - usually on leave of absence from our own universities. Nanjing University provides us with facilities and some supervision, but does not grant degrees. During the holidays we are permitted to travel.

The tenor of this trip, though, is beginning to worry me. It is well-organised - the transport, the board, the accommodation, the guides, everything that would be time-consuming and expensive for individuals to arrange has been thought of. Considering the problems of organisation (train tickets, for example, can be booked no earlier than three days in advance) things have gone smoothly. Yet the comfort of being cushioned from these practicalities has brought with it restrictions of two kinds.

The first is inherent in group travel, indeed in any form of organised group activity - a discipline, a punctuality, imposed upon the participants. Every minute I am late for the bus means fifteen wasted person-minutes for the group as a whole. It will not do, I realise, to stare at a stone when Claire and Carlo and Midoragawa and John and Wolfgang and ten others besides are slowly vaporising in the bus. And yet to be hustled by the Group Will into rushing from sight to sight, savouring nothing, is, I'm sure, irksome to all of us.

The second kind of restriction is peculiar to travel in China. The movement of foreigners is tightly controlled, and it is easier to keep an eye on a group than on its scattered members. A travel pass is needed for every place - outside Nanjing - that we foreign students go to. It has to be filled out and signed by the Public Security Bureau (the police). They will certainly refuse, for instance, to put Kashgar on it; the whole of rural China, except for famous scenic spots or - occasionally - model communes, is out of bounds. If you travel in a group, even what is shown within a town is effectively limited to those places to which the guide is willing to take you. By the engaging ploy of keeping you continuously occupied from dawn to sunset he leaves you no time to explore. Our avuncular guide, Abdurrahman, is particularly adept at this. This is stringent enough, but the situation is aggravated by the ever-present phenomenon of *lianxi* - a word as fundamental to an understanding of China as *guiding* (regulations), or *guanxi* (personal connections in official places). Roughly translatable as 'contact' or 'liaison', *lianxi* is absolutely essential for effective action where discretion, personal fiefdoms and a hierarchical system of command exist. Channels for lateral communication are poor in China. If your work-unit wants something done by another work-unit not in its direct line of command, you have one of two choices. Either apply upwards through your hierarchy to a common boss, and then have the order percolate downwards to the other unit, which is time-consuming; or, alternatively, try, through phone calls, visits, common friends, promises of future favours or some other form of *lianxi*, to get them to do what you want.

Since we foreign students are under the care of the Nanjing University teachers accompanying us, and since the group, during its stay in Turfan, travels under the aegis of the Turfan office of the Foreign Affairs Bureau, there are certain proprieties to be observed. If we want to see something - a museum, for instance - we cannot go to the curators ourselves. We speak to our teachers, who *lianxi* with the Foreign Affairs guide, who, after checking with his superiors, will *lianxi* with some representative of the Ministry of Culture, who will talk to the museum authorities. By that time, of course, we will probably have left for another destination. It is also worth noting that in this delicate concatenation a single reasoned, hostile, lazy or timorous 'no' is sufficient to stymie our efforts to do what we want to do, or to see what we want to see.

I do not think that I will be able to tolerate the limitations of group travel much longer. I have already committed myself at Turfan, but at Urumqi I will simply refuse to be shown the sights.

Seeing fewer monuments will not distress me. At the birth of this idea I pour a little baptismal water onto my head and feel the cool comfort as it steams off my hair. I drink the last of the water and, more cheerfully than before, face the constraints of the present and the heat of the desert.

A line of poplars appears suddenly to the right of the road, a crystal channel of water running alongside. 'Karez', says Abdurrahman. 'It's water from the mountains.'

We get out to inspect the stream. The water is ice-cold. We take off our hot shoes and wade gratefully across. A few members of a *karez* commune come forward to meet us. Three naked children splash about in the stream and pause to greet us with 'bye-byes' of great vigour and friendliness. They have met foreigners before.

As we look upstream, the channel cuts more and more deeply into the desert, and finally disappears underground into what appears to be a cave. This is in fact a narrow tunnel, or *karez*, part of a system of tunnels that brings water down to Turfan from the mountains to the north. A *karez* is usually less than ten kilometres long, but some are as long as forty kilometres. The same volume of water flows all the year round; there is little depletion in summer, even with temperatures of as much as 48°C. All this is explained by Abdurrahman with a note of justifiable pride; within China, the *karez* is unique to Xinjiang.

'What if the roof caves in somewhere?' I inquire.

'The *karez* can be repaired.'

'Repaired?' I ask.

Abdurrahman smiles indulgently. 'After all, it was built once.'

'But there doesn't appear to be anywhere to get in from apart from the mouth. What if damage occurs a good distance inside - say, a few kilometres?'

Abdurrahman points to a slight rise in the ground. 'We can't see it from here, but there's an entrance there too. It's a hole, like the entrance to a well. It's fifty metres upstream, and there are entrances of that kind all the way along the *karez*. Some are further apart, but you can always get to the damage and repair it.'

We walk over to the opening and I am intrigued. The stream gurgles about three metres below, its surface almost unruffled.

'This,' says Abdurrahman, 'is where the *karez* commune members enter to maintain the channels. It's quite simple.'

The water is too tempting. 'I think I'll be an honorary commune member,' I murmur, as I take off my shoes, slip off my shirt and drop my legs over the edge of the well. 'See you at the mouth of the *karez*.'

Abdurrahman drops his avuncular air. 'No - no -' he exclaims, 'there's nothing of interest inside. I wouldn't go down.' Then, yielding to the inevitable as I disappear downwards with a splash, he adds, 'Be careful!'

The walls are slippery, and I couldn't climb out even if I wanted to. There is not much light, which is something of a shock after the brilliant sunshine above. I notice how cold my feet are, and at first it feels comfortable. I walk slowly, groping along the slippery clay walls, bumping my head against the low roof. The light dies. I am guided solely by my hands and submerged feet, both suddenly numb with cold. There is a slight bend in the *karez*; I realise I had better feel the walls to make sure that there are no branches in the channel. It would be unpleasant to be lost here. The water washes up to my shorts, and when I speak aloud to myself my voice sounds hollow and garbled. Surely I must have gone more than fifty metres? In this unguided blackness the thought grips me that if the *karez* curves, it could still be a long way to the exit. Panic, I tell myself, is ridiculous - I can't be far from the mouth - and yet I feel it grow, so I talk myself forwards: a little further, a little further. Then there is another bend, a glimmer of light, then more light, and finally I run the last few steps into the lovely sunshine, chased, incidentally, by a small swarm of wasps whose nest I must have disturbed at the mouth of the *karez*.

I sit by the stream for a minute. There are more than two thousand kilometres of *karez* in the deserts of Xinjiang. Without them there would be no agriculture here, no grapes, melons or long-stapled cotton. Abdurrahman looks at me with relief, a little peeved with his ill-disciplined charge.

Greenery and flowing water: my father has always said that these form his idea of paradise. I would enjoy sitting here for a while, doing nothing in particular, but our guide is looking perturbedly at his watch. Almost everyone is back on the bus.

'Come along,' he says to me, 'we're going to see people buried in sand.'

This sounds inexplicable, if promising. We drive to a conical dune of dark sand. Umbrellas and tents protrude from its slopes, and people sit below, with their legs and sometimes their entire bodies submerged. They do not look unduly uncomfortable; some, indeed, appear relaxed, calm heads rising limbless like mushrooms from the sand. I take off my shoes for a better grip, and walk a few steps up the slope, only to run yelping down. As I nurse my scorched soles, I am told that the sand is not yet at its hottest. The best effect comes around two o'clock in the afternoon.

I have evidently missed part of the conversation. 'The best effect?' I ask, rubbing my traumatised feet.

'They do it to cure arthritis and other maladies,' says Abdurrahman with a gesture towards the dune. 'Why not go and have a picture of yourself taken sitting with them? Many of our foreign friends do.'

The status of a 'foreign friend' or 'foreign guest' in China is an interesting if unnatural one. Officialdom treats the foreigner as one would a valuable panda given to fits of mischief. On no account must any harm come to the animal. On the other hand, it must be closely watched at all times so that it does not see too much, do too much on its own, or influence the behaviour of the local inhabitants. 'We have friends all over the world,' announce banners slung up on the façades of hotels, but officialdom is disturbed by too much contact between Chinese and non-Chinese. They are horrified by affairs between Chinese and foreigners, especially if the woman is Chinese. From time to time this attitude bubbles over in tirades in the official press, but there is nothing like the xenophobia of the Cultural Revolution, when Beethoven was banned and diplomats beaten up by mobs.

As for the Chinese people, there is a general sense of friendliness and a curiosity towards the individual foreigner which is remarkable considering the anti-foreignness of the Chinese past, and indeed the stigma previously attached to contact with *waiguoren* (out-land persons). But the Chinese word for their country is simply 'Mid-land', an indication of their assumption of centrality in the scheme of things. One is often conscious of a minute examination of one's dress and behaviour upon first acquaintance; the impression is that one is considered not merely foreign, but in some sense weird. People passing one in the street stop to gape at dress and feature; on occasion even turning their heads round to stare and consequently bumping into bicycles or trees. Children yell, '*Waiguoren! waiguoren!*' as they catch sight of one; or, '*Waibin! waibin!*' (foreign guest) if they are old enough to combine etiquette with excitement.

> 'Papa, an Outlandman!' the toddler shrieks,
> Tugging his father's sleeve. 'Look, look,' he says,
> Gaping in shock at the unshaven cheeks,
> Long nose and camera and Outlandish ways.
> 'Look, look, a Midlandman,' I smile and say
> (In Midlandspeech). The toddler starts to cry.
> 'He spoke! He spoke! What is he anyway?'
> 'He is an Uncle,' is the sound reply.

Contact between Chinese and foreigners is permeated by the feeling that one's foreignness is the crucial element of one's character. With one's closest friends, however - and they are likely to be fairly knowledgeable about the world outside, or at least to be willing to conceive that Mid-land could be Out-land for Outlanders - one can share that acceptance, that tensionless and refreshing fellowship that makes one, through the enjoyment of their company, love the country from which they come.

One of the most unexpected features of my stay in Turfan is that it leads to my going to Tibet.

When I first came to China a year ago I wished to visit Tibet, but I soon put this idea aside as being impossible. The only people who obtain official stamps for Lhasa on their travel passes are wealthy groups of tourists whose programme is so carefully packed as to preclude the time for individual initiative or exploration. They pay about US$200 a day. Student friends, more eager than I to see Tibet, who were convinced that they could avoid the high prices, have tried to get their passes endorsed for Lhasa at a large number of police stations along the routes of their summer travels, but to no avail. I managed to get this permission because of two unlikely events: a song and a walk.

Late in the evening a troupe of local musicians perform a programme of songs and dances in the vine-covered courtyard of the guest house. We form a square under the trellis - the audience on three sides, the orchestra on the fourth, the dancers taking up the middle. It is wonderful to watch, and the music itself is beautiful, akin in spirit to that of the Middle East. Many of the songs are based on repartee between lovers - usually a tubby man with a wicked moustache and a woman with flashing eyes. Her manner consists in equal parts of affection and contempt. The orchestra yells out the chorus, rebuking this side, encouraging the other, commenting on the scene - or so I assume from their expressions, since I cannot understand the Uighur songs. The townspeople, who make up most of the audience, roll about in fits at the more outrageous verses.

When the troupe has performed, the townsfolk and musicians compel the foreign students to put on a show for them. A Japanese student plays the flute, the Italians sing revolutionary and feminist songs with their usual raucous aplomb. John Moffett, a lean and eccentric Englishman who talks like Bertie Wooster, interrupts his whimsical commentary on the proceedings to sing 'Ye Banks and Braes of Bonny Doon' in a pleasant and rich tenor.

It is now my turn to sing. There is no real choice. It will have to be the theme-song from *Awara (The Wanderer)*, a sentimental Indian movie from the 1950s that is astonishingly popular in China. It comes as a shock to me sometimes to hear it hummed on the streets of Nanjing - to be transported without warning back to both India and childhood. No sooner have I begun than I find that the musicians have struck up the accompaniment behind me: they know the tune better than I do. The tubby man with the twirling moustaches is singing along with me, in Hindi at that. I am entranced, and, carried forward by their momentum, pour out the lyrics with abandon.

> 'No family, no world have I
> And nobody's love...'

411

I sing happily.

> 'Ah! My chest is covered with wounds.
> I am struck by the arrows of fate!'

When the song ends the orchestra and audience cheer me back to my seat. I am giddy with euphoria. This performance is to have certain repercussions the next day.

I would not normally have gone for a walk the next morning, but Claire is leaving the school trip for Nanjing, and later France. I know I will miss her good-natured company; I wander along with her to the market. She wants to buy a cap, and I a knife. The melons lie in huge heaps on the ground. A man brushes his teeth in the ditch by the side of the street. An old woman sits in a doorway reading a letter, occasionally fanning her face with it. Two soldiers go by, cracking sunflower seeds between their teeth.

We examine the wares of the pavement hawkers: dates and figs and grapes and vegetables as well as an assortment of clothes and shoes, utensils and other household goods. I buy something that looks like a crude wooden pipe from a Uighur woman, who holds up three fingers to indicate the price. It will make a good present for a smoker friend, I think, and on impulse buy two more, asking, in a mixture of Chinese and puffing gestures, whether I am holding it properly. The woman looks at me with incomprehension. A small crowd gathers, as it usually does around something as entertaining as a foreigner making a purchase, but there is an undercurrent of hilarity that I cannot fathom. Only later do I learn that the 'pipe' is a device for diverting a baby's urine out of its cot so that it does not soil its nightclothes.

Claire finds a cap that she likes, and I look at one in dark velvet with a bead design. I am about to go off in search of a knife when I notice a board in Chinese: Local Police Station. John and I have recently been discussing ways and means of getting to Tibet, so it is on my mind. I tell Claire I am going to try to have Lhasa stamped on my travel pass. She laughs with amiable scepticism and says she will see me at lunch. I enter the police station.

There is the kind of confusion within that could prove fertile: paper, files, maps, forms, and bilingual exchanges in loud voices.

No one knows what to do with me. Finally a woman officer, kind and helpful beyond the call of duty, suggests that I follow her to the General Police Station, where they may be empowered to endorse passes; they certainly aren't at the local one. We walk halfway across town; the sun by now is unbearable. She is Han Chinese, has lived in Turfan for twenty years, speaks Uighur fluently, and has no fear of the heat; nevertheless she keeps telling me to walk in the spindly shade of the poplars lining the main street. At the General Police Station it is discovered that Akbar, the young officer who endorses travel passes, is not in. No one else can do it for him, as he has the key to the seals.

I sit down in the cool thick-walled corridor. Half an hour passes. Akbar finally enters with a friend of his. I am ushered into an office and asked what I have come for.

'I thought I would like to add a few more places to my travel pass,' I reply.

'Can I have a look at it?' I hand it over. 'You're from Nanjing, I see. Why didn't you get these places stamped at Nanjing?'

'Well, I would have liked to, but the Nanjing police were only willing to write sixteen places on the pass.'

'Sixteen?' Akbar looks surprised at the apparent arbitrariness of the number.

'There are four lines on the left-hand side of the page; they won't write more than four place-names on each line. They want things to look neat.' Akbar raises his eyebrows. 'In fact,' I continue, 'if one of your destinations has three or four characters, in its name, you may be penalised for its length: they will then only fit three place-names on each line.'

Akbar allows himself a smile. 'I see. But they don't mind how many names are written on the facing page by another police station?'

'Oh no. That's for endorsements. When I asked them to continue the list on the right-hand page, they argued that the issuing station couldn't endorse itself.'

'Very logical,' says Akbar wryly. 'And where do you want to go?'

'Oh, I was thinking of going to Chengdu and Chongqing and Emei Shan and perhaps to Lhasa, and, oh yes, also to Wuhan and...'

'Well, write it all down on this form.' He gets one out from a drawer. When I have completed it he looks it over.

'And why do you want to go to Lhasa?' he homes in.

'I am interested in minority areas. I've always wanted to go, but I didn't think I'd have the time.' I examine a paper clip with interest.

'Please wait here. I may have to get permission from Urumqi - the provincial capital. This make take some time. I'm sorry for any delay.' He walks out with the form.

When he comes back half an hour later, he finds me and his friend deep in conversation about Indian movies. His friend was in the audience last night; we discuss *Awara* - its artistic merits and social significance. Because one of the themes of the movie is the question of whether 'a judge's son has to be a judge and a criminal's son a criminal', the movie was attacked during the Cultural Revolution, when pure proletarian antecedents were considered a guarantee of correctness of thought.

Akbar joins in the conversation. 'I hear that Lita died earlier this year.' (He is referring to Nargis, the actress who played the role of Rita.)

'What?' This is news to me. 'Where did you read this?'

'In a film magazine. I was very sorry to read about it. We take a lot of interest in Lita and Laz.' (Raj Kapoor, the director and leading actor.) 'Laz, it said in the magazine, is a big capitalist in real life, and has his own film company.' He says this with evident approval. Everyone I have ever talked to in China approves of Raj Kapoor. In fact he has a large body of fans in Russia and the Middle East as well.

The three of us talk in eccentric and exhilarating circles for another twenty minutes. Finally Akbar gets up.

'I think the telephone line to Urumqi is down. They've been having trouble with it recently. I doubt we can get through.' He pauses; I can see him swaying delicately towards a decision. 'Could you wait till tomorrow?' he asks, intending to defer it.

'We're leaving tomorrow,' I say, disappointed.

'Oh, well. Then I will endorse your pass now.' He goes to a cupboard, unlocks it and takes out the magic seal.

I can hardly believe my good luck. Outside in the searing sunshine I examine the inked characters and red official stamp on my travel pass. The endorsement is numbered '00001', and as it is already July, I conclude that the volume of endorsements through this police station cannot be excessive. As I walk back for lunch, a series of questions runs through my mind.

The first is whether I will avail myself of this endorsement for Lhasa. The problem is that I have already bought a ticket to go home via Hong Kong to Delhi. But could I go to Lhasa at any other time than now? In winter it will be dangerously cold in Tibet, and next summer I plan to leave China by the Trans-Siberian Railway. Besides, it is extremely unlikely that today's luck will ever repeat itself. The travel pass expires towards the end of August. It will have to be this summer or not at all - this summer that I had earmarked for exemplary and fulfilling laziness. And money: I could do with more of it. Why did I buy that ticket in advance? Can I get a refund later? But money, however much of a problem, is finally just money, and I know the answer to this question almost as soon as it forms.

The second question is how I should get to Lhasa. There is no railway. I will have to go by air from Xian or Chengdu. Which would be more convenient? Which will be cheaper? Or - and here an idea begins to germinate - would it be possible for me to go by road? Are there buses? Will the floods in western China have disrupted road traffic as they have rail traffic? Trucks? Jeeps? Surely there must be some way of getting to Tibet through its neighbouring provinces (Xinjiang, Qinghai, Sichuan and Yunnan)? It would certainly be cheaper than flying. Perhaps I could hitch-hike. The idea has the quality of a pleasant hallucination. I see before my eyes yaks, and trucks, and a huge image of the Potala palace. Two lamas stand in front of me and ask to see my travel pass. I hand them my air ticket from Hong Kong.

Back at the guest house, I spread out a map of China over my bed. There are, I discover, five ways of getting to Lhasa by road. One is from the west, via Kashgar - that is definitely out. Two others begin in Sichuan and Yunnan respectively; there is no immediately obvious reason for rejecting these. Finally, the remaining routes enter from the north: from Liuyuan in Gansu Province and from Xining in Qinghai Province; both of these converge on Germu (also in Qinghai). These look possible too, and have the additional advantage of crossing remote Qinghai, a province I have not seen.

Finally, a third question presents itself: after Lhasa, what? Should I return to Nanjing and then use my Hong Kong-Delhi air-ticket after all? Or should I try to continue overland to India? The border with India is disputed, and as an Indian citizen I am unlikely to get permission to cross it. But the border with Nepal may provide a possible exit route.

The answer to the previous question will predetermine the answer to a related one: before Lhasa, what? For if I decide to go directly from Lhasa to Kathmandu, I will need to return to Nanjing to get my passport, and from there go to Beijing to obtain a Nepalese visa before setting out for Lhasa. This is a depressing thought when I am already so close to the western routes that lead into Tibet. However, the prospect of crossing the Himalayas is sufficiently exciting to warrant the expense and tedium of this huge eastward loop.

I realise as I turn these thoughts over in my mind that the chances of my getting through are very slight. I have not met anyone who has; I have heard of a number of foreigners who made it part of the way overland, only to be turned back by the police. But I do not know whether or not they had travel passes. The fact that I do certainly encourages me. I think it is worth a try.

After lunch (an exultant occasion: Claire is pleased and surprised by my documentary success) and a prolonged siesta (orchestrated by the buzz of flies and the whirr of an injured table-fan) we go off to see some more sights of Turfan - first the Grape Gorge, with its arbours and trellises and fast-flowing stone-lined canal. I threaten to swim in it, and Abdurrahman is disappointingly indifferent. 'Well, that's up to you,' he says. I look at the water for a while and realise that it is too dangerous. 'I think, after all, perhaps I won't take a swim.' Abdurrahman allows himself a fleeting smile and turns away.

Next comes the Emin Tower, a tall phallus of clay whose shifting shadow falls on the fields and roads around. We climb its spiral of narrowing steps for the fine view from the top.

Graffiti (in both Chinese and Uighur) have been carved into the lattice-work on the uppermost windows. Finally we go to Turfan's museum, where we see all kinds of objects dating from the time when Turfan first became a halt along the Silk Route: strips of cloth, shards of ceramic, coins, toys, ornaments, stones. There is even a map of the Buddhist monk Fa Xian's fifth-century travels to India as well as one of Xuan Zang's journey two centuries later. I recall that Fa Xian mentions in his account that it is possible for a foreigner to travel from one end of India to another without a passport or pass of any kind; it is clear that the travel passes that foreigners in China inveigh against are not recent and exceptional impositions.

Throughout the afternoon a debilitating heat has drained our energy; even the will to think is draining away. Two or three times a day I wonder what I am doing in Turfan at all. The heat is poignantly described by my pictorial guide to Turfan:

Turpan's tourism is not very prosperous but still, people come here to travel. The weather situation is unbearable since the temperature difference is really great. Turpan is also know as a 'Fire Place' in China. From the name, we can assume how hot the place is...

Turpan is so hot with daily temperatures of 40°C. The rocks, being heated by the sun, reach a temperature of 80°C. It is funny to see that people won't sweat since the sweat is evaporated before they come out to the outer layer of the skin.

But it is rather less funny to find oneself actually collapsing with heat-stroke. I wait until evening before wandering over to the market. Although this is a Muslim area, no women wear veils. A few children help their parents to load a donkey. Noticing my orange backpack they wave and shout the only foreign words they know: 'Bye-bye, bye-bye!' I return the greeting and turn to buy a couple of kilos of raisins and dates for future use. An old white-bearded man who has slung his bed over the pavement tells me to sit down. We talk for a while in Chinese over a glass of green tea. The talk drifts to the signs above the doors of shops around us. Apart from the Chinese characters, they are in the Latin and Arabic scripts.

'They're both Uighur,' says the old man.

'But I always thought Uighur was written in the Arabic script,' I say.

'It was, when I learned to read and write. I can't read any of this Latin stuff.' He pauses. 'But the script was changed, and my son learned the Latin script.'

I sip my tea meditatively. 'It must be sad to know that your way of writing is dying out.'

'But it isn't. They changed the script back again. My grandson learns the Arabic script at school.'

'Oh! Why did they change the script the first time round?' I ask.

'I think the government was afraid that too many people were reading Russian publications in Uighur - which use the Arabic script. By changing to Latin, the Chinese government made sure that the new generation wouldn't understand the books that the Russians publish for their Uighur population.'

'And why did they change the script back to Arabic?'

'I don't know,' says the old man. 'It's the new Minorities Policy.' He reflects for a bit. 'The Latin script wasn't very successful. People didn't like it.'

'But some people learned only the Latin script, didn't they?' I think of Akbar, who could barely sign his name in the Arabic script. A horrific thought occurs to me. 'You and your grandson, then, can write notes or letters to each other, but your son can write to neither?'

'Quite right. That's how it is,' says the old man happily. The date-seller comes over to listen in, and a couple of men to look at my watch. As townsfolk gather around us out of curiosity, the old man stops talking and sips his tea. Someone recognises me from last night and I am coerced and cajoled into a repeat performance of the movie song. Then someone else - the son of the date-seller - sings a song in Uighur, then someone else again: the marketplace takes a spontaneous break for music. On my way back to the guest house, a young soldier gives me a lift on the back of his bicycle. I fear that I am taking him out of his way - and indeed I am - but he insists that I must be too tired to walk. This instinctive kindness is something one encounters every day in China.

I sit down by a bright bed of zinnias in the centre of the courtyard as evening falls, and watch their colours dim and merge. At night, under the grape trellis, a few of us foreigners sit and talk. John has left to travel further up the northwest railway line, to Urumqi. Since that is where we are bound tomorrow, it is possible we will meet him. I like his unfettered manner of travelling; in spire of my congenital lethargy, I feel more than ever like breaking away from the guided comfort of the school trip.

As it is warm indoors, we pull our beds out and sleep under the vines, until, soon after dawn, the heat grows fierce again.

The Journey continues in **Skoob PACIFICA** *Anthology No: 2*
THE PEN IS MIGHTIER THAN THE SWORD.
Forthcoming winter 1993.

Harum!

Third Sutra Festival
Artistic Director: Ramli Ibrahim

Fragrant aroma for the entire month of November '93

End of Year SUTRA EXPLOSION!

Programme 1
FANTAMORGANA
Music Theatre by
Valerie Ross & Ramli Ibrahim

Programme 4
KRISHNA IN GUNA
Guna presents
Krishna, The Blue God
in an enchanting solo
Bharatha Natyam

Programme 2
THE OTHER...CAN'T
Sabera Shaik writes & stars
in her first play
Directed by Ramli Ibrahim

Programme 5
CHANDRABHANU IN
BHARATHA NATYAM

Programme 3
HOLY ALLIANCES
A celebration of new
Malaysian contemporary
works choreographed by
Ramli Inrahim,
Chandrabhanu & Guna

Programme 6
HALLOWED DIVERSIONS
Odissi at its best
SUTRA dance company

Enquiries: Sutra House, 12 Pesiaran Titiwangsa 3, 53200 Kuala Lumpur.
Tel No: 4211092, 2542655. Fax No: 7178093